Timber-Frame Buildi

Nottinghamshire

Jason Mordan

The Gables at Little Carlton near South Muskham

Nottinghamshire
County Council

Acknowledgements

For several years Graham Beaumont and I have discussed the idea of publishing a short book on the timber-frame buildings of the county akin to other County Council titles, like Windmills, Tudor Trail, Churches and Pinfolds. As is often the case with such things the original intention was much grander but constraints mean that only an abridged version is possible. That said this short book has still relied on the dedication and help of a number of people. Firstly, the recognition for the majority of the information and virtually all the illustrations used in this publication must go to other people, some of whom are not alive to read this. I have attempted to list the main contributors below, in no particular order, but I must make special reference to my predecessor Graham Beaumont without whose enthusiasm and knowledge I would not have been able to publish and whose illustrations pepper this book (thankfully he is still actively spreading the word). The investigations of Alison Arnold and Robert Howard, the dendrochronologists at The University of Nottingham Tree-ring Dating Laboratory, have provided the essential dating evidence to aid our understanding. The laboratory's key research in Newark has been recently published by English Heritage. I would also like to thank my colleagues at Nottinghamshire County Council for their help in producing the book, in particular David Littlewood and Rupert Vinnicombe for their essential inputs, also Virginia Baddeley for some timely suggestions and the members of the Publications Group and the Rowlands family for their time in commenting on early drafts of the text. Many thanks.....

The following people have very generously allowed their illustrations to be reproduced in this book. The copyright permission for the further reproduction of any of these illustrations must be obtained from them:

> **Richard Harris:** the first chapter of this book relies on the excellent illustrations from 'Discovering Timber Frame Buildings' which highlights that it is without a doubt the essential pocket guide for anyone with an interest in timber-frame buildings. Many thanks for allowing us to use them.
> **See figures marked *(1) in list of illustrations on page 4.**

> **Mary Charles:** for allowing us to reproduce some of the wonderful illustrations from 'Conserving Timber Buildings' written and illustrated in conjunction with her late husband Freddie.
> **See figures marked *(2)**

> **Maurice Barley:** with special reference to TIL House and The Gables, Little Carlton, we are very grateful to the publishers of 'The English Farmhouse' for permission to reproduce the late Professor Barley's illustrations. **See figures marked *(3)**

> **The Royal Commission for Historic Monuments of England (RCHME):** as always the National Monuments Record Centre in Swindon proved to be a valuable source of information. **See figures marked *(4)**

> **Guy St.John Taylor Architects, Newark:** for providing the very useful reconstruction illustrations for the Governor's House. **See figures marked *(5)**

(see 'Further Reading' section at the back for more information on books by the key contributors)

Contents

Illustrations		Page

* see Acknowledgements on page 3 for reference to original source

Historic Timber-frame Buildings

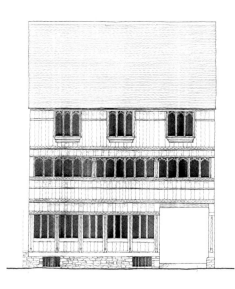

Introduction

This book is aimed at anyone who is interested in buildings, architecture or history in general. It is an introduction to some of the finest medieval buildings in the county of Nottinghamshire, with some basic information, a few line drawings and photographs to help explain each one in a little detail. Included is a very basic and straightforward introduction to the various components that make a 'timber-frame' building, so that the reader can appreciate the descriptions provided. In most cases there is also reference to the date of the building, for which we can thank the relatively new science of 'dendrochronology', otherwise known as tree-ring dating. For several of the buildings a more thorough account is available elsewhere (a list of sources is provided in the back for those who wish to read further) but for many this is the first time the new dating evidence and the architectural description have been published together. Some of the buildings listed here were described in publications many years ago with dates that were based on their architectural style alone, of which some have proved quite accurate, while others we now know to be wrong and misleading.

Historical background

The medieval period spans 500 hundred years from the time after the Norman invasion of 1066 up until the advent of the 'modern' period which technically begins during the later part of the 16th century. Most of us can name at least one or two of the most famous monarchs, Richard III or Henry VIII for instance, and will have a rudimentary understanding of events that shaped the time, like the Wars of the Roses and the Dissolution of the Monasteries. Our elementary education has also left us all with an appreciation of the lives of medieval people, the hardships of the plagues, the kinds of clothes they wore and the types of building they lived in.

What's so special?

The black and white appearance of oak frame buildings with 'wattle and daub' walls is probably a familiar concept to just about all of us. Nearly everyone, if asked, could think of at least one example that still survives in the city, town or village near where they live. These timber-frame buildings are all that is left of the homes of everyday people that lived in the medieval period. Those that survive are a testament to the enduring qualities of English oak as a building material and to the skill of the craftsmen that made these buildings by hand.

Medieval timber-frame buildings are rare and extremely old and provide a direct link to our ancestors, both those who built them and those that lived in them. Every example is different and contains unique information about the people who constructed it and all those that subsequently lived in it. They provide a superb opportunity for us to understand more closely what day-to-day life was actually like in the medieval period, although only for those who could afford to own one, or alternatively had to work in one.

What to look for

The black and white style of timber-frame buildings is immediately identifiable, but beware modern imitations! The style has been widely copied by builders and architects, especially since the Victorians, who began a resurgence of interest in medieval architecture, and as a result mock timber-framing is everywhere. Most are not true timber-frames as the wood is simply stuck onto the front of a solid building, usually brick, and provides no structural support. They are not always easy to tell from the real medieval timber-frames but in general terms the clues are that they appear much fresher and less weathered, and overall they are more square and less lop-sided than the true medieval building.

A basic introduction to medieval timber-frame construction

Fig. 1

BOXED HEART   HALVED   SLABBED

Without the aid of any powered tools the craftsman first felled and then split the oak tree trunks to achieve the desired section of timber, usually this meant halving or box sectioning it **(Fig. 1)**. He marked out and prepared all the joints at his yard during the first twelve months after the tree was felled, when the oak was 'green', otherwise it became too hard to work easily by hand **(Fig. 2)**. Oak becomes as hard as steel as it ages, anyone who has tried to hammer a nail into a piece of five hundred year old oak will testify to this! The joints a medieval carpenter used will be familiar to anyone who studied woodwork at school, but unlike modern joints no glue, nails or screws were used, only oak pegs hammered into pre-drilled holes secure the joints. The testament to the carpenters' skills are that the timbers they prepared in their yards invariably slotted together neatly and entirely by hand when the frame was assembled on site and have stood the test of time ever since.

Terminology

There are a variety of different types of medieval timber-frames, but they all have certain basic facts in common. Firstly, they are all made up of separate oak 'members': posts; beams; studs; rails; plates and rafters **(Fig. 3)**, and these are held together by pegged joints, such as mortice and tenon, scarfs and lap-dovetails **(Fig. 4)**. Secondly, each building can be split up into its constituent 'frames': wall; cross; roof and floor **(Fig. 5)** each of which is constructed of a set of oak members and is integral with others. So the roof frame for instance, is connected to a cross frame

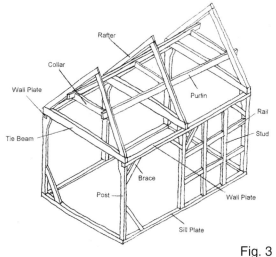

Fig. 3

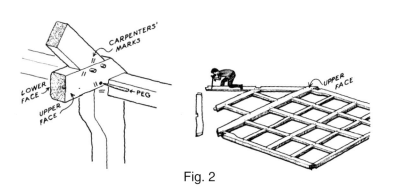

Fig. 2

6

and two wall frames via the most complex of all the joints used – the lap dovetail **(Fig. 4)**. In addition to these basic subdivisions of the timber-frame there are also a number of different types, so for instance the roof frame could be either a 'crown post' or 'side purlin' type, while the wall frame might be 'close studded' or 'box framed'. The most commonly used terms are explained below and are encountered in the descriptions of the buildings given later on.

Fig.4

Wall frame: as the name suggests this is the frame that makes up the front and back walls and is often the first and most clear indication that you are looking at a medieval timber-frame building. However, the wall frame is also the part of a medieval timber-frame building that was most commonly replaced, either by stone in the first part or later on during the 18th century by brick.

Cross frame: every timber building has to have frames running between the front and back walls. A minimum of two cross frames are needed to create a very basic single 'bay' building where each cross frame would be an end wall. Three or more cross frames make a longer building of two or more bays where one or more cross frames are internal and are not designed to act as end walls. A cross frame usually has a span of about 14 to 18 feet and on average the length of each bay, that is to say the space between each cross frame, is very similar.

Roof frame: supported on the wall and/or cross frame the roof frame is often one of the most interesting areas of a medieval timber-frame building where the carpenters' skills are most evident, especially in the best quality buildings. The principal timbers in the roof frame (principal rafters, purlins, king/crown & queen posts) are often supported by a cross frame and together they are referred to as a 'truss'.

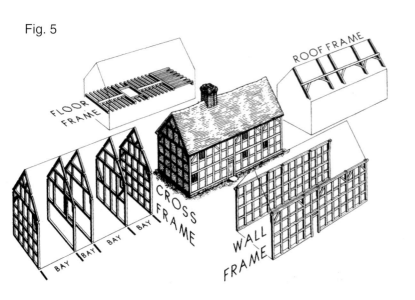

Fig. 5

Floor frame: evidence from surviving timber–frame buildings of the early medieval period show that floors were uncommon. Thirteenth and 14th century buildings were open to the rafters but later on, in the 15th and 16th centuries, floors became popular and were inserted into the earlier buildings. New buildings of the later medieval period were invariably designed with floors already built in. First floors have the benefit of doubling the floor space and also improve the strength of the building enabling it to be built taller.

Types of frame

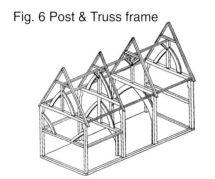

Fig. 6 Post & Truss frame

Post and truss frames vs Cruck frames (Fig. 6 & 7).
Most timber-frame buildings were constructed so that the roof slope was made of a separate set of timbers from the wall frame below. This is commonly termed 'post and truss' construction and contrasts the other type of construction know as the 'cruck frame'. Unlike post and truss frames the roof and walls of a cruck frame are constructed of a single length of timber. It is know as the 'cruck blade' and consists of a piece of oak suitably bent to allow the walls to be near vertical but still achieve the necessary roof pitch and bay width. On the whole cruck frames are less common than post and truss frame buildings except in parts of the north-west of Britain.

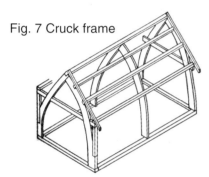

Fig. 7 Cruck frame

Roof frames
For any building ensuring the roof structure is capable of holding the weight of the roof covering is critical, whether it be thatch, clay tiles, or stone. Before the advent of first floors and ceilings in the later medieval period the early medieval carpenter also had to consider the fact that the roof frame would be completely on show to all those below. As a consequence the medieval roofs are often ornately moulded and shaped. The most common decorative themes are chamfered edges on the underside of the main beams where people could see them, and the deliberate use of naturally curved timbers. These were sometimes arranged in pairs to create 'pointed' arches or 'cusped' shapes that are common design themes in church architecture **(Fig. 8)**. As the medieval period progressed new buildings became increasingly partitioned and the roof structure lost its decorative role as it was hidden above bedroom ceilings. The basic roof types that are discussed in this book are:

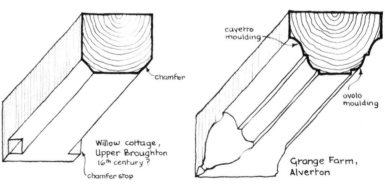

Fig. 9 Examples of Nottinghamshire Chamfers

Fig. 8 Cusped roof at Holme Pierrepont

Crown-post: **(Fig. 10 and Fig. 3)** this refers to a post that sits in the centre of the roof supported by the 'tie beam' of the cross frame below. The crown post supports a 'collar purlin' or 'crown plate' (usually via braces) which in turn supports 'collars' jointed between a pair of rafters. Every pair of rafters has a collar supported by the purlin making the roof very strong and stable. Nottinghamshire has 11 definite examples of crown post roofs, 6 of which are included later. It was the most popular form of roof construction in the early medieval period. The south range of the Old White Hart in Newark has the oldest example of a crown post roof in the county and has been dated to AD 1313. The Saracen's Head in Southwell is the latest known example of a crown post roof in Nottinghamshire dating to AD1463.

Fig.10 Old and new decorated Crown posts at South Muskham Prebend

Side purlin: (Fig. 11 and Fig. 3) Many more examples of side purlin roofs survive than crown-posts because they were most common in the later medieval period and are the only type used in Nottinghamshire after the 16th century. Unlike the crown-post roof there is no central support post in a side purlin roof. Instead each principal rafter supports a side purlin, one running along each side of the roof. These purlins support all the

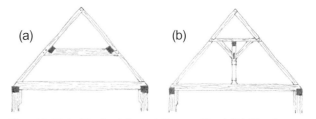

Fig. 11 Side Purlin (a) and Crown Post (b) Roof

other rafters, which are usually of smaller girth than the principal ones. Each pair of principal rafters has a collar running between them which is secured with a lap dovetail joint at the ends, on a crown-post roof this joint is often a mortice and tenon. Most of the timber-frame buildings discussed in this book have side purlin roofs.

Wall panels types and infill materials

Most people associate timber-frame buildings with the term 'wattle and daub' **(Fig. 12)**. Wattle consists of willow withies woven between the studs and the daub is a mud based render applied to the surface which is then protected with a lime based plaster and lime washed. This was most commonly used to infill between the large square openings of 'square panel' wall frames, like those shown in **Fig.12**. In truth there are very few recorded examples of wattle and daub panels in Nottinghamshire.

In fact daub was applied to a wide variety of materials especially where the wall frame was 'close studded' rather than a 'square panel' type **(Fig. 12 and 13)**. Thin slabs of local stone were used at The Saracen's Head in Southwell and plain roof tiles had been inserted and plastered at South Muskham Prebend, also in Southwell. In the case of square panels it appears to have been a more common practice to apply the daub to laths nailed across studs rather than on to wattle, as at The Woolpack in Newark.

Of course the core of an infill panel is covered by plaster and usually only seen when repairs are being carried out, or during alterations, so further information about original medieval infill panels may still come to light. As a general rule however, there was a tendency to replace medieval daubed panels with brick 'nogging' infill during the 17th and 18th centuries or otherwise their existence was hidden from view behind exterior brick walls and layers of internal modern plaster finishes.

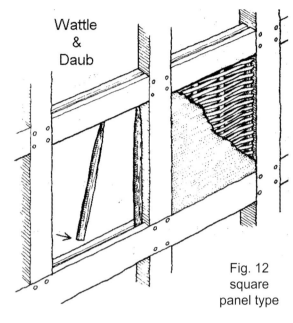

Wattle & Daub

Fig. 12 square panel type

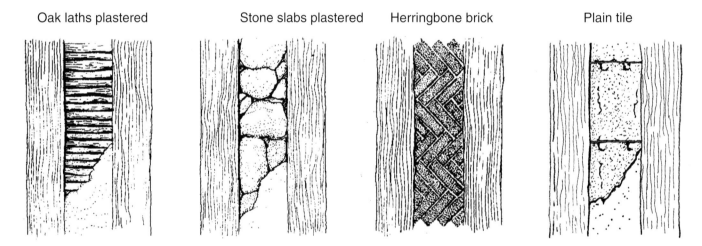

Oak laths plastered   Stone slabs plastered   Herringbone brick   Plain tile

Fig. 13 Close studding and examples of different types of infill found in Nottinghamshire

Other aspects of timber-frame technology

There are many aspects to timber-frame technology which are not discussed in this short book, such as carpenters marks, which is the system of Roman numerals used to identify individual timbers for assembly purposes, or the types of joints and their development through time. For anyone who is interested there are a number of excellent books available some of which are listed in the 'further reading' section at the back of the book.

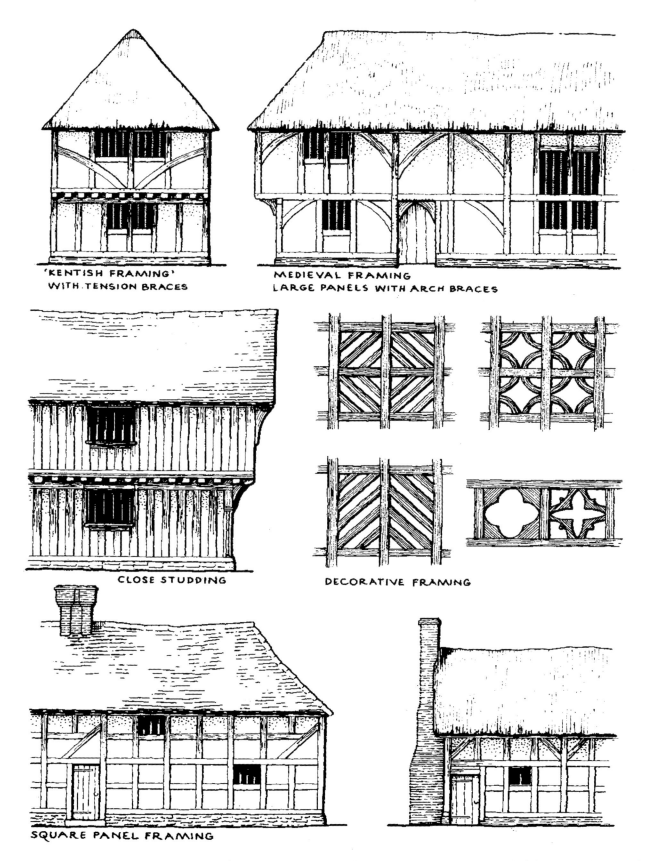

'KENTISH FRAMING'
WITH TENSION BRACES

MEDIEVAL FRAMING
LARGE PANELS WITH ARCH BRACES

CLOSE STUDDING

DECORATIVE FRAMING

SQUARE PANEL FRAMING

Fig. 14 Examples of the different types of timber frame that are found around the country, all of them can be seen in Nottinghamshire and are described in various examples discussed later in this book.

Dendrochronology (Fig. 15)

Much of the following information was gathered during surveys that accompanied tree-ring dating sampling of the timber-frame buildings. This usually involves taking pencil sized cores from at least six timbers each with at least 50 growth rings showing. The individual ring widths are measured and form a pattern for each sample which will show highs and lows related to the environmental and climatic conditions that affected the tree while it was growing. The same pattern will be seen in samples from trees that were growing in the same region at the same time. It is possible to match a sample, or set of samples, against a 'master chronology', built up over years from trees of known planting or felling dates. If there is a good match this gives a date for the last tree ring of the sample. If one or more of the samples contains bark this date is the year when the timber was felled. This date is likely to be very close to the year of the building's prefabrication and construction as medieval craftsmen worked the oak within the first year of its felling.

2. Medieval timber-frame buildings in Nottinghamshire

Nottinghamshire has many very fine medieval buildings, but most of these are stone built churches. As is the case elsewhere in the country relatively few of the ordinary houses and other buildings survive. The houses of the less well off who, as today, made up the majority of the population, have not survived. We have to look to archaeology and the very few old written accounts to understand their lives and occasionally we make assumptions, based on our best guesses, about their homes.

We only have to look around the historic centre of Newark-on-Trent to get some idea of how medieval towns and urban centers may have appeared. By no means all the timber-frame buildings of Newark are medieval in date, but views along some of its old streets, like Castle Gate, Kirk Gate, Stodman Street and Lombard Street, and of the Market Place, have a distinct character. These streets contain more examples of black and white timber-framing than most and help give Newark a distinct appearance unlike any other historic town in Nottinghamshire.

The occasional timber-frame buildings in settlements such as East Retford and Mansfield are less obvious to the passer by. In the case of Mansfield, this is very much the result of the abundant availability of good quality local building stone. Similarly, from the 18th century onwards the introduction of brick making in areas away from the local supplies of good building stone led to bricks becoming the ubiquitous material for new building or for cladding existing old timber frames. As a consequence, the influence of timber framing on the appearance of most of Nottinghamshire's towns is negligible. Even with its high number of surviving timber-frame buildings Newark is still largely a town of brick .

The building materials on show are not the only identifier of the medieval heritage of our towns. We often find narrow buildings tightly positioned alongside their neighbours on the main routes of the county's medieval settlements. One only has to pick up a current Ordnance Survey map to see the evidence in our towns of the long, narrow plot boundaries which were established in the medieval period. And of course, we can never be certain that there is not a medieval gem hidden behind the later layers of history which disguise the true origins of some of our towns' unexplored buildings.

The medieval open hall

The earliest type of timber-frame building built after the Norman invasion was the open hall. This type of building would most likely have been the standard form of house during the early stages of the medieval period in the 11th and 12th centuries. However in Britain, there is almost no known standing building evidence for the ordinary timber houses built before the 13th century. What evidence there is are stone buildings, like the Jews House in Lincoln with its upper hall living space at first floor level. Also the Bayeux Tapestry shows a timber upper hall building, set on fire by Norman invaders. Locally the best example of a timber upper hall building can be seen in Nottingham, on Castlegate, known as Severns and is described below. Another example of an early medieval building with a first floor is 22 – 24 Kirkgate, Newark which indicates that these buildings may not have been an uncommon type in the early post-conquest town, even if there are very few examples left. In the countryside on the other hand it is clear that the normal form of house type, for those that could afford them, was the ground floor open hall.

In its simplest form the medieval hall was only two bays long and open to the roof **(see Fig. 16)**. The cross-frames that support the roof could be either post and truss or a cruck type of construction. The middle frame was usually left open, and in some cases two open cross frames were used to create a longer three bay hall. Often the hall was widened through the use of an aisle (See 1. The Gables, Little Carlton). This was an economic way of extending the main living space with minimum impact on the roof structure. It meant the posts next to the aisle stood inside the hall space rather than acting as part of the outside wall frame, these are termed aisle or arcade posts.

The hearth was a simple arrangement in the centre of the hall with no chimney, the smoke making its own way out of the roof via the thatch or a louvre. This would have made for a very smokey atmosphere that is sometimes hinted at today when blackening is discovered on the underside of original medieval thatch (hidden under successive layers of new material) or more commonly as soot on rafters in a roof space. Both these types of evidence are easily removed and rarely discovered.

More often than not there would have been a bay at one or other end of the open hall, closed off to the hall with a door, creating a room for sleeping know as the

Fig.16 The White Hart's medieval hall

solar. Here the master of the house, the lord, would have slept while the rest of his household, knights and servants, found space in the hall itself.

The older the building the more likely it is that the original core is disguised and hidden behind later improvements and changes. These changes can be identified relatively simply in general terms. The basic communal hall building was continually refined during the medieval period, usually at first with the insertion of a floor and chimney, or smoke hood, and then if the site allowed, the floor plan of the building was extended. These developments provided increasingly sophisticated spaces for the inhabitants more akin to modern living. Some rooms had very specialist functions such as wine and beer storage (in the buttery) while others were simply bedrooms for the improved privacy of the household. In some instances services may have been housed in separate buildings, the kitchen for example may have been kept away from the main living area to provide a measure of protection from fire, but the general tendency was towards a building which functioned in a similar way as one does today.

1. The Gables, Little Carlton, South Muskham (Fig. 17 & 18). This is one of the most picturesque of

Fig. 17

Nottinghamshire's timber-frame buildings, but up until the 1980s it was hidden from view behind damaging cement render (see Figure inside rear cover). Now beautifully conserved the close studding of the wings is plain for all to see from the roadside. Tree ring analysis along with the in-depth analysis of the architecture, has established that the house began life as a medieval hall in 1266, with an aisle and cross passage. By the Tudor period the hall was floored over, with a fireplace and

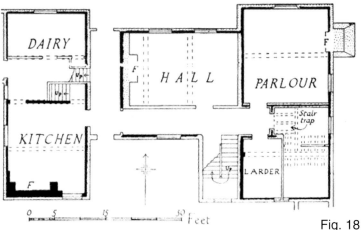

Fig. 18

chimney which gave improved heating and first floor accommodation. The house plan also expanded with the addition of two wings, set at right angles, one to each end of the hall, creating a symmetrical frontage and H plan layout that was fashionable at the time. One wing has been investigated through tree-ring dating and supports the theory that the wings were added around 1540.

2. Thatch Cottage, Main Street, South Collingham (Fig. 19) This is another beautiful building, with its dormer windows peeking through a thatched roof that descends almost to the ground. It contains at its core at least two bays of a medieval building. However, the dendrochronology dates were not conclusive and it has been much altered and repaired over the centuries. It has a narrow aisle that may be medieval, like that of The Gables mentioned above, and later additions that include a central fireplace, probably 16th or 17th century, and inserted first floors. When viewed from the road none of the timber-frame itself is obvious to the passer-by, but it makes a lovely photograph, with its tall brick chimney stacks and thatching that extends over the aisle to ground floor level.

Fig 19

The Wealden House

A Wealden House is type of medieval hall house that originally developed in the Weald area of Kent and Sussex, but is found in many parts of the country where timber-framing is common, such as Warwickshire. It is a very distinctive and efficient design having a central hall sandwiched between two bays which each have upper floors that project, or 'jetty', out above the ground floor. The whole building was constructed as a single unit, under a single span. The middle bays of the hall appear set back behind deep over-hanging eaves that have to extend out to cover the projecting bays either side. There are many variations on the basic design, but none are particularly common in the north of the country. Some examples still exist in York which probably represent about as far north as the style stretched and one example can still be seen in Nottinghamshire:

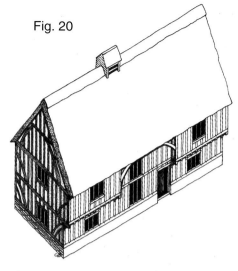

Fig. 20

3. The Woolpack, Stodman Street, Newark (Fig. 20 - 22) It is tightly sandwiched between two much later buildings, one of which occupies the position that would originally have been the third bay of the Wealden house. Unfortunately at some point in its history this bay was removed, by sawing off the building at the end of the hall, possibly because it had been damaged by fire. As a result of its 'shrinkage' the Woolpack has often been referred to as a 'half' or 'three-quarters' Wealden, but this is misleading since these terms refer to a type of Wealden building purposely constructed with a projecting jetty at only one end, not one that has been reduced in size at some later stage.

The roof construction of the building is also very special as it

The Woolpack Inn as it may have looked in about 1452

Fig. 22

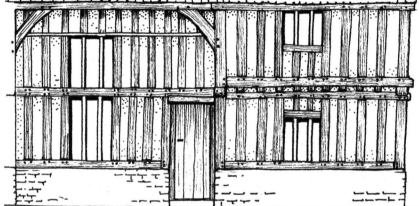

Fig. 21 Beneath the render there probably lies a 'close-studded' frame.

contains a set of original medieval rafters, with no replacements. All surviving 17 pairs have chiseled numbers applied by the original carpenter that ensured that they were all in exactly the right place when the building was raised. It is also strange for having an unusual side purlin roof, rather than the more common crown-post arrangement. The dendrochronology date of c.1452 has come from the roof timbers as the wall frame is obscured on the outside by render and brickwork and internally by modern finishes. The hall was floored over at some stage later in its history, but the location of an original louvre that would have acted as a vent to let the smoke out of the roof is indicated by a series of peg holes on two of the pairs of rafters.

Other Wealden houses are known to have existed in Newark such as some formerly on Millgate shown in Cornelius Brown's "A History of Newark on Trent "- Volume II (1907).

The upper hall

Ground floor halls are by far the most commonly surviving type of early medieval timber-frame dwelling and must have been present in almost every parish of the county, even if they are now few and far between. The 'upper hall' house is less common, but there are one or two good examples that have survived in Nottinghamshire: Severns in Nottingham and 22-24 Kirkgate in Newark . The former was restored to its medieval form in 1970 and is open to the public, providing an excellent opportunity to investigate and get a feel for this type of building. It is no surprise that the few examples in Nottinghamshire are to be found within the key medieval urban centres as they are generally associated with the merchant classes who used the ground floor for business transactions and storage and lived in the space above. Invariably the first floor had a jetty that protruded beyond the ground floor (this method of construction will be discussed a little fuller later), and a crown-post roof **(Fig. 11).** However, although there are other jettied buildings of the medieval period, the two buildings discussed here are ones that can be termed 'upper halls'. Their age (especially Severns) means they are more akin to the social status, functions and origins of the ground floor open hall than the purpose-built two storey town houses and inns that developed later on in the 15th and 16th centuries.

Fig. 23

4. Severns, Castlegate Nottingham (Fig. 23 & 24). In 1969, to save it from demolition, the remains of this upper hall timber-frame house were moved from Middle Pavement, restored and re-assembled where the building now stands at the end of Castlegate opposite the castle walls. Originally it formed the frontage of a merchant's house consisting of a three bay upper hall with shop space at ground floor and an extensive service range running off to the rear up to the sandstone cliff edge. As with almost every building of any age in Nottingham, beneath it were a set of cellars carved out of the sandstone which interconnect with caves of various dates and eventually led down to the foot of the cliff.

Walking into the Middle Pavement entrance to the Broadmarsh centre today you are passing the original location of the timber frame building and its rear range. The cave tours at the bottom of the escalators take you past the tannery site that was carved into the cliff face roughly below the location of the timber-frame building.

Severns underwent considerable reconstruction in 1969/70, some of it conjectural, under the expert supervision of F.W.B Charles who along with his wife was involved in the repair and restoration of many of the country's best timber-frame buildings. It provides the best opportunity in the county to see a 14th century crown-post roof, dated by

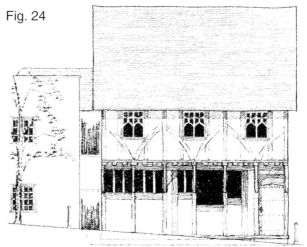

Fig. 24

CASTLE ROAD FRONT (WEST) scale

dendrochronology to 1334. Other aspects of the construction that are of particular interest include: the tracery windows which were re-installed based on examples from a building in Exeter; the jetty of the first floor; the curved down-braces; and the suspended wooden floor that was necessary to span the open cellars above which it was originally built. Usually the floor of a medieval building would be solid, possibly with flagstones or tiles or simply beaten earth with ox blood, lime or gypsum plaster added to improve its durability.

5. 22 – 24 Kirkgate, Newark (Fig.25 - 27). This building occupies a corner plot and has an original upper floor that projects on two sides which has been dated to 1337 by the dendrochronologists. It is easily visible from the road with its large downwards bracing with pronounced curves. Also visible on the projecting corner is the end of the 'dragon-beam' that runs diagonally to support floor joists running in two directions **(Fig.25 - 27).** It has been much restored in the past 150 years and the ground floor is mostly modern but it retains much of its original crown-post roof.

Fig. 25 Plan of first floor showing the dragon beam

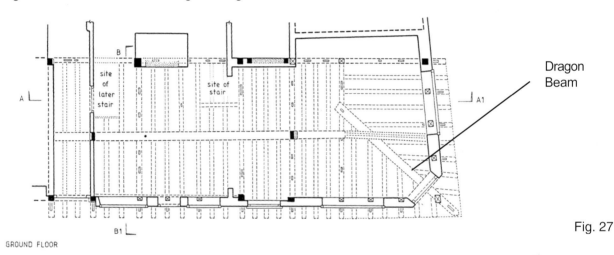

Dragon Beam

Fig. 27

GROUND FLOOR

Fig. 26 This cut-away shows the dragon beam and cross frame

AXONOMETRIC VIEW OF TIMBER
FRAME IN NORTH WEST END BAY

These two examples are not the only buildings with 'jetties' and first floors in the county and several other examples of medieval buildings with this type of floor arrangement are described below. However, most of them represent either later insertions into ground floor open hall buildings or 'multi-storeyed' 15th and 16th century buildings. None of them would generally be considered an upper hall structure as the definition is restricted to those buildings where the ground floor was a storage facility, not living space.

The cruck frame

A type of building technique often found used in medieval timber-frame buildings in the north and west of the country is the cruck frame. Cruck frames are quite distinctive as they use naturally curved oak beams but they are not found at all in the south-east parts of the country where oak woodland was plentiful in the medieval period. The system takes a bent piece of oak, splits it in half and secures it together at the top to create one pair of cruck blades. Pairs of cruck blades were arranged in the same way as a post and truss cross frame, at regular spacings to create roughly even sized rooms or bays. The cruck frame is different from a post and truss construction because the structural frame for the wall and the roof are formed by the same piece of timber. It is associated both with the open hall buildings of the manorial lords and also with the homes of people of a lesser status. Some examples show all the evidence of high quality workmanship, such as carving for purely decorative purpose, as in The Hollies described below, while others have the appearance of more rugged utilitarian construction, where frills were unnecessary or unaffordable to the owners.

Two examples of 'upper crucks' where the blades do not stretch fully to the ground were dated during the recent Newark tree-ring dating survey to the 17th and 18th centuries. They seem to prove that this type of construction had a very long history in this county. But for the most part the technique is much less common after the end of the medieval period. Around Nottinghamshire there is evidence of the widespread use of cruck frames in the medieval period, from the Wolds of the south to the borders with South Yorkshire in the north.

Fig. 28

There is a particular concentration in the south of Nottinghamshire, with many of the villages of the Wolds area having, or once having, examples. They appear to be part of a tradition of building that was also common in the adjacent area of north Leicestershire. Unfortunately, for those interested in seeing them for themselves several of the Nottinghamshire examples were demolished last century, including 'Cruck Frame Cottage'. This was one of the handful of buildings that made up the hamlet of Glapton that was cleared to make way for the new Clifton estate for Nottingham City in 1958 **(Fig. 28)**. One of the cruck blades of this building was saved and is now on display in the museum of the Department of Archaeology at the University of Nottingham where it offers probably the best opportunity to see a Nottinghamshire cruck at close quarters. The few examples still present in buildings are all hidden from the view of the passer-by. Others that have tragically been lost forever in recent times include a cottage in Sutton Bonnington and one in Kirkby-in-Ashfield, both of which were demolished in the 1930s.

Examples of cruck frames can be seen at:

6. TIL House, 56 Village Road, Clifton (Fig. 29 & 30). A private house which appears to the passer-by as a thatched brick building built and stamped with the initials of the owner 'TIL' and the date 1707. But this is misleading as its origins are actually much older. It contains the base of a single cruck, where the cruck blades never rose all the way to the roof apex, which has been dated by dendrochronology to 1319. The later alterations to the building, that include a fireplace addition to the back of the 'cross passage' and the addition of a side wing, are all good examples of the development of accommodation from a simple medieval open hall, through to a modern house of the 18th century period.

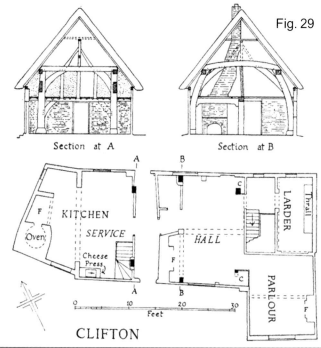

Fig. 29

CLIFTON

Fig. 30

Fig. 31

7. The Old Post Office, 75 Main Street, Normanton-on-Soar (Fig. 31). This building is part of the Wolds group but is considerably younger than TIL House above. According to the dendrochronologists the cruck blades date to c.1454. It shows that in southern Nottinghamshire at least, the cruck frame method of building continued throughout the medieval period.

There are 3 pairs of cruck blades plus some evidence that there was once at least one more pair, however, they unfortunately do not form part of an end wall that is visible to the passer-by. A slightly later timber-frame extension that faces on to the road contains a 'jetty'.

8. The Hollies, Main Street, Bathley (Fig. 32 & 33). This is a private house not very visible from the road, nor is the timber-frame immediately obvious as it is hidden behind later brick and render, as is so often the case. Here again there is a single base cruck representing one of the very oldest timber-frame buildings in the county dating to the late 13th century. The medieval open hall also had an aisle that provided the occupants with extra living space similar to that of The Gables, South Muskham mentioned above. In addition to being one of the oldest dated timber-frame buildings it also shows that the distribution of cruck frames is widespread in Nottinghamshire.

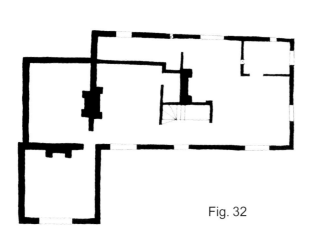

Fig. 32

Fig. 33

Examples of cruck frames also exist, or are known to have existed, in areas to the west such as Sookholme Lane Farm, Pleasley (one cruck still intact) and as far north as Blyth and Everton.

The medieval inn

Several of the county's best and most extensive examples of timber-framing technology were built as hostelries, and some, like The Saracen's Head in Southwell have remained so right through to modern times. As you would expect they are found in the busier medieval urban centres of the county: Nottingham, Newark and Southwell. None are known of in the villages of the rural parishes where the level of through trade would have been unlikely to warrant the investment in a dedicated inn building of this size.

The three described below are all quite different in their form but have similarities that are linked to their distinctive use, such as long ranges of two storey accommodation and displays of high quality workmanship (presumably to attract the more affluent traveller).

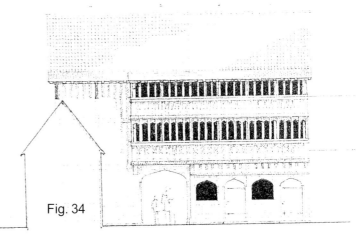

Fig. 34

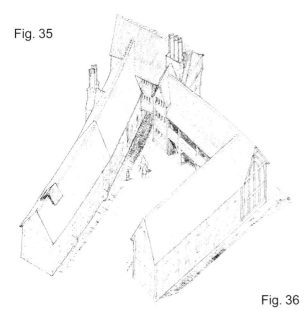

Fig. 35

Fig. 36

9. The Old White Hart, on the Market Place, Newark (Fig. 34 - 36). It is tucked away in the corner of the square but is clearly a very special timber-frame building. The painted front elevation with its tracery windows, similar to those seen at Severns in Nottingham, is actually the latest part of the building dating to the 15th century. The oldest part of the medieval inn is the wing to the rear, access to which is via the carriageway at the front. Considered by many to be one of the finest examples of its type in the Midlands, the crown-post roof has been dated to 1313. The 14th century building is unusual for

several reasons, firstly it is very wide, spanning over 20 feet, it also has a unique double wall frame with two layers of bracing that provides excellent strength to the structure. The beautiful reconstruction drawing by Mary Charles clearly shows all of the details of the main hall of the inn **(Fig. 16)**.

The three storey front range was added in 1459 and is interesting in its own right, especially because of the painted decoration which survives both internally and externally. The reconstruction of the window tracery and the repainting of the front were both based on surviving elements and give a splendid indication of how colourful medieval timber-framed buildings could and would have looked. The plaster niches containing figures of saints, one with a book and one with a palm, repeated 24 times.

10. The Saracen's Head, Southwell (Fig. 37 - 39). sits right at the centre of the medieval town fronting the Market Place, and would have indicated to any potential customers that it was a very high status establishment. In its time it was akin to the grandest hotels of our modern cities and played host to royalty. Charles I is said to have spent his very last night of freedom here during the 17th century Civil War.

Fig. 37

Fig. 38

Today the hotel includes the 18th century assembly hall building to the south, but the original timber-frame inn is clearly distinguishable, despite the later inserted sash windows, by the close studding of the upper floor.

Interestingly the inn is made up of three medieval timber-frame structures, a south range, a north range and a connecting east range that incorporates the carriageway.

The present uniform appearance is misleading as each range has a quite different type of roof construction even though all are of very similar ages. Before the tree-ring dating of the early 1980s experts considered the different styles of construction to be indicative of at least 100 years difference in age between the main north and south ranges, but according to the tree-ring dating results all the ranges probably date to the 1460s. Only the south range provided an exact date, 1463, but the other two are also contemporary. It seems that the inn was built and extended in very quick succession and that each wing was produced in a different style probably by different carpentry firms.

The south range of 1463 has a well-built side purlin roof, while the north range has a crown-post roof and the east range is also a side purlin construction, like the south, but with a ridge piece. The east range was clearly designed to link the upper floors of the other two ranges, but the south range is set back over six feet further from the road than the north range. As a result the east range link actually extends across the front of the south range hiding its gable end from view and giving a uniform appearance to the building. The roofs of the east and south ranges are also of slightly different heights, which can be seen at the southern end of the roof if you stand on the far side of the road and look at the very top of the roof.

The north range has a crown-post roof, the first two bays of which are turned to face the road. Upstairs these two bays form a single very high quality bedroom originally open to the rafters, known as the King Charles suite for obvious reasons. Both upstairs and downstairs spaces are highly decorated with wall paintings, some of which have been identified as Elizabethan by experts from the Courtauld Institute of Art **(Fig. 38)**.

Unfortunately none of the roof structure **(Fig. 39)** is visible to the casual visitor, but

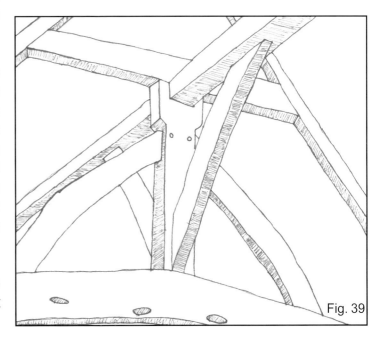

Fig. 39

there are many details which can be seen on request, including the wall paintings. Items of interest include the original over-hanging jetty braces which are clearly visible from the carriageway. These indicate that not only the sash windows but the whole ground floor frontage are part of an 18th century extension and explains why the timber-frame close-studding only survives at the first floor.

Parts of the original frame are still visible in the main bar and restaurant but they are not easily interpreted because of the subsequent alterations.

11, 12 & 13 The old inns of Nottingham: Ye Olde Salutation, Maid Marian Way; The Bell Inn, Long Row and The Trip to Jerusalem, Brewhouse Yard (Fig. 40) A debate about which of Nottingham's most famous inns is the oldest has run for years and even attracted the Channel 4 Time Team to investigate. The controversy continues however, as although a timber from the Bell Inn

Fig. 40

on Long Row produced the oldest tree-ring date it is disputed by some as being a 're-used' timber that must have come from a previous pub structure. Whatever the truth, it is clear that both the Salutation and Bell are considerably older timber-frame structures than the Trip to Jerusalem, even if brewing has been going on there as long as is claimed!

Medieval barns and others
Some very large timber-frame barn structures are found in parts of the country, but only really in the predominantly arable areas where the tithe system was strictly applied. Although they can be found across the Midlands there are very few of the archetypal 'aisled barns' in Nottinghamshire. There are one or two houses with aisles that may be early examples of a converted barn, such as Thorpe Farm,

Headon-cum-Upton in the north. But as with all the other types of timber-framing listed in this introduction to Nottinghamshire's traditions, a small number of exceptional examples survive that are worth mention. Also noted here two later, post-medieval, barns and one undated example as they help give a flavour of agricultural buildings which for the most part continued to be built in much the same way up until the early 18th century.

Fig. 41

14. The Barn at the Old Hall in Lowdham (Fig. 41) was dated by dendrochronolgy to 1541 . It is not really tall enough to constitute a threshing barn and probably indicates that the farm was not predominantly arable in production. Besides its age and rarity it is also very interesting because of the adjoining buildings and archaeological interest of the rest of the site. The barn is attached to the Old Hall which is a very impressive 17th century timber-frame building. Also nearby are the archaeological remains of the 'castle' site, with part of the original moat still able to hold water and a pronounced mound or building platform within. In fact this would best be thought of as a moated manor site and must have been where the medieval house stood when the barn was first constructed. It probably still existed and may have had a function up until the present Old Hall was built and replaced it in the 17th century. Unfortunately the barn is not easily visible from the lane that leads past the site to the church but the splendid Old Hall is quite noticeable and very much worth a look when passing (see 21 page 30).

15. Manor Farm Barn, Main Street, Askham (Fig. 42) was only very recently discovered to be medieval. Although a grade II listed structure, it had been described as an 18th century building in the official description, probably because the impressive internal timber-framing was not viewed at the time that it was inspected. It has now been tree-ring dated and is known to date to 1546, the last year

Fig.42

of Henry VIII's reign. This building really is special as not only is it one of the county's oldest barns but it also has a side aisle and an intact panel of daub on rough staves that separates one of the bays from the others. Also, instead of single braces between the posts and tie-beams there are two at each side. This type of arrangement is sometimes seen when there were a pair of aisles present, but a double aisled barn is very rare, the only example recorded in this county stood on Lover's Lane in Newark until 1960. The evidence that can be gleaned from the remaining timbers at Askham suggests it is unlikely to be another example. Although the roof is not original it has itself proved to be over 200 years old and is hipped at both ends as was the original. This replacement roof seems probably to be linked to the episode that led to the severe lean that particularly afflicts the east end of the barn. It has led to two of the main aisle posts cracking but farmer's repairs that have had been made in a truly agricultural and robust way, have proved basic but effective, and ensured the barn's survival and continued use. Recently it was bought and planning permission granted for conversion into a house. Thankfully this will ensure that the proper structural repairs essential to the barn's future will be carried out.

16. Aisled Barn, Ragnall (Fig. 43) is mentioned here in passing as it is one of only two other examples of aisled barns that we are aware of in this county. Although it appears from the evidence to be medieval as the presence of a side aisle generally indicates, the tree-ring analysis produced a date of 1717. This has led some to suggest that it is an indicator that the tradition of building large timber-frame barns with aisles continued for many centuries. Certain examples in Essex have been dated to the 18th century, but the lack of other similarly aged examples suggests that it was not a local tradition of this time in Nottinghamshire.

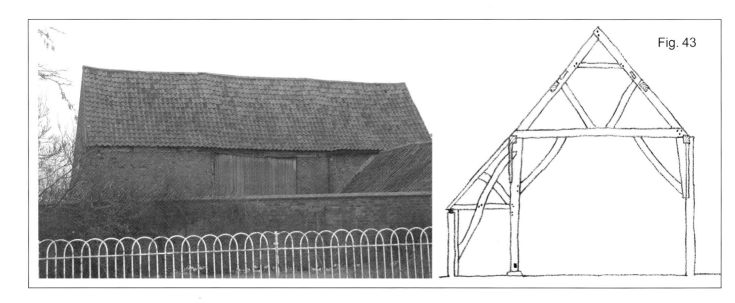

Fig. 43

17. Aisled barn at South Notts. Bus Depot, Gotham (Fig. 44) may provide the missing link between the aisled barn at Ragnall and the medieval example at Askham, but it has yet to be investigated by the dendrochronologists. It is certainly far from sure whether the side aisle is part of the original timber-frame or an addition, but until it is more thoroughly explored we will never know.

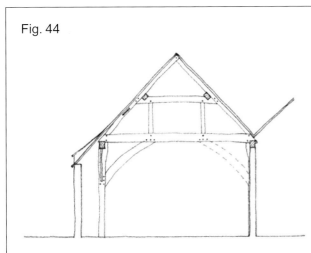
Fig. 44

Internal timbers at Gotham

Fig. 45

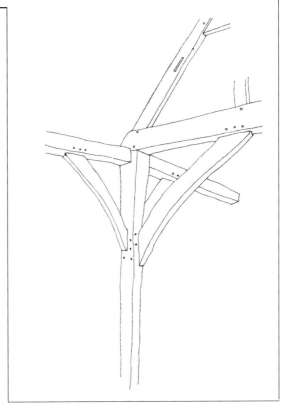

Fig. 46

18. Barn at 31 Main Street, Keyworth (Fig. 45 - 46)

is mentioned here along with the other key timber-frame barns. However, like Ragnall barn it is not actually medieval. It has been dated by dendrochronology to between 1635 and 1655 and is probably the grandest of all the county's surviving agricultural buildings. It sits right by the road and is easily walked past, but if you get the chance to go inside, which can be arranged through the owners, Rushcliffe Borough Council, you will find one of the largest oak pegged roofs in Nottinghamshire, spanning over 23 feet (usually a timber-frame barn will span about 18 – 20 feet). The roof has a double set of side purlins because of the sheer size of the span and length of the rafters. There are four surviving bays and there may originally have been one more. The original oak frame has survived and is infilled with the best example of brick nogging visible in the county. This is not the original walling material but probably dates to not long after the 1650s.

Jetties

A number of the buildings mentioned above have jetties, the Old White Hart and Saracen's Head Inns, Severns and 22-24 Kirk Gate, as well as many other examples, especially around Newark. The use of jetties was most common in urban settlements but they are not exclusively a town tradition as the example of The Old Post Office, 75 Main Street, Normanton-on-Soar shows. Explanations for the development of the jetty design are wide ranging, but the benefits of the increased living space within the high density urban context are obvious . It is clear that the jetty also became used as much as a status symbol as a practical device, applied as an architectural detail and indicator of taste. The jointing construction of a jetty is complex as the floor joists not only support the floor but also hold the weight of the outside wall and roof above. However, they are inherently stable and had the benefit of reducing the length needed for the main vertical posts (to that of a single floor). This meant each floor could be raised individually one stage at a time, never working with a main post timber much more than seven feet long. This must have been a distinct advantage when assembling the building as a main post is commonly 6 by 4 inches in section and solid oak is very heavy. An ordinary two storey building, built without a jetty, needs main posts that are 10 or 12 feet long at least, far more difficult to man-handle than a shorter length. Consequently a jettied building was presumably considerably less difficult to erect in the middle of a busy medieval town.

Fig. 47

19. The Governor's House, Lombard Street, Newark (Fig. 47 - 49). The name comes from the time of the Civil War when successive commanders of the town occupied and coordinated their operations from here. Nowadays it is a tea-room and bakery and provides a great opportunity to investigate and enjoy the interior of a 15th century timber-frame building. The building has actually been dated to c.1474 and is L shaped in plan with a splendid three-storey frontage, with each floor jettied out beyond the one below. It is without a doubt one of the most splendid and ornate timber-frame frontages in the

Fig. 48

Fig. 49 Elevation from Stodman St. and cross view showing jettying.

 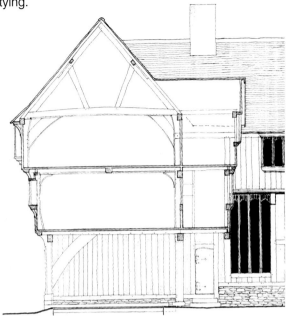

county. The first floor also has a long oriel gallery window beneath which the sill is coved, giving the impression of an extra jetty. The illustrations by Guy St. John Taylor Associates include a reconstruction of the original 1474 frontage and a very good illustration of the timber-frame skeleton. These provide a great opportunity to think about what lies behind the daubed and painted studs while you drink your tea in the café. The wall paintings that decorate the first floor interior are probably of the 16th century, a little before the time of the Civil War. It is worth taking the time to look at their design and colours to help get an idea of how colourful the interiors (and occasionally the exteriors) of these buildings could be. They are the best opportunity in the county to view 400 year old domestic wall paintings at one's leisure.

20. Manor House Wysall (Fig. 50).

In the south of the county there is yet another unique and very special example of a type of timber-frame building normally associated with other parts of the country. Manor House Wysall is one of a handful of examples in the county with 'herring-bone' pattern oak infill panels where the studs are set diagonally rather than perpendicular. But it is also has the only known example in the county of decorative panelling set within square panels above the front

Fig. 50

entrance. The herring-bone pattern framing is late Elizabethan in date and very decorative. The decorative panels take the form of four carved 'quatrefoils' which is a pattern often seen in the stone windows of medieval churches. This decorative panelling is unique in Nottinghamshire and would be much more at home in Derbyshire and areas to the west, especially in the West Midlands and Chester region. This unique survival probably dates to the 16th century but was only re-discovered in the late 1980s when the cement render obscuring the whole front of the building fell away. The building was then in a very poor state of repair but in recognition of its unique contribution to the heritage of the county and special character of Wysall the County Council helped fund its careful repair and restoration. It is still clearly visible set back off the Main Street to the east of the church although it is now slightly obscured by the unfortunate modern houses, some of which were built and sold to enable the repairs to the Manor House to be funded. When viewed from the front it is actually the stone gabled wing to the left of the entrance that hides the oldest part of the building. This north range retains a timber-frame that dates to the 15th century, at least 100 years before the part of the building with the decorative quatrefoils was added. The other examples in the county are all in the north, such as the White House in Blyth.

Timber-frame buildings after the medieval period

The Elizabethan period was a time of considerable change, especially in architecture. One of the most famous new Elizabethan buildings in the country is Wollaton Hall near Notttingham, completed in 1588 for Sir Francis Willoughby. This amazing building, designed by the architect Robert Smythson, was the ultimate in modern design and is about as far from a traditional timber-frame building as is a modern tower-block. Buildings of this size and quality are rare in the 16th century, the majority of the population continued to live in traditional buildings, which were largely unchanged from those of the medieval period, with a few notable exceptions.

Firstly, new timber-frame houses in Nottinghamshire of the late 16th century and early 17th century were invariably built with a large integral fireplace, commonly referred to as an inglenook. Secondly, they were almost always two storey in height. Thirdly, the new integral chimney and fireplace was increasingly built in brick, a material that had not been used since the Romans but which made a dramatic reappearance in the Tudor period. To begin with brick was an expensive and exotic material so for most its use was restricted to those areas where its qualities were best appreciated. Sometimes brick 'nogging' was used to replace earlier wattle and daub panels giving a more durable wall, as at the barn at 31 Main Street, Keyworth **(Fig. 45)**.

Another point that distinguishes timber-frame buildings of the 17th century from earlier examples is the layout and plan. Often we find that the chimney stack is placed in the middle of the building with a pair of back-to-back fireplaces heating two rooms. The entrance is also very often in the middle of the building and opens onto the side of the inglenook creating what is know as a 'lobby' entrance plan. Both The Old Hall, Lowdham and Raven's Farm, Misterton described below have inglenooks and lobbies.

Finally, although The Old Hall, Lowdham is a very finely built building akin in quality to several of the medieval buildings discussed earlier, both Raven's Farm and Yews Farmhouse are of much simpler construction. Presumably they were built by poorer farmers; this level of building is rarely found surviving from the earlier medieval period. They mark the end of the timber-frame building tradition as by the beginning of the 1700s brick had become the chosen building material for the majority of people in Nottinghamshire .

21. The Old Hall, Lowdham (Fig. 50 - 53). The medieval barn which stands immediately next to The Old Hall has already been described in this book. The barn was possibly originally a house that became down-graded when the new house was built next door in 1656. There is also a mound surrounded by a moat a few yards away that is probably older than either of the buildings, so The 'Old' Hall is in fact the newest building on the site! It is an excellent example of a 'baffle' entry house characterised by a central entrance that opens onto the side of a large centrally placed inglenook fireplace. This is built of stone but also included brick which was a very new material at the time. The building also has a front porch with a small room above it and a rear stair turret which together give the building a cross shaped plan form. The building has many elements of interest, one of which is the remains of an area of 'pargetting' hidden from view in the pantry. This is a very rarely seen method of decorating external lime

Fig. 51

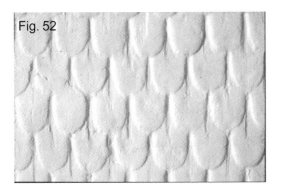

Fig. 52

Fig. 53

render, in this case with a fish-scale motif. It was quite common in East Anglia and probably would originally have covered the whole front of The Old Hall. This photo taken from the lane shows what a wonderfully picturesque image the house at the end of its tree lined driveway makes.

22. Yews Farmhouse, Styrrup (Fig. 54). This unusual little timber-frame building in the north of the county is a very good example of a lower status home. The owner who paid for its construction was a person of considerably less means than Peter Broughton, who it is believed built The Old Hall at Lowdham. Yews Farmhouse has none of the very fine details of The Old Hall. It is constructed of oak but the timbers are of much thinner section and has some very rough timbers, virtually un-worked, used as studs in the wall frame. However, like The Old Hall it is a mid 17th century timber-frame house with its original chimney, which in this case is at one end rather than in the middle. Also like The Old Hall the outside was originally completely rendered and may even have had some type of decoration, although it would never have had pargetting, the construction of Yews Farmhouse is much too functional for that. For instance, on close inspection of an original mud panel, uncovered during restoration of the building by Nottinghamshire Building Preservation Trust, the finger marks of the original builder were clearly visible. Spreading the daub onto the laths with bare hands, without applying a finishing top-coat of lime plaster, indicates that they were concerned solely with making the building wind and weather tight.

Fig. 54

Fig. 55

23. Raven's Farm, Church Street, Misterton (Fig. 55). Like The Old Hall in Lowdham this building is a baffle entry plan with a central fireplace of brick. Like both of the buildings above it was built in the mid 17th century. The roof was originally gabled on both ends and would have been thatched but now it is hipped at the road end. This is due to the rough alterations made to the roof structure when the building was later extended along the road front probably in the 18th century. Like Yews Farmhouse the roof structure is

not of high quality large sectioned timbers or constructed to especially high standards of workmanship. This reflects the lower status of the owners by comparison to those who paid to build the majority of the other timber-frame buildings that are noted in this book. It is no surprise that farmers would have had little time, or excess income, to spend it on indulging their homes on fashions from the south like pargetting.

Conclusion

This book is but a brief introduction to the timber-frame buildings of Nottinghamshire. The few examples listed are literally a handful of the total, they act as envoys for the rest and were picked for their extra-special status and genuine quality. They are the oldest, most elaborate, best preserved and generally the most accessible examples of the county's timber-frame buildings. Together they represent a period during which the craftsman's skills developed to their zenith in the 15th and 16th centuries. After this time, partly as a result of the increasing costs of oak, (much of which was diverted into ship building), timber-framing was gradually replaced by new 'modern' practices and materials. Most notably, from the Tudor Period the use of brick spread from Holland and became popular for new 'country houses' like Holme Pierrepont, especially in those parts of Britain where good building stone is not plentiful. Much of Nottinghamshire now has the appearance of a 'brick' county, especially along the Trent Valley and to the east of Sherwood.

Brick is by no means the whole picture. Many more examples of timber-frame buildings can be seen in the historic towns and villages of Nottinghamshire, especially in Newark, but few present themselves as obviously to the passer-by as those in this book. So many of the county's supposed brick and stone buildings hide remnants of an earlier timber-frame past that it is virtually impossible to calculate the full total. Some 'brick' buildings are very obviously hiding complete or near complete oak frames and are given away by their steeply pitched roofs, low eaves and small size. Even more brick buildings contain re-used oak frames, especially roof trusses, from earlier buildings making the most of the high quality materials, workmanship and the ease of disassembly. It is quite usual to find complete medieval roof trusses re-used in agricultural barns that were built in the 18th century. At Manor Farm Barn in Askham, the virtually complete medieval timber-frame aisled barn was only discovered in 2003 hidden behind the 18th century brick walls.

How many more hidden treasures still await discovery is not known and is part of the charm and interest of exploring historic buildings. The brief introduction to the technology given in this book is enough to enable anyone to make an accurate description and identification of a medieval timber-frame. Who knows, you may be the one who makes the discovery of an hither-to unknown medieval roof when you next go up in the attic.......

AUSTIN-HEALEY
100 SIX SERIES BN6

SERVICE PARTS LIST

SECOND ISSUE

This List cancels the Preliminary List (Part No. AKD855) and embodies all information issued up to and including Parts List Amendment No. PAU/541

WHEN ORDERING FURTHER COPIES OF THIS LIST PART No. **AKD855** (SECOND ISSUE) SHOULD BE QUOTED

Issued by

B.M.C. SERVICE LIMITED
COWLEY · OXFORD · ENGLAND

Telephone	- - - - - - - - - Oxford 77777
Telex	- - - - - - - Oxford Telex 83145 and 83146
Telegrams	- - - - - - - - Mowog, Telex, Oxford
Cables	- - - - - - - Mowog, Oxford, England
Codes	- - - - Bentley's, Bentley's Second Phrase, A.B.C.
	(5th and 6th Editions), Western Union, and Private

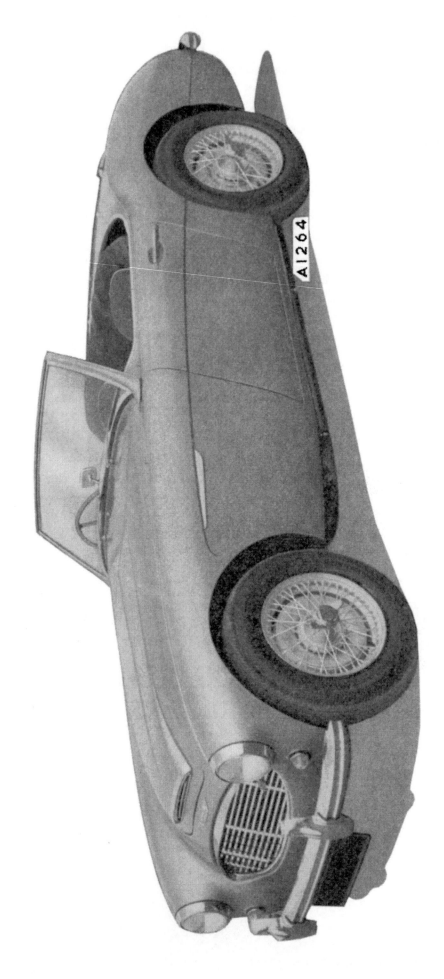

A1264

CONTENTS

LOCATION OF SERIAL NUMBERS

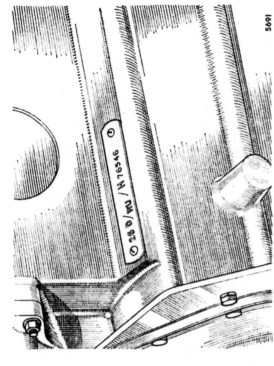

5691

The **Engine Number** is stamped on a plate secured to the front left-hand side of the cylinder block

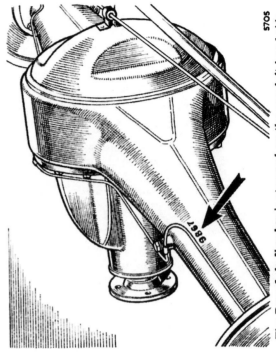

5705

The **Rear Axle Number** is stamped on the rear left-hand side of the axle

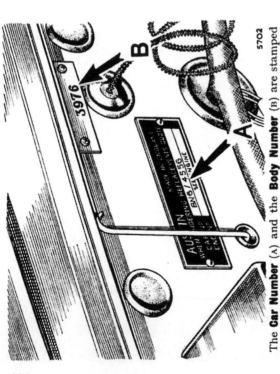

5702

The **Car Number** (A) and the **Body Number** (B) are stamped on plates secured to the right-hand side of the dash panel

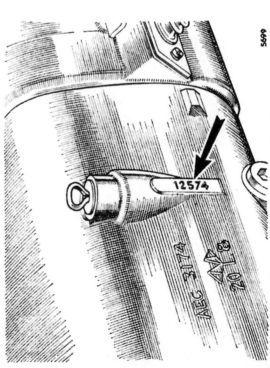

5699

The **Gearbox Number** is stamped on the right-hand side of the gearbox below the oil level indicator

4

Introduction

The range of parts in this List covers all serviceable components on all models to the standard specifications. Where the part is confined to one specification this is clearly defined in the 'Quantity' and/or 'Remarks' column, and where the part listed is not serviced, this is indicated by the letters N.S.P. in the 'Part Number' column.

The components in the plate illustrations are identified by numbers which correspond with the illustration reference appearing on the facing page in the column immediately following the part number.

It is essential first to identify the part against the illustration in the appropriate section of the List and make use of the illustration reference number to locate the part number and official description on the adjacent page.

When using the List it must be noted that each assembly (or sub-assembly) is shown as the **first item** and followed immediately by the individual components of the assembly, which are 'offset' for easy identification. It must be clearly understood that such assemblies (or sub-assemblies) will only be supplied complete with all their components when ordered against the assembly (or sub-assembly) part number. It will be appreciated, however, that the individual components of the assembly (which are listed immediately below and offset) can themselves be supplied separately, provided they are ordered against their individual part numbers. Note that the quantities shown are the quantity per vehicle, and not the quantity per component.

Example:

CONNECTING RODS—BEARINGS	AEC1092	6
Connecting rod and cap		
Bolt for cap	AEC268	12
Nut for bolt	AEC328	12
Bush—small-end	AEC797	6

We reserve the right to make changes or improvements in the construction or equipment of our products at any time. It is our general policy, however, to supply components to the latest specification.

Where a modification has taken place to a part, or a new part issued replacing the original part, this is indicated by the inclusion of the new part number under 'Modifications'.

Owner's Guide for Ordering Parts

Obtain your parts from the local B.M.C. Distributor or Dealer, who stocks only B.M.C. genuine and warranted parts.

(1) In order to ensure prompt and correct execution of orders it is essential that the following instructions are adhered to:

(*a*) Always state the **vehicle/chassis** and **engine numbers** complete with prefixes and suffixes (see page iii).

(*b*) Always **state the colour** of carpets, painted items, trim items, etc.

(*c*) Give **part numbers and description** (prefix letters to part numbers must always be quoted).

(*d*) **Quantity required**, bearing in mind that the quantities shown are the quantity per vehicle.

(*e*) **If ordering for dispatch give definite forwarding instructions**, i.e. sea, air freight, air parcel service, post, passenger/goods train, road service, or collection.

(2) When cabling or telegraphing the local Distributor or Dealer use the part number and give the **vehicle/chassis number. Confirm your cable or telegram by letter, or order**, at once. Give sufficient postal address for a parcel to find you. If you are away from home give **your home address in addition** to the dispatching instructions. Remember when sending a telegraphic order that **your name and address must be telegraphed as a message**. If this is not done the order will arrive without any indication of the sender's address, as your signature and address on the back of the telegram form is not telegraphed. Always write the quantity required of any particular part in words.

(3) **Claims under Warranty**

Claims for the replacement of material or parts under Warranty must always be submitted to the supplying Distributor or Dealer, or, when this is not possible, to the nearest Distributor or Dealer, informing them of the vendor's name and address.

(4) **Replacement Unit Schemes**

Where service replacement units are available this is clearly indicated by a bold letter (**R**) against the item at the end of the 'Description' line. Details of these and the terms and method of replacement are published in the local press and trade periodicals. You are advised to consult the local Distributor or Dealer for full details.

Instructions to Dealers

Modifications will be covered by the issue of Parts Amendment Sheets as required and also by the periodical reissue of the Part Number Index. Each issue of this Index is identifiable by its issue number and supersedes the previous issue, which should be destroyed. This Part Number Index should be kept with this List, for which purpose it is suitably punched.

In practice, first identify the items with the aid of the appropriate illustration. This provides a reference to the part number and official description appearing on the facing page. Now turn up the part number in the Part Number Index. Any modification will be indicated by the Parts Amendment Sheet number appearing in the adjacent column, and reference to this will provide the information necessary to ensure the issue of the correct part. If no Amendment Sheet number is indicated against the part number in the Part Number Index the part is clear for issue.

New parts introduced subsequent to the printing of this Parts List may be traced with the aid of the separate Index to Improvements and Alterations. They will be included in the Part Number Index as this is reissued and appropriately cross-referenced.

Certain classes of items are stocked and issued in **cartons, packets, etc., only,** and these are indicated in the Parts List by a figure in the 'Unit of Issue' column showing the quantity per package.

It is most important that orders should quote quite clearly the number of **packets** required, the word 'packets' (or the abbreviation 'pkt.') being used in every case.

If the word 'packet' is not used confusion may arise concerning the quantity actually required, with consequent delay in order handling.

While the quantity of units per pack indicated in the 'Unit of Issue' column in this Parts List provides a ready guide, it is always advisable to check the latest information regarding items in this category by referring to the Master Price List.

In addition a number of prices in the Price List are shown for a dozen (i.e. the abbreviation 'doz.' appears between the part number and units in the price), in which case the item is sold in 'dozens' only, and units

of one dozen must be ordered, quoting the word 'dozen' or the abbreviation 'doz.'; thus, should 48 be required, the order should state clearly '4 doz.'. Again, confusion can result if this is not done and over- or under-issue may occur.

NOTE.—Oversize and undersize replacement parts are tabulated at the end of the engine section.

The following abbreviations are used:

E indicates 'Export only'.
RHD indicates 'Right-hand drive'.
LHD indicates 'Left-hand drive'.
R/H indicates 'Right-handed'.
L/H indicates 'Left-handed'.
RHT indicates 'Right-hand thread'.
LHT indicates 'Left-hand thread'.
N.S.P. indicates 'Non-serviceable part'.
R at the end of the description indicates that reconditioned units are available under the B.M.C. Exchange Parts Service.

Where commencing and finishing numbers are quoted they are preceded by the following symbols to indicate the unit to which they apply:

(E) in the case of engine numbers.
(C) in the case of car/chassis numbers.
(G) in the case of gearbox numbers.
(FA) in the case of front axle numbers.
(RA) in the case of rear axle numbers.
(B) in the case of body numbers.

Bundy pipes are supplied completely finished and to the correct length but not shaped. They may be delivered straight or coiled according to their length and mode of delivery.

S.U. carburetter needles are supplied under the one part number AJH5292 and the individual needles are identified by the letter symbols stamped on the shoulder. When ordering replacement needles it is essential to quote the identification symbol in addition to and immediately following the part number.

IMPORTANT

B.M.C. SERVICE PARTS

When purchasing replacement parts or having repairs done owners are requested to see that a label similar to the one illustrated here is attached to the invoice rendered. These labels are issued by the Company and constitute a guarantee that genuine parts are supplied.

No better vehicle maintenance service exists in the world than that provided by the manufacturers and no vehicle demands less attention; but it is unfair to the manufacturers to expect the continuance of their support if the structure of the vehicle has been disturbed by the use of replacements that are not genuine B.M.C. parts.

Replacement parts that are not of genuine B.M.C. manufacture cannot be relied upon to be of B.M.C. specification, material, and workmanship, and therefore the manufacturers cannot be expected to extend their Warranty to vehicles which have been fitted with parts not of their manufacture.

All Authorized B.M.C. Distributors and Dealers are under contract to supply only genuine B.M.C. parts.

Alphabetical Index

Alphabetical Index

Alphabetical Index

Alphabetical Index

Part Number Index

The following is a complete index of parts in this list, giving the page reference of each part number.

Part Number	Page	Amdt. Number
1A1829	A.17	
1A1832	A.17	
1A1880	R.8	
1A2104	A.14	
1A2203	A.8	
1A3073	B.1	
1A3073	F.1	
1A4742	K.1	
1A4744	K.1	
1A4745	K.1	
1A4746	K.1	
1A4751	K.1	
1A4752	K.1	
1A4753	K.1	
1A4754	K.1	
1A4756	K.1	
1A4760	K.1	
1A4785	K.5	
1A4788	K.1	
1A9203	R.1	
1A9209	A.15	
1A9211	A.15	
1A9222	H.4	
1A9223	H.4	
1A9307	R.17	
1A9308	R.17	
2A880	D.2	
2A504	D.2	
2A587	B.2	
2A770	A.8	
2A780	A.8	
2A2088	D.2	
2A3254	F.4	
2A5006	H.4	
2A5346	M.8	
2A5893	H.4	
2A5412	S.1	
2A5419	S.1	
2A7227	M.2	
2A9039	O.1	
14A366	R.8	
14A3823	R.32	
ABZ0407	R.5	
ABZ0407	R.6	
ABZ0407	R.34	

Part Number	Page	Amdt. Number
ACA5297	J.1	
ACA5297	J.3	
ACA5814	R.8	
ACB5311	A.17	
ACB5311	A.18	
ACB5856	M.2	
ACC5187	A.16	
ACG5147	D.1	
ADA457	R.8	
ADA461	R.8	
ADA463	R.8	
ADA464	R.8	
ADA466	R.8	
ADA467	R.8	
ADA2450	R8	
ADB554	R.12	
ADB557	R.12	
ADB8657	R.12	
ADE539	R.30	
ADE565	R.30	
ADG709	R.12	
ADG1673	R.12	
ADG1811	R.12	
ADH456	R.8	
ADP610	A.6	
ADP610	A.14	
AEB3105	F.2	
AEB3105	F.6	
AEB3111	F.2	
AEB3111	F.6	
AEB3112	F.2	
AEB3112	F.6	
AEB3115	F.8	
AEB3115	F.6	
AEB3124	F.2	
AEB3124	F.6	
AEB3180	F.3	

Part Number	Page	Amdt. Number
AEB3180	F.7	
AEB3162	F.4	
AEB3163	F.4	
AEB3181	F.4	
AEB3202	F.4	
AEB3203	F.3	
AEB3203	F.6	
AEB3204	F.3	
AEB3204	F.7	
AEB3206	F.3	
AEB3209	F.7	
AEB3209	F.3	
AEB3212	F.7	
AEB3212	F.3	
AEB3214	F.2	
AEB3214	F.6	
AEC27	A.5	
AEC28	A.2	
AEC91	A.4	
AEC108	A.7	
AEC110	A.1	
AEC128	A.4	
AEC135	A.5	
AEC139	A.4	
AEC135	A.5	
AEC139	A.1	
AEC143	A.5	
AEC144	A.5	
AEC150	A.4	
AEC157	A.6	
AEC158	A.6	
AEC160	A.5	
AEC162	A.5	
AEC176	A.6	
AEC179	A.2	
AEC180	A.2	
AEC183	A.4	
AEC191	A.2	
AEC193	A.2	
AEC202	A.3	
AEC203	A.7	
AEC205	A.6	
AEC206	A.9	
AEC214	A.9	
AEC216	A.9	

Part Number	Page	Amdt. Number
AEC223	A.7	
AEC224	A.7	
AEC238	A.10	
AEC242	A.10	
AEC245	A.5	
AEC247	A.2	
AEC264	A.4	
AEC265	A.4	
AEC268	A.2	
AEC278	A.2	
AEC279	A.2	
AEC283	A.7	
AEC284	A.7	
AEC289	A.11	
AEC290	A.4	
AEC291	A.10	
AEC293	A.10	
AEC313	A.3	
AEC315	A.7	
AEC328	A.2	
AEC382	A.11	
AEC383	A.11	
AEC336	A.3	
AEC337	A.3	
AEC389	A.2	
AEC340	A.2	
AEC341	A.1	
AEC343	A.1	
AEC346	A.5	
AEC348	A.3	
AEC349	A.14	
AEC350	A.14	
AEC357	A.7	
AEC368	D.5	
AEC375	D.6	
AEC388	A.9	
AEC384	A.9	
AEC385	F.1	
AEC398	A.1	
AEC403	A.14	
AEC405	A.7	
AEC406	A.7	
AEC407	A.7	
AEC416	B.2	
AEC435	A.3	
AEC436	A.3	
AEC440	D.6	
AEC441	D.6	

Part Number Index—continued

Part Number	Page	Amdt. Number
AEC442	D.6	
AEC448	A.4	
AEC449	A.14	
AEC450	A.14	
AEC451	A.8	
AEC461	A.3	
AEC463	A.5	
AEC474	A.4	
AEC478	A.4	
AEC479	A.14	
AEC482	A.2	
AEC488	A.6	
AEC490	A.6	
AEC491	A.5	
AEC496	B.2	
AEC604	A.1	
AEC607	A.10	
AEC600	A.9	
AEC616	A.5	
AEC621	A.3	
AEC667	A.7	
AEC671	A.7	
AEC672	A.1	
AEC675	A.8	
AEC678	B.1	
AEC679	B.1	
AEC680	B.1	
AEC681	B.1	
AEC682	A.10	
AEC685	B.1	
AEC686	B.1	
AEC687	A.3	
AEC689	B.1	
AEC692	A.7	
AEC695	A.7	
AEC698	A.7	
AEC699	A.6	
AEC701	B.1	
AEC702	D.6	
AEC703	A.10	
AEC719	A.1	
AEC720	A.1	
AEC720	A.5	
AEC724	A.14	
AEC730	A.14	
AEC731	A.5	
AEC736	A.5	
AEC744	A.11	
AEC745	A.11	
AEC746	A.11	
AEC747	A.11	
AEC748	A.11	
AEC749	A.11	
AEC773	A.2	
AEC785	A.1	
AEC787	A.4	
AEC796	B.1	
AEC797	A.2	
AEC798	A.5	
AEC825	B.1	
AEC827	A.5	
AEC828	A.2	
AEC829	A.8	
AEC831	A.5	
AEC832	A.1	
AEC833	A.1	
AEC834	A.1	
AEC835	D.5	
AEC844	A.1	
AEC853	A.7	
AEC863	A.7	
AEC864	A.7	
AEC871	A.14	
AEC872	A.1	
AEC874	A.14	
AEC888	A.7	
AEC897	A.8	
AEC1011	A.3	
AEC1024	A.11	
AEC1025	A.11	
AEC1092	A.2	
AEC1097	A.5	
AEC1117	A.1	
AEC1229	D.5	
AEC1230	D.5	
AEC1266	A.5	
AEC1289	A.1	
AEC1290	A.1	
AEC1291	A.1	
AEC1292	A.5	
AEC1293	A.14	
AEC1294	A.14	
AEC1295	A.14	
AEC1804	A.6	
AEC1856	A.9	
AEC3000	F.1	
AEC3000	F.5	
AEC3003	F.8	
AEC3009	F.6	
AEC3015	F.1	
AEC3015	F.2	
AEC3067	F.6	
AEC3067	F.5	
AEC3071	F.3	
AEC3071	F.6	
AEC3072	F.2	
AEC3072	F.6	
AEC3102	F.1	
AEC3102	F.5	
AEC3104	F.1	
AEC3104	F.5	
AEC3105	F.1	
AEC3105	F.5	
AEC3106	F.1	
AEC3106	F.5	
AEC3109	F.1	
AEC3109	F.5	
AEC3112	F.2	
AEC3112	F.6	
AEC3113	F.3	
AEC3113	F.7	
AEC3115	F.3	
AEC3116	F.7	
AEC3116	F.3	
AEC3119	F.3	
AEC3121	F.6	
AEC3121	F.3	
AEC3142	F6.	
AEC3168	F.2	
AEC3168	F.8	
AEC3170	F.1	
AEC3176	F.5	
AEC3176	F.2	
AEC3177	F.4	
AEC3178	F.2	
AEC3178	F.6	
AEC3180	F.2	
AEC3180	F.6	
AEC3181	F.2	
AEC3181	F.6	
AEC3182	F.2	
AEC3182	F.6	
AEC3183	F.2	
AEC3183	F.6	
AEC3184	F.2	
AEC3184	F.6	
AEC3185	F.2	
AEC3185	F.6	
AEC3186	F.2	
AEC3186	F.6	
AEC3187	F.3	
AEC3187	F.7	
AEC3188	F.8	
AEC3188	F.7	
AEC3189	F.3	
AEC3189	F.7	
AEC3193	F.2	
AEC3193	F.6	
AEC3195	F.1	
AEC3195	F.5	
AEC3198	F.4	
AEC3207	F.1	
AEC3207	F.5	
AEC3208	F.2	
AEC3208	F.3	
AEC3210	F.6	
AEC3210	F.2	
AEC3211	F.6	
AEC3211	F.8	
AEC3221	F.6	
AEC3221	F.1	
AEC3224	F.5	
AEC3224	F.4	
AEC3259	F.11	
AEC3259	F.2	
AEC3264	F.6	
AEC3298	E.1	
AEC3822	F.1	
AEC3822	F.5	
AEC3823	F.3	
AEC3824	F.7	
AEC3824	F.1	
AEC3840	F.5	
AEC3842	F.3	
AEC3842	F.6	
AEC3843	F.3	
AEC3850	F.7	
AEC3850	F.3	
AEC3504	F.10	
AEC3507	F.3	
AEC3507	F.7	
AEC3520	F.3	
AEC013510	F.6	
AEC024510	F.7	
AEC083202	A.11	
AEC083204	A.11	

Part Number Index—continued

Part Number	Page	Amdt. Number
AEC083206	A.11	
AEC083310	A.11	
AEC083320	A.11	
AEC083380	A.11	
AEC083340	A.11	
AEC083410	A.11	
AEC083420	A.11	
AEC083430	A.11	
AEC083440	A.11	
AEC083510	A.11	
AEC083520	A.11	
AEC083530	A.11	
AEC083540	A.11	
AEC111710	A.11	
AEC111720	A.11	
AEC111730	A.11	
AEC111740	A.11	
AED159	A.5	
AED161	A.5	
AED808	D.5	
AEK113	A.5	
AHB5366	D.2	
AHB5367	A.17	
AHB5870	A.18	
AHB5872	A.18	
AHB5891	R.2	
AHB5392	R.2	
AHB5393	R.2	
AHB5394	R.2	
AHB5395	R.2	
AHB5396	R.2	
AHB5397	A.14	
AHB5398	R.18	
AHB5401	C.1	
AHB5402	C.1	
AHB5406	R.31	
AHB5407	R.28	
AHB5410	R.22	
AHB5411	R.22	
AHB35412	R.22	
AHB35413	R.22	
AHB35414	R.22	
AHB35415	R.22	
AHB35416	R.22	
AHB5417	R.22	
AHB5418	R.22	
AHB5419	R.22	
AHB5420	R.22	
AHB5421	R.22	

Part Number	Page	Amdt. Number
AHB35434	R.23	
AHB35435	R.23	
AHB35436	R.23	
AHB35437	R.23	
AHB35438	R.23	
AHB35439	R.23	
AHB35440	R.23	
AHB5441	R.23	
AHB35442	R.23	
AHB35443	R.23	
AHB35444	R.23	
AHB35445	R.23	
AHB35446	R.23	
AHB35447	R.24	
AHB35448	R.24	
AHB35449	R.24	
AHB35450	R.24	
AHB35451	R.24	
AHB35452	R.24	
AHB35453	R.24	
AHB35454	R.24	
AHB35455	R.24	
AHB35456	R.24	
AHB35457	R.24	
AHB35458	R.24	
AHB35459	R.24	
AHB35460	R.24	
AHB35461	R.24	
AHB35462	R.24	
AHB35463	R.24	
AHB35464	R.24	
AHB35465	R.24	
AHB35466	R.24	
AHB35407	R.24	
AHB35468	R.24	
AHB35469	R.24	
AHB35470	R.24	
AHB35471	R.24	
AHB35472	R.24	
AHB35473	R.24	
AHB35474	R.24	
AHB35475	R.24	
AHB35476	R.24	
AHB35477	R.24	
AHB35478	R.25	
AHB35479	R.25	
AHB35480	R.25	
AHB5481	R.25	
AHB35482	R.25	
AHB35483	R.25	
AHB35484	R.25	
AHB35485	R.25	

Part Number	Page	Amdt. Number
AHB5486	R.25	
AHB5487	R.25	
AHB5488	R.25	
AHB5489	R.25	
AHB5490	R.25	
AHB5491	R.25	
AHB5492	R.25	
AHB5493	R.25	
AHB5494	R.25	
AHB5495	R.25	
AHB5496	R.25	
AHB5497	R.25	
AHB5498	R.26	
AHB5499	R.26	
AHB5500	R.26	
AHB5501	R.26	
AHB5502	R.26	
AHB5503	R.26	
AHB5504	R.26	
AHB5505	R.26	
AHB5506	R.26	
AHB5507	R.26	
AHB5508	R.26	
AHB5509	R.26	
AHB5510	R.26	
AHB5511	R.26	
AHB5512	R.26	
AHB5513	R.26	
AHB5514	R.26	
AHB5515	R.26	
AHB5516	R.26	
AHB5517	R.26	
AHB5518	R.27	
AHB5519	R.27	
AHB5520	R.27	
AHB5521	R.27	
AHB5522	R.27	
AHB5523	R.27	
AHB5524	R.27	
AHB5525	R.27	
AHB5526	R.27	
AHB5527	R.27	
AHB5528	R.27	
AHB5529	R.27	
AHB5530	R.27	
AHB5531	R.27	
AHB5532	R.27	
AHB5533	R.27	
AHB5534	R.27	
AHB5535	R.27	
AHB5536	R.27	
AHB5537	R.27	

Part Number	Page	Amdt. Number
AHB5538	R.18	
AHB5539	R.18	
AHB5540	R.18	
AHB5541	R.18	
AHB5542	R.18	
AHB5543	R.18	
AHB5544	R.18	
AHB5545	R.18	
AHB5546	R.18	
AHB5547	R.18	
AHB5548	R.18	
AHB5549	R.18	
AHB5550	R.18	
AHB5551	R.18	
AHB5552	R.18	
AHB5553	R.18	
AHB5554	R.18	
AHB5555	R.17	
AHB5556	R.18	
AHB5557	R.18	
AHB5558	R.18	
AHB5559	R.19	
AHB5560	R.19	
AHB5561	R.19	
AHB5562	R.19	
AHB5563	R.19	
AHB5564	R.19	
AHB5565	R.19	
AHB5566	R.19	
AHB5567	R.19	
AHB5568	R.19	
AHB5569	R.19	
AHB5570	R.19	
AHB5571	R.19	
AHB5572	R.19	
AHB5573	R.20	
AHB5574	R.20	
AHB5575	R.20	
AHB5576	R.20	
AHB5577	R.20	
AHB5578	R.20	
AHB5579	R.20	
AHB5580	R.20	
AHB5581	R.20	
AHB5582	R.20	
AHB5583	R.20	
AHH5584	R.20	
AHB5585	R.20	
AHB5586	R.28	
AHB5594	R.28	
AHB5595	R.28	
AHB5596	R.28	

Part Number Index—continued

Part Number	Page	Amdt. Number	Part Number	Page	Amdt. Number	Part Number	Page	Amdt. Number	Part Number	Page	Amdt. Number
AHB5597	R.28		AHB88382	R.11		AKD970	S.5		ATC7155	H.2	
AHB5598	R.28		AHB88384	R.21		ANK4646	N.3		ATC7156	H.2	
AHB5599	R.28		AHB88388	J.1		ANK4646	R.10		ATC7157	H.2	
AHB5600	R.28		AHB88389	J.1		ARH1039	C.1		ATC7158	H.2	
AHB5601	R.28		AHB38749	R.29		ATA7043	H.2		ATC7172	H.2	
AHB5602	R.29		AHB38782	R.30		ATB7198	H.2		ATC7182	H.1	
AHB5603	R.29		AHB38783	R.20		ATC4178	K.1		ATC7189	H.2	
AHB5604	R.29		AHB38859	R.23		ATC7060	H.2		ATC7194	H.2	
AHB5605	R.1		AHB38860	R.23		ATC7061	H.2		ATC7236	H.2	
AHB5606	R.29		AHB38871	R.23		ATC7062	H.1		ATC7237	M.4	
AHB5748	R.3		AHB88872	R.23		ATC7065	H.2		ATC7251	H.2	
AHB5790	R.28		AHB88886	R.25		ATC7071	G.1		ATC7256	H.2	
AHB5800	R.28		AHB88887	R.25		ATC7083	H.3		ATC7257	H.1	
AHB5833	R.11		AHB88888	R.25		ATC7084	H.1		ATC7262	H.1	
AHB5866	D.2		AHH5417	N.7		ATC7085	H.1		ATC7263	H.1	
AHB5895	R.22		AHH5714	R.35		ATC7089	H.2		ATC7266	H.1	
AHB5896	R.22		AHH5759	R.32		ATC7091	H.2		ATC7267	H.1	
AHB5897	R.22		AHH8008	P.1		ATC7092	H.2		ATC7268	H.1	
AHB5898	R.22		AHH8009	P.1		ATC7093	H.2		ATC7288	H.1	
AHB5899	R.22		AJA5006	N.6		ATC7094	H.2		ATC7289	H.1	
AHB5900	R.28		AJA5081	N.4		ATC7095	H.2		ATC7290	H.1	
AHB5943	R.28		AJA5083	N.4		ATC7096	H.2		ATC7309	H.1	
AHB5944	R.11		AJC5011	A.8		ATC7097	H.2		ATC7310	H.1	
AHB5945	R.11		AJC5033	A.2		ATC7098	H.2		ATC7315	H.1	
AHB5947	R.22		AJC5095	B.1		ATC7099	H.2		ATC7343	H.2	
AHB5948	R.22		AJC5116	N.5		ATC7100	F.2		ATC7344	H.2	
AHB5949	R.22		AJC5128	N.1		ATC7100	H.2		ATC7357	H.2	
AHB5950	R.23		AJC5159	A.2		ATC7101	H.2		ATC7394	H.2	
AHB8285	N.8		AJC6042	A.1		ATC7104	H.1		AUA72	D.1	
AHB8286	N.8		AJC515910	A.11		ATC7106	H.1		AUA847	D.1	
AHB8287	N.8		AJC515920	A.11		ATC7107	H.1		AUA868	D.1	
AHB8288	N.9		AJC515930	A.11		ATC7108	H.1		AUA869	D.1	
AHB8289	N.9		AJC515940	A.11		ATC7109	H.2		AUA878	D.1	
AHB8290	N.6		AJD7626	A.4		ATC7110	H.1		AUA1433	D.1	
AHB8293	R.22		AJH5079	N.7		ATC7111	H.1		AUA1435	D.1	
AHB8294	R.22		AJH5177	O.1		ATC7112	H.1		AUA1453	D.1	
AHB8295	R.22		AJH5178	O.1		ATC7113	H.1		AUA1455	D.1	
AHB8296	R.23		AJH5182	O.1		ATC7114	H.1		AUA1456	D.1	
AHB8297	R.23		AJH5182	O.2		ATC7115	H.1		AUA1459	D.1	
AHB8298	R.23		AJH5292	D.8		ATC7116	H.1		AUA1466	D.1	
AHB8299	R.23		AKD650	S.5		ATC7124	H.1		AUA1468	D.1	
AHB8301	R.8		AKD693	S.5		ATC7125	H.1		AUA1500	D.1	
AHB8302	R.27		AKD855	S.5		ATC7152	H.2		AUA1661	D.1	
AHB8303	R.27		AKD858B	S.5		ATC7153	H.2		AUA1662	D.1	
AHB8304	R.27		AKD947	S.5		ATC7154	H.2		AUA1785	D.1	
AHB8305	R.27		AKD967	S.5					AUA1863	D.1	
AHB8307	R.18		AKD969	S.5					AUA4083	D.1	
AHB8308	R.18								AUA4007	D.1	
AHB8300	R.18								AUA4609	D.1	
AHB8312	J.3								AUA4611	D.1	
AHB8314	J.3								AUA4643	D.1	
AHB8315	D.2										

Part Number Index—continued

Part Number	Amdt. Number	Page
AUA4643		D.3
AUA4643		D.4
AUA4644		D.1
AUA4645		D.1
AUA4646		D.1
AUA4647		D.1
AUA4850		D.1
AUA6003		D.1
AUA6012		D.1
AUA6021		D.1
AUA6084		D.1
AUA6086		D.1
AUC1037		D.4
AUC1123		D.4
AUC1147		D.4
AUC1152		D.4
AUC1167		D.3
AUC1196		A.18
AUC1196		D.4
AUC1358		D.4
AUC1557		D.4
AUC1867		D.4
AUC1928		D.5
AUC1980		D.4
AUC2001		D.3
AUC2002		D.3
AUC2006		D.4
AUC2006		D.4
AUC2010		D.3
AUC2014		D.3
AUC2018		D.3
AUC2019		D.3
AUC2020		D.3
AUC2023		D.4
AUC2027		D.4
AUC2028		D.4
AUC2029		D.4
AUC2030		D.4
AUC2081		D.4
AUC2044		D.3
AUC2057		D.3
AUC2062		D.4
AUC2065		D.3
AUC2066		D.3
AUC2096		D.3
AUC2097		D.3
AUC2098		D.4
AUC2108		D.5
AUC2109		D.5
AUC2110		D.4
AUC2139		D.4

Part Number	Page	Amdt. Number
AUC2140	D.1	
AUC2141	D.1	
AUC2141	D.4	
AUC2156	D.1	
AUC2175	D.5	
AUC2246	D.8	
AUC2256	D.4	
AUC2419	D.5	
AUC2451	D.3	
AUC2521	D.3	
AUC2672	D.4	
AUC2673	D.5	
AUC2673	D.4	
AUC2694	D.4	
AUC2698	D.4	
AUC2867	D.3	
AUC3071	D.3	
AUC3280	D.4	
AUC3464	D.8	
AUC3481	A.18	
AUC4067	D.4	
AUC4260	D.4	
AUC4261	D.4	
AUC4334	D.5	
AUC4386	D.3	
AUC4490	D.3	
AUC4612	D.4	
AUC4612	D.8	
AUC4771	D.3	
AUC4781	D.4	
AUC4790	D.3	
AUC4790	D.3	
AUC4839	D.4	
AUC4859	D.4	
AUC4900	D.4	
AUC4943	D.4	
AUC4944	D.4	
AUC8075	D.4	
AUC8102	D.3	
AUC8149	D.3	
AUC8155	D.4	
AUC8170	D.3	
AUC8206	D.3	
AUC8242	D.3	
AUC8248	D.3	
AUC8366	D.5	
AUC8367	D.5	
AUC9040	D.4	
AUC9041	D.3	

Part Number	Page	Amdt. Number
AWZ105	R.8	
1B1033	A.2	
1B1219	A.2	
1B1283	A.8	
1B1814	A.15	
1B1815	A.15	
1B1424	A.9	
1B1714	A.4	
1B2178	A.10	
1B2261	A.10	
1B2697	A.18	
1B2721	N.3	
1B2736	D.2	
1B2796	N.9	
1B2800	N.9	
1B2801	N.9	
1B2804	N.3	
1B2810	N.9	
1B2836	N.3	
1B2837	N.3	
1B2847	N.8	
1B2897	A.8	
1B3346	F.1	
1B3346	F.5	
1B3363	F.4	
1B3363	F.7	
1B3632	F.4	
1B3632	F.7	
1B3634	F.4	
1B3650	F.7	
1B3655	F.9	
1B3701	F.6	
1B3705	E.2	
1B3705	F.1	
1B3706	F.5	
1B3706	F.4	
1B3707	F.7	
1B3707	F.8	
1B3708	F.7	
1B3708	F.3	
1B3709	F.7	
1B3709	F.3	
1B3710	F.7	
1B3713	F.4	
1B3720	F.7	
1B3721	F.6	
1B3728	F.6	
1B3728	F.3	
1B3728	F.7	

Part Number	Page	Amdt. Number
1B8736	F.4	
1B8736	F.7	
1B8753	F.8	
1B8755	F.5	
1B8757	F.1	
1B8760	F.4	
1B8760	F.7	
1B8763	F.1	
1B8765	F.2	
1B8766	F.2	
1B8767	F.2	
1B8836	F.4	
1B8836	F.7	
1B8839	F.8	
1B4316	K.2	
1B4839	S.1	
1B4865	K.1	
1B4866	K.1	
1B4892	K.2	
1B4899	K.2	
1B4400	K.2	
1B4407	K.1	
1B4409	K.1	
1B4411	K.1	
1B4416	K.2	
1B4421	A.15	
1B4422	A.15	
1B4423	A.15	
1B4428	A.15	
1B4451	K.3	
1B4453	K.3	
1B4454	K.3	
1B4457	K.3	
1B4459	K.2	
1B4475	K.1	
1B4476	K.1	
1B4478	K.2	
1B4481	K.2	
1B4486	K.5	
1B4490	K.4	
1B4496	K.8	
1B4497	K.3	
1B4501	K.5	
1B4518	K.5	
1B4517	K.1	
1B4525	K.5	
1B4526	K.5	
1B4527	K.2	
1B4528	K.2	
1B4529	K.2	
1B4530	K.2	
1B4552	K.1	

Part Number Index—*continued*

Part Number	Amdt. Number	Page
1B4569		K.5
1B4570		K.4
1B5829		M.4
1B6127		J.2
1B6137		J.2
1B6188		J.2
1B6195		J.2
1B6199		J.2
1B6214		J.3
1B6226		N.6
1B6256		J.2
1B6257		J.1
1B6257		J.3
1B6257		J.2
1B6258		J.1
1B6274		J.1
1B6276		J.1
1B6277		J.2
1B6278		J.1
1B6278		J.2
1B6281		J.2
1B6282		J.2
1B6286		J.2
1B6287		J.2
1B6292		J.2
1B6299		J.3
1B6300		J.3
1B6301		J.3
1B6303		N.6
1B6340		J.2
1B6346		N.6
1B6348		J.1
1B6350		J.1
1B7354		K.5
1B7355		K.5
1B7356		K.5
1B7362		M.4
1B7364		M.4
1B7366		H.4
1B7386		G.1
1B7422		K.4
1B7424		M.4
1B7437		H.8
1B7438		H.3
1B7463		L.1
1B7464		H.4
1B7470		L.1
1B7472		M.2
1B7473		S.1
1B7474		S.1
1B7489		N.3
1B7490		H.3
1B7526		H.8
1B7527		M.8
1B8036		P.1
1B8037		P.1
1B8038		P.1
1B8039		P.1
1B8040		P.1
1B8041		P.1
1B8048		P.1
1B8057		P.1
1B8077		P.1
1B8078		P.1
1B8347		A.15
1B8358		K.4
1B8641		R.1
1B8648		R.1
1B8658		R.1
1B8670		R.1
1B8672		R.1
1B8685		R.1
1B8688		R.1
1B8689		R.1
1B8693		R.1
1B8698		R.1
1B8699		R.1
1B8703		R.1
1B8731		R.1
1B8750		E.2
1B8750		M.1
1B8751		E.2
1B8762		M.1
1B8763		H.4
1B8764		H.4
1B8766		H.4
1B8777		R.1
1B8811		R.1
1B8811		A.15
1B8882		H.4
1B8839		A.15
1B8840		R.1
1B8895		R.1
1B8896		M.4
1B8926		M.4
1B8930		M.2
1B8937		H.4
1B8940		R.16
1B8965		R.16
1B8995		M.2
1B8997		S.1
1B9030		N.3
1B9031		N.3
1B9056		N.5
1B9057		O.1
1B9058		O.1
1B9059		O.1
1B9060		O.1
1B9061		O.2
1B9064		O.1
1B9074		M.4
1B9078		N.9
1B9095		N.4
1B9096		N.4
1B9098		N.4
1B9099		N.4
1B9100		N.5
1B9101		N.8
1B9102		N.9
1B9104		O.2
1B9140		O.2
1B9141		N.8
1B9179		N.9
1B9180		O.1
1B9188		
4B1083		R.5
4B1085		R.3
4B1087		R.5
4B1088		R.3
4B1089		R.7
4B1090		R.6
4B1091		R.6
4B1092		R.7
4B2048		R.2
4B2050		R.5
4B2053		J.2
4B2502		R.23
4B3172		R.9
4B3178		R.23
4B3179		R.22
4B3180		R.22
4B3181		R.22
4B3182		R.23
4B3183		R.24
4B3207		R.23
4B3208		R.24
4B3215		R.24
4B3217		R.24
4B3218		R.24
4B3219		R.24
4B3220		R.24
4B3221		R.24
4B3222		R.25
4B3223		R.8
4B3247		R.24
4B4119		R.25
4B4124		R.23
4B4204		R.15
4B4205		R.18
4B4206		R.19
4B4207		R.27
4B4210		R.25
4B4211		R.28
4B4216		R.1
4B4922A		R.27
4B5118		R.27
4B5119		R.27
4B5120		R.27
4B5121		R.26
4B5122		R.25
4B5123		R.23
4B5124		R.26
4B5125		R.26
4B5126		R.26
4B5127		R.26
4B5128		R.26
4B5133		R.28
4B5134		R.27
4B5139		R.27
4B5140		R.27
4B5142		R.27
4B5143		R.2
4B7427		R.2
4B7428		R.3
4B8521		R.3
4B8646		R.2
4B9353		R.5
4B9354		R.2
4B9355		R.2
4B9356		R.2
4B9357		R.2
4B9358		R.2
4B9359		R.2
4B9364		R.2
4B9365		R.2
4B9366		R.2
11B121		A.5
11B174		B.1
11B206		B.1
11B511		A.5
11B618		D.6
11B619		D.6
11B621		D.6
11B622		D.6

Part Number Index—*continued*

Part Number	Page	Amdt. Number
11B3623	D.6	
11B6024	R.35	
11B2011	D.2	
11B2115	C.1	
11B2116	C.1	
11B2117	R.35	
11B2118	C.1	
11B2119	C.1	
11B2120	A.16	
11B2122	A.16	
11B2187	D.2	
11B2143	A.17	
11B2145	A.17	
11B2146	A.17	
11B2151	A.17	
11B2155	A.17	
11B2156	A.17	
11B2157	A.17	
11B2159	A.17	
11B2163	N.3	
11B2186	O.1	
11B2188	O.1	
11B2207	A.17	
11B2301	C.1	
11B2348	A.18	
11B2349	A.18	
11B2350	A.18	
11B2351	N.3	
11B2352	A.18	
11B2356	A.16	
11B2357	A.16	
11B2365	A.18	
11B2366	A.18	
11B2375	D.2	
11B2380	D.2	
11B5068	H.4	
11B5070	H.4	
11B5071	H.4	
11B5074	A.15	
11B5113	A.15	
11B5115	A.15	
11B5117	R.1	
11B5119	R.1	
11B5120	R.1	
11B5123	R.1	
11B5126	R.1	
11B5128	R.1	
11B5138	M.1	
11B5148	R.1	
11B5149	R.9	
11B5166	S.1	
11B5188	A.15	
11B5196	S.1	
11B5199	H.4	
11B5202	R.1	
11B5205	R.1	
11B5212	R.1	
11B5214	R.1	
11B5217	R.1	
11B5218	R.1	
11B5220	R.1	
11B5223	R.1	
11B5224	R.1	
11B5225	R.1	
11B5228	R.1	
11B5236	R.1	
11B5251	R.1	
11B5252	R.1	
11B5254	R.1	
11B5264	R.1	
11B5265	R.1	
11B5266	H.4	
11B5268	M.1	
11B5271	E.2	
11B5273	M.1	
11B5277	M.1	
11B5279	M.4	
11B5282	M.1	
11B5283	E.2	
11B5294	E.2	
11B5298	R.17	
11B5303	R.17	
11B5308	R.17	
11B5309	E.2	
11B5312	M.4	
11B5323	M.1	
11B5338	E.2	
11B5509	M.2	
11B5510	M.2	
11B5521	R.1	
11B5522	R.1	
11B5529	M.2	
11B5580	R.1	
11B5584	R.1	
11B5543	M.2	
14B766	R.3	
14B1882	R.18	
14B1883	R.19	
14B1385	R.28	
14B1386	R.20	
14B1387	R.18	
14B1388	R.20	
14B1708	R.21	
14B1718	R.7	
14B1719	R.7	
14B1721	R.10	
14B1722	R.10	
14B1723	R.21	
14B1725	R.10	
14B1726	R.10	
14B1727	R.21	
14B1728	R.21	
14B1729	R.31	
14B1730	R.28	
14B1815	R.9	
14B1867	R.32	
14B1884	R.7	
14B1917	R.33	
14B1941	R.17	
14B1963	R.10	
14B1964	R.10	
14B1998	R.21	
14B2005	R.3	
14B2006	R.3	
14B2016	R.32	
14B2036	D.2	
14B2038	R.7	
14B2465	R.28	
14B2512	R.9	
14B2513	R.9	
14B2531	R.7	
14B2544	R.13	
14B2546	R.6	
14B2547	R.9	
14B2742	R.16	
14B2749	R.33	
14B2767	R.20	
14B2768	R.20	
14B2774	R.20	
14B2809	R.7	
14B2841	R.12	
14B2842	R.12	
14B2843	R.12	
14B2845	R.8	
14B2846	R.8	
14B2871	R.8	
14B2877	R.20	
14B2878	R.25	
14B3462	R.11	
14B3463	R.10	
14B8732	R.5	
14B8823	R.10	
14B4466	R.12	
14B5588	N.7	
14B5589	N.7	
14B5596	N.7	
14B5597	N.7	
14B5598	N.7	
14B5623	R.28	
14B5722	R.3	
14B5723	R.3	
14B5724	R.3	
14B5725	R.3	
14B5726	R.3	
14B5727	R.3	
14B5728	R.9	
14B5735	R.9	
14B5739	R.7	
14B5759	R.21	
14B5772	R.21	
14B5773	R.21	
14B5775	R.31	
14B5776	R.31	
14B5777	R.21	
14B5779	R.21	
14B5796	R.21	
14B5811	R.2	
14B5812	R.3	
14B5861	R.21	
14B5876	R.21	
14B5877	R.11	
14B5889	R.11	
14B5890	R.11	
14B5891	R.11	
14B5892	R.5	
14B5896	R.5	
14B6453	R.2	
14B6461	R.2	
14B6462	R.7	
14B6467	R.7	
14B6597	R.34	
14B6598	R.34	
14B6599	R.34	
14B6600	R.85	
14B6601	R.35	
14B6602	R.35	
14B6603	R.35	
14B6632	R.9	
14B6729	R.21	
14B6740	R.81	
14B6743	R.11	
14B6754	R.8	
14B6759	R.30	
14B6760	R.30	
14B6761	R.30	
14B6805	R.8	
14B6806	R.4	

Part Number Index—continued

Part Number	Page	Amdt. Number
14B6816	R.23	
14B6817	R.7	
14B6822	R.5	
14B6823	R.5	
14B6824	R.21	
14B6825	R.21	
14B6828	R.30	
14B6877	R.9	
14B7458	R.9	
14B7466	R.10	
14B7474	R.30	
14B7475	R.30	
14B7476	R.30	
14B7481	R.5	
14B7482	R.5	
14B7483	R.5	
14B7484	R.5	
14B7544	R.9	
14B7545	R.9	
14B7550	R.34	
14B7554	R.12	
14B7555	R.12	
14B7556	R.12	
14B7557	R.12	
14B7562	R.12	
14B7563	R.12	
14B7564	R.12	
14B7565	R.12	
14B7566	R.12	
14B7579	R.31	
14B7581	R.28	
14B7584	R.30	
14B7585	R.30	
14B7586	R.30	
14B7587	R.30	
14B7648	R.18	
14B7649	R.13	
14B7651	R.13	
14B7660	R.11	
14B7661	R.8	
14B7662	R.8	
14B7711	R.33	
14B7712	R.33	
14B7744	R.14	
14B7755	R.14	
14B7756	R.14	
14B7762	R.14	
14B7764	R.14	
14B7776	R.34	
14B7777	R.34	
14B7779	R.33	
14B7780	R.34	
14B7781	R.23	
14B7782	R.88	
14B7784	R.11	
14B7785	R.21	
14B7804	R.30	
14B7810	R.34	
14B8472	R.28	
14B8634	R.11	
14B8635	R.11	
14B8692	R.10	
14B8699	R.28	
14B8712	R.14	
14B8713	R.14	
14B8780	R.38	
14B8781	R.38	
14B8812	R.3	
14B8813	R.8	
14B9476	R.12	
14B9484	R.21	
14B9820	R.34	
14B9821	R.35	
24B508	R.11	
24B540	R.18	
24B553	R.14	
24B554	R.15	
24B601	R.12	
24B612	R.12	
24B617	R.12	
24B618	R.14	
24B624	R.11	
24B625	R.11	
24B682	R.84	
24B633	R.34	
24B635	R.14	
24B636	R.14	
24B637	R.14	
24B638	R.14	
24B690	R.18	
24B691	R.18	
24B697	R.31	
24B725	R.31	
24B726	R.32	
24B747	R.8	
24B758	R.4	
24B773	R.21	
24B774	R.26	
24B785	R.26	
24B787	R.28	
24B789	R.32	
24B811		
24B876	R.21	
24B877	R.21	
24B878	R.21	
24B879	R.21	
24B880	R.21	
24B881	R.21	
24B1588	R.28	
24B1656	R.18	
24B1677	R.21	
24B1678	R.21	
24B1679	R.21	
24B1682	R.2	
24B1683	R.2	
24B1684	R.2	
24B1709	R.28	
24B1709	R.29	
24B1710	R.28	
24B1710	R.29	
24B1711	R.28	
24B1712	R.28	
24B1714	R.28	
24B1715	R.28	
24B1716	R.28	
24B1717	R.28	
24B1777	R.28	
24B1791	R.30	
24B1792	R.30	
24B1793	R.30	
24B1794	R.30	
24B1795	R.22	
24B1796	R.22	
BHA4066	R.32	
BHA4073	E.2	
BHA4081	O.1	
BHA4112	E.2	
BLS108	F.9	
BLS110	F.2	
BLS110	F.3	
BLS110	F.6	
BLS110	F.7	
BLS110	F.9	
BNN104	A.14	
BNN105	A.14	
CCN120	F.6	
CLS2516	A.14	
CLZ0313	R.8	
CLZ0511	R.8	
CLZ0513	E.2	
CLZ0518	M.1	
CMN0308	R.4	
CMN0308	R.6	
CMN0308	R.7	
CMN0310	R.4	
CMN0410	R.6	
CMZ0208	R.32	
CMZ0307	O.1	
CMZ0308	R.8	
CMZ0308	R.5	
CMZ0408	R.33	
CMZ0412	H.2	
CMZ0414	R.7	
CMZ0414	H.3	
CMZ0428	K.4	
CMZ0516	H.3	
CNZ102	N.3	
CNZ102	N.4	
CNZ102	N.5	
CPS0806	D.2	
CTP605	R.25	
CTZ610	R.25	
CWN804	R.28	
CWZ806	R.25	
1D1780	R.34	
1D1963	B.2	
1D1977	A.5	
1D6182	J.3	
5D8518	R.30	
5D8627	R.30	
5D8826	R.30	
5D8827	R.30	
5D8828	R.30	
8D5768	D.2	
1E504	A.3	

Part Number Index—*continued*

Part Number	Page	Amdt. Number
1F1298	A.17	
1F6153	J.8	
1F9026	N.4	
1F9026	N.5	
2F15	A.17	
2F3040	F.4	
2F3040	F.7	
2F3151	F.4	
2F3151	F.4	
2F3152	F.7	
2F3152	F.4	
2F3154	F.7	
2F3154	F.4	
2F3166	F.4	
2F3166	F.7	
2F3198	F.4	
2F3198	F.7	
3F90	N.9	
8F2408	R.28	
8F2409	R.28	
8F2480	R.25	
FNN103	R.4	
FNN103	R.6	
FNN103	R.7	
FNN104	F.10	
FNN104	R.6	
FNN104	R.7	
FNN104	A.1	
FNN105	A.3	
FNN105	A.6	
FNN105	A.10	
FNN105	R.9	
FNN106	F.4	
FNN106	F.11	
FNN106	N.2	
FNN107	A.10	
FNN107	H.1	
FNN206	A.5	
FNN505	F.8	
FNN506	A.5	
FNZ103	A.17	
FNZ103	A.18	
FNZ103	D.5	
FNZ103	M.2	
FNZ103	N.3	
FNZ103	N.8	
FNZ103	N.9	
FNZ103	O.1	
FNZ103	R.8	
FNZ103	R.4	
FNZ103	R.5	
FNZ103	R.8	
FNZ103	R.11	
FNZ103	R.12	
FNZ103	R.18	
FNZ103	R.15	
FNZ103	R.21	
FNZ103	R.23	
FNZ103	R.26	
FNZ103	R.27	
FNZ103	R.31	
FNZ103	R.33	
FNZ103	R.35	
FNZ104	A.17	
FNZ104	B.2	
FNZ104	E.2	
FNZ104	F.1	
FNZ104	F.5	
FNZ104	F.8	
FNZ104	H.4	
FNZ104	J.2	
FNZ104	K.1	
FNZ104	K.3	
FNZ104	M.1	
FNZ104	M.2	
FNZ104	N.9	
FNZ104	R.8	
FNZ104	R.5	
FNZ104	R.7	
FNZ104	R.8	
FNZ104	R.9	
FNZ104	R.10	
FNZ104	R.11	
FNZ104	R.15	
FNZ104	R.16	
FNZ104	R.20	
FNZ104	R.21	
FNZ104	R.31	
FNZ105	A.14	
FNZ105	A.15	
FNZ105	A.16	
FNZ105	C.1	
FNZ105	D.1	
FNZ105	F.8	
FNZ105	F.11	
FNZ105	J.2	
FNZ105	K.3	
FNZ105	K.5	
FNZ105	M.8	
FNZ105	M.4	
FNZ106	A.8	
FNZ106	A.14	
FNZ106	A.15	
FNZ106	A.16	
FNZ106	G.1	
FNZ106	H.1	
FNZ106	H.4	
FNZ106	J.2	
FNZ106	K.2	
FNZ106	L.1	
FNZ107	R.17	
FNZ107	A.15	
FNZ107	H.4	
FNZ204	L.1	
FNZ205	M.4	
FNZ205	D.2	
FNZ205	F.8	
FNZ205	H.3	
FNZ206	K.3	
FNZ206	A.15	
FNZ206	E.2	
FNZ206	H.4	
FNZ206	M.2	
FNZ207	A.9	
FNZ307	J.2	
FNZ407	K.2	
FNZ408	K.5	
FNZ506	L.1	
FNZ507	K.2	
FNZ507	K.3	
FNZ612	F.2	
FNZ612	H.2	
1G838	A.4	
1G1865	A.6	
1G1814	A.4	
1G2175	A.18	
1G2268	D.6	
1G2842	A.10	
1G2673	B.2	
1G2673	N.8	
1G2697	A.17	
1G2984	A.4	
1G3410	B.1	
1G3581	F.4	
1G3581	F.7	
1G3668	H.1	
1G3709	F.4	
1G3709	F.7	
1G3710	F.1	
1G3710	F.5	
1G3804	F.1	
1G3804	F.5	
1G4116	H.3	
1G4271	K.1	
1G4276	K.5	
1G4279	K.1	
1G4345	K.1	
1G4346	K.1	
1G4348	K.2	
1G4349	K.1	
1G4350	K.1	
1G4400	K.1	
1G4505	H.4	
1G5753	J.1	
1G6286	J.2	
1G6286	J.2	
1G6853	J.2	
1G6354	K.1	
1G7435	M.4	
1G7484	M.4	
1G7485	M.4	
1G7549	M.4	
1G7574	H.2	
1G8075	K.1	
1G8075	P.1	
1G8084	E.2	
1G9310	M.1	
1G9310	M.1	
1G9314	H.4	
1G9820	H.4	
1G9321	A.15	
1G9382	A.15	
1G9384	E.2	
1G9516	E.2	
1G9529	E.2	
1G9622	R.17	
1G9707	R.17	
1G9799		
4G2541	R.32	
4G3575	R.32	
4G4920	R.9	
4G6492	R.32	
4G6575	R.33	
4C7614	R.21	
4C8595	R.8	
4C8595	R.14	
8G500	F.1	
8G500	F.5	
8G505	D.2	
8G507	A.1	

Part Number Index—continued

Part Number	Page	Amdt. Number	Part Number	Page	Amdt. Number	Part Number	Page	Amdt. Number	Part Number	Page	Amdt. Number
8G511	C.1		18G2	S.2		18G134AQ	S.4		2H1046	R.3	
8G531	R.35		18G2A	S.2		18G134K	S.4		2H1046	R.7	
8G548	N.9		18G3	S.2		18G174D	S.2		2H1082	D.2	
8G554	K.1		18G8	S.8		18G177	S.3		2H1641	M.4	
8G554	K.2		18G8H	S.3		18G178	S.3		2H1683	S.1	
8G612	A.6		18G8J	S.3		18G179	S.3		2H2099	S.1	
8G616	B.2		18G8K	S.3		18G180	S.3		2H3271	B.2	
8G621	K.2		18G8L	S.2		18G181	S.3		2H4340	A.8	
8G622	K.5		18G16	S.2		18G182	S.3		2H4500	A.9	
8G624	J.1		18G21	S.2		18G183	S.3		2H4605	H.4	
8G627	A.9		18G27	S.2		18G184	S.3		2H4614	S.1	
8G637	O.1		18G29	S.2		18G185	S.3		2H4685	A.7	
8G654	D.2		18G29A	S.4		18G186	S.3		2H4732	N.6	
8G2121	A.2		18G34A	S.3		18G187	S.2		2H4817	N.5	
8G2228	A.12		18G37	S.2		18G191	S.4		2H4933	A.10	
8G2229	A.12		18G42A	S.2		18G191A	S.4		2H4935	A.14	
8G2285	G.1		18G42B	S.2		18G207	S.4		2H4978	N.6	
8G3001	H.3		18G47C	S.4		18G220	S.4		2H6136	R.22	
8G7067	H.3		18G47R	S.2		18G220A	S.4		2H6136	R.23	
8G7069	K.3		18G55A	S.3		18G220D	S.4		2H6961	R.22	
8G7069	H.3		18G56	S.2		18G220E	S.4		2H8445	R.22	
8G7070	H.3		18G61	S.3		18G251	S.3		2H8445	R.23	
8G7102	A.18		18G64	S.3		18G251A	S.3		2H9215	R.23	
8G8021	K.4		18G65	S.3		18G251B	S.3		2H9215	R.8	
8G8145	K.3		18G68	S.3		18G251C	S.3		2H9215	R.10	
8G8159	K.3		18G69	S.2		18G258	S.4				
8G8160	K.4		18G75A	S.3		18G262	S.2		3H599	M.2	
8G8201	E.2		18G79	S.2		18G263	S.2		3H660	J.1	
8G8219	E.2		18G85	S.3		18G264	S.4		3H743	D.5	
8G8249	R.84		18G89	S.3		18G264D	S.4		3H804	A.10	
8G9048	A.11		18G99A	S.2		18G264H	S.4		3H852	N.3	
8G212110	A.11		18G106	S.2		18G264K	S.2		3H921	N.4	
8G212120	A.11		18G123A	S.2		18G372	S.2		3H964	B.1	
8G212130	A.11		18G123AA	S.2		18G389	S.2		3H993	N.4	
8G212140			18G123AB	S.2		18G389D	S.2		3H1281	N.2	
			18G123AL	S.2		18G512	S.2		3H1454	N.6	
11G291	A.6		18G123C	S.2		18G536	S.3		3H1589	H.2	
11G2007	N.3		18G123D	S.2		18G537	S.4		3H1655	B.2	
11G2100	D.2		18G123E	S.2					3H1656	B.2	
11G3062	F.5		18G123F	S.2		1H55	A.17		3H1657	B.2	
11G9093	N.6		18G123L	S.2		1H722	A.5		3H1658	B.2	
			18G123R	S.2		1H723	A.5		3H1659	B.2	
14G800	R.33		18G123T	S.2		1H726	A.5		3H1660	B.2	
14G800	R.35		18G124A	S.2		1H3131	F.4		3H1709	J.2	
14G3499	R.34		18G124C	S.2		1H3131	F.11		3H1813	N.5	
14G3692	R.3		18G124D	S.2		1H5286	H.4		3H1836	N.3	
14G3693	R.3		18G124E	S.2		1H9049	O.1		3H1892	N.4	
14G8722	N.7		18G124F	S.2					3H1893	N.4	
14G56630	R.35		18G124H	S.2		2H10	C.1		3H1894	M.2	
14G5854	R.31		18G124L	S.3		2H174	M.2		3H1910	N.3	
14G6451	R.38		18G125	S.4		2H400	M.2		3H2006	A.5	
						2H731	A.4		3H2092	A.10	
									3H2138	B.1	

Part Number Index—*continued*

Part Number	Amdt. Number	Page
3H2144		N.9
3H2192		K.1
3H2192		M.4
3H2287		E.2
3H2287		M.2
3H2502		A.1
3H2506		R.32
3H2615		O.1
3H2648		S.1
3H2695		B.2
3H2696		B.2
3H2765		N.6
3H2824		N.3
3H2962		N.4
3H3028		K.1
3H3058		N.3
3H3050		N.6
3H3060		N.6
3H3076		A.16
3H3079		H.4
3H3079		K.5
3H3095		N.3
3H3096		N.3
3H3098		N.3
3H3099		N.3
3H3100		N.3
7H25		A.8
7H28		A.8
7H147		A.8
7H157		A.8
7H1709		P.1
7H1756		A.8
7H1758		A.8
7H1759		A.8
7H1761		A.8
7H1762		A.8
7H1763		A.8
7H1764		A.8
7H1765		A.8
7H1804		P.1
7H1805		P.1
7H1806		P.1
7H1840		A.8
7H3001		E.1
7H3006		E.1
7H3042		E.1
7H3048		E.1
7H3067		E.1
7H3069		E.1
7H3072		E.1
7H3078		E.1
7H3171		E.1
7H3174		E.1
7H3196		E.1
7H3240		E.1
7H3251		E.1
7H3325		E.1
7H3885		G.1
7H3886		G.1
7H3858		G.1
7H3858		H.4
7H3859		G.1
7H3902		G.1
7H3905		G.1
7H3912		G.1
7H3913		G.1
7H3918		G.1
7H3956		G.1
7H3962		G.1
7H4030		H.3
7H4030		K.4
7H4259		K.3
7H4339		H.3
7H4379		M.2
7H4406		K.3
7H4419		H.3
7H4419		K.4
7H4419		H.3
7H4429		K.3
7H4429		K.3
7H4439		H.3
7H4461		K.3
7H4461		K.3
7H4581		K.3
7H4583		K.3
7H4584		K.3
7H4585		H.3
7H4596		K.3
7H4600		M.2
7H4726		K.3
7H4745		M.2
7H4867		K.3
7H4868		K.4
7H4873		K.3
7H4904		H.3
7H4906		H.3
7H4907		H.3
7H4917		H.3
7H4918		E.2
7H4944		M.1
7H4944		E.2
7H4970		E.2
7H4973		E.2
7H4973		H.3
7H4973		K.4
7H4988		H.8
7H4989		H.3
7H4989		K.3
7H4990		H.3
7H4992		H.3
7H4997		H.3
7H4998		H.3
7H4999		H.3
7H5000		N.2
7H5001		N.2
7H5002		N.2
7H5004		N.2
7H5005		N.2
7H5006		N.2
7H5007		N.2
7H5008		N.2
7H5009		N.2
7H5010		N.2
7H5011		N.2
7H5012		N.2
7H5013		N.2
7H5016		N.1
7H5020		N.1
7H5021		N.1
7H5023		N.1
7H5025		N.3
7H5062		N.3
7H5066		N.5
7H5067		N.5
7H5121		N.5
7H5122		N.3
7H5123		N.7
7H5128		N.6
7H5130		N.6
7H5138		N.6
7H5139		N.6
7H5140		N.6
7H5142		N.5
7H5143		N.5
7H5156		N.4
7H5164		N.5
7H5182		N.5
7H5182		N.6
7H5185		N.2
7H5339		N.6
7H5468		N.6
7H5469		N.6
7H5471		N.6
7H5472		N.4
7H5483		N.4
7H5485		N.4
7H5486		N.4
7H5498		N.2
7H5512		N.6
7H5522		N.8
7H5525		N.1
7H5528		N.1
7H5540		N.3
7H5563		N.7
7H5582		N.4
7H5820		F.9
7H5821		F.8
7H5822		F.8
7H5825		F.8
7H5827		F.8
7H5829		F.8
7H5830		F.8
7H5831		F.8
7H5832		F.8
7H5833		F.8
7H5834		F.11
7H5836		F.9
7H5837		F.9
7H5838		F.9
7H5839		F.9
7H5840		F.9
7H5841		F.9
7H5842		F.9
7H5843		F.9
7H5844		F.9
7H5845		F.9
7H5846		F.8
7H5849		F.8
7H5851		F.8
7H5852		F.8
7H5853		F.9
7H5856		F.9
7H5857		F.9
7H5860		F.10
7H5861		F.10
7H5862		F.10
7H5863		F.10
7H5866		F.10
7H5867		F.10
7H5868		F.10
7H5870		F.10
7H5872A		F.9
7H5872B		F.9
7H5872C		F.9
7H5872D		F.9
7H5872E		F.9
7H5872F		F.9

Part Number Index—continued

Part Number	Page	Amdt. Number
7H5872G	F.9	
7H5873	F.9	
7H5877	F.10	
7H5879	F.10	
7H5881	F.10	
7H5882	F.10	
7H5888	F.10	
7H5884	F.10	
7H5885E	F.10	
7H5885F	F.10	
7H5885G	F.10	
7H5885H	F.10	
7H5885J	F.10	
7H5888	F.11	
7H5889	F.11	
7H5894	F.11	
7H5897	F.8	
7H5898	F.9	
7H6024	J.1	
7H6024	J.8	
7H6079	J.1	
7H6079	J.8	
7H6116	J.1	
7H6116	J.8	
7H6118	J.1	
7H6118	J.3	
7H6128	J.1	
7H6128	J.8	
7H6129	J.1	
7H6129	J.8	
7H6130	J.1	
7H6130	J.8	
7H6155	J.1	
7H6155	J.8	
7H6167	J.1	
7H6167	J.8	
7H6220	J.1	
7H6267	J.1	
7H6267	J.8	
7H6391	J.1	
7H6391	J.8	
7H6392	J.1	
7H6392	J.8	
7H6436	J.1	
7H6436	J.8	
7H6460	J.1	
7H6507	J.1	
7H6507	J.8	
7H6515	J.1	
7H6515	J.8	
7H6589	J.1	
7H6589	J.8	
7H6598	J.1	
7H6598	J.8	
7H6599	J.1	
7H6599	J.3	
7H6604	J.1	
7H6606	J.1	
7H6607	J.1	
7H6608	J.1	
7H6609	J.1	
7H6610	J.1	
7H6620	J.1	
7H6620	J.8	
7H7553	A.8	
7H9770	R.11	
7H9782	R.11	
7H9785	R.11	
7H9830	N.3	
7H9830	R.10	
18H50	S.1	
18H59	R.33	
18H76	R.84	
18H77	R.84	
18H78	R.84	
18H137	F.8	
17H3	A.8	
17H841	A.13	
17H842	A.2	
17H577	R.11	
17H578	R.11	
17H579	R.11	
17H581	R.11	
17H680	O.2	
17H689	O.1	
17H690	O.1	
17H775	A.8	
17H786	M.4	
17H787	M.4	
17H788	M.4	
17H789	M.4	
17H790	R.84	
17H819	O.1	
17H844	O.1	
17H932	O.2	
17H932	A.8	
17H940	O.1	
17H1068	O.2	
17H1068	A.8	
17H1148	A.8	
17H1150	A.8	
17H1152	A.8	
17H1167	A.8	
17H1168	A.8	
17H1173	A.8	
17H1304	O.1	
17H1341	O.1	
17H1343	O.2	
17H1476	A.8	
17H1493	R.33	
17H1494	R.84	
17H1496	O.1	
17H1591	R.84	
17H1597	R.84	
17H1642	O.1	
17H1642	O.2	
17H1658	O.1	
17H1684	O.1	
17H1822	O.2	
17H4003	K.8	
17H4004	K.8	
17H4006	K.8	
17H4010	E.2	
17H4011	E.2	
17H4082	K.3	
17H4180	M.2	
17H4238	M.2	
17H4327	E.2	
17H4358	H.8	
17H4415	M.1	
17H4481	K.8	
17H4513	E.2	
17H4513	M.2	
17H4514	M.1	
17H4515	M.1	
17H4515	M.2	
17H4516	E.2	
17H4517	E.2	
17H4518	M.2	
17H4519	M.2	
17H4528	M.2	
17H4528	K.8	
17H4553	E.2	
17H4554	M.2	
17H4556	M.2	
17H4557	M.2	
17H4558	M.2	
17H4559	M.3	
17H4560	M.3	
17H5065	B.1	
17H5069	B.1	
17H5095	B.1	
17H5110	B.1	
17H5118	B.1	
17H5117	B.1	
17H5146	N.4	
17H5158	B.1	
17H5166	B.1	
17H5180	N.4	
17H5205	N.1	
17H5238	B.1	
17H5243	N.4	
17H5244	N.7	
17H5255	N.6	
17H5259	N.4	
17H5806	N.4	
17H5375	B.1	
17H5884	N.7	
17H5896	B.1	
17H5898	N.4	
17H5427	N.5	
17H5427	N.7	
17H5431	N.1	
17H5433	N.1	
17H5434	B.1	
17H5437	N.7	
17H5441	N.7	
17H5442	N.1	
17H5453	N.6	
17H5594	F.10	
17H5804	F.8	
17H5808	F.8	
17H5809	F.8	
17H5810	F.8	
17H5811	F.11	
17H5815	F.11	
17H5816	F.11	
17H5818	F.11	
17H5819	F.11	
17H5820	F.11	
17H5821	F.11	
17H5822	F.10	
17H5823	F.10	
17H5824	F.8	
17H5825	F.8	
17H5826	F.9	
17H5827	F.10	
17H5829	F.8	
17H5830	F.9	
17H5833	F.10	
17H5835	F.10	
17H5836	F.10	
17H5837	F.10	
17H5844	F.10	
17H5845	F.10	
17H5846	F.10	
17H5847	F.7	

Part Number Index—continued

Part Number	Page	Amdt. Number
17H5848	F.8	
17H5849	F.7	
17H6098	J.1	
17H6103	J.1	
17H6103	J.3	
17H6105	J.3	
17H6106	J.1	
17H6106	J.8	
17H6107	J.1	
17H6108	J.1	
17H6109	J.1	
17H6110	J.1	
17H6120	J.1	
17H6121	J.3	
17H6161	J.3	
17H6162	J.8	
17H6163	J.3	
17H6164	J.1	
17H6214	J.1	
17H6215	J.1	
17H6216	J.1	
17H9099	R.17	
17H9700	R.17	
17H9701	R.17	
17H9702	R.17	
17H9832	R.32	
27H387	O.1	
27H387	O.2	
27H397	O.1	
27H397	O.1	
27H429	R.34	
27H611	R.34	
27H614	O.2	
27H1084	O.2	
27H1085	O.1	
27H992	A.8	
27H1135	A.8	
27H1139	A.8	
27H1140	A.8	
27H1141	A.8	
27H1142	A.8	
27H1143	A.8	
27H1144	B.1	
27H1171	R.34	
27H1172	R.34	
27H1173	R.34	
27H1174	R.34	
27H1176	R.34	
27H1177	R.34	
27H1178	R.34	
27H1179	R.34	
27H1242	R.34	
27H3178	E.1	
27H3179	E.1	
27H5309	N.7	
27H5316	B.1	
27H5545	N.4	
27H5545	N.5	
27H5555	N.6	
27H5556	N.6	
27H5557	N.6	
27H7466	A.8	
27H9587	R.29	
27H9588	R.29	
27H9591	R.29	
27H9592	R.29	
27H9594	R.29	
27H9595	R.29	
27H9597	R.29	
27H9598	R.29	
27H9601	R.29	
27H9622	R.11	
27H9628	R.11	
27H9625	R.11	
27H9626	R.11	
27H9654	R.11	
27H9655	R.11	
27H9662	R.11	
27H9671	R.11	
27H9673	R.29	
27H9674	R.29	
27H9772	R.29	
27H9773	R.29	
27H9774	R.29	
27H9776	R.29	
27H9777	R.29	
27H9893	R.29	
27H9894	R.29	
27H9895	R.29	
37H5169	N.7	
87H5288	N.7	
37H5308	N.7	
37H5487	N.7	
37H5445	B.1	
37H5519	N.4	
37H5527	N.5	
87H5527	N.4	
87H5580	N.5	
87H5531	N.5	
47H5010	N.6	
47H5011	N.6	
47H5240	N.6	
47H5241	N.6	
47H5242	N.6	
47H5248	N.6	
47H5244	N.6	
47H5245	N.6	
47H5246	N.6	
47H5247	B.1	
47H5250		
97H510	R.21	
97H1489	S.5	
HBN0509	A.10	
HBN0509	F.1	
HBN0509	F.5	
HBN0510	A.3	
HBN0510	A.10	
HBN0510	F.2	
HBN0512	F.1	
HBN0512	F.5	
HBN0518	F.1	
HBN0518	F.5	
HBN0522	F.1	
HBN0522	F.5	
HBN0611	F.4	
HBN0611	F.11	
HBN0612	F.4	
HBN0612	F.11	
HBN0632	A.8	
HBZ0410	M.2	
HBZ0411	E.2	
HBZ0512	J.1	
HBZ0512	J.3	
HBZ0516	C.1	
HBZ0524	J.2	
HBZ0611	R.17	
HBZ0612	R.17	
HBZ0616	K.2	
HBZ0618	K.5	
HBZ0620	K.2	
HBZ0620	K.5	
HBZ0624	J.2	
HBZ0626	J.2	
HBZ0636	A.8	
HBZ0638	J.2	
HBZ0726	K.8	
HBZ0728	K.3	
HCN0631	A.8	
HNS0408	A.3	
HNS0404	B.1	
HNS0405	A.10	
HNS0405	R.7	
HNS0406	A.7	
HNS0406	R.6	
HNS0407	A.7	
HNS0407	A.10	
HNS0503	A.1	
HNS0505	R.9	
HNS0506	A.3	
HNS0506	J.1	
HNS0506	J.3	
HNS0507	A.2	
HNS0507	A.8	
HNS0507	A.11	
HNS0615	E.1	
HNS0615	N.2	
HZS0408	M.2	
HZS0408	M.4	
HZS0408	N.9	
HZS0404	M.2	
HZS0404	M.3	
HZS0404	R.16	
HZS0405	A.15	
HZS0405	K.5	
HZS0405	N.6	
HZS0405	R.8	
HZS0405	R.16	
HZS0405	R.17	
HZS0406	F.8	
HZS0406	R.8	
HZS0406	R.5	
HZS0406	R.9	
HZS0406	R.12	
HZS0406	R.15	
HZS0407	R.7	
HZS0407	R.8	
HZS0408	B.2	
HZS0408	R.11	
HZS0409	A.17	
HZS0410	R.11	
HZS0505	A.15	
HZS0505	C.1	
HZS0505	M.1	
HZS0506	A.15	
HZS0506	A.16	
HZS0506	D.6	
HZS0506	J.2	
HZS0506	K.5	
HZS0506	M.3	
HZS0506	M.4	
HZS0507	A.16	

Part Number Index—continued

Part Number	Amdt. Number	Page
HZS0508		M.1
HZS0508		R.5
HZS0510		R.11
HZS0604		N.9
HZS0606		A.15
HZS0606		A.15
HZS0607		A.16
HZS0607		H.4
HZS0608		E.2
HZS0608		K.5
HZS0608		R.17
HZS0610		R.17
1K21		B.1
1K51		A.1
1K141		A.7
1K204		B.2
1K369		A.2
1K372		A.5
1K618		A.16
1K711		A.16
1K756		A.9
1K759		A.9
1K800		A.5
1K1754		F.1
1K1754		F.5
1K3055		F.2
1K3055		F.6
2K1201		F.9
2K1209		F.9
2K1345		F.1
2K1858		A.1
2K1858		N.3
2K2163		B.1
2K2561		A.5
2K4909		F.4
2K4909		F.7
2K4954		A.1
2K4954		C.1
2K4958		A.9
2K4970		B.1
2K4974		K.1
2K4975		C.1
2K5107		A.3
2K5197		A.7
2K5213		M.4
2K5215		D.5
2K5215		O.1
2K5217		M.3
2K5218		M.3
2K5221		M.4

Part Number	Amdt. Number	Page
2K5243		M.4
2K5291		M.4
2K5319		A.3
2K5319		A.10
2K5505		F.2
2K5507		F.10
2K5578		A.2
2K5578		A.4
2K5616		M.4
2K5622		E.2
2K5863		H.3
2K5914		G.1
2K5928		A.5
2K6012		A.1
2K6057		J.1
2K6167		N.9
2K6192		A.14
2K6192		B.2
2K6193		A.14
2K6193		B.2
2K6584		A.5
2K6650		A.1
2K6842		H.4
2K6842		K.5
2K6930		M.4
2K7056		A.9
2K7181		A.15
2K7181		E.2
2K7181		M.2
2K7440		A.3
2K7500		F.4
2K7552		A.4
2K7914		F.5
2K8209		J.2
2K8232		R.5
2K8377		A.7
2K8600		R.10
2K8609		R.12
2K8609		R.14
2K8645		N.1
2K8725		A.2
2K8910		D.2
2K8929		J.1
2K8951		K.1
2K9005		R.5
2K9051		R.5
2K9798		R.28
2K9799		F.1
2K9799		F.5
2K9932		A.10
2K9993		R.5
2K9993		R.6

Part Number	Amdt. Number	Page
6K35		E.2
6K35		M.2
6K35		O.1
6K56		B.1
6K431		A.7
6K432		F.1
6K432		F.5
6K433		A.6
6K433		A.14
6K467		A.17
6K499		F.1
6K499		F.5
6K499		A.5
6K638		D.2
6K639		A.7
6K649		B.2
6K650		B.2
6K681		F.2
6K681		F.6
6K777		F.2
6K777		F.6
6K780		F.2
6K780		F.6
6K803		A.9
6K9062		R.24
6K9062		R.25
6K9062		R.26
6K9062		R.27
6K9426		R.10
6K9433		R.34
6K9582		K.5
6K9588		N.3
6K9717		R.5
6K9817		R.5
6K9817		R.6
6K9817		R.34
6K9818		R.5
6K9823		R.15
6K9829		F.1
6K9829		F.5
11K100		N.1
11K9095		N.8
11K9181		N.8
51K320		J.2
51K329		K.1
51K330		K.1
51K330		K.2
51K865		J.2
51K370		J.2
51K490		A.6

Part Number	Amdt. Number	Page
51K505		F.8
51K562		A.14
51K590		A.5
51K591		A.5
51K1764		K.1
51K1770		K.1
52K1551		J.2
53K122		R.12
53K124		R.28
53K128		A.18
53K129		N.3
53K155		R.33
53K155		R.34
53K165		D.2
53K462		F.1
53K485		F.5
53K485		A.1
53K507		A.14
53K525		A.3
53K563		A.14
53K564		A.14
53K1023		A.18
53K1025		L.1
53K1048		G.1
53K1191		R.12
53K1302		R.34
53K1393		H.4
53K1435		F.1
53K1435		F.5
53K1452		A.9
53K1661		R.10
53K1662		K.1
53K1662		R.10
53K1712		R.12
53K3061		D.2
53K3151		R.30
53K3157		R.9
54K195		R.11
54K1723		F.4
54K1723		F.7
54K2995		R.27
54K3014		R.13
54K3014		R.24
54K3016		R.24
54K3024		R.21
54K3215		R.27
54K3418		R.18
54K3495		R.12
LNN208		A.1

Part Number Index—*continued*

Part Number	Page	Amdt. Number
LNZ205	M.1	
LNZ206	A.10	
LNZ206	G.1	
LNZ206	H.3	
LNZ206	H.4	
LNZ206	K.5	
LNZ305	K.5	
LWN203	F.9	
LWN203	R.4	
LWN203	R.6	
LWN203	R.7	
LWN204	A.7	
LWN204	A.10	
LWN204	B.2	
LWN204	F.1	
LWN204	F.5	
LWN204	R.6	
LWN204	R.7	
LWN205	A.1	
LWN205	A.2	
LWN205	A.3	
LWN205	A.6	
LWN205	A.10	
LWN205	A.11	
LWN205	E.1	
LWN205	F.1	
LWN205	F.2	
LWN205	F.3	
LWN205	F.5	
LWN205	F.6	
LWN205	F.8	
LWN205	J.1	
LWN205	R.9	
LWN205	A.5	
LWN206	A.8	
LWN206	F.4	
LWN206	F.11	
LWN206	N.2	
LWN206	A.9	
LWN207	A.10	
LWZ102	N.5	
LWZ106	L.1	
LWZ107	L.1	
LWZ203	A.17	
LWZ203	A.18	
LWZ203	F.8	
LWZ203	M.2	
LWZ203	M.4	
LWZ203	N.3	
LWZ208	N.6	
LWZ203	N.8	
LWZ203	N.9	
LWZ203	O.1	
LWZ203	R.3	
LWZ203	R.4	
LWZ203	R.5	
LWZ203	R.8	
LWZ203	R.12	
LWZ203	R.13	
LWZ203	R.15	
LWZ203	R.21	
LWZ203	R.23	
LWZ203	R.26	
LWZ203	R.27	
LWZ203	R.28	
LWZ203	R.30	
LWZ203	R.31	
LWZ203	R.33	
LWZ203	R.35	
LWZ204	B.1	
LWZ204	F.1	
LWZ204	F.5	
LWZ204	F.8	
LWZ204	K.1	
LWZ204	M.2	
LWZ204	M.4	
LWZ204	N.6	
LWZ204	N.9	
LWZ204	R.3	
LWZ204	R.5	
LWZ204	R.8	
LWZ204	R.9	
LWZ204	R.10	
LWZ204	R.11	
LWZ204	R.15	
LWZ204	R.16	
LWZ204	R.17	
LWZ204	R.20	
LWZ204	R.31	
LWZ205	A.14	
LWZ205	A.15	
LWZ205	A.16	
LWZ205	A.18	
LWZ205	C.1	
LWZ205	D.2	
LWZ205	D.6	
LWZ205	F.8	
LWZ205	F.11	
LWZ205	J.1	
LWZ205	J.8	
LWZ205	K.8	
LWZ205	K.5	
LWZ205	M.1	
LWZ205	M.8	
LWZ205	M.4	
LWZ205	R.11	
LWZ206	A.14	
LWZ206	A.15	
LWZ206	H.4	
LWZ206	N.9	
LWZ206	R.17	
LWZ206	R.20	
LWZ207	A.15	
LWZ212	H.4	
LWZ212	F.2	
LWZ302	H.2	
LWZ302	N.3	
LWZ302	N.4	
LWZ303	A.17	
LWZ303	A.18	
LWZ303	D.5	
LWZ304	A.15	
LWZ304	E.2	
LWZ304	J.2	
LWZ304	K.5	
LWZ304	M.1	
LWZ304	M.2	
LWZ304	M.8	
LWZ304	N.6	
LWZ304	R.12	
LWZ305	D.1	
LWZ305	J.2	
LWZ305	M.4	
LWZ306	A.15	
LWZ306	A.16	
LWZ306	E.2	
LWZ306	G.1	
LWZ306	H.1	
LWZ306	H.4	
LWZ306	J.2	
LWZ306	K.2	
LWZ306	K.3	
LWZ306	K.5	
LWZ307	H.1	
LWZ307	K.2	
NCS0606	A.4	
NZS103	M.4	
PCR0807	O.1	
PCR0807	R.38	
PCR0811	N.9	
PCR0407	N.8	
PCR0407	N.9	
PCR0507	D.2	
PCR0507	N.8	
PCR0607	N.9	
PCR0607	N.8	
PCR0007	N.9	
PCR0009	M.4	
PCR0009	N.9	
PCR0707	N.8	
PCR0707	N.9	
PCR0713	N.8	
PCR0807	N.9	
PCR1007	N.8	
PFS106	R.10	
PFS106	R.32	
PFS514	R.5	
PFS528	R.8	
PMN0310	R.6	
PMP0308	R.21	
PMP0308	R.23	
PMP0308	R.31	
PMP0312	R.31	
PMZ0207	N.3	
PMZ0207	N.4	
PMZ0207	N.5	
PMZ0304	N.8	
PMZ0305	D.5	
PMZ0306	A.17	
PMZ0306	M.4	
PMZ0306	N.3	
PMZ0306	N.8	
PMZ0306	R.10	
PMZ0306	R.27	
PMZ0307	D.5	
PMZ0307	M.2	
PMZ0307	O.1	
PMZ0308	R.23	
PMZ0308	F.8	
PMZ0308	F.9	
PMZ0308	N.3	
PMZ0308	N.6	
PMZ0308	N.8	
PMZ0308	N.9	
PMZ0308	R.3	
PMZ0308	R.4	
PMZ0308	R.15	

Part Number Index—*continued*

Part Number	Page	Amdt. Number	Part Number	Page	Amdt. Number	Part Number	Page	Amdt. Number	Part Number	Page	Amdt. Number
PMZ0308	R.28		PWN105	R.9		PWZ104	R.31		RMP0308	R.12	
PMZ0308	R.80		PWN106	A.5		PWZ105	A.14		RMP0308	R.26	
PMZ0308	R.83		PWN106	A.14		PWZ105	A.15		RMP0310	R.12	
PMZ0308	R.35		PWN106	A.17		PWZ105	C.1		RMP0810	R.26	
PMZ0308	R.8		PWN107	A.1		PWZ105	D.6		RMP0812	R.12	
PMZ0310	R.30		PWN107	A.9		PWZ105	E.2		RMP0416	R.11	
PMZ0310	R.33		PWN112	F.11		PWZ105	F.8		RMZ0810	R.5	
PMZ0310	R.35		PWN203	R.6		PWZ105	M.4		RMZ0410	R.10	
PMZ0314	M.2		PWN204	B.2		PWZ105	N.1				
PMZ0816	R.11		PWZ102	N.3		PWZ105	R.3		RPP0810	R.13	
PMZ0820	N.3		PWZ102	N.4		PWZ105	R.10		RPP0812	R.21	
PMZ0828	R.35		PWZ102	N.5		PWZ105	R.32		RPP0812	R.32	
PMZ0408	N.6		PWZ103	N.3		PWZ106	A.14		RPW606	R.27	
PMZ0410	R.8		PWZ103	R.8		PWZ106	A.15				
PMZ0510	A.16		PWZ103	R.4		PWZ106	A.17		RTP604	R.27	
			PWZ103	R.5		PWZ106	K.5		RTP606	R.25	
PPZ0806	R.5		PWZ108	R.8		PWZ106	R.11		RTP806	R.21	
			PWZ108	R.11		PWZ106	R.17				
PTN805	R.6		PWZ108	R.12		PWZ106	R.20		RWP605	R.24	
			PWZ103	R.13		PWZ107	H.4				
PTZ603	R.5		PWZ108	R.14		PWZ112	J.2		TPS0405	F.8	
PTZ603	R.9		PWZ103	R.15		PWZ203	A.18		TP30610	F.1	
PTZ603	R.28		PWZ103	R.21		PWZ203	R.3		TPS0610	F.5	
PTZ603	R.38		PWZ103	R.23		PWZ203	R.8		TPS0710	A.9	
PTZ803	R.8		PWZ103	R.26		PWZ204	R.11				
PTZ803	R.28		PWZ103	R.27		PWZ204	R.16		UHN805	M.4	
PTZ804	R.23		PWZ103	R.28		PWZ204	R.20				
PTZ806	R.9		PWZ103	R.31		PWZ204	R.27		WKN305	F.4	
PTZ806	R.23		PWZ103	R.88		PWZ205	R.31		WKN405	N.1	
PTZ808	R.28		PWZ103	R.85		RFN803	M.1		WKN606	A.2	
PTZ1003	R.83		PWZ104	A.17		RFN803	N.8				
PTZ1004	D.2		PWZ104	B.1		RFN403	R.32		WNZ104	N.1	
PTZ1004	M.2		PWZ104	N.6		RFN403	A.18		WNZ104	R.32	
PTZ1004	N.9		PWZ104	R.8		RFN408	O.1				
PWN103	R.4		PWZ104	R.5		RFN408	O.2		ZCS0505	A.18	
PWN108	R.6		PWZ104	R.7		RFN405	N.8				
PWN108	R.7		PWZ104	R.8		RFR106	D.5		ZPS0204	R.8	
PWN104	A.7		PWZ104	R.10		RJP604	R.26				
PWN104	A.14		PWZ104	R.11		RJP1005	R.21		45223	B.2	
PWN104	R.6		PWZ104	R.12							
PWN104	R.7		PWZ104	R.16							

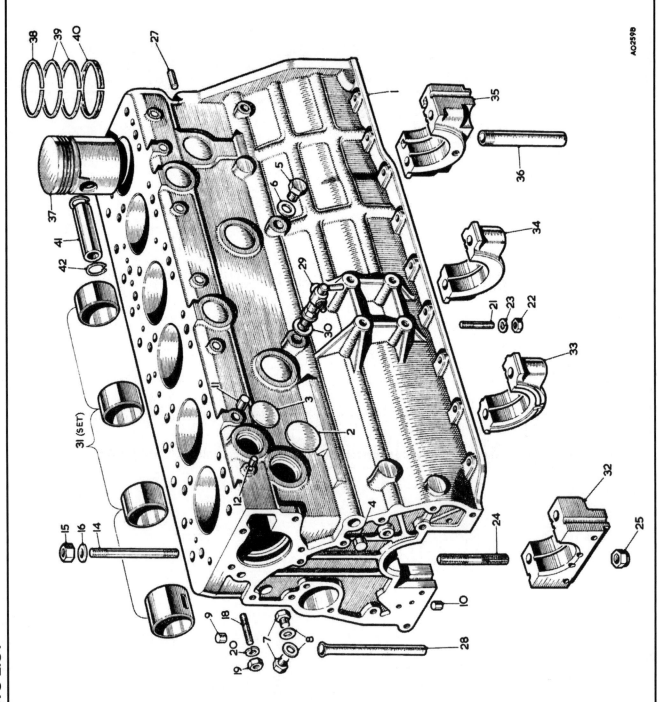

A0259B

SERVICE PARTS LIST

AUSTIN-HEALEY 100 SIX (SERIES BN6)

Item No.	DESCRIPTION	Part Number Commencing (E) 60049	Illus. No.	Qty. per Vehicle RHD	Qty. per Vehicle LHD	Unit of Issue	Type of Vehicle	New Part Number	Change Point	Amdt. No.	REMARKS
	ENGINE										
	ENGINE UNIT										
1	**Stripped engine** (R)	AEC1291		1	1						
2	**Half-engine**	AEG1290		1	1						
3	**Block assembly—cylinder and pistons**	AEG1289	A1	1	1						
4	Plug for core hole (large)	AEC719	A2	5	5	12.					
5	Plug for core hole (small)	AEC720	A3	4	4						
6	Plug for oil gallery	8G507	A4	2	2						
7	Plug for oil filter feed hole	AEC110	A5	1	1						
8	Washer for plug	AEC343	A6	1	1						
9	Plug for oil pump feed hole	HNS0508	A7	2	2						
10	Washer for plug	AEC398	A8	2	2						
11	Plug for oil pump boss	2K6012	A9	1	1						
12	Plug for tensioner feed hole	2K6650	A10	1	1						
13	Plug for water gallery (large)	2K1358	A11	5	5						
14	Plug for water gallery (small)	2K6650	A12	2	2						
15	Stud for cylinder head	AEC604	A14	16	16						
16	Nut for stud	AEC139	A15	16	16						
17	Washer for stud (steel)	PWN107	A16	16	16						
18	Stud for water pump	53K485	A18	4	4						
19	Nut for stud	FNN105	A19	4	4						
20	Washer for stud (spring)	LWN205	A20	4	4						
21	Stud for oil pump	AEC341	A21	3	3						
22	Nut for stud	FNN105	A22	3	3						
23	Washer for stud (spring)	LWN205	A23	8	8						
24	Stud for main bearing cap	AEC872	A24	8	8						
25	Nut for stud (self-locking)	LNN208	A25	8	8						
26	Dowel—rear plate to block	1K51	A27	2	2						
27	Tube—oil level indicator	AEC672	A28	1	1						
28	Tap—water drain	3H2502	A29	1	1						
29	Washer for tap	2K4054	A30	1	1	36.					
30	Liner for camshaft	AJC6042	A31	1	1	set					
31	Cap for main bearing (front)	N.S.P.	A32								
32	Cap for main bearing (No. 2)	N.S.P.	A33								
33	Cap for main bearing (No. 3)	N.S.P.	A34								
34	Cap for main bearing (rear)	N.S.P.	A35								
35	Tube—drain	AEC853	A36	1	1						
36	**Piston assembly—standard**	AEG1117	A37	6	6						
37	Ring—compression	AEC833	A38	6	6			AEC834	Com. (E) 64300		
38	Ring—compression (taper)	AEC834	A39	12	12						
39	Ring—scraper	AEC835	A40	6	6						
40	Pin—gudgeon	AEC832	A41	6	6						
41	Circlip for gudgeon pin	AEC785	A42	12	12						

29

A.1

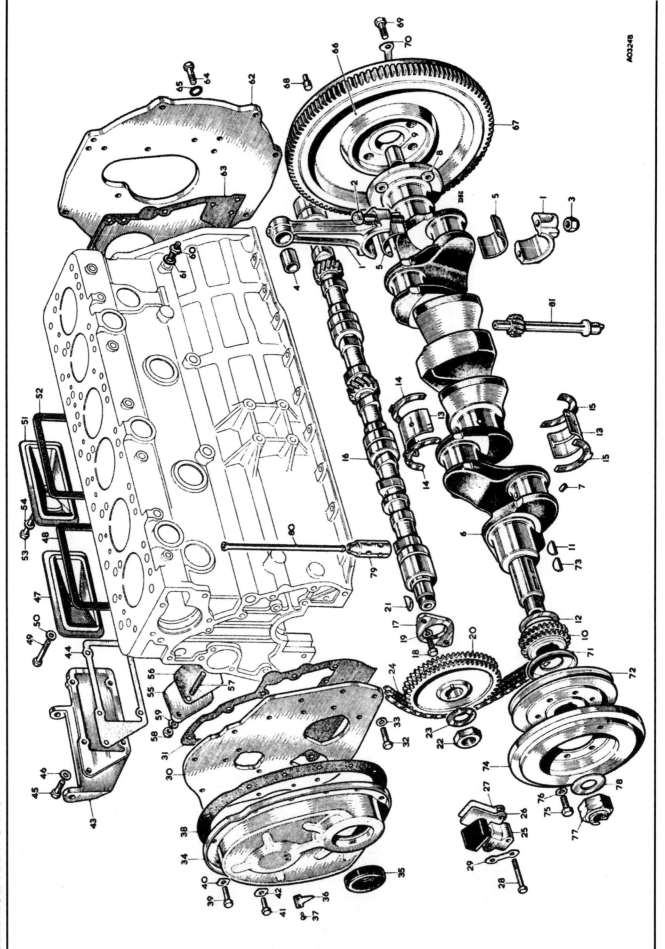

AO324B

SERVICE PARTS LIST

ENGINE

ENGINE UNIT

Item No.	DESCRIPTION	Part Number (Commencing (E) 60949)	Illus. No.	Qty. per Vehicle RHD	Qty. per Vehicle LHD	Unit of Issue	Type of Vehicle	New Part Number	Change Point	Amdt. No.	REMARKS
1	Stripped engine (R)	**AEC1291**		1	1						
2	Half-engine	**AEC1290**		1	1						
3	**Block assembly—cylinder and pistons**	**AEC1289**	**A1**	1	1						
4	Plug for core hole (large)	AEC719	A2	5	5	12					
5	Plug for core hole (small)	AEC720	A3	4	4						
6	Plug for oil gallery	8G507	A4	2	2						
7	Plug for oil filter feed hole	AEC110	A5	1	1						
8	Washer for plug	AEC343	A6	1	1						
9	Plug for oil pump feed hole	HNS0503	A7	2	2						
10	Washer for plug	AEC398	A8	2	2						
11	Plug for oil pump boss	2K6012	A9	1	1						
12	Plug for tensioner feed hole	2K6650	A10	1	1						
13	Plug for water gallery (large)	2K1858	A11	5	5						
14	Plug for water gallery (small)	2K6650	A12	2	2						
15	Stud for cylinder head	AEC604	A14	16	16						
16	Nut for stud	AEC139	A15	16	16						
17	Washer for stud (steel)	PWN107	A16	16	16						
18	Stud for water pump	53K485	A18	4	4						
19	Nut for stud	FNN105	A19	4	4						
20	Washer for stud (spring)	LWN205	A20	4	4						
21	Stud for oil pump	AEC341	A21	3	3						
22	Nut for stud	FNN105	A22	3	3						
23	Washer for stud (spring)	LWN205	A23	3	3						
24	Stud for main bearing cap	AEC872	A24	8	8						
25	Nut for stud (self-locking)	LNN208	A25	8	8						
26	Dowel—rear plate to block	1K51	A27	2	2						
27	Tube—oil level indicator	AEC672	A28	1	1						
28	Tap—water drain	3H2502	A29	1	1						
29	Washer for tap	2K4954	A30	1	1	36					
30	Liner for camshaft	AJC6042	A31	1	1	set					
31	Cap for main bearing (front)	N.S.P.	A32								
32	Cap for main bearing (No. 2)	N.S.P.	A33								
33	Cap for main bearing (No. 3)	N.S.P.	A34								
34	Cap for main bearing (rear)	N.S.P.	A35								
35	Tube—drain	AEC853	A36	1	1						
36	**Piston assembly—standard**	**AEC1117**	**A37**	6	6						
37	Ring—compression	AEC833	A38	6	6			AEC834	Com. (E) 64300		
38	Ring—compression (taper)	AEC834	A39	12	12						
39	Ring—scraper	AEC835	A40	6	6						
40	Pin—gudgeon	AEC832	A41	6	6						
41	Circlip for gudgeon pin	AEC785	A42	12	12						

A.2

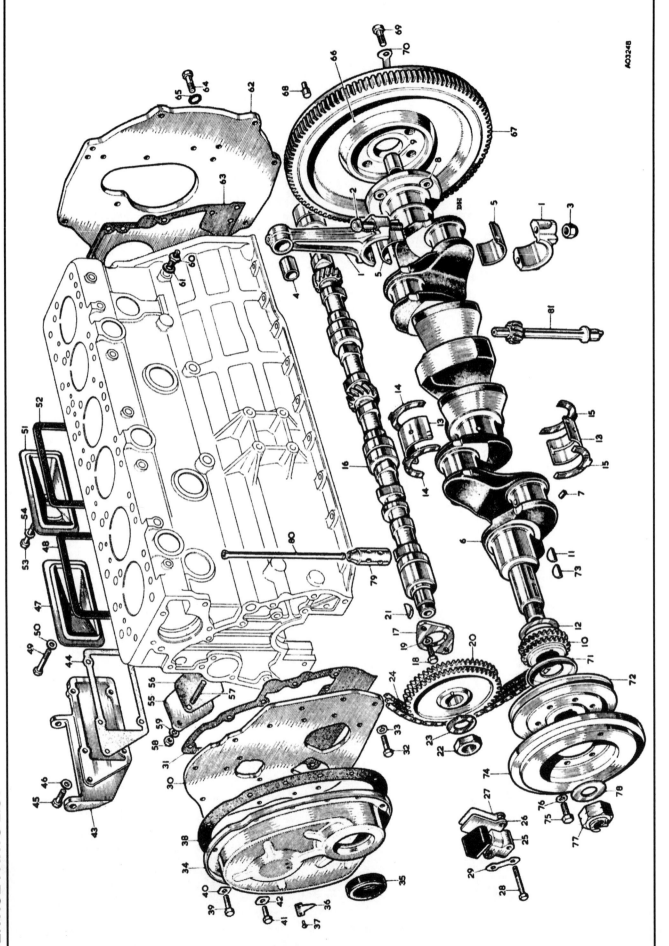

A0324B

Item No.	DESCRIPTION	Commencing (E) 60949 Part Number	Illus. No.	Qty. per Vehicle RHD	Qty. per Vehicle LHD	Unit of Issue	Type of Vehicle	New Part Number	Change Point	Amdt. No.	REMARKS
	CONNECTING RODS—BEARINGS										
1	**Connecting rod and cap**	**AEC1092**	**AA1**	**6**	**6**						
2	Bolt for cap	AEC268	AA2	12	12						
3	Nut for bolt	AEC328	AA3	12	12	12					
4	Bush—small-end	AEC797	AA4	6	6						
5	**Bearing for connecting rod—big-end (standard)**	**AJC5159**	**AA5**	**1**	**1**	**set**					
	CRANKSHAFT GEAR										
6	**Crankshaft with oil restrictor and bush**	**AEC28**	**AA6**	**1**	**1**						
7	Restrictor	1B1033	AA7	6	6						
8	Nut for flywheel bolt	AEC179	AA8	4	4						
9	Bush for drive gear	1K369	AA9	1	1						
10	**Gear for crankshaft**	**AEC180**	**AA10**	**1**	**1**						
11	Key for gear	2K5578	AA11	1	1						
12	Washer—packing	2K8725	AA12	A/R	A/R						
13	**Bearing—main (standard)**	**8G2121**	**AA13**	**1**	**1**	**set**					
14	Washer—thrust—upper (standard)	AEC278	AA14	A/R	A/R						
15	Washer—thrust—lower (standard)	AEC279	AA15	A/R	A/R						
	CAMSHAFT—GEAR										
16	**Camshaft**	**AEC828**	**AA16**	**1**	**1**						
17	Plate—locating	AEC778	AA17	1	1						⎤ Alternatives
18	Plate—locating	AEC810		1	1						⎦
19	Screw—plate to crankcase	HNS0507	AA18	2	2						
20	Washer for screw (spring)	LWN205	AA19	2	2						
21	**Gear for camshaft**	**AEC482**	**AA20**	**1**	**1**						
22	Key for gear	WKN606	AA21	1	1						
23	Nut for gear	AEC247	AA22	1	1						
24	Washer for nut (lock)	1B1219	AA23	1	1						
25	**Chain for camshaft drive**	**AEC191**	**AA24**	**1**	**1**						
26	**Tensioner—chain**	**17H342**	**AA25**	**1**	**1**						
27	Back plate—body	AJC5038	AA26	1	1						
28	Joint for tensioner	AEC389	AA27	1	1	12					
29	Bolt—tensioner to block	AEC108	AA28	2	2						
30	Washer for bolt (lock)	AEC840	AA29	1	1						

A.3

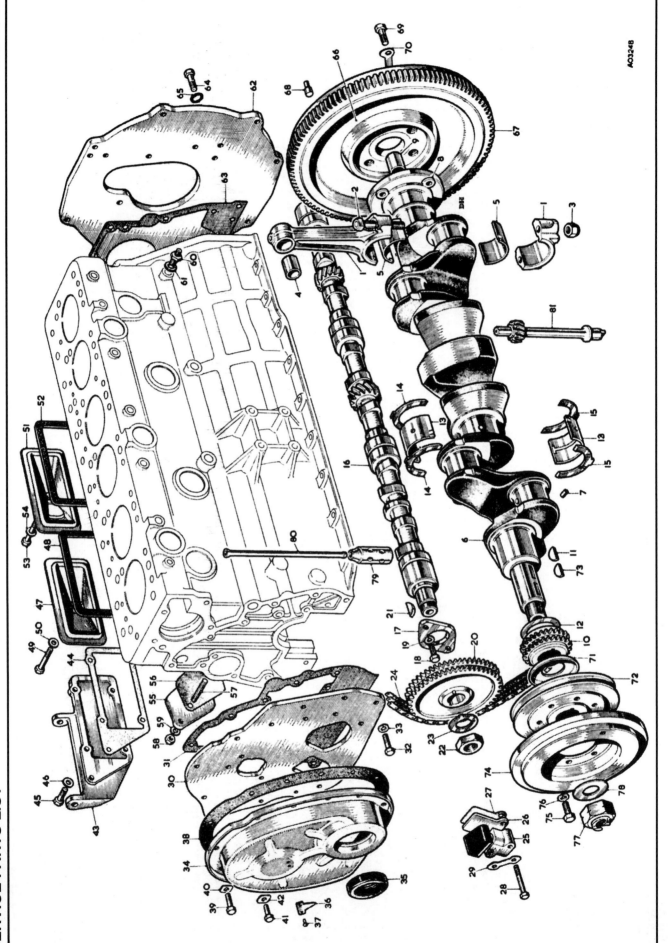

AO3248

SERVICE PARTS LIST

AUSTIN-HEALEY 100 SIX (SERIES BN6)

Item No.	DESCRIPTION	Part Number Commencing (E) 60949	Illus. No.	Qty. per Vehicle RHD	Qty. per Vehicle LHD	Unit of Issue	MODIFICATIONS Type of Vehicle	MODIFICATIONS New Part Number	MODIFICATIONS Change Point	MODIFICATIONS Amdt. No.	REMARKS
	FRONT ENGINE MOUNTING PLATE										
1	**Plate—engine mounting—front.**	**AEG336**	**AA30**	1	1						
2	Washer—joint—mounting plate to crankcase	AEC337	AA31	1	1						
3	Screw—plate to crankcase	HNS0506	AA32	5	5	12					
4	Screw—plate to bearing	HNS0506	AA32	1	1						
5	Washer for screw	2K5819	AA33	6	6						
	OIL PUMP SPINDLE										
6	Spindle for oil pump—driving	AEC829	AA81	1	1						
	CYLINDER FRONT AND SIDE COVERS										
7	**Cover—front**	**AEG1011**	**AA34**	1	1						
8	Seal for cover	AEC621	AA35	1	1						
9	Pointer—timing	AEC848	AA36	1	1						
10	Rivet for pointer	AEC349	AA87	2	2						
11	Joint for front cover	AEC202	AA38	1	1	12					
12	Screw—cover to mounting plate (long)	HNS0507	AA39	7	7						
13	Washer for screw	2K7440	AA40	7	7						
14	Screw—cover to mounting plate (short)	HNS0403	AA41	5	5						
15	Washer for screw	2K5197	AA42	5	5	24					
16	**Cover for cylinder side (front)**	**AEG689**	**AA43**	1	1						
17	Joint for cover	AEC813	AA44	1	1						
18	Screw—cover to crankcase	HNS0506	AA45	5	5	12					
19	Washer for screw	AEC435	AA46	5	5						
20	**Cover for cylinder side (centre)**	**2A770**	**AA47**	1	1						
21	Joint—cover to crankcase	1A2203	AA48	1	1	12					
22	Bolt—cover to crankcase	HBN0510	AA49	1	1						
23	Washer for bolt	AEC461	AA50	1	1						
24	**Cover for cylinder side (rear)**	**AEG436**	**AA51**	1	1						
25	Joint—cover to block	1A2203	AA52	1	1	12					
26	Bolt—cover to block	HBN0510	AA53	1	1						
27	Washer for bolt	AEC461	AA54	1	1						
28	**Plate—cylinder block blanking (R/H)**	**AEG451**	**AA55**	1	1						
29	Joint for blanking plate	1E504	AA56	1	1	12					
30	Stud for blanking plate	53K525	AA57	2	2						
31	Nut for stud	FNN105	AA58	2	2						
32	Washer for stud (spring)	LWN205	AA59	2	2						

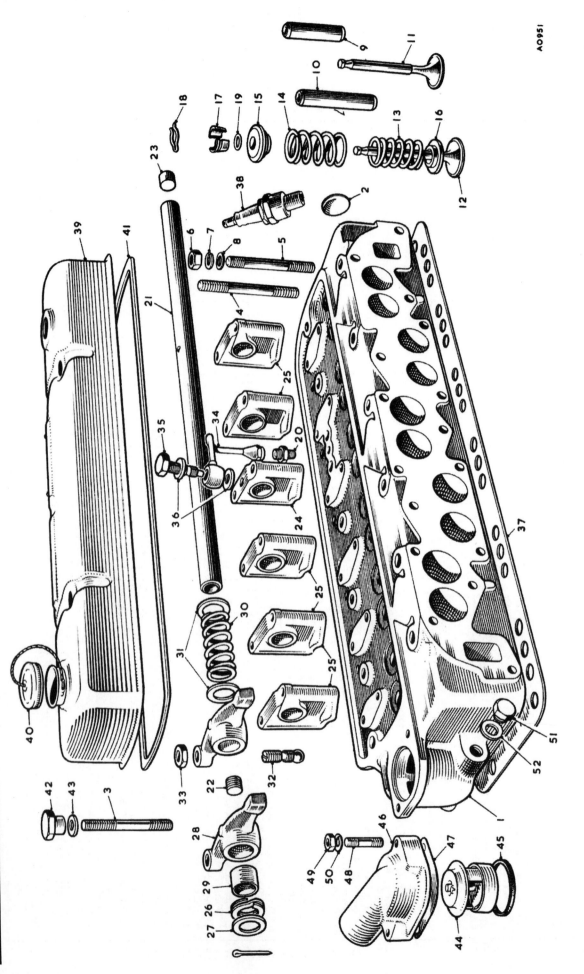

AUSTIN-HEALEY 100 SIX (SERIES BN6)

Item No.	DESCRIPTION	Commencing (E) 60949 Part Number	Illus. No.	Qty. per Vehicle RHD	Qty. per Vehicle LHD	Unit of Issue	Type of Vehicle	New Part Number	Change Point	Amdt. No.	REMARKS
	CYLINDER HEAD—VALVES—GUIDES—SPRINGS—ROCKERS										
1	Cylinder head with valve assembly	**AEG1292**	**AB1**	1	1						
2	Cylinder head with valve guides—assembly	**AEG1266**	AB2	1	1						
3	Plug for core hole	AEC720	AB3	2	2						
4	Stud for rocker bracket and cover	AEC491	AB4	6	6						
5	Stud for rocker bracket (long)	51K591	AB5	4	4						
6	Stud for rocker bracket (short)	51K590	AB6	12	12						
7	Nut for stud	FNN506	AB7	12	12						
8	Washer for stud (spring)	LWN206	AB8	12	12						
9	Washer for stud (plain)	PWN106	AB9	6	6						
10	Guide—inlet valve	AEC135	AB10	6	6						
11	Guide—exhaust valve	AEC245	AB11	6	6						
12	Valve—inlet	**AEG724**	**AB11**	6	6						
13	Valve—exhaust	**AEG631**	**AB12**	6	6						
14	Spring for valve (inner)	1H728	AB13	12	12	8					
15	Spring for valve (outer)	1H722	AB14	12	12	8					
16	Cap for spring	AEC786	AB15	12	12						
17	Collar for spring (lower)	1H726	AB16	12	12						
18	Retainer for spring	1K800	AB17	24	24	72					
19	Circlip for retainer	1K872	AB18	12	12						
20	Grommet for valve stem	AEK113	AB19	12	12	144					
21	Union for rocker oil feed pipe	AEC463	AB20	1	1						
22	**Shaft assembly—valve rocker**	**AEG1097**	AB21	1	1						
23	Shaft—rocker	AEC27	AB22	1	1						
24	Plug—screwed	2K6534	AB23	1	1						
25	Plug—plain	1D1977	AB24	1	1						
26	Bracket for rocker shaft (tapped)	AEG616	AB25	1	1						
27	Bracket for rocker shaft (plain)	11B121	AB26	5	5						
28	Washer for rocker shaft (spring)	2K2561	AB27	2	2						
29	Washer for rocker shaft (plain)	AEC144	AB28	2	2						
30	**Rocker assembly**	**AED159**	**AB28**	**12**	**12**						
31	Bush	11B511	AB29	12	12						
32	Spring—rocker spacing	2K5923	AB30	5	5	36					
33	Washer—rocker spacing	AEC143	AB31	12	12						
34	Screw—rocker adjusting	AED161	AB32	12	12						AED260 alternative
35	Lock nut for adjusting screw	FNN206	AB33	12	12						
36	**Pipe—rocker oil feed**	**AEG160**	**AB34**	1	1						
37	Bolt—pipe to rocker bracket	AEC162	AB35	1	1						
38	Washer for bolt	AEC346	AB36	2	2						
39	Joint for cylinder head	AEC827	AB37	1	1						For use with low-octane fuel
40	Joint for cylinder head	AEC798		1	1						
41	Plug—sparking	3H2006	AB88	6	6						

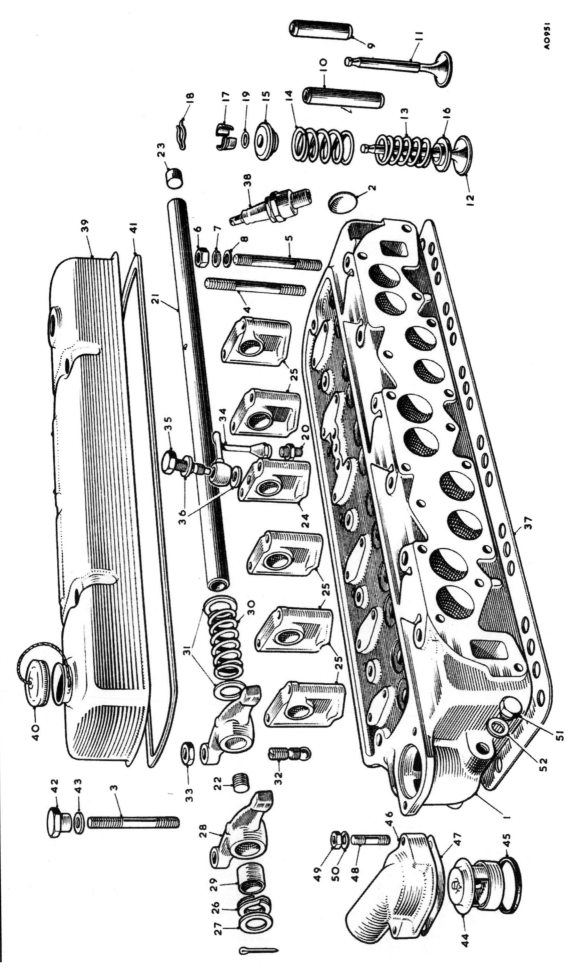

A0951

Item No.	DESCRIPTION	Commencing (E) 60040		Qty. per Vehicle		Unit of Issue	MODIFICATIONS				REMARKS
		Part Number	Illus. No.	RHD	LHD		New Part Number	Type of Vehicle	Change Point	Amdt. No.	
	VALVE ROCKER COVER—OIL FILLER										
1	**Cover—valve rocker (with filler cap)**	**AEG1304**	**AB39**	1	1						
2	Cap—oil filler	8G612	AB40	1	1						
3	Joint—cover to head	AEC176	AB41	1	1	12					
4	Nut for rocker cover	AEC488	AB42	2	2						
5	Washer for nut	AEC400	AB43	2	2						
6	**Thermostat**	**11G291**	**AB44**	1	1						
7	Joint for thermostat	1G1365	AB45	1	1	12					
8	**Elbow—water outlet**	**AEG158**	**AB46**	1	1						
9	Joint for elbow	AEC157	AB47	1	1	12					
10	Stud—elbow to cylinder head	51K490	AB48	2	2						
11	Nut for stud	FNN105	AB49	2	2						
12	Washer for stud (spring)	LWN205	AB50	2	2						
13	Plug—thermal indicator boss	ADP610	AB51	1	1				Fin. (E) 66672		
14	Washer for plug	6K488	AB52	1	1						

39

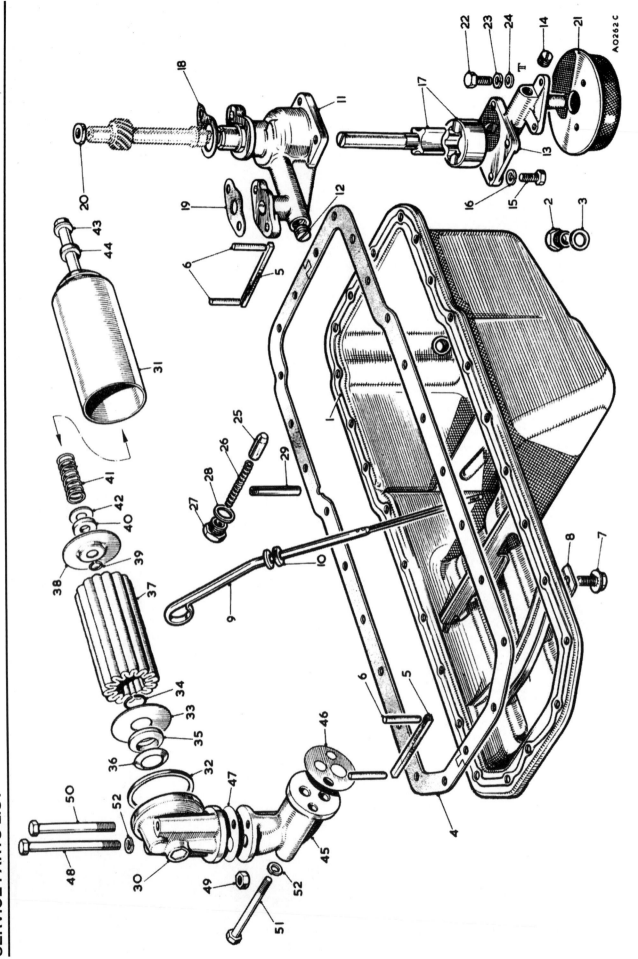

A0262C

SERVICE PARTS LIST

Item No.	DESCRIPTION	Commencing (E) 60949 — Part Number	Illus. No.	Qty. per Vehicle — RHD	Qty. per Vehicle — LHD	Unit of Issue	Type of Vehicle	MODIFICATIONS — New Part Number	MODIFICATIONS — Change Point	MODIFICATIONS — Amdt. No.	REMARKS
	SUMP—OIL LEVEL INDICATOR										
	Sump—oil	**AEC203**	**AC1**	1	1						
1	Plug for sump—drain	2H4485	AC2	1	1						
2	Washer for plug (copper)	AEC699	AC3	1	1						
3	Joint—sump to crankcase	AEC205	AC4	1	1	12.					
4	Seal—front and rear main bearing cap	AEC108	AC5	2	2	12.					
5	Plug—front and rear main bearing cap	AEC357	AC6	4	4			AEC888	Com. (E) 60629		
6	Bolt—sump to crankcase	6K689	AC7	25	25	12.					
7	Washer for bolt	2K5197	AC8	25	25	24.					
8	**Indicator—oil level**	**AEC667**	**AC9**	1	1						
9	Washer for indicator (rubber)	AEC671	AC10	1	1						
	OIL PUMP—OIL RELEASE VALVE										
11	**Pump assembly—oil** (R)	**AEG692**	**AC11**	1	1						
12	Body with plug	AEC695	AC12	1	1						
13	Plug for body	AEC405	AC13	1	1						
14	Cover for body	AEC407	AC14	1	1						
15	Plug for cover	AEC405	AC15	1	1						
16	Screw—cover to body	HNS0407	AC16	4	4						
17	Washer for screw (spring)	LWN204	AC17	4	4						
18	**Shaft—driving—with inner and outer rotors**	**AEC406**	**AC18**	1	1						
19	Joint for pump	AEC698	AC19	1	1						
20	Joint for pump filter flange	AEC315	AC20	1	1						
21	Washer for driving spindle (thrust)	AEC223	AC21	1	1	12.					
22	**Strainer assembly—oil**	**AEC224**	**AC22**	1	1						
23	Screw—strainer to pump	HNS0406	AC23	8	8						
24	Washer for screw (spring)	LWN204	AC24	8	8						
25	Washer for screw (plain)	PWN104	AC25	8	8						
26	**Valve—oil release**	**AEC283**	**AC26**	1	1			**AEC863**	Com. (E) 67464 except 67501 to 67505		] Supply in sets after (E) 67464
27	Spring for valve	AEC284	AC27	1	1			AEC864			
28	Plug for valve	2K8377	AC28	1	1						
29	Washer for plug	6K431	AC29	1	1	72.					
30	**Pipe—valve drain**	**1K141**		1	1						

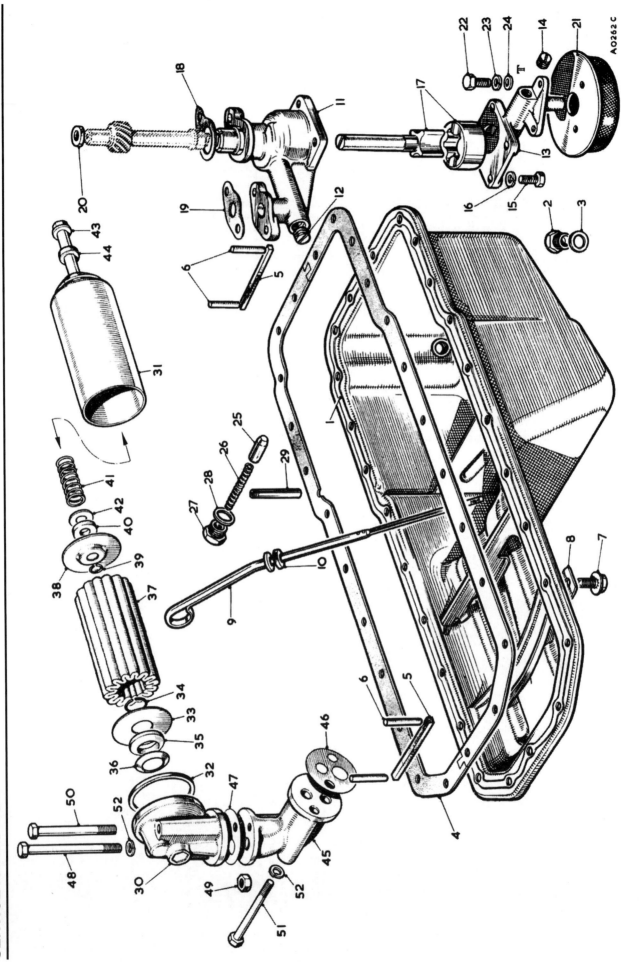

A0262 C

Item No.	DESCRIPTION	Part Number Commencing (E) 600949	Illus. No.	Qty. per Vehicle RHD	Qty. per Vehicle LHD	Unit of Issue	Type of Vehicle	New Part Number	Change Point	Amdt. No.	REMARKS
	OIL FILTER (EXTERNAL)										
1	**Filter—oil (Tecalemit)**	**1B2897**		1	1						**Alternative**
2	Head assembly (for use with ·875″ B.S.F. centre-bolt)	AJC5011	AC30	1	1						
3	Head assembly (for use with ·875″ U.N.F. centre-bolt)										
4	Sump	17H940		1	1						
5	Seal—sump to head	17H3	AC31	1	1						
6	Plate—element clamp	2A780	AC32	1	1	12					
7	Circlip—plate to head	7H147	AC33	1	1						
8	Washer for clamp plate (felt)	7H157	AC34	1	1						
9	Washer for clamp plate (dished)	7H1756	AC35	1	1						
10	Element	7H1761	AC36	1	1						
11	Plate—pressure	2H4840	AC37	1	1						
12	Circlip—plate to centre-bolt	7H1763	AC38	1	1						
13	Washer for pressure plate (felt)	7H1840	AC39	1	1						
14	Spring for pressure plate	7H1758	AC40	1	1						
15	Washer for spring	7H1764	AC41	1	1						
16	Bolt—centre (·875″ B.S.F.)	7H1765	AC42	1	1						
17	Bolt—centre (·875″ U.N.F.)	7H1762	AC43	1	1						
18	Seal—bolt to sump	17H775	AC44	1	1						
19	**Plate—adaptor**	7H1759 / **AE6675**	**AC45**	1	1						
20	Joint—plate to crankcase	1B1233	AC46	1	1						
21	Joint—filter to plate	1B1233	AC47	1	1						
22	Bolt—oil filter to plate	HBZ0636	AC48	1	1						
23	Nut for bolt	FNZ106	AC49	1	1						
24	Screw—oil filter to plate	HCN0631	AC50	1	1						
25	Bolt—adaptor plate to crankcase	HBN0682	AC51	2	2						
26	Washer—spring	LWN206	AC52	4	4						
27	**Filter—oil (Purolator)**	**AE6897**		1	1						**Alternative**
28	Element assembly	27H1185		1	1						
29	Spring	7H25		1	1						
30	Seal	7H28		1	1						
31	Plate—pressure	17H1148		1	1						
32	Plate—clamping	17H1150		1	1						
33	Gasket	17H1152		1	1						
34	Ring—snap	17H1167		1	1						
35	Seal	17H1168		1	1						
36	Sump	27H1144		1	1						
37	Collar	27H1143		1	1						
38	Seal—'O' section	17H1173		1	1						
39	Seat—relief valve	27H1139		1	1						
40	Spring—relief valve	27H1140		1	1						
41	Head	27H1141		1	1						
42	Bolt—centre	27H1142		1	1						
43	Circlip	17H1476		1	1						
44	Washer	7H7553		1	1						
45	Ball	27H7466		1	1						

9887A

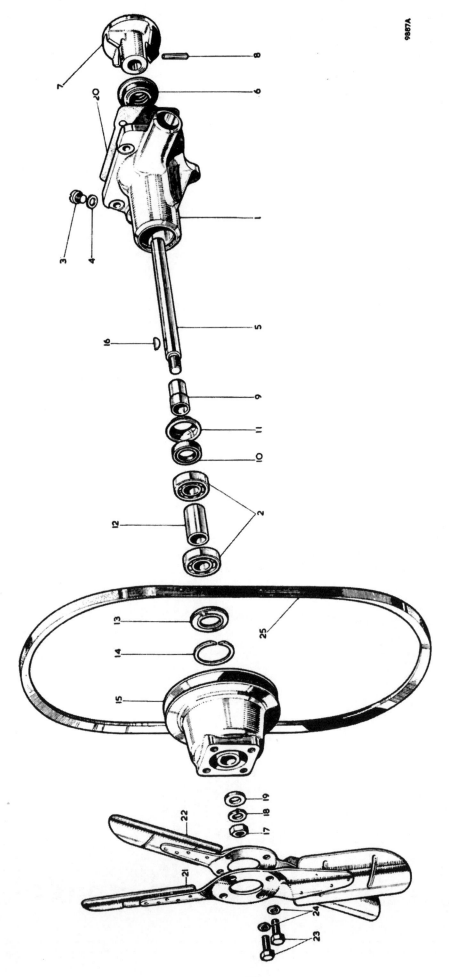

WATER PUMP—FAN PULLEY

Item No.	DESCRIPTION	Commencing (E) 60049 Part Number	Illus. No.	Qty. per Vehicle RHD	Qty. per Vehicle LHD	Unit of Issue	Type of Vehicle	New Part Number	Change Point	Amdt. No.	REMARKS
1	Pump assembly—water (R)	AEC1356		1	1						
2	Body	AEC206	AD1	1	1						
3	Bearing—ball	6K803	AD2	1	1						
4	Plug—oil filler screw	53K1452	AD3	2	2						
5	Washer for plug (fibre)	2K4958	AD4	1	1	36					
6	Spindle	AEC383	AD5	1	1						
7	Seal	8G627	AD6	1	1						
8	Vane	AEC609	AD7	1	1						
9	Pin for vane (taper)	TPS0710	AD8	1	1						
10	Distance piece for vane	AEC384	AD9	1	1						
11	Seal—bearing oil	2H4500	AD10	1	1	12					
12	Housing for oil seal	1B1424	AD11	1	1						
13	Distance piece for bearing	1K756	AD12	1	1						
14	Retainer—bearing oil	AEC214	AD13	1	1						
15	Circlip for bearing	1K759	AD14	1	1						
16	Key for pulley	2K7056	AD16	1	1						
17	Nut for spindle	FNZ207	AD17	1	1	12					
18	Washer for nut (spring)	LWN207	AD18	1	1						
19	Washer for nut (plain)	PWN107	AD19	1	1						
20	Joint—pump to crankcase	AEC216	AD20	1	1	12					
21	Pulley	AEC292	AD15	1	1						

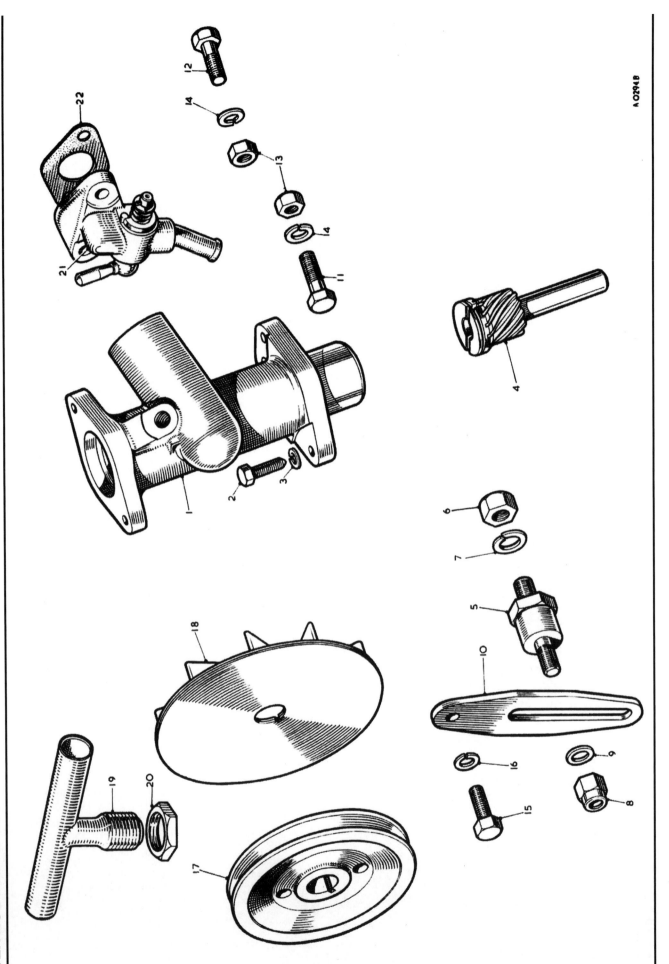

A0294B

46

SERVICE PARTS LIST

AUSTIN-HEALEY 100 SIX (SERIES BN6)

Item No.	DESCRIPTION	Commencing (E) 60949 Part Number	Illus. No.	Qty. per Vehicle RHD	Qty. per Vehicle LHD	Unit of Issue	Type of Vehicle	New Part Number	Change Point	Amdt. No.	REMARKS
	DISTRIBUTOR AND DYNAMO MOUNTINGS										
1	Housing for distributor and tachometer	**AEC685**	**AE1**	1	1						
2	Screw—housing to crankcase	HNS0407	AE2	3	3						
3	Washer for screw (spring)	LWN204	AE3	3	3						
4	**Gear—distributor driving**	**AEC242**	**AE4**	1	1						
5	Pillar—dynamo adjusting link	AEC298	AE5	1	1						
6	Nut—pillar to engine	FNN107	AE6	1	1						
7	Washer for nut (spring)	LWN207	AE7	1	1						
8	Nut—adjusting link to pillar	LNZ206	AE8	1	1						
9	Washer for nut (plain)	2K9932	AE9	1	1						
10	Link—dynamo adjusting	AEC288	AE10	1	1						
11	Bolt—dynamo to cylinder side cover (front)	HBN0510	AE11	1	1						
12	Bolt—dynamo to cylinder side cover (rear)	HBN0509	AE12	1	1						
13	Nut for bolt	FNN105	AE13	2	2						
14	Washer for bolt (spring)	LWN205	AE14	2	2						
15	Screw—dynamo to adjusting link	3H2092	AE15	1	1						
16	Washer for screw (spring)	2K5819	AE16	1	1						
17	Pulley for dynamo	AEC291	AE17	1	1						
18	Fan for dynamo	1B2178	AE18	1	1						
	CYLINDER LINER										
19	Liner for cylinder block	**AEC607**		6	6						For service purposes only
	BREATHER PIPE										
20	Pipe—breather	**AEC703**	**AE19**	1	1						
21	Locknut for breather pipe	1B2261	AE20	1	1						
	HEATER CONTROL TAP										
22	Tap—heater control	**2H4933**	**AE21**	1	1						
23	Tap—heater control	8H804	AE22	1	1						Alternatives
24	Washer for tap	1G2342	AE23	1	1	12					
25	Screw for tap	HNS0405	AE24	2	2						
26	Washer for screw (spring)	LWN204		2	2						

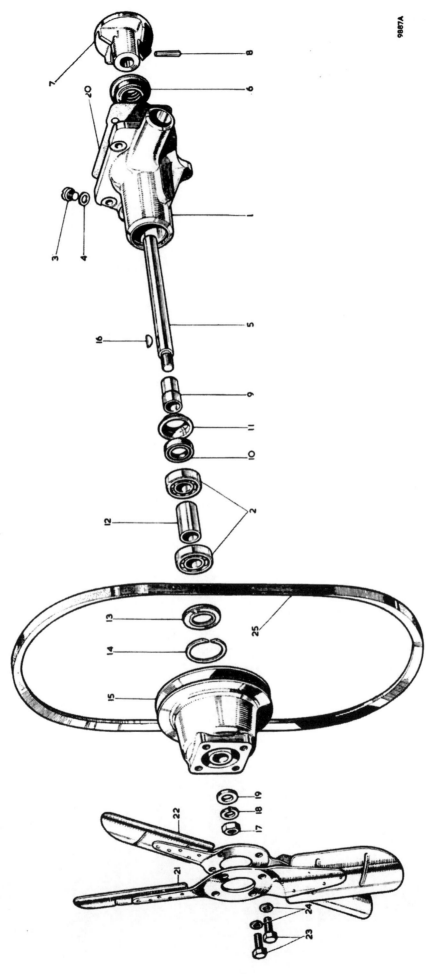

9867A

48

AUSTIN-HEALEY 100 SIX (SERIES BN6)

Item No.	DESCRIPTION	Part Number (Commencing (E) 60040)	Illus. No.	Qty. per Vehicle RHD	Qty. per Vehicle LHD	Unit of Issue	Type of Vehicle	New Part Number	Change Point	Amdt. No.	REMARKS
	FAN BLADE—BELT										
1	**Blade assembly—fan (front)**	**AEC1025**	**AD21**	1	1						
2	Blade assembly—fan (rear)	AEC1024	AD22	1	1						
3	Screw—blade to pulley	HNS0507	AD23	4	4						
4	Washer for screw (spring)	LWN205	AD24	4	4						
5	**Belt for fan—wedge type**	**AEC289**	**AD25**	1	1						
	OVERSIZE AND UNDERSIZE SERVICE COMPONENTS										
6	**Piston assembly (-010" O/S)**	**AEG111710**		6	6						
7	Piston assembly (-020" O/S)	AEC111720		6	6						
8	Piston assembly (-030" O/S)	AEC111730		6	6						
9	Piston assembly (-040" O/S)	AEC111740		6	6						
10	Ring—compression (-010" O/S)	AEC083310		6	6						
11	Ring—compression (-020" O/S)	AEC083320		6	6			AEC083410	Com. (E) 64800		
12	Ring—compression (-030" O/S)	AEC083330		6	6			AEC083420			
13	Ring—compression (-040" O/S)	AEC083340		6	6			AEC083430			
14	Ring—compression—taper (-010" O/S)	AEC083410		12	12			AEC083440			
15	Ring—compression—taper (-020" O/S)	AEC083420		12	12						
16	Ring—compression—taper (-030" O/S)	AEC083430		12	12						
17	Ring—compression—taper (-040" O/S)	AEC083440		12	12						
18	Ring—scraper (-010" O/S)	AEC083510		6	6						
19	Ring—scraper (-020" O/S)	AEC083520		6	6						
20	Ring—scraper (-030" O/S)	AEC083530		6	6						
21	Ring—scraper (-040" O/S)	AEC083540		6	6						
22	Pin—gudgeon (-002" O/S)	AEC083202		6	6						
23	Pin—gudgeon (-004" O/S)	AEC083204		6	6						
24	Pin—gudgeon (-006" O/S)	AEC083206		6	6						
25	**Bearing for connecting rod—big-end (-010" U/S)**	**AJC515910**		1	1	set					
26	Bearing for connecting rod—big-end (-020" U/S)	AJC515920		1	1	set					
27	Bearing for connecting rod—big-end (-030" U/S)	AJC515930		1	1	set					
28	Bearing for connecting rod—big-end (-040" U/S)	AJC515940		1	1	set					
29	**Bearing—main (-010" U/S)**	**8G212110**		1	1	set					
30	Bearing—main (-020" U/S)	8G212120		1	1	set					
31	Bearing—main (-030" U/S)	8G212130		1	1	set					
32	Bearing—main (-040" U/S)	8G212140		1	1	set					
33	**Washer—thrust—crankshaft upper (-0025" O/S)**	**AEC332**		A/R	A/R						
34	Washer—thrust—crankshaft upper (-005" O/S)	AEC744		A/R	A/R						
35	Washer—thrust—crankshaft upper (-0075" O/S)	AEC746		A/R	A/R						
36	Washer—thrust—crankshaft upper (-010" O/S)	AEC748		A/R	A/R						
37	Washer—thrust—crankshaft lower (-0025" O/S)	AEC333		A/R	A/R						
38	Washer—thrust—crankshaft lower (-005" O/S)	AEC745		A/R	A/R						
39	Washer—thrust—crankshaft lower (-0075" O/S)	AEC747		A/R	A/R						
40	Washer—thrust—crankshaft lower (-010" O/S)	AEC749		A/R	A/R						
41	Guide—inlet valve (-010" O/S)	AEC013510		6	6						
42	Guide—exhaust valve (-010" O/S)	AEC024510		6	6						

SERVICE PARTS LIST

Item No.	DESCRIPTION	Commencing (E) 60049 Part Number	Illus. No.	Qty. per Vehicle RHD	LHD	Unit of Issue	MODIFICATIONS Type of Vehicle	New Part Number	Change Point	Amdt. No.	REMARKS
	ENGINE SERVICE KITS										
1	**Joint washer kit for engine decarbonizing**	8G2228				set					
2	Gasket—cylinder head to block			1	1						
3	Joint—valve rocker cover to head			1	1						
4	Joint for exhaust pipe flange			2	2						
5	Grommet for valve stem			12	12						
6	Joint—inlet and exhaust manifold			1	1						Quantity reduced at (E) 66448
7	Joint—inlet manifold to exhaust manifold			4/2	4/2						
8	Joint—heat shield to carburetter			2	2						
9	**Joint washer kit for engine (supplementary)**	8G2229		1	1						Use together with decarbonizing joint washer kit for complete engine overhaul
10	Washer for drain tap			1	1						
11	Seal for front and rear main bearing cap			2	2						
12	Plug for front and rear main bearing cap			4	4						
13	Joint—front plate to block			1	1						
14	Joint—rear plate to block			1	1						
15	Joint—front cylinder cover to block			1	1						
16	Joint—centre cylinder cover to block			1	1						
17	Joint—rear cylinder cover to block			1	1						
18	Joint for timing cover			1	1						
19	Joint—chain tensioner to block			1	1						
20	Joint—sump to block			1	1						
21	Washer—oil sump drain plug			1	1						
22	Joint—oil pump to block			1	1						
23	Joint—pump filter flange to block			1	1						
24	Joint—filter to block			1	1						
25	Joint—water pump to block			1	1						
26	Joint—water outlet elbow			1	1						
27	Joint—fuel pump to block			1	1						
28	Joint—heater control tap			1	1						
29	Joint—thermostat			1	1						

A.12

SERVICE PARTS LIST

AUSTIN-HEALEY 100 SIX (SERIES BN6)

Item No.	DESCRIPTION	Commencing (E) 60949 Part Number	Illus. No.	Qty. per Vehicle RHD	Qty. per Vehicle LHD	Unit of Issue	Type of Vehicle	New Part Number	Change Point	Amdt. No.	REMARKS
	Engine Service Kits—*continued*										
	Chain tensioner servicing kit	**17H341**									
1	Spring			1	1						
2	Bottom plug			1	1						
3	Tab washer			1	1						
4	Cylinder			1	1						
5				1	1						
	Water pump repair kit	**8G8021**									
6	Retainer—bearing—oil			1	1						
7	Circlip for bearing			1	1						
8	Seal—bearing oil			1	1						
9	Seal			1	1						
10	Washer for plug			1	1						
11	Joint—pump to crankcase			1	1						
12											

A0952

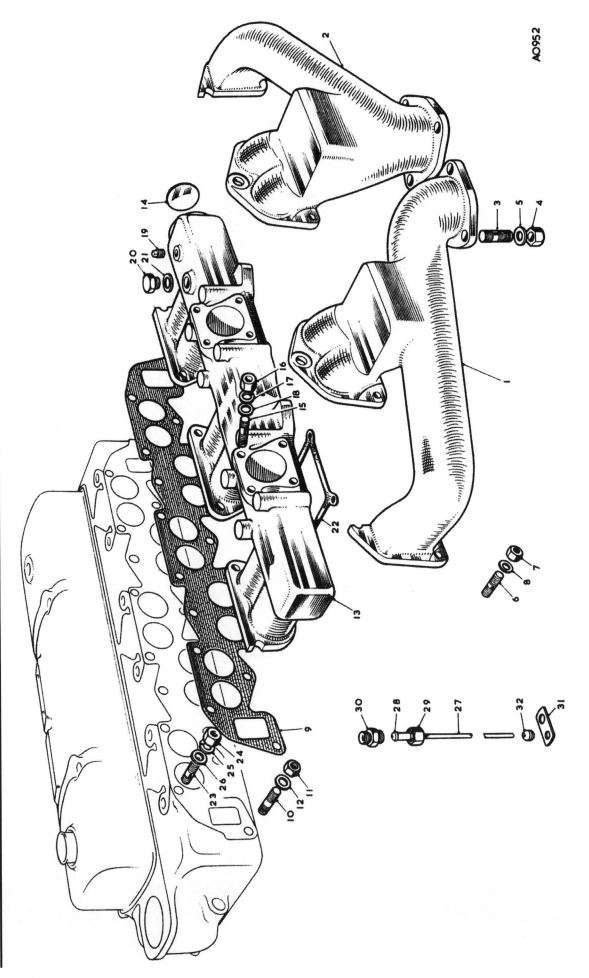

INLET AND EXHAUST MANIFOLD

Item No.	Description	Commencing (E) 60649 Part Number	Illus. No.	Qty RHD	Qty LHD	Unit of Issue	Type of Vehicle	New Part Number	Change Point	Amdt. No.	REMARKS
1	**Manifold—exhaust (front)**	**AEC1294**	**AF1**	1	1						
2	**Manifold—exhaust (rear)**	**AEC1295**	**AF2**	1	1						
3	Stud for outlet flange	58K507	AF3	6	6						
4	Nut for stud	BNN105	AF4	6	6						
5	Washer for stud (plain)	PWZ105	AF5	6	6						
6	Stud for heat shield	AEC403	AF6	2	2						
7	Nut for stud	BNN104	AF7	2	2						
8	Washer for stud (plain)	PWN104	AF8	2	2						
9	**Joint—inlet and exhaust manifold to cylinder head**	**AEC731**	**AF9**	1	1						
10	Stud for exhaust manifold	58K564	AF10	10	10						
11	Nut for stud	AEC850	AF11	10	10						
12	Washer for stud (plain)	PWN106	AF12	10	10						
13	Clip—retainer—thermo capillary pipe			2	2	12		AHB5397	Com. (E) 66673		
14	**Manifold—inlet**	**AEC1293**	**AF13**	1	1						
15	Plug for inlet manifold (welch)	AEC871	AF14	1	1						
16	Stud—carburetter to manifold	CLS2516	AF15	8	8						
17	Nut for stud	FNZ105	AF16	8	8						
18	Washer for nut (spring)	LWZ205	AF17	8	8	24					
19	Washer for nut (plain)	PWZ105	AF18	8	8						
20	Plug for vacuum take-off	AEC479	AF19	1	1						
21	Plug for servo boss	ADP610	AF20	1	1						
22	Washer for plug	6K433	AF21	1	1						
23	**Joint—inlet to exhaust manifold**	**AEC730**	**AF22**	4	4						
24	**Joint—inlet to exhaust manifold**			2	2			AEC874	Fin. (E) 66442 Com. (E) 66443		
25	Stud—inlet manifold to cylinder head (short)	51K562	AF23	7/5	7/5						Quantity reduced at (E) 66673
26	Stud—inlet manifold to cylinder head (long)			2	2			58K563	Com. (E) 66673		
27	Nut for stud	FNZ106	AF24	7	7						
28	Washer for stud (spring)	LWZ206	AF25	7	7						
29	Washer for stud (plain)	PWZ106	AF26	7	7						
30	**Pipe—petrol drain**	**AEC449**	**AF27**	2	2						
31	Nipple for pipe	2K6192	AF28	2	2						
32	Nut for pipe	2K6193	AF29	2	2						
33	Union for drain pipe	AEC450	AF30	2	2						
34	Clip for pipe	1A2104	AF31	2	2						
35	Ferrule for clip	2H4985	AF32	2	2						

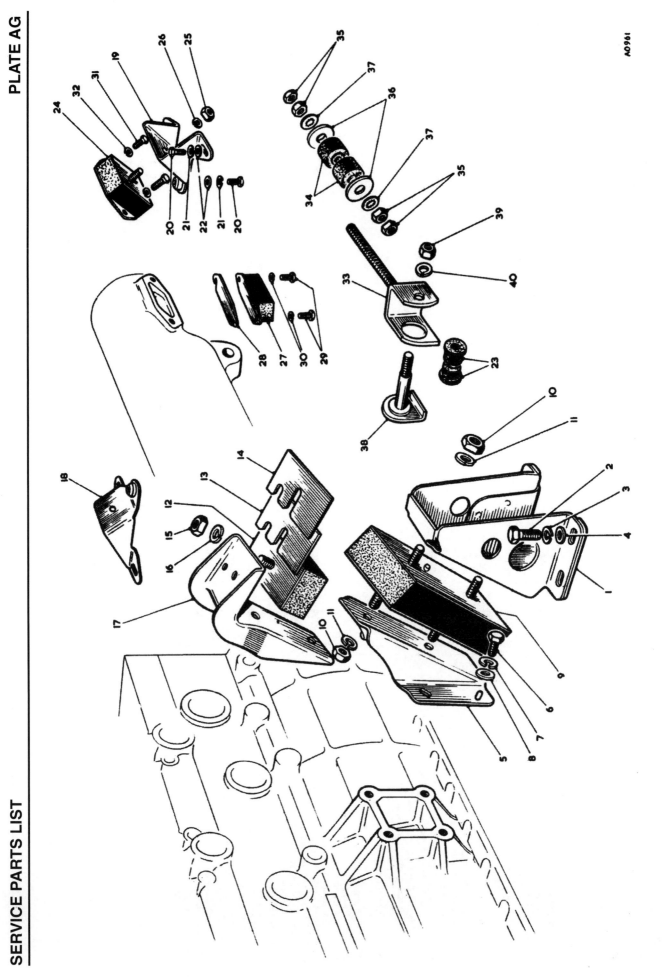

A0961

AUSTIN-HEALEY 100 SIX (SERIES BN6)

Item No.	DESCRIPTION	Part Number Commencing (E) 60949	Illus. No.	Qty. per Vehicle RHD	Qty. per Vehicle LHD	Unit of Issue	Type of Vehicle	New Part Number	Change Point	Amdt. No.	REMARKS
	ENGINE MOUNTINGS										
1	**Bracket—engine mounting (front)**	**11B5188**	**AG1**	2	2						
2	Screw—bracket to side-member	HZS0607	AG2	8	8						
3	Washer for screw (spring)	LWZ306	AG3	8	8						
4	Washer for screw (plain)	PWZ106	AG4	8	8						
5	**Bracket—mounting—rubber to crankcase**	**1B4421**	**AG5**	2	2						
6	Set screw—bracket to crankcase	HZS0606	AG6	8	8						
7	Washer for set screw (spring)	LWZ206	AG7	8	8						
8	Washer for set screw (plain)	PWZ106	AG8	8	8						
9	**Rubber—engine mounting (front)**	**1B4423**	**AG9**	2	2						
10	Nut—mounting to brackets	FNZ107	AG10	8	8						
11	Washer for nut (spring)	LWZ207	AG11	8	8						
12	**Rubber—rebound—engine mounting (front)**	**1B4428**	**AG12**	2	2						
13	Packing piece for rebound rubber	1B1814	AG13	A/R	A/R						
14	Packing piece for rebound rubber	1B1815	AG14	A/R	A/R						
15	Nut—rebound rubber to bracket	FNZ105	AG15	2	2						
16	Washer for nut (spring)	LWZ205	AG16	2	2	24.					
17	**Bracket—rebound rubber**	**1B4422**	**AG17**	2	2						
18	**Bracket—engine mounting—R/H (rear)**	**11B5113**	**AG18**	1	1						
19	**Bracket—engine mounting—L/H (rear)**	**11B5115**	**AG19**	1	1						
20	Set screw—bracket to frame	HZS0505	AG20	6	6						
21	Washer for set screw (spring)	LWZ205	AG21	6	6	24.					
22	Washer for set screw (plain)	PWZ105	AG22	6	6						
23	Bush—gearbox rear cover (rubber)	1B8847	AG23	2	2						
24	**Rubber—engine mounting (rear)**	**11B5074**	**AG24**	2	2						
25	Nut for mounting bolt	FNZ105	AG25	2	2						
26	Washer for nut (spring)	LWZ205	AG26	2	2	24.					
27	**Rubber—rebound—engine mounting (rear)**	**1A9209**	**AG27**	1	1						
28	Shim for rebound rubber	1A9211	AG28	A/R	A/R						
29	Set screw—rebound rubber to gearbox rear cover	HZS0405	AG29	2	2						
30	Washer for set screw (spring)	LWZ304	AG30	4	4						
31	Set screw—mounting to gearbox rear cover	HZS0506	AG31	4	4						
32	Washer for set screw (spring)	LWZ205	AG32	4	4	24.					
33	**Tie-rod—engine**	**1G9382**	**AG33**	1	1						
34	Bush for tie-rod (rubber)	1B8882	AG34	2	2	12.					
35	Nut for tie-rod	FNZ206	AG35	4	4						
36	Washer for nut	1B8811	AG36	2	2						
37	Washer for nut (shakeproof)	2K7131	AG37	2	2						
38	Hinge pin—tie-rod to gearbox extension	1G9384	AG38	1	1						
39	Nut for hinge pin	FNZ106	AG39	1	1						
40	Washer for nut (spring)	LWZ306	AG40	1	1						

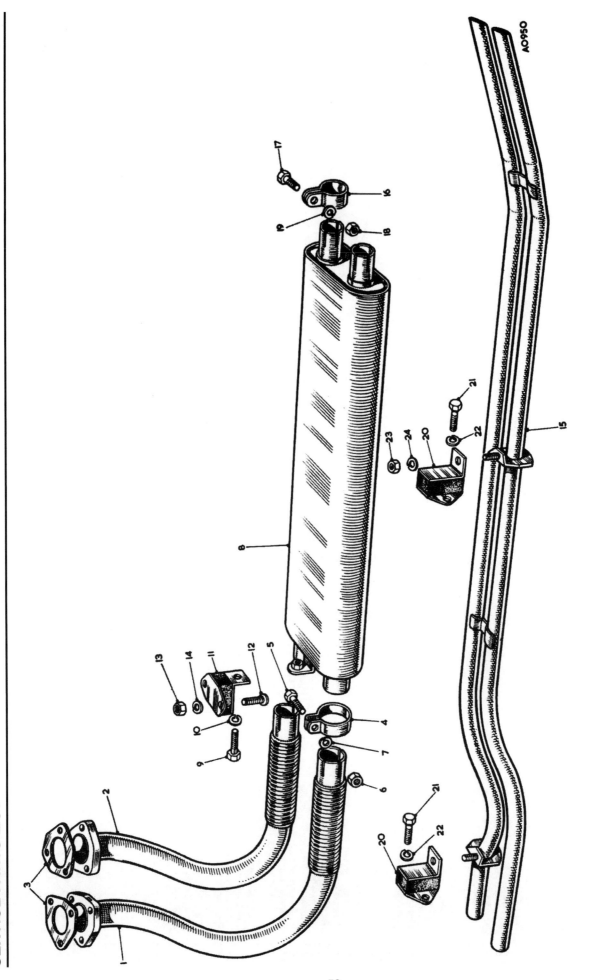

AO950

SERVICE PARTS LIST

Item No.	DESCRIPTION	Part Number Commencing (C) 501	Illus. No.	Qty. per Vehicle RHD	LHD	Unit of Issue	Type of Vehicle	New Part Number	Change Point	Amdt. No.	REMARKS
	EXHAUST SYSTEM										
1	**Pipe assembly—front**	**11B2120**	**AH1**	1	1						
2	**Pipe assembly—rear**	**11B2122**	**AH2**	1	1						
3	Gasket—pipe to manifold	ACC5187	AH3	2	2	12					
4	Clip—pipe to silencer	1K618	AH4	2	2						
5	Bolt for clip	HZS0507	AH5	2	2						
6	Nut for bolt	FNZ105	AH6	2	2						
7	Washer for nut (spring)	LWZ205	AH7	2	2	24					
8	**Silencer assembly**	**11B2356**	**AH8**	1	1						
9	Bolt—silencer to mounting assembly	HZS0506	AH9	1	1						
10	Washer for bolt (spring)	LWZ205	AH10	1	1	24					
11	**Mounting for silencer—front**	**3H3076**	**AH11**	1	1						
12	Screw—mounting to frame	PMZ0510	AH12	2	2						
13	Nut for screw	FNZ105	AH13	2	2						
14	Washer for nut (spring)	LWZ205	AH14	2	2	24					
15	**Pipe assembly—tail**	**11B2357**	**AH15**	1	1						
16	Clip—pipe to silencer	1K711	AH16	2	2						
17	Bolt for clip	HZS0607	AH17	2	2						
18	Nut for bolt	FNZ106	AH18	2	2						
19	Washer for nut (spring)	LWZ306	AH19	2	2						
20	**Mounting for silencer and tail pipe—rear**	**3H3076**	**AH20**	2	2						
21	Bolt—mounting to frame	HZS0506	AH21	4	4						
22	Washer for bolt (spring)	LWZ205	AH22	4	4	24					
23	Nut—tail pipe to frame	FNZ105	AH23	2	2						
24	Washer for nut (spring)	LWZ205	AH24	2	2	24					

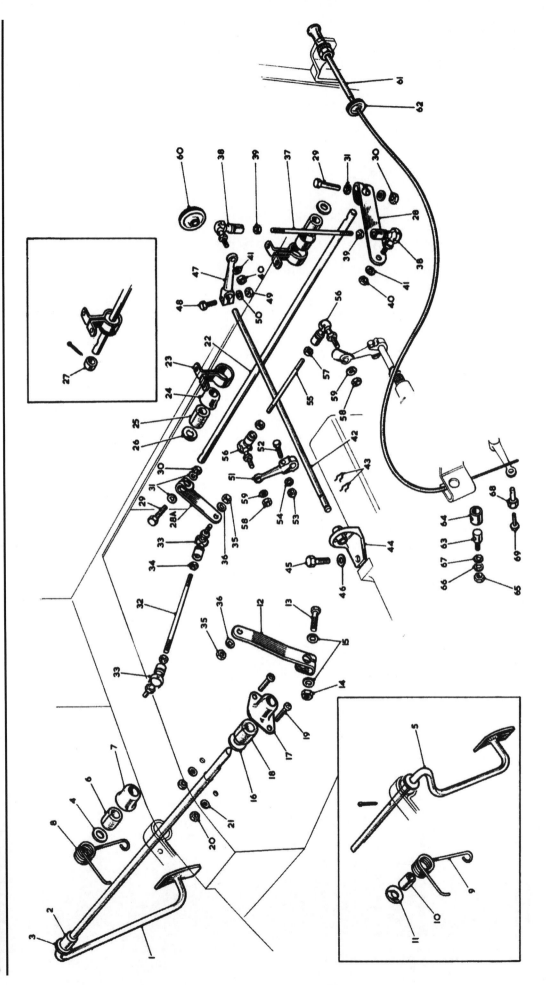

SERVICE PARTS LIST

AUSTIN-HEALEY 100 SIX (SERIES BN6)

Item No.	DESCRIPTION	Commencing (C) 501 Part Number	Illus. No.	Qty. per Vehicle RHD	Qty. per Vehicle LHD	Unit of Issue	Type of Vehicle	MODIFICATIONS New Part Number	MODIFICATIONS Change Point	MODIFICATIONS Amdt. No.	REMARKS
	ENGINE CONTROLS										
1	**Pedal—accelerator**	**11B2151**	**A11**	1							
2	Collar for pedal rod	11B2207	A12	1							
3	Washer for collar	6K467	A13	1							
4	Washer for pedal rod	PWN106	A14	1							
5	**Pedal—accelerator**	**11B2143**	**A15**		1						
6	Washer for pedal rod	PWN106			1						
7	Bush—accelerator shaft (felt)	1A1832	A16	1	1	12					
8	Cup for felt—accelerator shaft	1H55	A17	1	1						
9	Spring—accelerator pedal	1G2697	A18	1	1						
10	Spring—pedal return	11B2146	A19		1						
11	Collar—return spring location	1F1293	A110		1						
12	Washer—return spring location	6K467	A111		1						
13	**Lever—pedal shaft**	**11B2145**	**A112**	1	1						
14	Bolt—lever to pedal shaft	HZS0409	A113	1	1						
15	Nut for bolt	FNZ104	A114	1	1						
16	Washer for nut (plain)	PWZ104	A115	2	2	12					
17	Washer—accelerator shaft (plain)	PWN106	A116	1	1						
18	Cup for felt—accelerator shaft	2F115	A117	1	1						
19	Bush accelerator shaft (felt)	1A1832	A118	1	1	12					
20	Screw—felt cup to pedal box	PMZ0306	A119	2	2						
21	Nut for screw	FNZ103	A120	2	2						
22	Washer for nut (spring)	LWZ2308	A121	2	2						
23	**Shaft—accelerator relay**	**11B2155**	**A122**	1	1						
24	Bracket—mounting	11B2159	A123	2	2						
25	Cup for felt—accelerator relay shaft	1H55	A124	2	2						
26	Bush—accelerator relay shaft (felt)	1A1832	A125	2	2	12					
27	Washer—accelerator relay shaft (plain)	PWZ106	A126	2	2						
28	Collar—accelerator relay shaft	1A1829	A127	2	2						
29	Lever—accelerator relay shaft (short)	11B2156	A128A	1	1						
30	**Lever—accelerator relay shaft (long)**	**11B2157**	**A128**	1	1						
31	Bolt—lever to relay shaft	HZS0409	A129	2	2						
32	Nut for bolt	FNZ104	A130	2	2						
33	Washer for nut (plain)	PWZ104	A131	4	4	12					
34	**Rod—control—pedal to relay shaft**	**AHB5367**	**A132**	1	1						
35	Ball joint	ACB5311	A133	2	2						
36	Locknut for ball joint to control rod	FNZ103	A134	2	2						
37	Nut for ball joint at lever	FNZ103	A135	2	2						
38	Washer for nut (spring)	LWZ2208	A136	2	2						

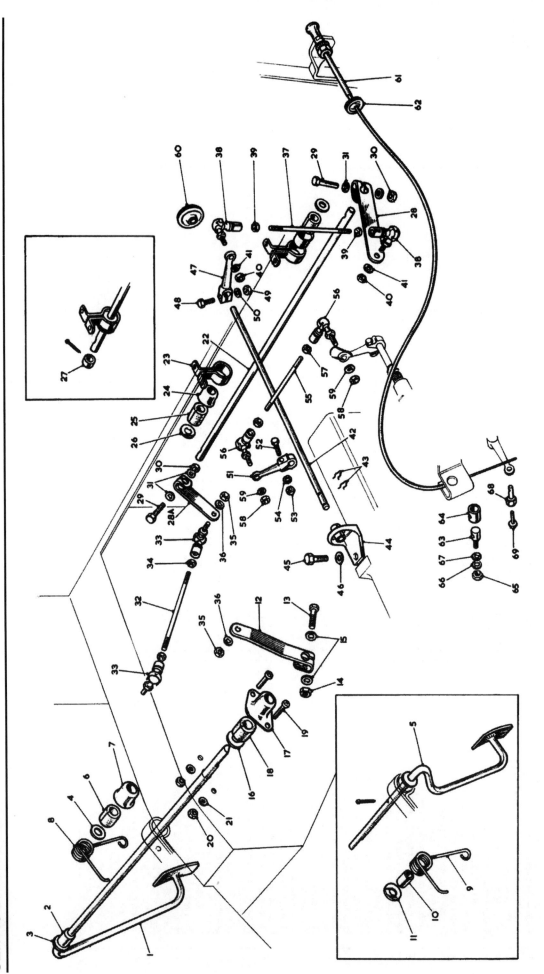

Item No.	DESCRIPTION	Commencing (C) 501 Part Number	Illus. No.	Qty. per Vehicle RHD	Qty. per Vehicle LHD	Unit of Issue	Type of Vehicle	New Part Number	Change Point	Amdt. No.	REMARKS
	Engine Controls—*continued*										
	Rod—control—relay shaft to throttle shaft										
1		**AHB5370**	**AI37**	1	1						
2	Ball joint	ACB5811	AI38	2	2						
3	Locknut—ball joint to control rod	FNZ103	AI39	2	2						
4	Nut for ball joint at lever	FNZ103	AI40	2	2						
5	Washer for nut (spring)	LWZ203	AI41	2	2						
	Shaft—throttle relay										
6		**11B2349**	**AI42**	1	1						
7	Circlip—throttle relay shaft	11B2350	AI43	2	2						
8	Bracket—relay shaft bearing	11B2348	AI44	1	1						
9	Screw—bearing bracket to induction manifold	ZCS0505	AI45	1	1						
10	Washer for screw (spring)	LWZ205	AI46	1	1						
	Lever—throttle relay shaft										
11		**AUC3481**	**AI47**	1	1						
12	Screw—lever to throttle relay shaft	53K128	AI48	1	1						
13	Nut for screw	FNZ103	AI49	1	1						
14	Washer for nut (spring)	LWZ303	AI50	1	1						
	Lever—throttle relay shaft grooved end										
15		**AUC1196**	**AI51**	1	1						
16	Screw—lever to throttle relay shaft	53K128	AI52	1	1						
17	Nut for screw	FNZ103	AI53	1	1						
18	Washer for nut (spring)	LWZ303	AI54	1	1						
	Rod—control—throttle relay shaft to carburetter										
19		**AHB5372**	**AI55**	1	1						
20	Ball joint	ACB5811	AI56	2	2						
21	Locknut—ball joint to control rod	FNZ103	AI57	2	2						
22	Nut for ball joint to lever	FNZ103	AI58	2	2						
23	Washer for nut (spring)	LWZ303	AI59	2	2						
24	Bearing—throttle relay shaft in dash	1G2175	AI60	1	1						
	Control—air strangler										
25		**11B2352**	**AI61**	1	1						
26	Grommet—air strangler control	RFN403	AI62	1	1						
27	Trunnion for choke cable (inner)	11B2365	AI63	1	1						
28	Trunnion for choke cable (outer)	11B2366	AI64	1	1						
29	Nut for trunnion (inner)	FNZ103	AI65	1	1						
30	Washer for nut (spring)	LWZ303	AI66	1	1						
31	Washer for nut (plain)	PWZ203	AI67	1	1						
32	Trunnion—choke lever and connecting wire	1B2697	AI68	1	1						
33	Bolt for trunnion	53K1023	AI69	1	1						

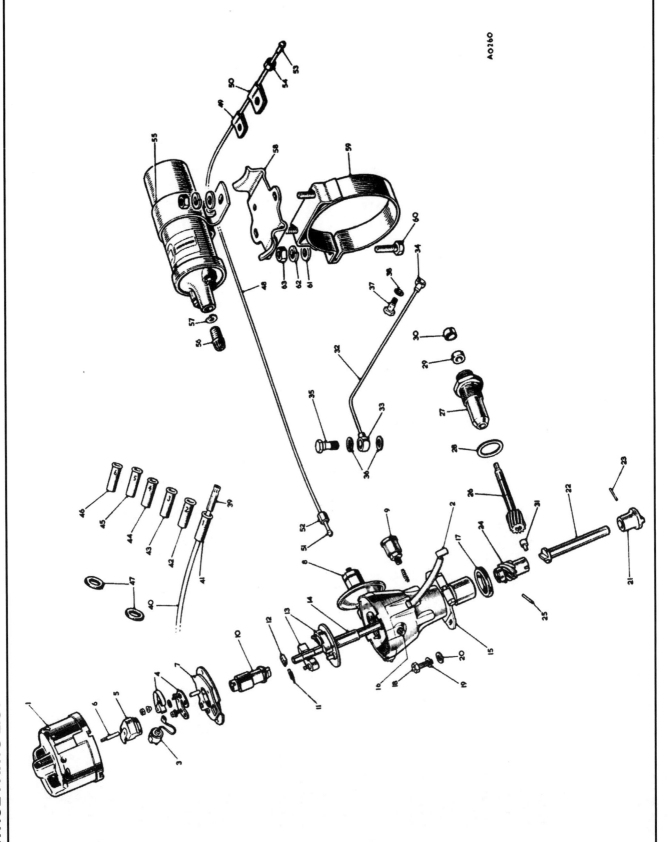

A0260

SERVICE PARTS LIST

IGNITION EQUIPMENT

DISTRIBUTOR

Item No.	Description	Commencing (E) 60940 Part Number	Illus. No.	Qty. RHD	Qty. LHD	Unit of Issue	Type of Vehicle	New Part Number	Change Point	Amdt. No.	REMARKS
	Distributor	**AEC925**		1	1						
1	Cover	17H5158	B1	1	1						
2	Clip—cover retaining	87H5445	B2	2	2						
3	Condenser	47H5250	B3	1	1						
4	Contact set	17H5248	B4	1	1						
5	Arm—rotor	17H5110	B5	1	1						
6	Carbon and spring	17H5065	B6	1	1						
7	Plate—fixing	3H2138	B7	1	1						
8	Vacuum unit	17H5884	B8	1	1						
9	Lubricator	AJC5095	B9	1	1						
10	Cam assembly	17H5113	B10	1	1						
11	Spring—auto advance	27H5816	B11			set					
12	Toggle—spring	17H5069	B12	2	2						
13	Weight	17H5095	B13	2	2						
14	Shaft and action plate	17H5166	B14	1	1						
15	Base plate	17H5487	B15	1	1						
16	Pin—terminal—L.T.	17H5898	B16	1	1						
17	Sundry parts	17H5117	B17			set					
18	Seal—oil	AEC681	B18	1	1						
19	Screw—distributor to housing	HNS0404	B19	2	2						
20	Washer for screw (spring)	LWZ204	B20	2	2						
21	Washer for screw (plain)	PWZ104		2	2	12.					

DISTRIBUTOR AND TACHOMETER DRIVE

Item No.	Description	Commencing (E) 60940 Part Number	Illus. No.	Qty. RHD	Qty. LHD	Unit of Issue	Type of Vehicle	New Part Number	Change Point	Amdt. No.	REMARKS
23	**Dog—driving**	**AEC6678**	**B21**	1	1						
24	**Extension—driving spindle**	**AEC686**	**B22**	1	1						
25	Peg for spindle	2K2163	B23	1	1						
26	**Gear—tachometer driving**	**AEC679**	**B24**	1	1						
27	Peg for gear	2K2163	B25	1	1						
28	**Pinion—tachometer**	**AEC680**	**B26**	1	1						
29	Bush for pinion	AEC701	B27	1	1						
30	Joint—bush to housing	2K4970	B28	1	1						
31	Seal—pinion oil	3H964	B29	1	1	12.					
32	Ring—oil seal retaining	1G3410	B30	1	1						
33	Button—tachometer pinion thrust	1A8078	B31	1	1						
34	**Pipe—tachometer drive oil feed**	**AEC687**	**B32**	1	1						
35	Union—banjo—tachometer end	1K21	B33	1	1						
36	Union—banjo—crankcase end	11B174	B34	1	1						
37	Bolt for tachometer end banjo union	AEC706	B35	1	1						
38	Washer for bolt	6K56	B36	2	2	72.					
39	Bolt for crankcase end banjo union	AEC682	B37	1	1						
40	Washer for bolt	11B206	B38	2	2						

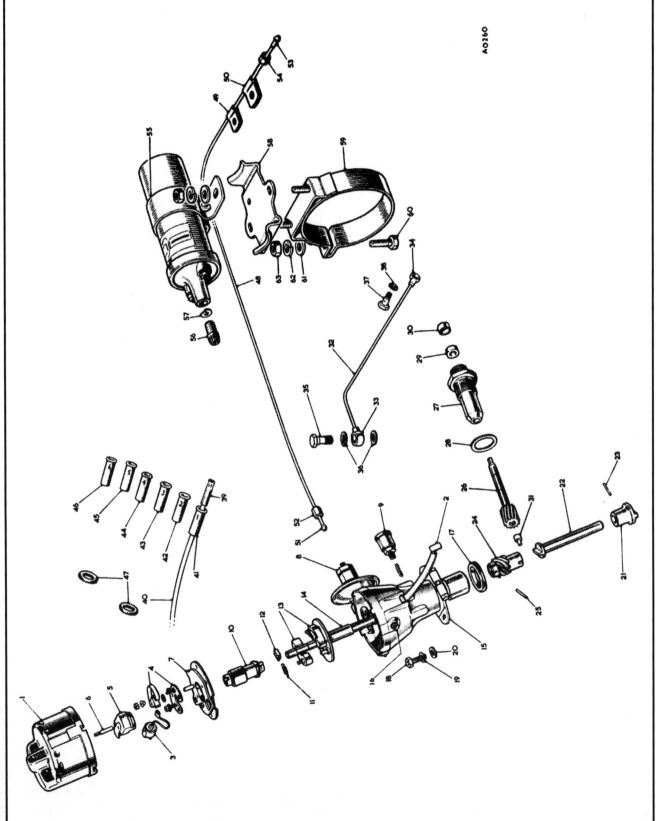

A0260

SERVICE PARTS LIST

AUSTIN-HEALEY 100 SIX (SERIES BN6)

Item No.	DESCRIPTION	Part Number Commencing (E) 60940	Illus. No.	Qty. per Vehicle RHD	Qty. per Vehicle LHD	Unit of Issue	Type of Vehicle	New Part Number	Change Point	Amdt. No.	REMARKS
	H.T. CABLES, ETC.										
1	**Terminal—sparking plug**	**8G616**	**B39**	**6**	**6**						
2	Cable—No. 1 H.T. (13″ long)	45223	B40	A/R	A/R	100'					
3	Cable—No. 2 H.T. (11″ long)	45223		A/R	A/R						
4	Cable—No. 3 H.T. (10″ long)	45223		A/R	A/R						
5	Cable—No. 4 H.T. (9″ long)	45223		A/R	A/R						
6	Cable—No. 5 H.T. (10″ long)	45223		A/R	A/R						
7	Cable—No. 6 H.T. (15″ long)	45223		A/R	A/R						
8	Ferrule for H.T. cable No. 1 (rubber)	3H1655	B41	1	1						
9	Ferrule for H.T. cable No. 2 (rubber)	3H1656	B42	1	1						
10	Ferrule for H.T. cable No. 3 (rubber)	3H1657	B43	1	1						
11	Ferrule for H.T. cable No. 4 (rubber)	3H1658	B44	1	1						
12	Ferrule for H.T. cable No. 5 (rubber)	3H1659	B45	1	1						
13	Ferrule for H.T. cable No. 6 (rubber)	3H1660	B46	1	1						
14	Ring for H.T. cable (rubber)	1G2073	B47	2	2						
	VACUUM CONTROL										
15	**Pipe—ignition control**	**AEC416**	**B48**	**1**	**1**						
16	Clip—small	2H8271	B49	1	1						
17	Clip—large	1K204	B50	1	1						
18	Olive	6K649	B51	1	1						
19	Nut—distributor end	6K650	B52	1	1	12					
20	Nipple	2K6192	B53	1	1						
21	Nut—carburetter end	2K6193	B54	1	1						
	IGNITION COIL										
22	**Coil—ignition**	**1D1963**	**B55**	**1**	**1**						
23	Nut—H.T. terminal	3H2695	B56	1	1						
24	Washer—H.T. terminal	3H2696	B57	1	1						
25	Plate—coil steady	2A537	B58	1	1						
26	Bracket—coil to dynamo	AEC496	B59	1	1						
27	Bolt for bracket—clamping	HZS0408	B60	1	1						
28	Washer for clamp and bracket bolt (plain)	PWN204	B61	3	3						
29	Washer for clamp and bracket bolt (spring)	LWN204	B62	3	3						
30	Nut for bolt	FNZ104	B63	3	3						

PLATE C

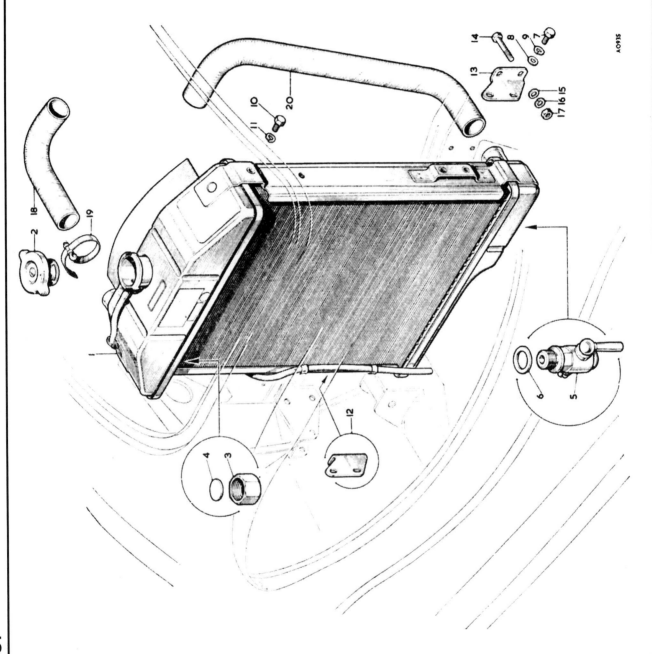

Item No.	DESCRIPTION	Part Number	Illus. No.	RHD	LHD	Unit of Issue	Type of Vehicle	New Part Number	Change Point	Amdt. No.	REMARKS
	COOLING SYSTEM										
	RADIATOR										
1	Core—radiator	11B2301	C1	1	1						After (C) 2030 supply also 1 off AHB5401 and 1 off AHB5402
2	Cap—filler	ARH1089	C2	1	1						
3	Plug for radiator tank		C3	1	1			AHB5401	Com. (C) 2080		
4	Washer for plug		C4	1	1			AHB5402			
5	Tap—drain	2H10	C5	1	1						
6	Washer for drain tap (·0625" thick)	2K4954	C6	1	1	36					Optional thickness to determine position
7	Washer for drain tap (·09375" thick)	2K4975		1	1						
8	Screw—radiator to support bracket	HZS0505	C7	4	4						
9	Washer for screw (plain)	PWZ105	C8	4	4						
10	Washer for screw (spring)	LWZ205	C9	4	4	24					
11	Screw—radiator to top fixing bracket	HZS0505	C10	2	2						
12	Washer for screw (spring)	LWZ205	C11	2	2	24					
13	Bracket—radiator support—R/H	11B2118	C12	1	1						
14	Bracket—radiator support—L/H	11B2119	C13	1	1						
15	Bolt—bracket to front suspension support	HBZ0516	C14	4	4						
16	Washer for bolt (plain)	PWZ105	C15	4	4						
17	Washer for bolt (spring)	LWZ205	C16	4	4	24					
18	Nut for bolt	FNZ105	C17	4	4						
19	Hose for radiator (top)	11B2115	C18	1	1						
20	Clip for hose	8G511	C19	2	2						
21	Hose—radiator to water pump	11B2216	C20	1	1						
22	Clip for hose	8G511		2	2						

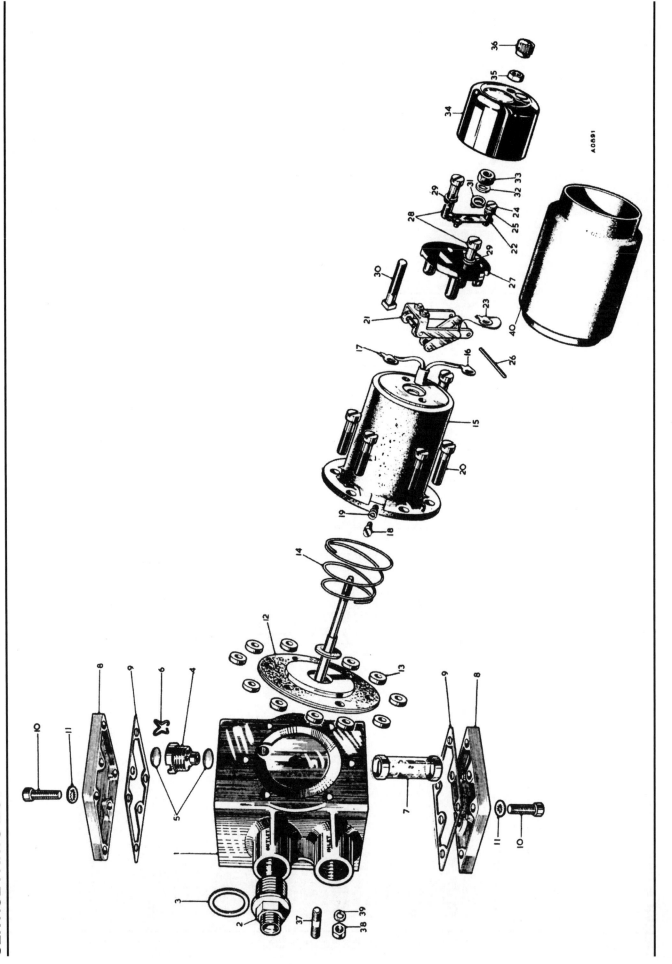

A0691

SERVICE PARTS LIST

AUSTIN-HEALEY 100 SIX (SERIES BN6)

Item No.	DESCRIPTION	Commencing (C) 501 Part Number	Illus. No.	Qty. per Vehicle RHD	Qty. per Vehicle LHD	Unit of Issue	Type of Vehicle	New Part Number	Change Point	Amdt. No.	REMARKS
	FUEL SYSTEM										
	FUEL PUMP										
	Pump assembly	**AUA72**									
1	Body	AUA4644	D1	1	1						
2	Union—inlet and outlet	AUC2140	D2	2	2						
3	Washer—union to body	AUC2141	D3	2	2						
4	Cage—valve	AUA4607	D4	1	1						
5	Disc—valve	AUA4611	D5	2	2						
6	Clip—valve cage	AUA4609	D6	1	1						
7	Filter	AUA4647	D7	1	1						
8	Lid—top and bottom	AUA4645	D8	2	2						
9	Washer for lid	AUA4646	D9	2	2						
10	Screw for lid	AUA4083	D10	12	12						
11	Washer for screw	AUA4643	D11	12	12						
12	**Diaphragm assembly**	**AUA6012**	D12	1	1						
13	Roller	AUA1483	D13	11	11						
14	Spring	AUA1785	D14	1	1						
15	**Coil housing**	**AUA6003**	D15	1	1						
16	Tag—5 B.A.—terminal	AUA1455	D16	1	1						
17	Tag—2 B.A.—terminal	AUA1456	D17	1	1						
18	Screw—earth	AUA4850	D18	1	1						
19	Washer for earth screw (spring)	AUA1863	D19	1	1						
20	Screw—housing to body	AUA1453	D20	6	6						
21	**Rocker and blade**	**AUA6021**	**D21**	1	1						
22	Blade	AUA6086	D22	1	1						
23	Tag—2 B.A.—terminal	AUA1456	D23	1	1						
24	Screw for blade	AUA847	D24	1	1						
25	Washer for screw (spring)	AUA868	D25	1	1						
26	Spindle for contact breaker	AUA1435	D26	1	1						
27	**Pedestal**	**AUA6034**	**D27**	1	1						
28	Screw—pedestal to housing	AUA1459	D28	2	2						
29	Washer for screw (spring)	AUA1863	D29	2	2						
30	Screw for terminal	AUA1468	D30	1	1						
31	Washer for screw (spring)	AUA1863	D31	1	1						
32	Washer for screw (lead)	AUA1662	D32	1	1						
33	Nut for screw	AUA1661	D33	1	1						
34	Cover—end	AUA1466	D34	1	1						
35	Nut for cover	AUA878	D35	1	1						
36	Knob—terminal	AUA869	D36	1	1						
37	Stud—pump to body	AUA1500	D37	2	2						
38	Nut for stud	FNZ105	D38	2	2						
39	Washer for nut (spring)	LWZ305	D39	2	2						
40	Cover for pump	ACG5147	D40	1	1						
41											

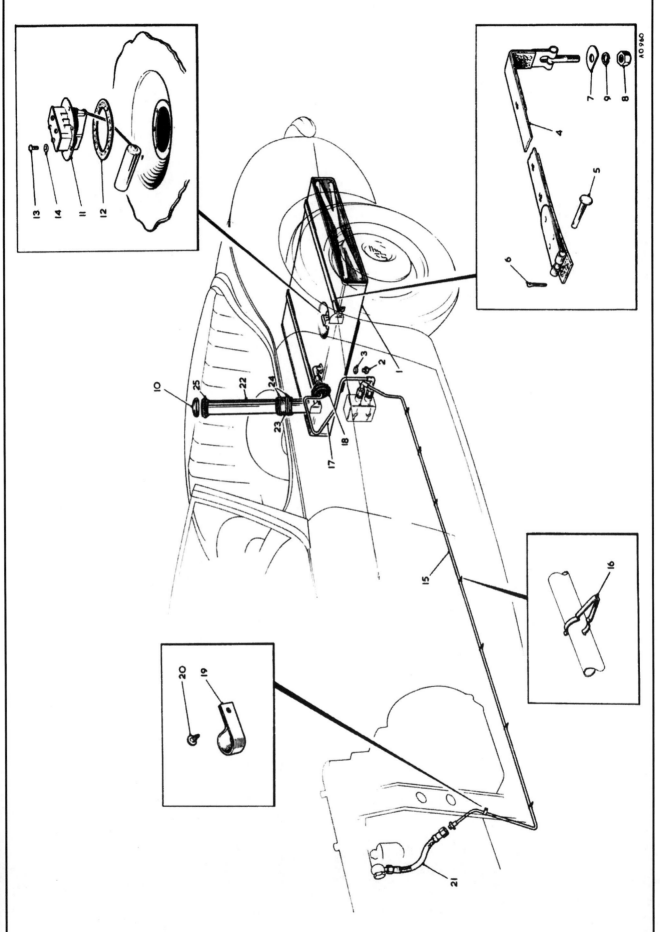

AO 960

SERVICE PARTS LIST

AUSTIN-HEALEY 100 SIX (SERIES BN6)

Item No.	DESCRIPTION	Commencing (C) 501 Part Number	Illus. No.	Qty. per Vehicle RHD	Qty. per Vehicle LHD	Unit of Issue	Type of Vehicle	New Part Number	Change Point	Amdt. No.	REMARKS
	FUEL TANK										
1	**Tank—fuel**	**11B2375**	**DA1**	1	1						
2	Plug—drain	2A880	DA2	1	1						
3	Washer for plug	6K688	DA3	1	1						
4	Strap—tank to body	11B2187	DA4	2	2	12					
5	Joint pin for strap	53K3061	DA5	2	2						
6	Split pin for joint pin	CPS0806	DA6	2	2						
7	'D' washer for 'T' bolt	14B2036	DA7	2	2						
8	Nut for 'T' bolt	FNZ205	DA8	4	4						
9	Washer for nut (spring)	LWZ205	DA9	2	2	24					
10	Tube—filler	AHB8815	DA22	1	1						
11	Connection—filler tube	11B2011	DA23	1	1						
12	Clip for tube	8G505	DA24	2	2						
13	Collar—tube to body	11G2100	DA25	1	1						
14	Cap—filler	8G654	DA10	1	1						
15	Cap—filler (complete with lock)	2A504		1	1						Optional extra
16	**Tank unit for petrol gauge**	**1B2736**	**DA11**	1	1						
17	Washer for tank unit	2H1082	DA12	1	1						
18	Screw fixing unit to tank	53K165	DA13	6	6						
19	Washer for screw (copper)	2A2088	DA14	6	6						
	FUEL PIPES										
20	**Pipe—pump to flexible pipe**	**11B2380**	**DA15**	1	1						
21	Clip—pipe to side-member	2K8910	DA16	7	7						
22	**Pipe—tank to pump**	**AHB5866**	**DA17**	1	1						
23	Grommet for pipe (rubber)	8D5768	DA18	1	1						
24	Clip—pipe to bonnet support	PCR0507	DA19	1	1						
25	Screw for clip	PTZ1004	DA20	1	1						
26	**Pipe—flexible**	**AHB5366**	**DA21**	1	1						

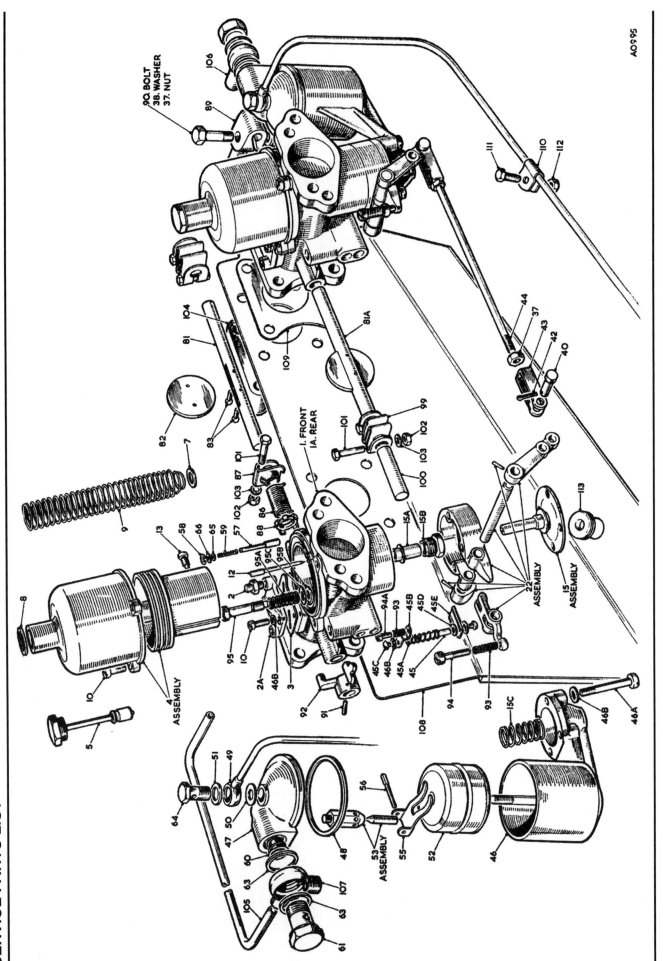

90. BOLT
38. WASHER
37. NUT

I. FRONT
IA. REAR

AO965

SERVICE PARTS LIST

AUSTIN-HEALEY 100 SIX (SERIES BN6)

Item No.	DESCRIPTION	Part Number (Commencing (E) 60949)	Illus. No.	Qty. per Vehicle RHD	Qty. per Vehicle LHD	Unit of Issue	Type of Vehicle	New Part Number	Change Point	Amdt. No.	REMARKS
	CARBURETTER										
1	**Carburetter assembly—front**	**AUC9040**		1	1						
2	**Carburetter assembly—rear**	**AUC9041**		1	1						
3	**Body—carburetter—front**	**AUC8243**	**DB1**	1	1						
4	**Body—carburetter—rear**	**AUC8242**	**DB1A**	1	1						
5	Washer—throttle spindle (brass)	AUC2096		4	4						
6	Washer—throttle spindle (Langite)	AUC2098		4	4						
7	Spring for gland washer	AUC2097		4	4						
8	Cap for spring	AUC2010		4	4						
9	Pin—piston lifting	AUC2065	DB57	2	2						
10	Spring for pin	AUC2066	DB59	2	2						
11	Washer for pin (paroid)	AUC4943	DB65	2	2						
12	Washer for pin (brass)	AUC4944	DB66	2	2						
13	Circlip for pin	AUC4886	DB58	2	2						
14	Union—auto ignition	AUC4490	DB2	1	1						
15	Adaptor for union	AUC2044	DB2A	1	1						
16	Gasket for adaptor	AUC2014	DB8	1	1						
17	Screw for adaptor	AUC2175	DB10	2	2						
18	Washer for screw	AUA4648	DB46B	2	2						
19	**Chamber and piston assembly—suction**	**AUC8075**	**DB4**	2	2						
20	Cap assembly	AUC8102	DB5	2	2						
21	Washer for cap (fibre)	AUC4000	DB8	2	2						
22	Spring for piston (yellow)	AUC1167	DB9	2	2						
23	Washer for piston spring	AUC3071	DB7	2	2						
24	Screw—chamber to body	AUC2175	DB10	6	6						
25	**Jet assembly**	**AUC8155**	**DB15**	2	2						
26	Bearing for jet	AUC2001	DB15A	2	2						
27	Screw—jet locking	AUC2002	DB15B	2	2						
28	Spring—jet	AUC2006	DB15C	2	2						
29	Needle	AJH5292	DB12	2	2						For sizes see Workshop Manual
30	Screw for needle (locking)	AUC2057	DB13	2	2						
31	Housing assembly—jet (front carburetter)	AUC8149	DB22	1	1						
32	Housing assembly—jet (rear carburetter)	AUC8206	DB22	1	1						
33	Screw—jet adjusting	AUC2521	DB94	2	2						
34	Spring for screw	AUC2451	DB93	2	2						
35	Rod—sliding	AUC2018	DB45	2	2						
36	Spring for rod	AUC2020	DB45A	2	2						
37	Plate—stop	AUC2019	DB45B	2	2						
38	Screw for stop plate	AUC4790	DB45C	2	2						
39	Washer for screw (shakeproof)	AUA4648	DB46B	4	4						
40	Screw—adjusting	AUA3464	DB94A	2	2						
41	Spring for adjusting screw	AUC2451	DB93	2	2						

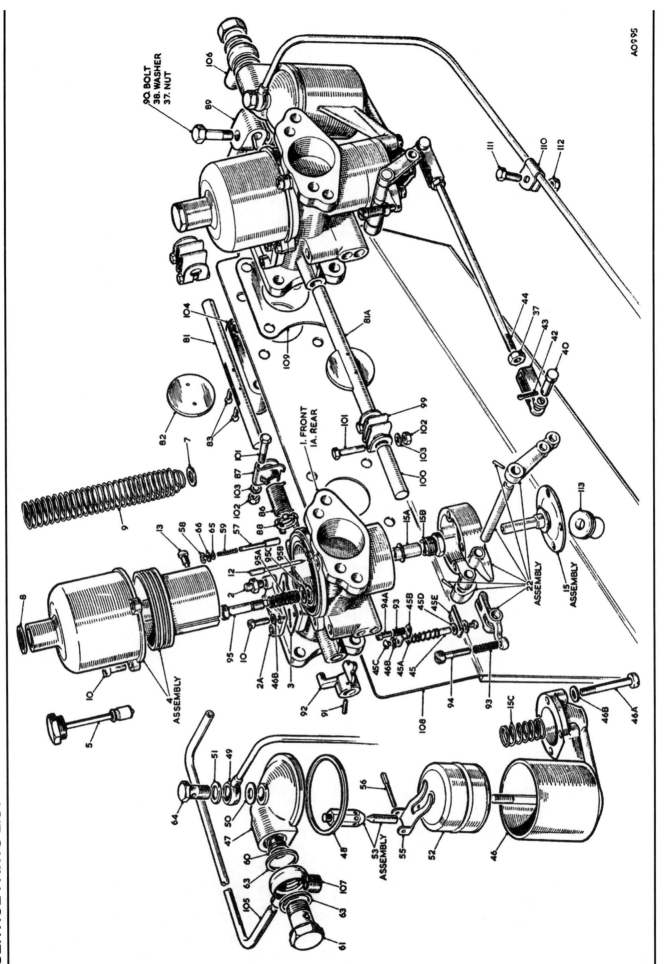

90. BOLT
38. WASHER
37. NUT

I. FRONT
IA. REAR

AO595

74

SERVICE PARTS LIST

Item No.	DESCRIPTION	Commencing (E) 60040 Part Number	Illus. No.	Qty. per Vehicle RHD	LHD	Unit of Issue	Type of Vehicle	New Part Number	Change Point	Amdt. No.	REMARKS
	Carburetter—*continued*										
1	Shoe for cam	AUC2031	DB45E	2	2						
2	Screw for shoe	AUC4790	DB45C	2	2						
3	Washer for screw (shakeproof)	AUA4648	DB46B	4	4						
4	**Spindle-throttle (front carburetter)**	AUC4859	DB81	1	1						
5	**Spindle-throttle (rear carburetter)**	AUC4839	DB81A	1	1						
6	Disc	AUC3280	DB82	2	2						
7	Screw for disc	AUC1858	DB83	4	4						
8	Stop—throttle	AUC2023	DB92	2	2						
9	Pin for stop	AUC2106	DB91	2	2						
10	Spring—throttle return	AUC4781	DB86	2	2						
11	Plate—anchor—spring	AUC1037	DB88	2	2						
12	Clip—end	AUC4771	DB87	2	2						
13	Bolt for clip	AUC2672	DB101	2	2						
14	Nut for bolt	AUC2678	DB102	2	2						
15	Washer for bolt	AUC4612	DB103	2	2						
16	**Lever—throttle (rear carburetter)**	AUC1196	DB89	1	1						
17	Bolt for lever	AUC2694	DB90	1	1						
18	Nut for bolt	AUC2156	DB87	1	1						
19	Washer for bolt (spring)	AUC2246	DB88	1	1						
20	Valve—slow-running adjusting	AUC2028	DB95	2	2						
21	Spring for valve	AUC2027	DB95A	2	2						
22	Washer for valve (brass)	AUC2080	DB95C	2	2						
23	Washer for valve (neoprene)	AUC2029	DB95B	2	2						
24	**Chamber—float (front carburetter)**	AUC4067	DB46	1	1						
25	**Chamber—float (rear carburetter)**	AUC2062	DB46	1	1						
26	Bolt—fixing—float-chamber	AUC2110	DB46A	8	8						
27	Washer for bolt (shakeproof)	AUA4643	DB46B	8	8						
28	Float	AUC1123	DB52	2	2						
29	Lid (front carburetter)	AUC4260	DB47	1	1						
30	Lid (rear carburetter)	AUC4261	DB47	1	1						
31	Washer for lid	AUC1147	DB48	2	2						
32	Needle and seat assembly	AUC8170	DB58	2	2						
33	Lever—hinged	AUC1980	DB55	2	2						
34	Pin for hinged lever	AUC1152	DB56	2	2						
35	Filter	AUC2139	DB60	2	2						
36	Bolt—banjo	AUC2698	DB61	2	2						
37	Washer for banjo bolt (fibre)	AUC2141	DB63	4	4						
38	Cap nut for lid	AUC1867	DB64	2	2						
39	Washer for cap nut (aluminium)	AUC1557	DB51	2	2						

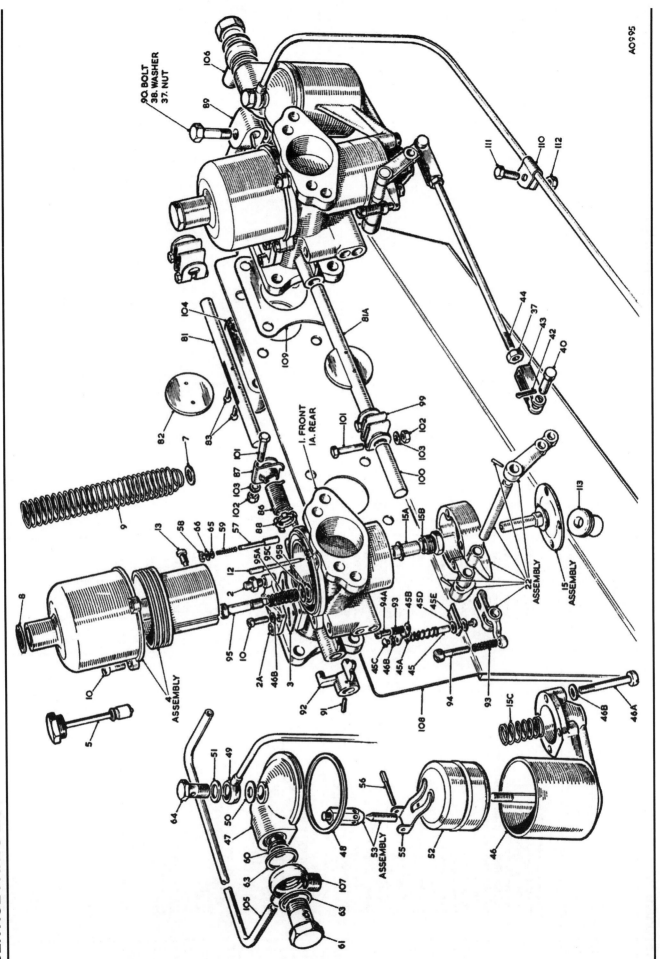

90. BOLT
38. WASHER
37. NUT

I. FRONT
IA. REAR

ASSEMBLY

ASSEMBLY

ASSEMBLY

ASSEMBLY

AO995

Item No.	DESCRIPTION	Part Number Commencing (E) 60949	Illus. No.	Qty. per Vehicle RHD	LHD	Unit of Issue	Type of Vehicle	New Part Number	Change Point	Amdt. No.	REMARKS
	Carburetter—*continued*										
1	Washer for cap nut (fibre)	AUC1928	DB50	2	2						
2	Pipe—overflow (front carburetter)	AUC8366	DB49	1	1						
3	Pipe—overflow (rear carburetter)	AUC8367	DB49	1	1						
4	**Rod—connecting—throttle spindles**	**AUC2419**	**DB100**	1	1						
5	Coupling—rod to spindle	AUC4384	DB99	2	2						
6	Bolt for coupling	AUC2672	DB101	4	4						
7	Nut for bolt	AUC2673	DB102	4	4						
8	Washer for bolt	AUC4012	DB103	4	4						
9	**Rod—connecting—jet levers**	**AUC2867**	**DB44**	1	1						
10	Fork for rod	AUC2256	DB43	2	2						
11	Nut—adjusting—fork	AUC2156	DB87	2	2						
12	Pin—pivot—fork to lever	AUC2108	DB40	2	2						
13	Split pin for pivot pin	AUC2109	DB42	2	2						
14	Distance piece—insulating	AEC368	DB104	3	3						
15	**Pipe—carburetter to carburetter**	**AEC1230**	**DB105**	1	1						
16	Union—banjo—single	3H743	DB106	1	1						
17	Union—banjo—double	AEC844	DB107	1	1						
18	**Shield—heat**	**AEC1229**	**DB108**	1	1						
19	Joint—heat shield to carburetters	AED808	DB109	2	2						
20	Clip—overflow pipe to heat shield	2K5215	DB110	1	1						
21	Screw—clip to heat shield	PMZ0805	DB111	1	1						
22	Screw—clip to heat shield							PMZ0307	Fin. (E) 67663		
23	Washer for screw (spring)							LWZ303	Com. (E) 67664		
24	Nut for screw	FNZ103	DB112	1	1						
25	Grommet for heat shield	RFR106	DB113	1	1						

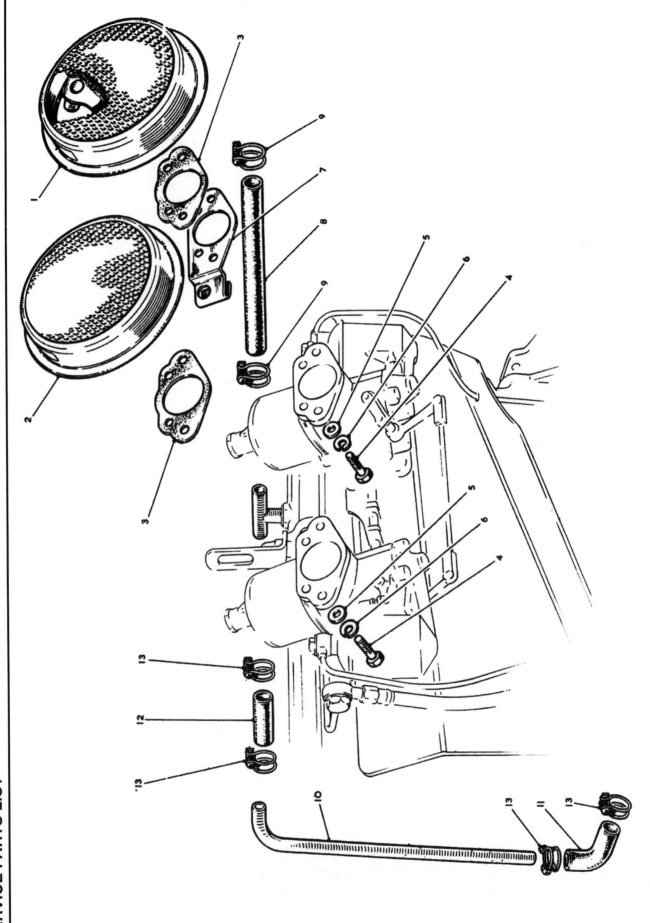

AUSTIN-HEALEY 100 SIX (SERIES BN6)

Item No.	DESCRIPTION	Part Number (Commencing (E) 60949)	Illus. No.	Qty. per Vehicle RHD	Qty. per Vehicle LHD	Unit of Issue	Type of Vehicle	New Part Number	Change Point	Amdt. No.	REMARKS
	AIR CLEANER										
1	**Cleaner with tube for rear carburetter**	11B619	DC1	1	1						⎫ Alternatives
2	Cleaner with tube for rear carburetter	11B622		1	1						⎭
3	**Cleaner less tube for front carburetter**	11B618	DC2	1	1						⎫ Alternatives
4	Cleaner less tube for front carburetter	11B621		1	1						⎭
5	Washer—cleaner to carburetter	AEC875	DC3	2	2						
6	Screw—cleaner to carburetter	HZS0506	DC4	4	4						
7	Washer for screw (plain)	PWZ105	DC5	4	4						
8	Washer for screw (spring)	LWZ205	DC6	4	4	24					
9	Bracket for choke cable trunnion	11B623	DC7	1	1						
10	Connection—cleaner to cover (rubber)	1G2268	DC8	1	1						
11	Clip for connection	AEC442	DC9	2	2						
12	Pipe—breather	AEC702	DC10	1	1						
13	Elbow for pipe	AEC440	DC11	1	1						
14	Hose for vent pipe	AEC441	DC12	1	1						
15	Clip for hose	AEC442	DC13	4	4						

SERVICE PARTS LIST

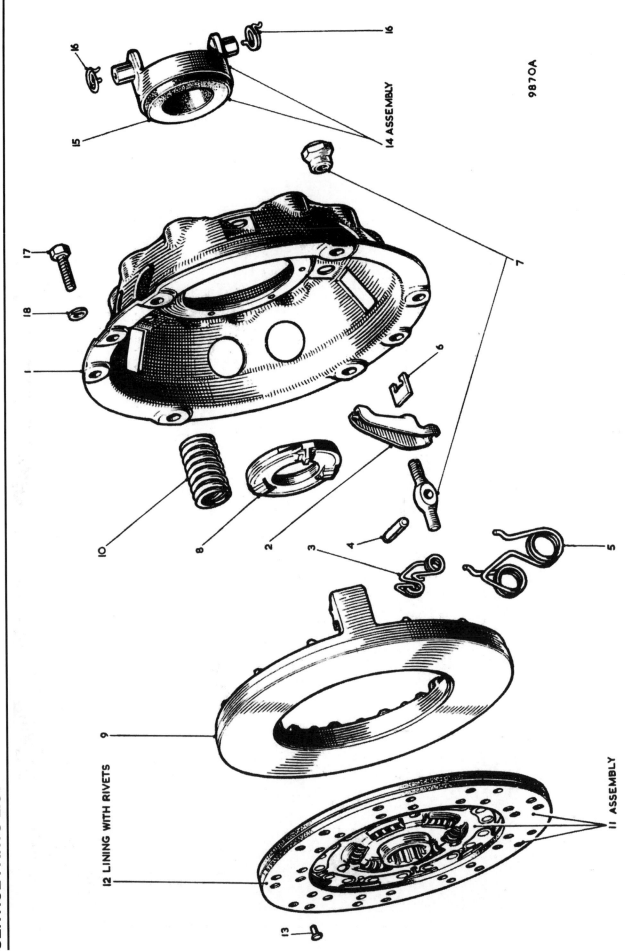

14 ASSEMBLY

9870A

12 LINING WITH RIVETS

11 ASSEMBLY

80

SERVICE PARTS LIST

AUSTIN-HEALEY 100 SIX (SERIES BN6)

CLUTCH

CLUTCH COMPONENTS

Item No.	Description	Part Number (Commencing (E) 60949)	Illus. No.	Qty. per Vehicle RHD	Qty. per Vehicle LHD	Unit of Issue	Type of Vehicle	New Part Number	Change Point	Amdt. No.	REMARKS
1	Clutch cover assembly	27H3178	E1	1	1						
2	Cover—clutch	N.S.P.	E2	1	1						
3	Lever—release	7H3196	E3	3	3	12.					
4	Retainer for lever	7H3001	E4	3	3	72.					
5	Pin for lever	7H3067	E5	3	3	12.					
6	Spring—anti-rattle	7H3171	E6	3	3	36.					
7	Strut—release lever	7H3069	E7	3	3						
8	Eyebolt and nut	7H3240	E8	3	3						
9	Plate—release lever	7H3042	E9	1	1						
10	Plate—pressure	7H3072	E10	1	1						
11	Spring—pressure plate (white)	7H3006		6	6	12.					
12	Spring—pressure plate (black)	7H3325		3	3						
13	Plate assembly—driven (R)	27H3179	E11	1	1						
14	Lining and rivets	7H3174	E12	1	1	set					
15	Rivet	7H3078	E13	38	38.						
16	Bearing assembly—release	AE63264	E14	1	1						
17	Bearing	7H3251	E15	1	1						
18	Retainer—bearing to clutch fork	7H3048	E16	2	2	36.					
19	Screw—clutch to flywheel	HNS0507	E17	6	6						
20	Washer for screw (spring)	LWN205	E18	6	6						

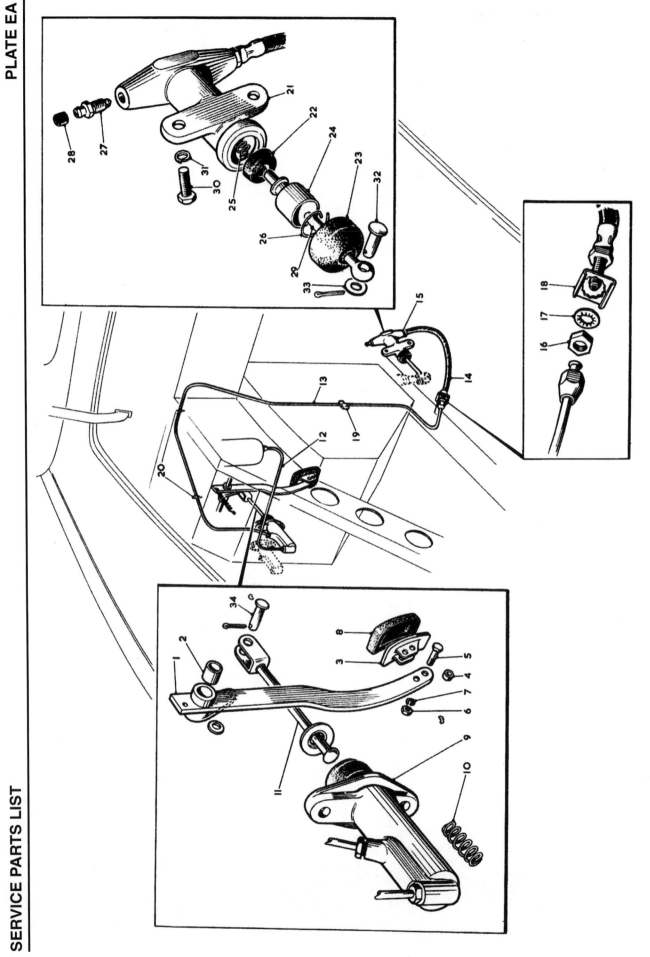

SERVICE PARTS LIST

CLUTCH PEDAL AND LINKAGE

Item No.	Description	Part Number Commencing (C) 501	Illus. No.	Qty. RHD	Qty. LHD	Unit of Issue	Type of Vehicle	New Part Number	Change Point	Amdt. No.	Remarks
1	Lever—clutch pedal	11B5271	EA1	1	1						
2	Bush	1G9310	EA2	1	1						
3	Pad—pedal	1B8750	EA3	1	1						
4	Distance piece—clutch pedal pad	11B5823	EA4	2	2						
5	Bolt—pad to lever	HBZ0411	EA5	2	2						
6	Nut for bolt	FNZ104	EA6	2	2						
7	Washer for nut (spring)	LWZ304	EA7	2	2						
8	Rubber—clutch pedal pad	1B8751	EA8	1	1						
9	Master cylinder assembly	11B5510	EA9	1	1						
10	Spring	7H4944	EA10	1	1						
11	Push-rod	17H4518	EA11	1	1						
12	Service kit for master cylinder	8G8219		1	1						
13	Service kit for master cylinder	17H4416	EA12	1	1						
14	Pipe—supply tank to master cylinder	17H4517		1							
15	Pipe—supply tank to master cylinder	17H4516	EA18		1						
16	Pipe—master cylinder to flexible hose	11B5294		1							
17	Pipe—master cylinder to flexible hose	11B5298	EA18		1						
18	Hose—flexible	1G9516	EA14	1	1						
19	Gasket for hose	3H2287	EA15	1	1						
20	Nut for hose	FNZ206	EA16	1	1						
21	Washer for nut (shakeproof)	2K7131	EA17	1	1						
22	Plate—locking	1G9622	EA18	1	1						
23	Clip—clutch pipe to pedal box	1G9529	EA19	1	1						
24	Clip—clutch pipe to dash	6K35	EA20	2	2						
25	Cylinder—clutch operating	BHA4073	EA21	1	1			BHA4112	Com. (C) 2878		
26	Body	N.S.P.	EA22	1	1						
27	Seal	17H4327	EA23	1	1						
28	Cover—dust	17H4010	EA24	1	1						
29	Plunger	17H4554	EA25	1	1						
30	Spring	7H4970	EA26	1	1						
31	Circlip	17H4011	EA27	1	1						
32	Screw—bleeder	7H4973	EA28	1	1						
33	Cover—dust—bleeder screw	7H4419	EA29	1	1						
34	Push-rod—clutch operating cylinder	1B8701	EA80	1	1						
35	Set screw fixing cylinder	HZS0608	EA31	2	2						
36	Washer for set screw (spring)	LWZ306		2	2						
37	Joint pin—clutch withdrawal lever to operating cylinder	2K5022	EA32	1	1						
38	Service kit for clutch operating cylinder	8G8249	EA33	1	1						
39	Washer for joint pin (plain)	PWZ105		1	1						
40	Joint pin—pedal lever to master cylinder	CLZ0513	EA34	1	1						

E.2

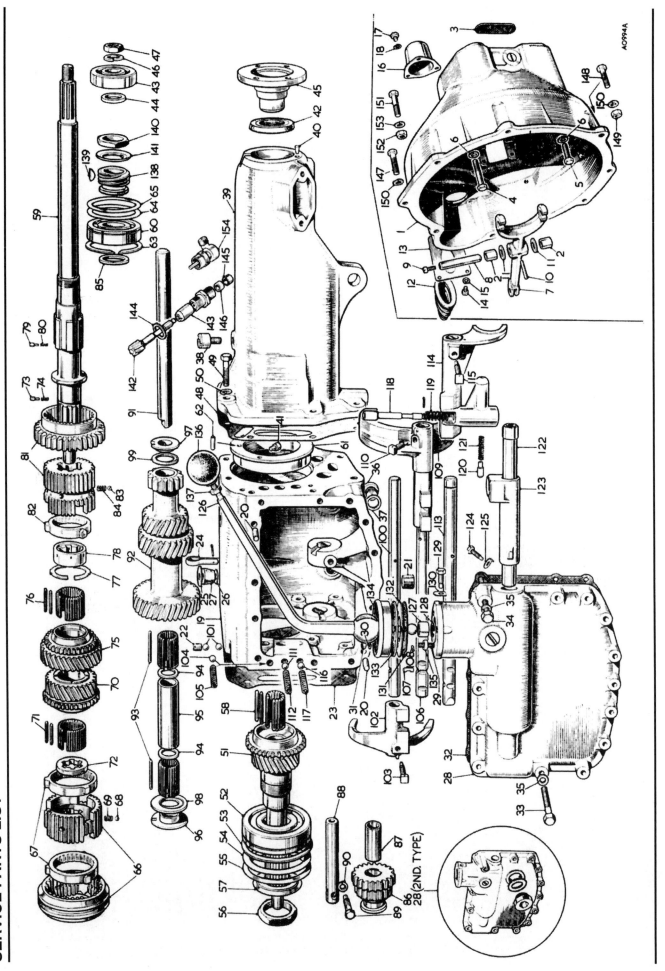

28 (2ND. TYPE)

A0994A

GEARBOX

Item No.	DESCRIPTION	Commencing (E) 60949 Part Number	Illus. No.	Qty. per Vehicle RHD	Qty. per Vehicle LHD	Unit of Issue	Type of Vehicle	New Part Number	Change Point	Amdt. No.	REMARKS
1	Gearbox assembly	1B3757									
	Housing—clutch										
2	Housing—clutch	AEC3067	F1	1	1						
3	Bush—fork and lever shaft	AEC8102	F2	2	2						
4	Pad—buffer	AEC8298	F3	1	1						
5	Bolt—housing to gearbox (long)	HBN0518	F4	1	1						
6	Bolt—housing to gearbox (short)	HBN0509	F5	7	7						
7	Washer for bolt (spring)	LWN205	F6	8	8						
8	Fork and lever—clutch	AEC3324	F7	1	1						
9	Shaft—fork and lever	AEC8104	F8	1	1						
10	Screw for clutch withdrawal fork	AEC3221	F9	1	1						
11	Taper pin—fork and lever to shaft	TPS0610	F10	1	1						
12	Washer for fork and lever (thrust)	AEC8105	F11	2	2						
13	Seal for fork and lever	AEC8106	F12	1	1						
14	Plate—seal retaining	AEC8168	F13	1	1						
15	Screw for retaining plate	53K1435	F14	3	3						
16	Washer for screw (spring)	LWN204	F15	3	3						
17	Cover—starter end	1B3846	F16	1	1						
18	Screw—cover to housing	AEC3207	F17	3	3						
19	Washer for screw (spring)	LWN204	F18	3	3						
20	**Case—gearbox**	AEC3000	F19	1	1						
21	Dowel—side cover	1K1754	F20	2	2						
22	Plug—oil drain	6K499	F21	1	1						
23	Plug for interlock ball hole	1G3710	F22	1	1						
24	Joint—case to clutch housing	AEC3195	F23	1	1	12					
25	**Indicator—oil level**	AEC3109	F24	1	1						
26	Washer (large)	2K9799	F25	1	1						
27	Washer (small)	6K9829	F26	1	1						
28	Washer (felt)	1G3804	F27	1	1	12					
29	**Cover—gearbox side**	1B3705	F28	1	1			AEC3323	Com. (G) 2857		**When supplying AEC3323 supply also 1 off 8G500 and 1 off 6K432**
30	Plug for side cover (small)	AEC385		1	1			8G500	] Com. (G) 2857		
31	Plug for side cover (large)		F29	1	1			6K432			
32	Washer for plug	53K462	F30	3	3	72					
33	Stud for change speed lever cover	LWZ204	F31	3	3						
34	Washer for stud (spring)	FNZ104	F32	3	3						
35	Nut for stud	AEC3176	F33	1	1						
36	Joint—cover to gearbox	HBN0522	F34	1	1	72					
37	Bolt—cover to gearbox (long)	HBN0512	F35	12	12						
38	Bolt—cover to gearbox (short)	LWN205	F36	13	13						
39	Washer for bolt (spring)	8G500	F37	2	2						
40	Cap—control shaft boss	6K432	F38	2	2	72					
41	Washer for cap	AEC3009	F39	1	1						
42	Breather—gearbox	1B3763		1	1						
43	**Casing—gearbox extension**	2K1845	F40	1	1						
44	Taper plug for casing	1A3073	F41	1	1						
45	Button—speedometer pinion thrust			1	1						

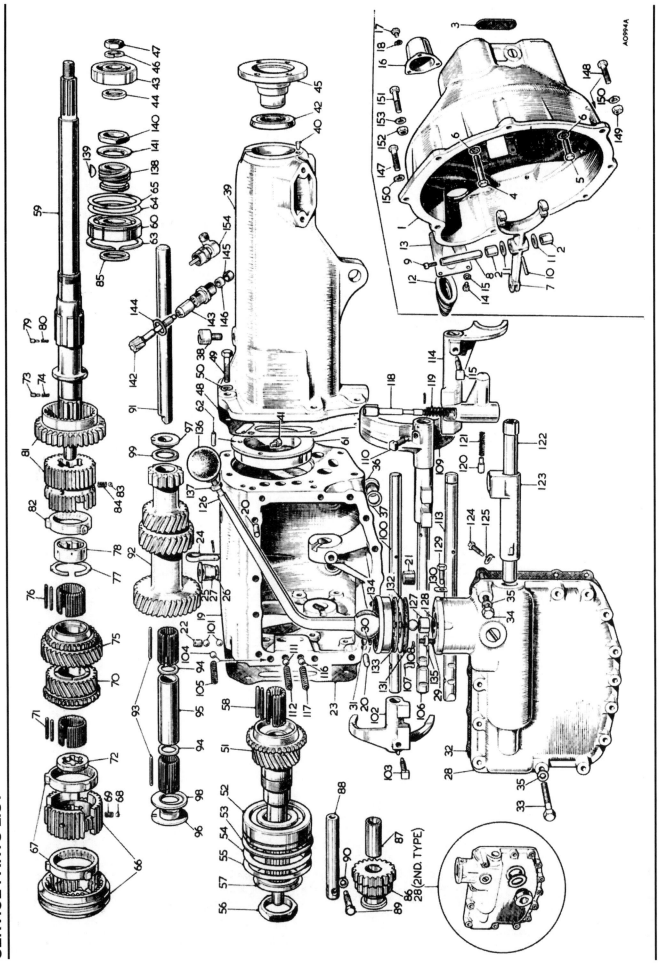

28 (2ND. TYPE)

AO94A

SERVICE PARTS LIST

Item No.	DESCRIPTION	Commencing (E) 60949 Part Number	Illus. No.	Qty. per Vehicle RHD	Qty. per Vehicle LHD	Unit of Issue	Type of Vehicle	New Part Number	Change Point	Amdt. No.	REMARKS
	Gearbox—*continued*										
1	Seal—oil	1B8767	F42	1	1						
2	Bearing	2K5505	F43	1	1						
3	Washer for bearing	1B8766	F44	1	1						
4	Flange—coupling	ATC7100	F45	1	1						
5	Washer for flange (spring)	LWZ212	F46	1	1						
6	Nut for flange	FNZ612	F47	1	1						
7	Joint—casing to gearbox	AEC8142	F48	1	1	12					
8	Bolt—casing to gearbox	HBN0510	F49	8	8						
9	Washer for bolt (spring)	LWN205	F50	8	8						
10	**Gear—drive**	AEC3259	F51	1	1						
11	Bearing for drive gear	6K777	F52	1	1						
12	Circlip for bearing	6K780	F53	1	1						
13	Plate for bearing	AEC8184	F54	1	1						
14	Plate for bearing (spring)	AEC8183	F55	1	1						
15	Nut for bearing	AEB8124	F56	1	1						
16	Washer for nut (lock)	AEC8185	F57	1	1						
17	Roller—drive gear (needle)	AEC8186	F58	16	16						
18	**Mainshaft**	1B3765	F59	1	1						
19	Bearing for mainshaft	6K681	F60	1	1						
20	**Housing for bearing**	AEC3015	F61	1	1						
21	Peg—locating	AEC3112	F62	1	1						
22	Circlip for bearing	1K8055	F63	1	1						
23	Plate for bearing	AEB8105	F64	1	1						
24	Plate for bearing (spring)	AEC8178	F65	1	1						
25	**Hub with striking dog—top and third (sliding)**	AEC3072	F66	1	1						
26	Interceptor—sliding hub	AEB3214	F67	2	2						
27	Ball for sliding hub	BLS110	F68	3	3	12					
28	Spring for ball	AEC8208	F69	3	3						
29	**Gear—third speed**	AEC3170	F70	1	1						
30	Roller—gear	AEC8180	F71	32	32						
31	Plate (locking)	AEC8198	F72	1	1						
32	Plunger—gear	AEC8181	F73	1	1						
33	Spring for plunger	AEC8182	F74	1	1						
34	**Gear—second speed**	AEC3210	F75	1	1						
35	Roller—gear	AEC8180	F76	33	33						
36	Washer for gear	AEB8111	F77	2	2						
37	Plate (locking)	AEB8112	F78	1	1						
38	Plunger—gear	AEC8181	F79	1	1						
39	Spring for plunger	AEC8182	F80	1	1						

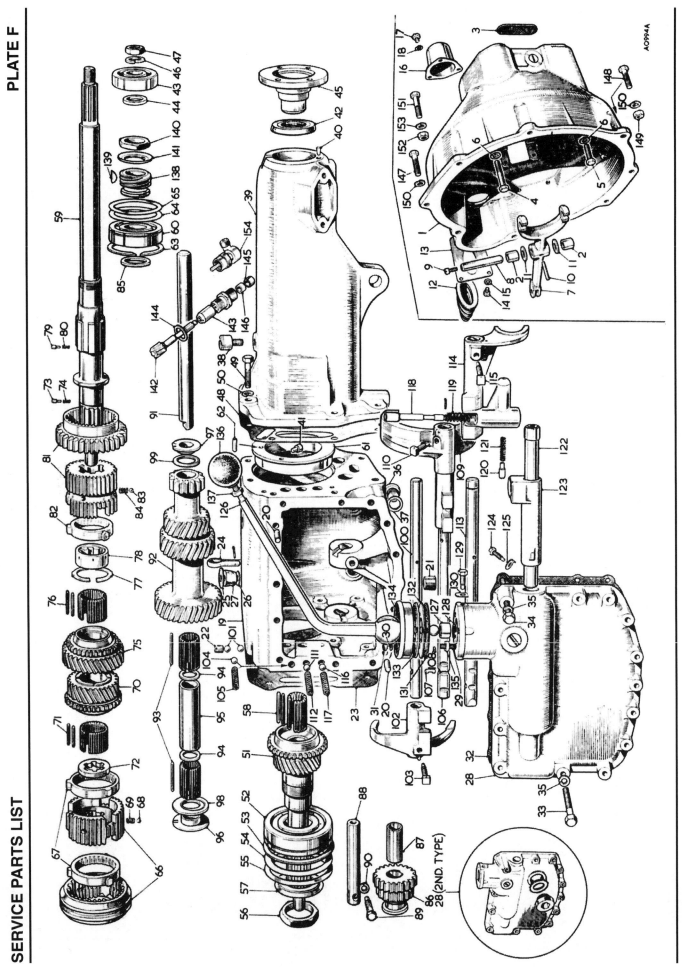

A0994A

SERVICE PARTS LIST

Item No.	DESCRIPTION	Commencing (E) 60049 Part Number	Illus. No.	Qty. per Vehicle RHD	LHD	Unit of Issue	Type of Vehicle	New Part Number	Change Point	Amdt. No.	REMARKS
	Gearbox—continued										
1	Gear with first and second sliding hub—first speed	AEC3071	F81	1	1			AEC3507	Com. (G) 2794		
2	Interceptor—sliding hub	AEC3211	F82	1	1						
3	Ball for sliding hub	BLS110	F83	8	8	12					
4	Spring for ball	AEC3208	F84	3	3						
5	Collar—distance—mainshaft	AEB3115	F85	1	1						
6	Gear—reverse	AEC3003	F86	1	1						
7	Bush	AEC3119	F87	1	1						
8	Shaft—gear	AEC8840	F88	1	1						
9	Screw—shaft retaining	AEC8121	F89	1	1						
10	Washer for screw (spring)	LWN205	F90	1	1						
11	Layshaft	AEB3203	F91	1	1						
12	Gear unit—layshaft	1B3728	F92	1	1						
13	Roller—gear unit	AEB3212	F93	46	46						
14	Washer for roller	AEB3204	F94	2	2						
15	Spacer for roller	AEC3113	F95	1	1						
16	Plate—gear unit (front thrust)	AEC3115	F96	1	1						
17	Plate—gear unit (rear thrust)	AEC3116	F97	1	1						
18	Washer—gear unit (front thrust)	AEB3209	F98	1	1						
19	Washer—gear unit (rear thrust)	AEB3206	F99	1	1			AEC3850	Com. (G) 3326		
20	Shaft—top and third shifter	AEC3342	F100	1	1						
21	Ball—shaft interlocking	BLS110	F101	2	2	12					
22	Fork—top and third (striking)	1B3707	F102	1	1						
23	Screw—fork to shaft	AEB3180	F103	1	1						
24	Ball for shaft	BLS110	F104	1	1	12					
25	Spring for ball	AEC3189	F105	1	1	12					
26	Shaft—first and second shifter	AEC3504	F106	1	1						
27	Pin—shaft interlocking	AEC3187	F107	1	1						
28	Rivet—interlocking pin	AEC3188	F108	1	1						
29	Fork—first and second (striking)	1B3708	F109	1	1						
30	Screw—fork to shaft	AEB3180	F110	1	1						
31	Ball for shaft	BLS110	F111	1	1	12					
32	Spring for ball	AEC3189	F112	1	1	12					
33	Shaft—reverse shifter	AEC3343	F113	1	1						
34	Fork—reverse (striking)	1B3709	F114	1	1			AEC3822	Com. (G) 2955		
35	Screw—fork to shaft	AEB3180	F115	1	1						
36	Ball for shaft	BLS110	F116	1	1	12					
37	Spring for ball	AEC3189	F117	1	1	12					

MODIFICATIONS

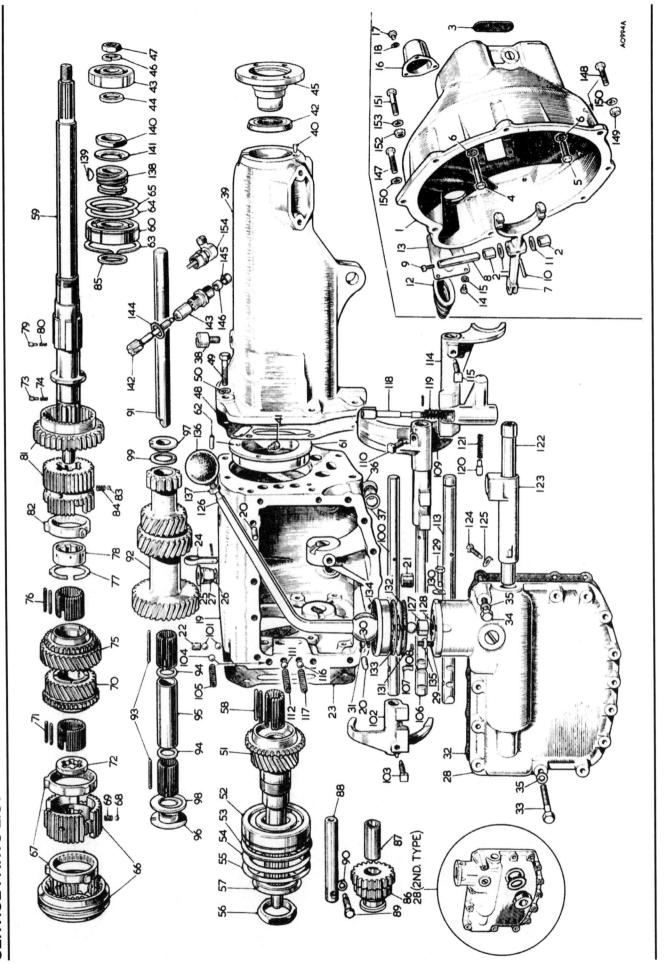

AO94A

SERVICE PARTS LIST

Item No.	DESCRIPTION	Part Number (Commencing (E) 60940)	Illus. No.	Qty. per Vehicle RHD	LHD	Unit of Issue	Type of Vehicle	New Part Number	Change Point	Amdt. No.	REMARKS
	Gearbox—*continued*										
1	Plunger—reverse selector	1B3710	F118	1	1						
2	Spring for plunger	2F3198	F119	1	1						
3	Plunger—detent	1B3836	F120	1	1						
4	Spring—detent plunger	2K4909	F121	1	1	36.					
5	Shaft—control	1B8713	F122	1	1						
6	Lever—control	1B8706	F123	1	1						
7	Screw—shaft locking	1G3581	F124	1	1						
8	Washer for screw (lock)	1B3363	F125	1	1						
9	**Lever—change speed**	**1B3760**	**F126**	1	1						
10	Bush for lever	AEC3520	F127	pr.	pr.						
11	Circlip for bush	1G3709	F128	1	1						
12	Screw—lever locating	2F8166	F129	1	1						
13	Washer for screw (tab)	2F3040	F130	1	1						
14	Washer—change speed lever sealing	1B3632	F181	1	1						
15	Seat—change speed lever	2F3151	F182	1	1						
16	Pad—change speed lever packing	2F3152	F183	1	1						
17	Cover—change speed lever	2F3154	F184	1	1						
18	Distance piece for cover.	1B3634	F185	8	8						
19	Knob—change speed lever	1B3736	F186	1	1						
20	Nut for knob (lock)	54K1723	F187	1	1						
21	**Gear—speedometer**	**AEG3177**	**F138**	1	1						
22	Key for gear	WKN805	F189	1	1						
23	Nut for gear (lock)	AEB3162	F140	1	1						
24	Washer for gear (lock)	AEB3163	F141	1	1						
25	**Pinion—speedometer**	**AEB3181**	**F142**	1	1						
26	Bearing—pinion	AEC3198	F143	1	1						
27	Washer for bearing	2K7500	F144	1	1						
28	Collar—pinion distance	AEB3202	F145	1	1						
29	Seal—pinion oil	2A3254	F146	1	1	12.					
30	Bolt—clutch housing to crankcase (long)	HBN0612	F147	1	1						
31	Bolt—clutch housing to crankcase (short)	HBN0611	F148	4	4						
32	Nut for bolt	FNN106	F149	4	4						
33	Washer for bolt (spring)	LWN206	F150	5	5						
34	Dowel bolt to rear plate	AEC3224	F151	2	2						
35	Nut for bolt	FNN106	F152	2	2						
36	Washer for bolt (spring)	LWN206	F153	2	2						
37	Adaptor box—speedometer drive	1H8181	F154	1	1						

F.4

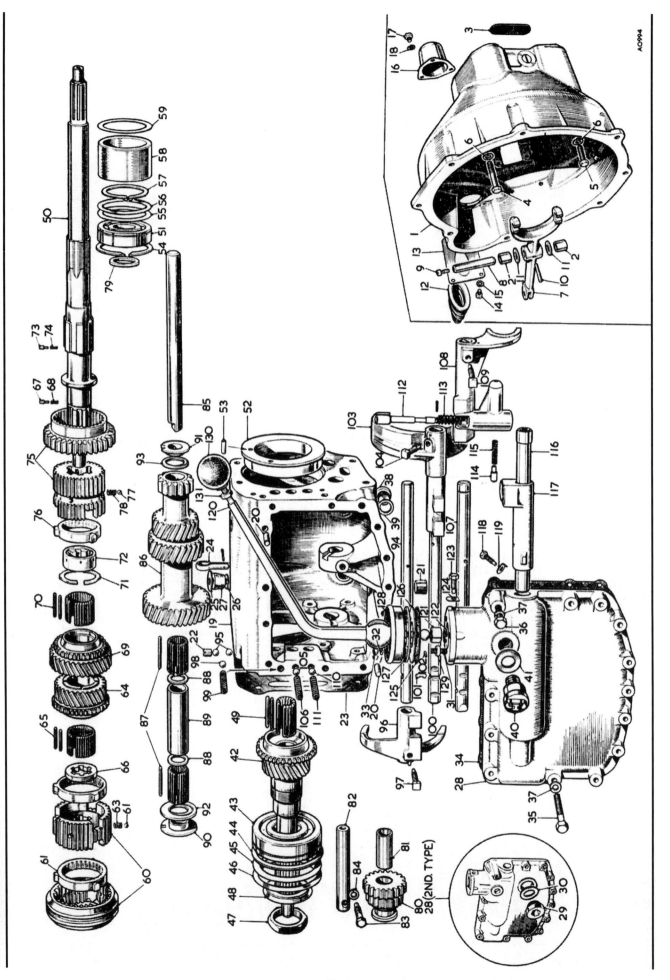

SERVICE PARTS LIST

GEARBOX WITH OVERDRIVE (Optional Extra)

Item No.	DESCRIPTION	Commencing (E) 60949 Part Number	Illus. No.	Qty. per Vehicle RHD	Qty. per Vehicle LHD	Unit of Issue	Type of Vehicle	New Part Number	Change Point	Amdt. No.	REMARKS
	Gearbox assembly	**1B3755**		1	1						
	Housing—clutch	**AEC3067**	**FA1**	1	1						
1	Bush—fork and lever shaft	AEC8102	FA2	2	1						
2	Pad—buffer	AEC8298	FA3	1	1						
3	Bolt—housing to gearbox (long)	HBN0518	FA4	7	7						
4	Bolt—housing to gearbox (short)	HBN0509	FA5	8	8						
5	Washer for bolt (spring)	LWN205	FA6	1	1						
6	Fork and lever—clutch	AEC8824	FA7	1	1						
7	Shaft for fork and lever	AEC8104	FA8	1	1						
8	Screw—shaft blanking	AEC8221	FA9	2	2						
9	Pin—taper—fork and lever to shaft	TPS0610	FA10	1	1						
10	Washer—thrust—fork and lever	AEC8105	FA11	1	1						
11	Seal for fork and lever	AEC8106	FA12	8	8						
12	Plate—seal retaining	AEC8168	FA13	8	8						
13	Screw for retaining plate	53K1435	FA14	1	1						
14	Washer for screw (spring)	LWN204	FA15	8	8						
15	Cover—starter end	1B8346	FA16	3	3						
16	Screw—cover to housing	AEC8207	FA17	3	3						
17	Washer for screw (spring)	LWN204	FA18	1	1						
18	**Case—gearbox**	**AEC3000**	**FA19**	2	2						
19	Dowel—side cover	1K1754	FA20	1	1						
20	Plug—oil drain	6K499	FA21	1	1						
21	Plug for interlock ball hole	1G3710	FA22	1	1		Overdrive				
22	Joint—case to clutch housing	AEC8195	FA23	1	1	12.					
23	**Indicator—oil level**	**AEC3109**	**FA24**	1	1						
24	Washer—large	2K9799	FA25	1	1						
25	Washer—small	6K9829	FA26	1	1						
26	Washer—felt	1G8804	FA27	1	1	12.					
27	**Cover—gearbox side**	**1B3705**	**FA28**	1	1			AEC3323	Com. (G) 9274		When supplying AEC3323 supply also 1 off 8G500 and 1 off 6K432
28	Plug for side cover		FA29	1	1						
29	Washer for plug		FA30	1	1	72.					
30	Stud—change speed lever cover	58K462	FA31	8	8						
31	Washer for stud (spring)	LWZ204	FA32	3	3						
32	Nut for stud	FNZ104	FA33	8	8						
33	Joint—cover to gearbox	AEC3176	FA34	1	1						
34	Bolt—cover to gearbox (long)	HBN0522	FA35	12	12						
35	Bolt—cover to gearbox (short)	HBN0512	FA36	13	18						
36	Washer for bolt (spring)	LWN205	FA37	2	2						
37	Cap—control shaft boss	8G500	FA38	2	2			8G500	Com. (G) 9274		
38	Washer for cap	6K482	FA39	1	1	72.		6K432	Com. (G) 9274		
39	**Switch—overdrive**	**11G3062**	**FA40**	1	1						
40	Joint for switch	2K7914	FA41	1	1						

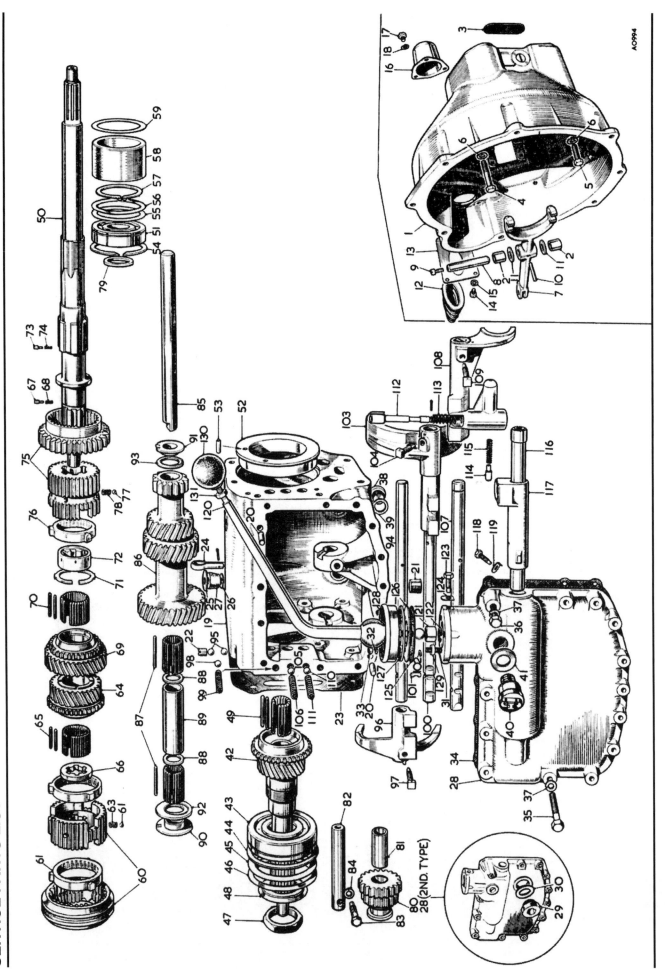

A0994

Item No.	DESCRIPTION	Part Number Commencing (E) 60949	Illus. No.	Qty. per Vehicle RHD	Qty. per Vehicle LHD	Unit of Issue	Type of Vehicle	New Part Number	Change Point	Amdt. No.	REMARKS
	Gearbox with Overdrive—*continued*										
	Gear—drive	**AEC3259**	**FA42**	1	1						
1	Bearing for drive gear	6K777	FA43	1	1						
2	Circlip for bearing	6K780	FA44	1	1						
3	Plate for bearing	AEC3184	FA45	1	1						
4	Plate—spring—for bearing	AEC3183	FA46	1	1						
5	Nut for bearing	AEB3124	FA47	1	1						
6	Washer for nut (lock)	AEC3185	FA48	1	1						
7	Roller—needle—for drive gear	AEC3186	FA49	16	16						
8	**Mainshaft**	**1B3720**	**FA50**	1	1						
9	Bearing for mainshaft	6K681	FA51	1	1						
10	**Housing—bearing**	**AEC3015**	**FA52**	1	1						
11	Peg—locating	AEC3112	FA53	1	1						
12	Circlip for bearing	1K3055	FA54	1	1						
13	Plate for bearing	AEB3105	FA55	1	1						
14	Plate—spring—for bearing	AEC3178	FA56	1	1						
15	Circlip for mainshaft	CCN120	FA57	1	1						
16	Piece—distance—circlip to bearing	1B3721	FA58	1	1						
17	Shim for distance piece	1B3655	FA59	A/R	A/R						
18	**Hub—sliding—top and third**	**AEC3072**	**FA60**	1	1						
19	Interceptor—sliding hub	AEB8214	FA61	2	2						
20	Ball for sliding hub	BLS110	FA62	3	3						
21	Spring for ball	AEC3208	FA63	3	3	12					
22	**Gear—third speed**	**AEC3170**	**FA64**	1	1						
23	Roller for gear	AEC3180	FA65	32	32		Overdrive				
24	Plate—gear locking	AEC3103	FA66	1	1						
25	Plunger for gear	AEC3181	FA67	1	1						
26	Spring for plunger	AEC3182	FA68	1	1						
27	**Gear—second speed**	**AEC3210**	**FA69**	1	1						
28	Roller for gear	AEC3180	FA70	33	33						
29	Washer for gear	AEB3111	FA71	1	1						
30	Plate for gear—locking	AEB3112	FA72	2	2						
31	Plunger for gear	AEC3181	FA73	1	1						
32	Spring for plunger	AEC3182	FA74	1	1						
33	**Gear—first speed**	**AEC3071**	**FA75**	1	1			AEC3507	Com. (G) 9041		
34	Interceptor—sliding hub	AEC3211	FA76	1	1						
35	Ball for sliding hub	BLS110	FA77	3	3	12					
36	Spring for ball	AEC3208	FA78	3	3						
37	Collar—distance—for mainshaft	AEB3115	FA79	1	1						
38	**Gear—reverse**	**AEC3003**	**FA80**	1	1						
39	Bush for gear	AEC3119	FA81	1	1						
40	Shaft—reverse gear	AEC3340	FA82	1	1						
41	Screw—shaft retaining	AEC3121	FA83	1	1						
42	Washer for screw (spring)	LWN205	FA84	1	1						
43	**Layshaft**	**AEB3203**	**FA85**	1	1						

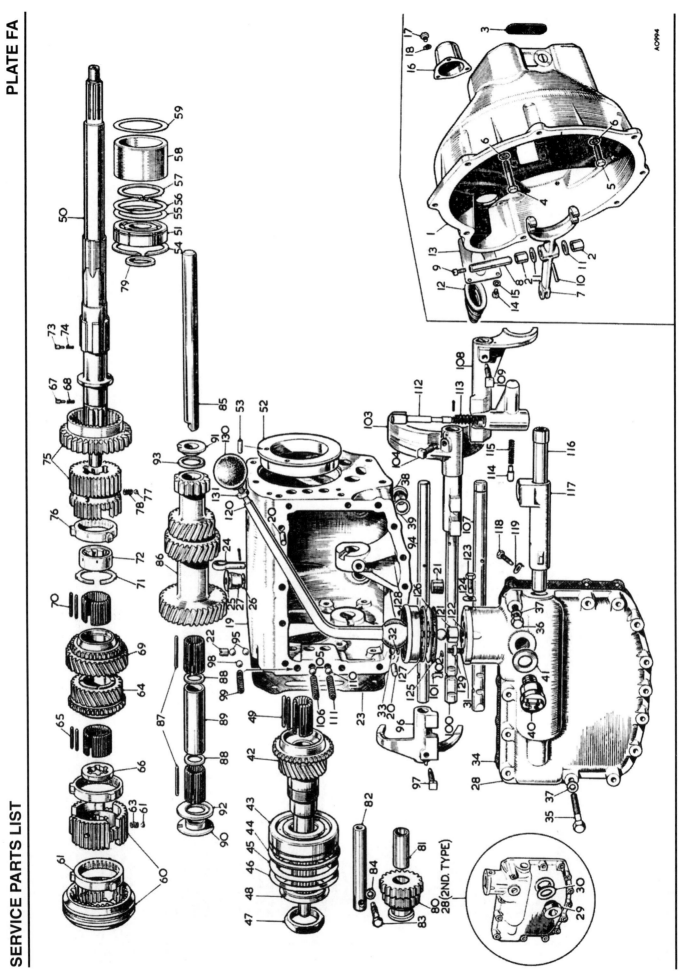

A0994

Item No.	DESCRIPTION	Commencing (E) 60049 Part Number	Illus. No.	Qty. per Vehicle RHD	Qty. per Vehicle LHD	Unit of Issue	Type of Vehicle	New Part Number	Change Point	Amdt. No.	REMARKS
	Gearbox with Overdrive—*continued*										
	Gear unit—layshaft	**1B3728**	**FA86**	1	1						
1	Roller for gear unit	AEB8212	FA87	46	46						
2	Washer for roller	AEB8204	FA88	2	2						
3	Spacer for roller	AEC3113	FA89	1	1						
4	Plate—thrust (front)	AEC3115	FA90	1	1						
5	Plate—thrust (rear)	AEC3116	FA91	1	1						
6	Washer—thrust (front)	AEB8209	FA92	1	1						
7	Washer—thrust (rear)	AEB8206	FA93	1	1			AEC3350	Com. (G) 10392		
8	**Shaft—top and third shifter**	**AEC3342**	**FA94**	1	1						
9	Ball—shaft interlocking	BLS110	FA95	2	2	12.					
10	Fork—striking—top and third	1B3707	FA96	1	1						
11	Screw—fork to shaft	AEB8180	FA97	1	1						
12	Ball for shifter shaft	BLS110	FA98	1	1	12.					
13	Spring for ball	AEC3189	FA99	1	1	12.					
14	**Shaft—first and second shifter**	**AEC3504**	**FA100**	1	1						
15	Pin—shaft interlocking	AEC3187	FA101	1	1						
16	Rivet—interlocking pin	AEC3188	FA102	1	1						
17	Fork—striking—first and second	1B3708	FA103	1	1						
18	Screw—fork to shaft	AEB8180	FA104	1	1						
19	Ball for shifter shaft	BLS110	FA105	1	1	12.					
20	Spring for ball	AEC3189	FA106	1	1	12.					
21	**Shaft—reverse shifter**	**AEC3343**	**FA107**	1	1		Overdrive	AEC3322	Com. (G) 9447		
22	Fork—striking—reverse	1B3709	FA108	1	1						
23	Screw—fork to shaft	AEB8180	FA109	1	1						
24	Ball for shifter shaft	BLS110	FA110	1	1	12.					
25	Spring for ball	AEC3189	FA111	1	1	12.					
26	**Plunger—reverse selector**	**1B3710**	**FA112**	1	1						
27	Spring for plunger	2F3198	FA113	1	1						
28	Plunger—detent	1B8836	FA114	1	1						
29	Spring for plunger	2K4909	FA115	1	1	36.					
30	Shaft—control	1B3713	FA116	1	1						
31	Lever—control	1B3706	FA117	1	1						
32	Screw for shaft (locking)	1G3581	FA118	1	1						
33	Washer for screw (lock)	1B3363	FA119	1	1						
34	**Lever—change speed**	**1B3760**	**FA120**	1	1						
35	Bush for lever	AEC3520	FA121	pr.	pr.						
36	Circlip for bush	1G3709	FA122	1	1						
37	Screw for lever (locating)	2F3166	FA123	1	1						
38	Washer for locating screw (tab)	2F3040	FA124	1	1						
39	Washer for change speed lever (sealing)	1B3632	FA125	1	1						
40	Seat for change speed lever	2F3151	FA126	1	1						
41	Pad for change speed lever (packing)	2F3152	FA127	1	1						
42	**Cover for change speed lever**	**2F3154**	**FA128**	1	1						
43	Distance piece for cover	1B3634	FA129	3	3						
44	**Knob for change speed lever**	**1B3736**	**FA130**	1	1						
45	Nut for knob (locking)	54K1723	FA131	1	1						

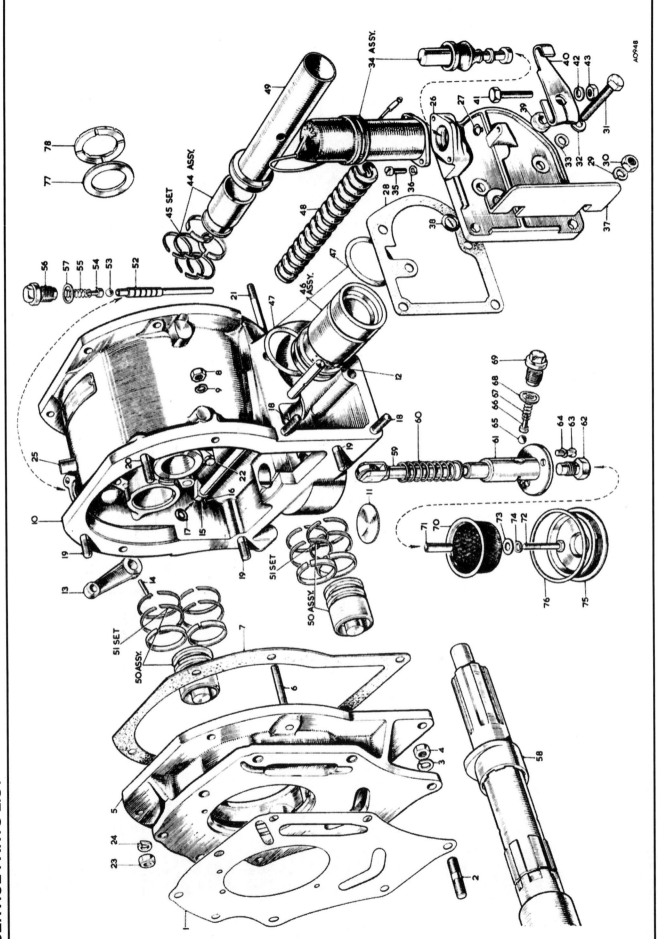

A0948

AUSTIN-HEALEY 100 SIX (SERIES BN6)

Item No.	DESCRIPTION	Commencing (E) 60949 Part Number	Illus. No.	Qty. per Vehicle RHD	Qty. per Vehicle LHD	Unit of Issue	Type of Vehicle	New Part Number	Change Point	Amdt. No.	REMARKS
	Gearbox with Overdrive—continued										
1	Joint—overdrive unit to gearbox	AEC3142	FB1	1	1	12					
2	Stud—overdrive unit to gearbox	51K505	FB2	8	8						
3	Washer for stud (spring)	LWN205	FB3	8	8						
4	Nut for stud	FNN505	FB4	8	8						
5	**Overdrive unit assembly** (R)	1B3839	**FB5**	1	1						
6	**Plate—adaptor**	1B3753	FB6	1	1						
7	Stud—plate to front casing	7H5829	FB6	2	2						
8	Joint—adaptor plate to front casing	7H5825	FB7	1	1						
9	Nut—plate stud to casing	FNZ105	FB8	2	2						
10	Washer for stud (spring)	LWZ205	FB9	2	2	24.					
11	**Casing—front**	**17H5830**	**FB10**	1	1						
12	Plug—welch	7H5897	FB11	1	1						
13	Shaft—valve operating	7H5821	FB12	1	1						
14	Lever for shaft	7H5822	FB13	1	1						
15	Pin—lever to shaft (taper)	TPS0405	FB14	1	1						
16	Cam—valve operating	7H5827	FB15	1	1						
17	Pin for cam (taper)	TPS0405	FB16	1	1						
18	Seal for shaft—oil	17H5815	FB17	1	1						
19	Stud for solenoid bracket	7H5832	FB18	2	2						
20	Stud for adaptor plate—long	7H5830	FB19	3	3						
21	Stud for adaptor plate—short	7H5831	FB20	1	1						
22	Stud to rear casing	7H5833	FB21	2	2						
23	Peg—guide for oil pump plunger	7H5851	FB22	1	1						
24	Nut—casing to adaptor plate	FNZ205	FB23	4	4						
25	Washer for nut (spring)	LWZ205	FB24	4	4	24.	Overdrive				
26	**Breather**	**17H5825**	**FB25**	1	1						
27	Bracket—solenoid	17H5826	FB26	1	1						
28	Stop—rubber	17H5811	FB27	1	1						
29	Joint—bracket to case	7H5852	FB28	1	1						
30	Washer—bracket to casing (spring)	LWZ205	FB29	2	2	24.					
31	Nut—bracket to casing	FNZ105	FB30	2	2						
32	Screw—bracket to casing	7H5853	FB31	2	2						
33	Washer for screw (plain)	PWZ105	FB32	2	2						
34	Washer for screw (spring)	LWZ205	FB33	2	2	24					
35	**Solenoid**	**13H137**	**FB34**	1	1						
36	Screw—solenoid to bracket	PMZ0308	FB35	2	2						
37	Washer for screw (spring)	LWZ203	FB36	2	2						
38	Guard for solenoid	17H5810	FB87	1	1						
39	Seal for shaft—oil	17H5815	FB88	1	1						
40	Collar for shaft—distance	17H5809	FB39	1	1						
41	Lever—solenoid	17H5808	FB40	1	1						
42	Screw—lever to spindle	HZS0406	FB41	1	1						
43	Washer for screw (spring)	LWZ204	FB42	1	1						
44	Nut for screw	FNZ104	FB43	1	1						
45	**Piston assembly—accumulator**	**17H5847**	**FB44**	1	1						
46	Ring—piston	7H5849	FB45	2	2	set					
47	Housing assembly—accumulator	17H5848	FB46	1	1						
48	Ring—rubber	7H5846	FB47	2	2						

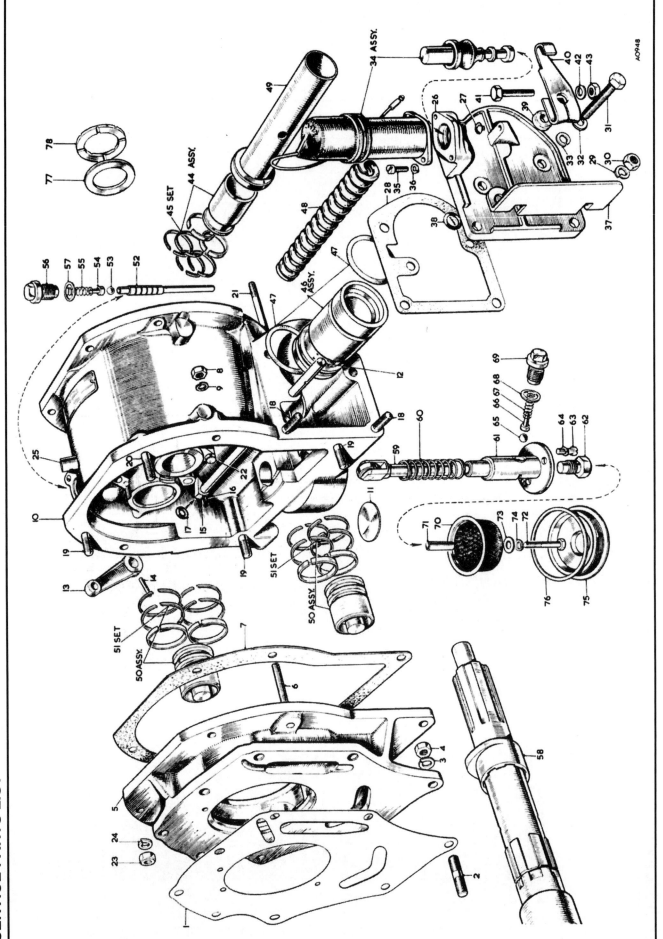

AO948

SERVICE PARTS LIST

AUSTIN-HEALEY 100 SIX (SERIES BN6)

Item No.	DESCRIPTION	Part Number Commencing (E) 60049	Illus. No.	Qty. per Vehicle RHD	Qty. per Vehicle LHD	Unit of Issue	Type of Vehicle	New Part Number	MODIFICATIONS Change Point	Amdt. No.	REMARKS
	Gearbox with Overdrive—*continued*										
1	Spring—accumulator pressure	17H5833	FB48	1	1						
2	Tube for spring	7H5845	FB49	1	1						
	Piston—operating										
3		17H5849	FB50	2	2						
4	Ring—piston	7H5860	FB51	2	2	set					
	Valve—operating										
5		17H5827	FB52	1	1						
6	Ball for valve	BLS110	FB53	1	1	12					
7	Plunger—ball	7H5837	FB54	1	1						
8	Spring for plunger	7H5836	FB55	1	1						
9	Plug for valve (screwed)	7H5820	FB56	1	1						
10	Washer for plug	7H5898	FB57	1	1						
	Cam—oil pump										
11		1B3650	FB58	1	1						
12	Plunger assembly—oil pump	7H5838	FB59	1	1						
13	Spring for plunger	7H5839	FB60	1	1						
	Body—oil pump										
14		7H5840	FB61	1	1						
15	Plug for body (screwed)	7H5841	FB62	1	1						
16	Screw—body to front casing	PMZ0808	FB63	2	2	24					
17	Washer for screw (spring)	LWN203	FB64	2	2	144					
18	Ball—valve	BLS108	FB65	1	1						
19	Plunger—ball	7H5837	FB66	1	1						
20	Spring for plunger	7H5836	FB67	1	1						
21	Washer for valve plug (copper)	7H5898	FB68	1	1						
22	Plug—valve	7H5820	FB69	1	1		Overdrive				
	Strainer—oil pump										
23		7H5842	FB70	1	1						
24	Distance tube for strainer	7H5843	FB71	1	1						
25	Bolt for strainer	7H5844	FB72	1	1						
26	Washer for bolt (plain)	2K1201	FB73	1	1						
27	Washer for bolt (spring)	2K1209	FB74	1	1						
28	Plug for front casing—oil drain	7H5856	FB75	1	1						
29	Washer for plug	7H5857	FB76	1	1						
30	Washer—steel—sun wheel adjusting—front—·118 to ·114"	7H5872A	FB77	A/R	A/R						
31	Washer—steel—sun wheel adjusting—front—·107 to ·108"	7H5872B		A/R	A/R						
32	Washer—steel—sun wheel adjusting—front—·101 to ·102"	7H5872C		A/R	A/R						
33	Washer—steel—sun wheel adjusting—front—·095 to ·096"	7H5872D		A/R	A/R						
34	Washer—steel—sun wheel adjusting—front—·089 to ·090"	7H5872E		A/R	A/R						
35	Washer—steel—sun wheel adjusting—front—·083 to ·084"	7H5872F		A/R	A/R						
36	Washer—steel—sun wheel adjusting—front—·077 to ·078"	7H5872G		A/R	A/R						
37	Washer—phosphor-bronze—sun wheel thrust—front	7H5873	FB78	1	1						

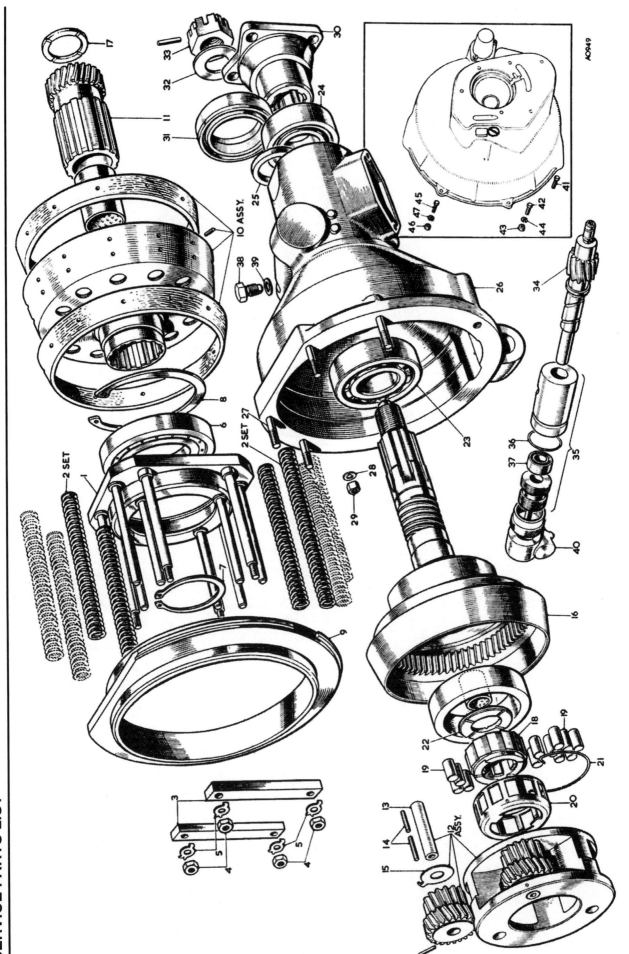

AO49

10 ASSY.

2 SET 27

2 SET

ASSY.

SERVICE PARTS LIST

AUSTIN-HEALEY 100 SIX (SERIES BN6)

Gearbox with Overdrive—continued

Item No.	Description	Part Number Commencing (E) 60949	Illus. No.	Qty. per Vehicle RHD	Qty. per Vehicle LHD	Unit of Issue	Type of Vehicle	New Part Number	Change Point	Amdt. No.	REMARKS
	Ring assembly—clutch thrust										
1	Spring—clutch	17H5804	FC2	1	1	set					
2	Bridge piece—thrust ring	7H5862	FC3	2	2						
3	Nut for thrust ring	FNN104	FC4	4	4						
4	Washer for nut (tab)	7H5863	FC5	4	4						
5	**Bearing for thrust ring**	7H5866	FC6	1	1						
6	Circlip for bearing (small)	7H5867	FC7	1	1						
7	Circlip for bearing (large)	7H5868	FC8	1	1						
8	Ring—clutch brake	17H5824	FC9	1	1						
9	**Member with lining—clutch sliding**	7H5870	FC10	1	1						
10	**Annulus assembly**	17H5829		1	1						
11	Sun wheel assembly	17H5885	FC11	1	1						
12	Carrier assembly—planet.	17H5836	FC12	1	1						
13	Shaft—planet wheel	17H5844	FC13	8	8						
14	Needle-rollers for wheel	17H5846	FC14	6	6	set					
15	Washer—thrust	17H5845	FC15	8	8						
16	**Annulus**	17H5837	FC16	1	1		Overdrive				
17	Washer—phosphor-bronze—sun wheel thrust—rear	7H5877	FC17	1	1						
18	**Inner member—roller clutch**	7H5879	FC18	1	1						
19	Roller for clutch	17H5828	FC19	1	1	set					
20	Cage for roller	7H5881	FC20	1	1						
21	Ring—spring—for clutch	7H5882	FC21	1	1						
22	Washer—thrust—phosphor-bronze—clutch to annulus	7H5888	FC22	1	1						
23	**Bearing for annulus—front**	2K5507	FC23	1	1						
24	**Bearing for annulus—rear**	7H5884	FC24	1	1						
25	Washer—steel—annulus end-float—.146"	7H5885E	FC25	A/R	A/R						
26	Washer—steel—annulus end-float—.151"	7H5885F		A/R	A/R						
27	Washer—steel—annulus end-float—.156"	7H5885G		A/R	A/R						
28	Washer—steel—annulus end-float—.161"	7H5885H		A/R	A/R						
29	Washer—steel—annulus end-float—.166"	7H5885J		A/R	A/R						

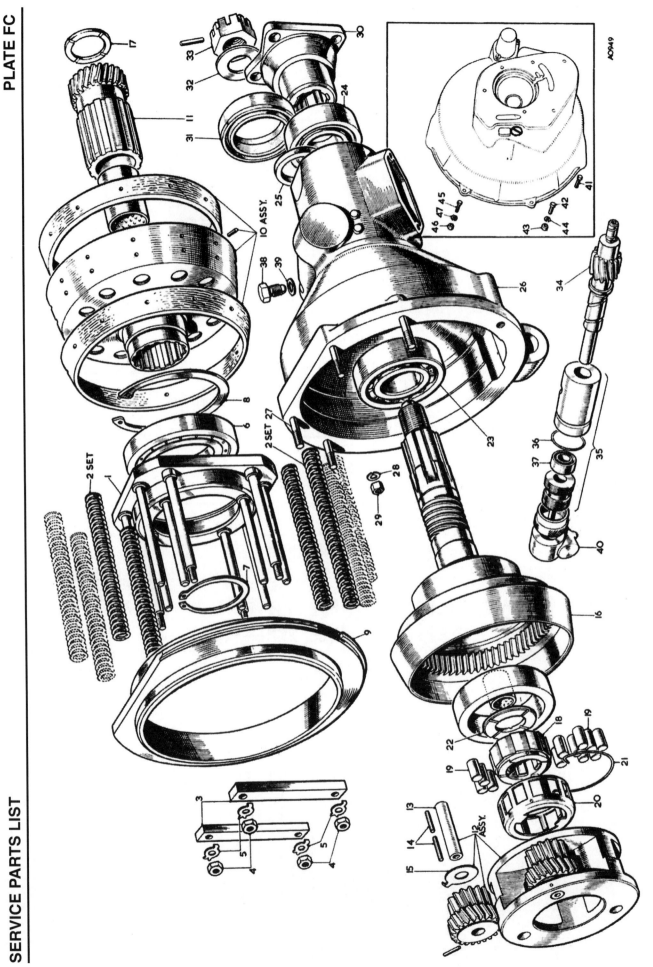

Item No.	DESCRIPTION	Part Number Commencing (E) 60049	Illus. No.	Qty. per Vehicle RHD	Qty. per Vehicle LHD	Unit of Issue	Type of Vehicle	New Part Number	Change Point	Amdt. No.	REMARKS
	Gearbox with Overdrive—*continued*										
	Casing—rear.										
1	Casing—rear	17H5822	FC26	1	1						
2	Stud to front casing	7H5884	FC27	4	4						
3	Washer to front casing (spring)	LWZ205	FC28	6	6	24					
4	Nut to front casing	FNZ105	FC29	6	6						
5	**Flange—coupling**	17H5821	FC30	1	1						
6	Seal for flange—oil	7H5888	FC31	1	1						
7	Washer for flange (plain)	PWN112	FC32	1	1						
8	Nut for flange (slotted)	7H5889	FC33	1	1						
9	**Pinion assembly—speedometer**	17H5820	FC34	1	1						
10	Pinion—speedometer	17H5816	FC35	1	1						
11	Bearing assembly	17H5819	FC36	1	1		Overdrive				
12	'O' ring for bearing	17H5818	FC37	1	1						
13	Seal—oil	N.S.P.	FC38	1	1						
14	Screw—pinion locking	7H5894	FC39	1	1						
15	Washer for screw (spring)	LWZ205	FC40	1	1	24					
16	Adaptor box—speedometer drive	1H8181	FC41	1	1						
17	Bolt—clutch housing to engine (long)	HBN0612	FC42	4	4						
18	Bolt—clutch housing to engine (short)	HBN0611	FC43	4	4						
19	Nut for bolt	FNN106	FC44	5	5						
20	Washer for bolt (spring)	LWN206	FC45	2	2						
21	Dowel bolt—clutch housing to rear plate	AEC3224	FC46	2	2						
22	Nut for dowel bolt	FNN106	FC47	2	2						
23	Washer for nut (spring)	LWN206		2	2						

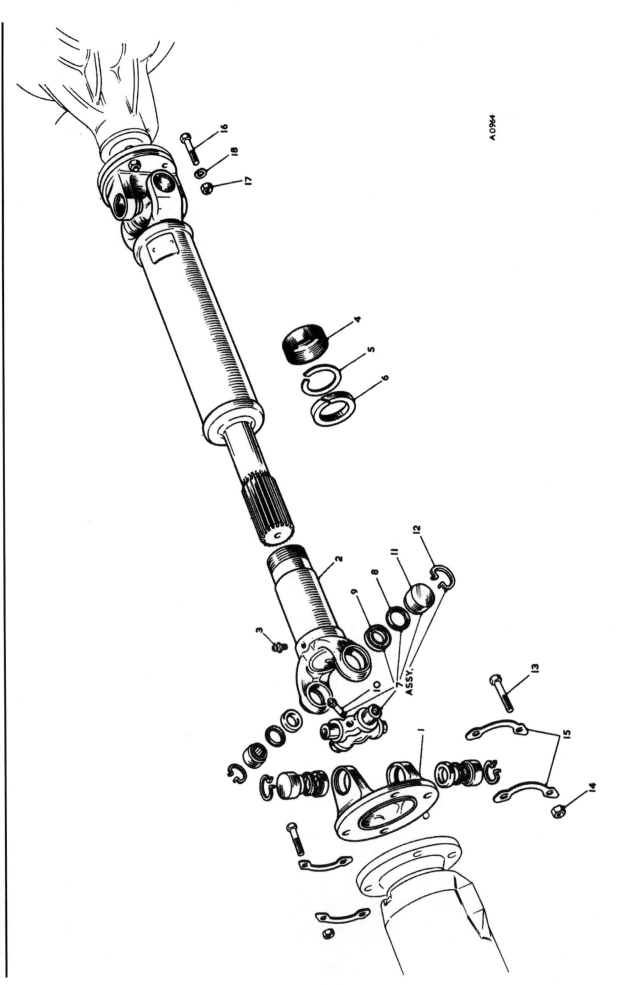

A0964

PROPELLER SHAFT

Item No.	Description	Commencing (C) 501 Part Number	Illus. No.	Qty. per Vehicle RHD	Qty. per Vehicle LHD	Unit of Issue	Type of Vehicle	New Part Number	Change Point	Amdt. No.	Remarks
1	Shaft—propeller .... (R)	1B7439		1	1						
2	Yoke—flange	7H8902	G1	1	1						
3	Yoke—sleeve	7H8905	G2	1	1						
4	Lubricator—sleeve yoke	7H8859	G3	1	1						
5	Cap—dust—for sleeve yoke	7H8835	G4	1	1						
6	Washer for dust cap (steel)	7H8886	G5	1	1						
7	Washer for dust cap (cork)	7H8956	G6	1	1						
8	Journal assembly	8G3001	G7	2	2						
9	Gasket	7H8962	G8	8	8						
10	Retainer—gasket	7H8918	G9	8	8						
11	Lubricator—journal	7H8858	G10	2	2						
12	Bearing assembly—needle	7H8912	G11	8	8						
13	Circlip—bearing	7H8918	G12	8	8						
14	Bolt—flange to gearbox	ATC7071	G13	4	4						
15	Nut for bolt	FNZ106	G14	4	4						
16	Lock washer for nut	1B7886	G15	4	4						
17	Bolt—flange to overdrive	1B7474		4	4		Overdrive				
18	Nut for bolt	FNZ106		4	4		Overdrive				
19	Lock washer for nut	2K5914		4	4		Overdrive				
20	Bolt—flange to bevel pinion	58K1048	G16	4	4						
21	Nut for bolt	LNZ206	G17	4	4						
22	Washer for nut (spring)	LWZ806	G18	4	4						

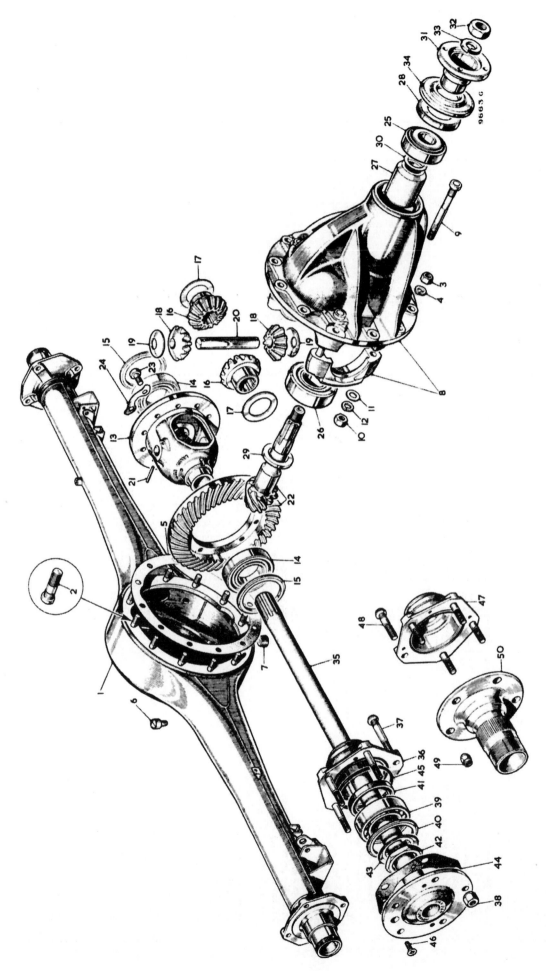

9663 G

SERVICE PARTS LIST

AUSTIN-HEALEY 100 SIX (SERIES BN6)

Item No.	DESCRIPTION	Part Number Commencing (C) 501	Illus. No.	Qty. per Vehicle RHD	LHD	Unit of Issue	Type of Vehicle	New Part Number	Change Point	Amdt. No.	REMARKS
	REAR AXLE AND SUSPENSION										
1	**Rear axle assembly**	**N.S.P.**									
2	**Case assembly**	**AT07315**	**H1**	1	1						
3	Nut—bearing retaining—R.H.T.	ATC7062	H42	1	1						
4	Nut—bearing retaining—L.H.T.	ATC7309		1	1						
5	Bolt—differential carrier	ATC7125	H2	12	12						
6	Nut for bolt	FNZ106	H3	12	12						
7	Washer for nut (spring)	LWZ306	H4	12	12						
8	Washer for bearing retaining nut	ATC7810	H48	2	2						
9	Joint to axle case	ATC7124	H5	1	1	12.					
10	**Breather assembly**	**1G3668**	**H6**	1	1						
11	Plug—drain	6K499	H7	1	1						
12	Plug—filler	6K499		1	1						
13	**Differential assembly** (R)	**AT07290**		1	1						
14	**Differential assembly** (R)	**AT07289**		1	1						
15	**Carrier assembly**	**AT07288**	**H8**	1	1		**Overdrive**				
16	Bolt—serrated—cap	ATC7083	H9	4	4						
17	Nut for bolt	FNN107	H10	4	4						
18	Washer for nut (plain)	ATC7084	H11	4	4						
19	Washer for nut (spring)	LWZ307	H12	4	4						
20	Cage—differential	ATC7189	H18	1	1						
21	Bearing—differential	ATC7110	H14	2	2						
22	Washer—bearing packing—·108″	ATC7268	H15	2	2						
23	Washer—bearing packing—·191″	ATC7267		2	2						
24	Washer—bearing packing—·189″	ATC7266		2	2						
25	Washer—bearing packing—·187″	ATC7061		2	2						Two used of selected size
26	Washer—bearing packing—·185″	ATC7111		2	2						
27	Washer—bearing packing—·183″	ATC7112		2	2						
28	Washer—bearing packing—·181″	ATC7113		2	2						
29	Washer—bearing packing—·179″	ATC7114		2	2						
30	Washer—bearing packing—·177″	ATC7115		2	2						
31	Washer—bearing packing—·175″	ATC7116		2	2						
32	Gear—thrust gear	ATC7262	H16	2	2						
33	Washer—thrust gear	ATC7106	H17	2	2						
34	Pinion	ATC7263	H18	2	2						
35	Washer—thrust pinion	ATC7104	H19	2	2						
36	Pin—pinion	ATC7107	H20	1	1						
37	Peg—pinion pin	ATC7108	H21	1	1						

MODIFICATIONS

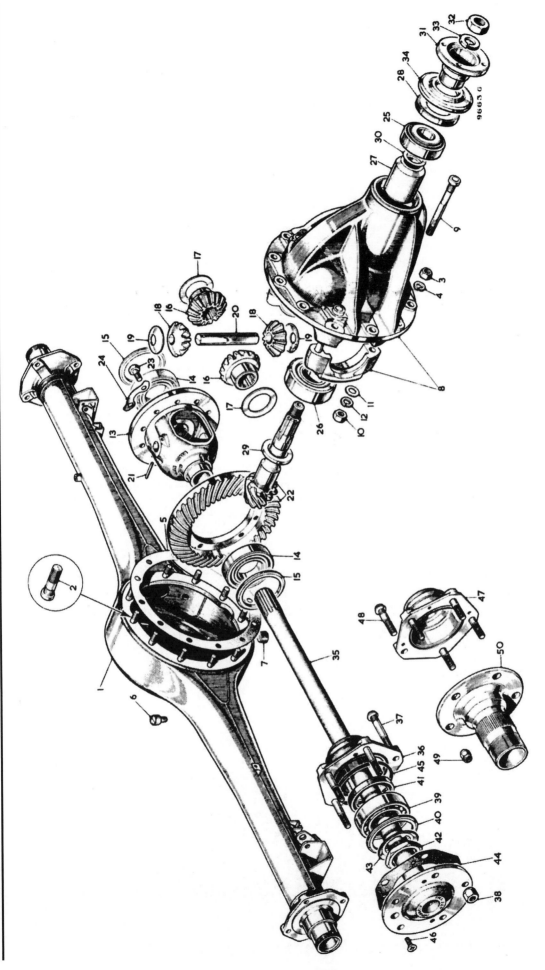

MODIFICATIONS

Item No.	Description	Part Number (Commencing (C) 501)	Illus. No.	Qty. per Vehicle RHD	Qty. per Vehicle LHD	Unit of Issue	Type of Vehicle	New Part Number	Change Point	Amdt. No.	REMARKS
	Rear Axle and Suspension—*continued*										
1	**Crown wheel and pinion**	**ATG7182**	**H22**	1	1						
2	**Crown wheel and pinion**	**ATG7194**		1	1		**Overdrive**				
3	Bolt to cage	ATA7048	H23	10	10						
4	Washer for bolt (lock)	ATC7109	H24	5	5						
5	Washer—pinion thrust—·222″	ATC7092	H29	1	1						One used of selected size
6	Washer—pinion thrust—·220″	ATC7093		1	1						
7	Washer—pinion thrust—·218″	ATC7094		1	1						
8	Washer—pinion thrust—·216″	ATC7095		1	1						
9	Washer—pinion thrust—·214″	ATC7096		1	1						
10	Washer—pinion thrust—·212″	ATC7097		1	1						
11	Washer—pinion thrust—·210″	ATC7098		1	1						
12	Washer—pinion thrust—·208″	ATC7099		1	1						
13	**Bearing—pinion—inner**	**ATG7089**	**H26**	1	1						
14	Distance piece—bearing	ATC7172	H27	1	1						
15	**Bearing—pinion—outer**	**ATG7091**	**H25**	1	1						
16	Shim—outer bearing—·004″	ATC7152	H30	A/R	A/R						
17	Shim—outer bearing—·006″	ATC7153		A/R	A/R						
18	Shim—outer bearing—·008″	ATC7154		A/R	A/R						
19	Shim—outer bearing—·010″	ATC7155		A/R	A/R						
20	Shim—outer bearing—·012″	ATC7156		A/R	A/R						
21	Shim—outer bearing—·020″	ATC7157		A/R	A/R						
22	Shim—outer bearing—·030″	ATC7158		A/R	A/R						
23	Seal—oil	ATC7085	H28	1	1	6.					
24	Cover—dust	ATC7101	H34	1	1						
25	Flange—universal joint	ATC7100	H31	1	1						
26	Nut—flange to pinion	FNZ612	H32	1	1						
27	Washer for nut (spring)	LWZ2212	H33	1	1						
28	**Shaft—axle**	**ATG7394**	**H35**	2	2						
29	Joint—shaft to hub	ATC7065	H44	2	2	12.					
30	Screw—shaft to hub	CMZ0408	H46	2	2						
31	**Hub assembly**	**ATG7343**	**H36**	2	2						
32	Stud—wheel	ATC7344	H87	10	10						Disc wheels only
33	Nut—wheel stud	1G8075	H88	10	10	12.					
34	**Hub assembly**	**ATG7256**	**H47**	2	2						Wire wheels only
35	Stud	ATC7257	H48	10	10						
36	Nut for stud (conical)	ATB7198	H49	10	10						
37	Extension—hub—R/H	ATC7286	H50	1	1						
38	Extension—hub—L/H	ATC7237		1	1						
39	Seal—oil—ring	ATC7857	H45	2	2	12.					
40	Seal—oil	3H1589	H41	2	2	6.					
41	**Bearing**	**ATG7060**	**H39**	2	2						
42	Spacer—bearing	ATC7061	H40	2	2						

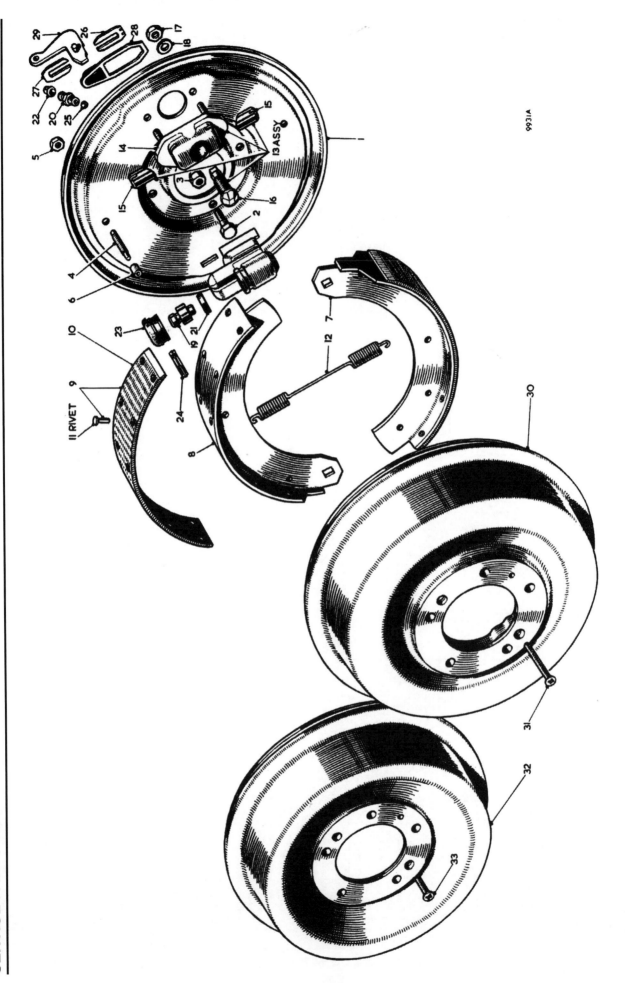

9931A

SERVICE PARTS LIST

AUSTIN-HEALEY 100 SIX (SERIES BN6)

Item No.	DESCRIPTION	Part Number (Commencing (C) 501)	Illus. No.	Qty. per Vehicle RHD	Qty. per Vehicle LHD	Unit of Issue	Type of Vehicle	New Part Number	Change Point	Amdt. No.	REMARKS
	BRAKES										
1	**Plate—brake—R/H**	**1B7437**	**HA1**	1	1						
2	**Plate—brake—L/H**	**1B7438**		1	1						
3	Bolt—brake plate to axle case	ATC7071	HA2	8	8						
4	Nut for bolt	LN2206	HA3	8	8						
5	Post—steady	7H4461	HA4	4	4						
6	Nut for steady post	FN2205	HA5	4	4						
7	Bush for steady post (felt)	7H4429	HA6	4	4						
8	**Shoe assembly—rear brake**	**8G7102**	**HA7**	2	2	set					
9	Shoe assembly	N.S.P.	HA8	4	4						
10	**Liner with rivets**	**8G7069**	**HA9**	1	1	set					
11	Liner	N.S.P.	HA10	4	4						
12	Rivet	7H4089	HA11	48	48						
13	Spring—brake-shoe return	7H4596	HA12	4	4						
14	**Adjuster assembly**	**7H4997**	**HA13**	2	2						
15	Body for adjuster	17H4858	HA14	2	2						
16	Tappet for adjuster	7H4998	HA15	4	4						
17	Wedge for adjuster	1G4116	HA16	2	2						
18	Nut—adjuster to brake plate	7H4999	HA17	4	4						
19	Washer for nut (spring)	2K5863	HA18	4	4	144.					
20	**Cylinder assembly—wheel**	**7H4988**	**HA19**	2	2						
21	Piston for wheel cylinder	7H4992	HA20	2	2						
22	Screw—bleed—for wheel cylinder	7H4973	HA21	2	2						
23	Seal for wheel cylinder	7H4839	HA22	2	2						
24	Cover—dust—for wheel cylinder bleed screw	7H4419	HA23	2	2						
25	Cover—dust—for wheel cylinder piston	7H4917	HA24	2	2						
26	Retainer for piston dust cover	7H4918	HA25	2	2						
27	Ball—bleed	7H4080	HA26	2	2						
28	Spring—retainer wheel cylinder	7H4904	HA27	2	2						
29	Plate—locking—retaining spring	7H4907	HA28	2	2						
30	Cover—dust—wheel cylinder to brake plate	7H4906	HA29	2	2						
31	Lever assembly for hand brake	7H4990	HA30	2	2						
32	**Drum—brake**	**1B7490**	**HA31**	2	2	set					
33	Screw—drum to hub	CMZ0428	HA32	4	4						Disc wheels only
34	**Drum—brake**	1B7526		2	2	set					Wire wheels only
35	Screw—drum to hub	CMZ0414		4	4						
36	**Kit—wheel cylinder repair**	**8G7067**		1	1	set					
37	Seal for wheel cylinder			2	2						
38	Cover—dust—for wheel cylinder bleed screw			2	2						
39	Cover—dust—for wheel cylinder piston			2	2						
40	Retainer for piston dust cover			2	2						
41	Ball—bleed			2	2						
42	**Kit—adjuster**	**8G7070**		2	2	set					
43	Tappet for adjuster			4	4						
44	Wedge for adjuster			2	2						

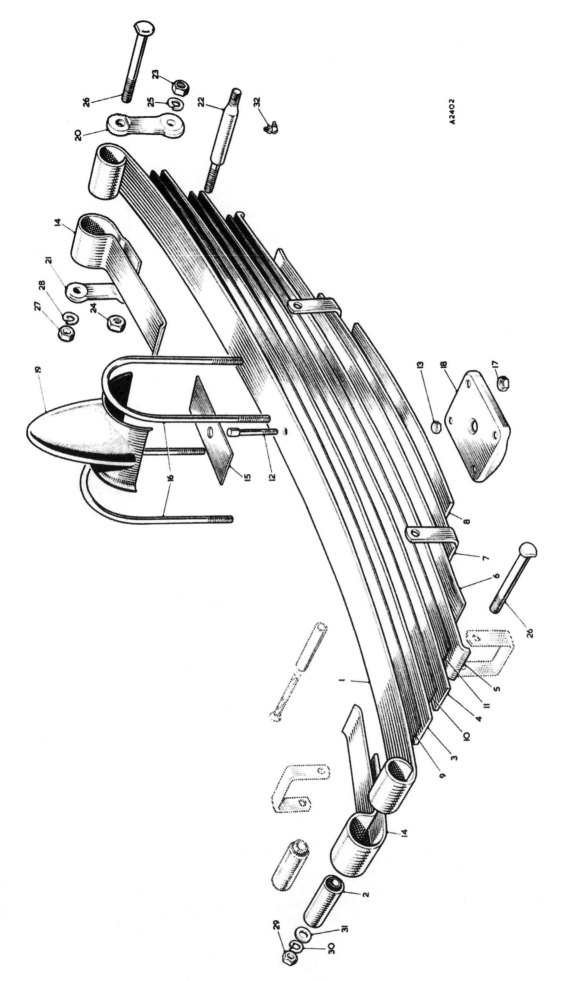

A2402

AUSTIN-HEALEY 100 SIX (SERIES BN6)

Item No.	Description	Commencing (C) 501 Part Number	Illus. No.	Qty. RHD	Qty. LHD	Remarks
	REAR SPRING					
1	**Spring assembly**	**11B5266**		2	2	
2	Leaf—main	1B8930	HB1	2	2	
3	Bush	2H4605	HB2	2	2	⎫ Alternatives
4	Bush	1H5286		4	4	⎭
5	Leaf—second	N.S.P.	HB3	2	2	
6	Leaf—third	N.S.P.	HB4	2	2	
7	Leaf—fourth	N.S.P.	HB5	2	2	
8	Leaf—fifth	N.S.P.	HB6	2	2	
9	Leaf—sixth	N.S.P.	HB7	2	2	
10	Leaf—seventh	N.S.P.	HB8	2	2	
11	Leaf—zinc—top	1B8762	HB9	2	2	
12	Leaf—zinc—second	1B8763	HB10	2	2	
13	Leaf—zinc—third	1B8764	HB11	2	2	
14	Toe bolt	2A5006	HB12	2	2	
15	Nut for toe bolt	FNZ104	HB13	4	4	
16	Spring eye reinforcement	11B5199	HB14	4	4	
17	Pad (fibre)	1G5758	HB15	2	2	
18	Clip for spring	11B5070	HB16	4	4	
19	Nut for clip	LNZ206	HB17	8	8	
20	Plate for spring clip	11B5071	HB18	2	2	
21	Buffer for spring	11B5068	HB19	2	2	
22	Shackle—rear spring outer	1A9222	HB20	2	2	
23	Shackle—rear spring inner	1A9223	HB21	2	2	
24	Pin—shackle bottom	1G9820	HB22	2	2	
25	Nut for pin	FNZ106	HB23	2	2	
26	Locknut	FNZ206	HB24	4	4	
27	Washer for nut (spring)	LWZ206	HB25	2	2	
28	Pin—rear spring—top and front	1G9821	HB26	4	4	
29	Nut for top pin	FNZ107	HB27	2	2	
30	Washer for nut (spring)	LWZ207	HB28	2	2	
31	Nut for front pin	FNZ107	HB29	2	2	
32	Washer for nut (spring)	LWZ207	HB30	2	2	
33	Washer for nut (plain)	PWZ107	HB31	2	2	
34	Nipple—grease	2A5893	HB32	2	2	
	TIE-ROD					
35	Rod assembly—tie	1B7866		1	1	
36	Nut (lock)	58K1893		2	2	
37	Bush (rubber)	3H8079		4	4	
38	Bush for bush	2K6842		2	2	
39	Washer for bush	1B8811		2	2	
40	Bracket for tie-rod	1B7470		1	1	
41	Bolt fixing bracket	HZS0407		2	2	
42	Nut for bolt	FNZ106		2	2	
43	Washer for nut (spring)	LWZ306		2	2	

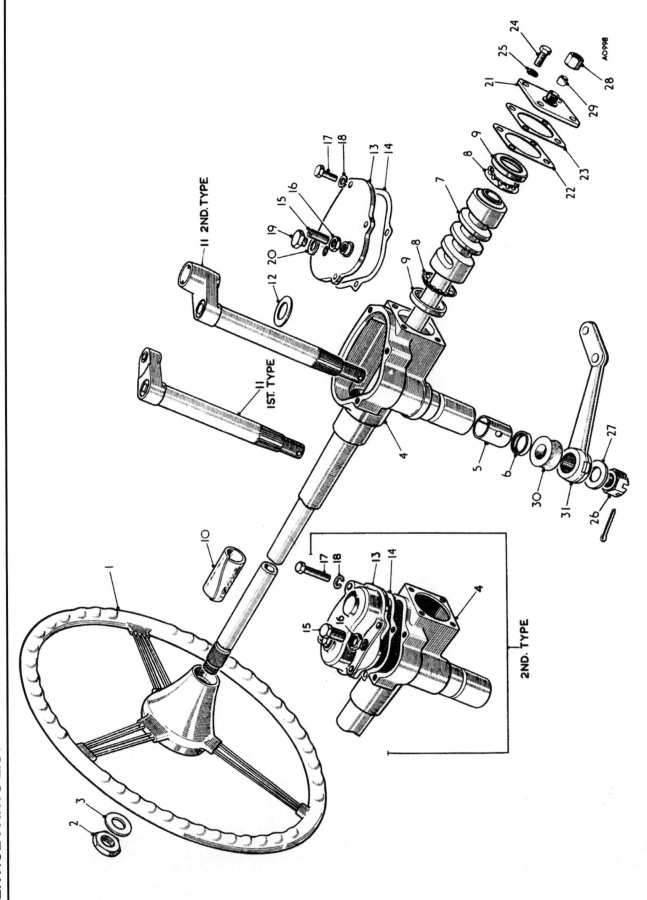

AUSTIN-HEALEY 100 SIX (SERIES BN6)

S T E E R I N G

Item No.	Description	Commencing (C) 501 Part Number	Illus. No.	RHD	LHD	Unit of Issue	Type of Vehicle	New Part Number	Change Point	Amdt. No.	Remarks
1	Wheel—steering	8G624	J1	1	1						
2	Nut for steering-wheel	2K6057	J2	1	1						
3	Washer for nut (shakeproof)	2K8929	J3	1	1						
4	Gear assembly—steering	1B6274		1				1B6348; AHB8388	Com. (C) 1995; Com. (C) 3395		
5	Gear assembly—steering	1B6276			1			1B6350; AHB8389	Com. (C) 1995; Com. (C) 3395		
6	Box and outer column	17H6120	J4	1				17H6214; 17H6109	Com. (C) 1995; Com. (C) 3395		
7	Box and outer column	17H6121			1			17H6216; 17H6107	Com. (C) 1995; Com. (C) 3395		
8	Bush	1B6257	J5	1	1						
9	Seal—oil	7H6589	J6	1	1						
10	Column with cam	7H6607	J7	1	1			17H6215; 17H6110	Com. (C) 1995; Com. (C) 3395		
11	Column with cam	7H6608	J8	1	1			17H6108	Com. (C) 1995		
12	Cage assembly—ball	7H6079	J9	2	2	12.					
13	Cup for ball cage	7H6116	J10	2	2	6.					
14	Bush (felt)	ACH5297		1	1						
15	Shaft—rocker	7H6609	J11	1	1			17H6106; 7H6507	Com. (C) 1995		
16	Roller assembly—cam	7H6620	J12	1	1						
17	Washer (Belleville)			6	6						
18	Cover—side	7H6606	J13	1	1			7H6599			
19	Cover—side	7H6610						7H6598; 7H6515	Com. (C) 1995		
20	Joint washer for side cover	7H6604	J14	1	1			17H6108			
21	Screw—thrust	17H6098	J15	1	1			7H6155			
22	Nut for screw (lock)	7H6229	J16	1	1			HB20512			
23	Bolt for side cover	HNS0506		2	2						
24	Bolt for side cover	HNS0506	J17	4/2	4/2						Quantity reduced at (C) 1995
25	Washer for bolt (spring)	LWZ205	J18	4	4	24.					
26	Plug—oil	7H6391	J19	1	1						
27	Washer for plug	7H6392	J20	1	1						
28	Cover—end	7H6267	J21	1	1						
29	Joint washer for end cover	7H6180	J22	1	1						
30	Shim—.0024" thick	7H6118	J23	A/R	A/R						
31	Shim—.005" thick	7H6128		A/R	A/R						
32	Shim—.010" thick	7H6129		A/R	A/R						
33	Bolt for end cover	HNS0506		4	4	24.					
34	Washer for bolt (spring)	LWZ205	J24	4	4						
35	Nut—lever to gear	7H6436	J25	1	1						
36	Washer for nut	7H6024	J26	1	1						
37	Nut for stator tube	7H6167	J27	1	1						
38	Olive	3H660	J28	1	1						
39	Cover—dust—for oil seal (rubber)	1G6286	J29	1	1						
40	Lever for steering side- and cross-tube	1B6277	J30	1	1						
41	Lever for steering side- and cross-tube	1B6278	J31	1	1						

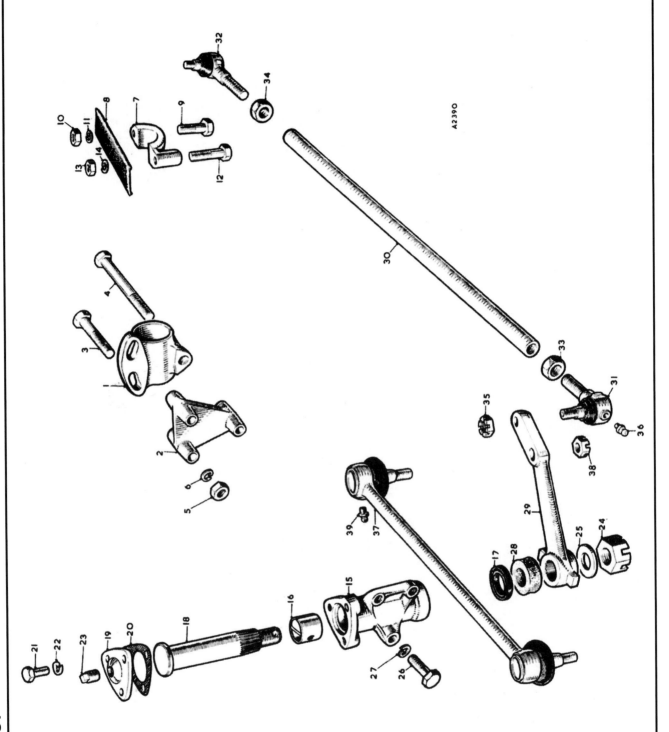

A2390

SERVICE PARTS LIST

AUSTIN-HEALEY 100 SIX (SERIES BN6)

Item No.	DESCRIPTION	Commencing (C) 501 Part Number	Illus. No.	Qty. per Vehicle RHD	Qty. per Vehicle LHD	Unit of Issue	Type of Vehicle	MODIFICATIONS New Part Number	MODIFICATIONS Change Point	MODIFICATIONS Amdt. No.	REMARKS
	Steering—*continued*										
1	**Bracket—steering box**	**1B6127**	**JA1**	1	1						
2	Spacer for bracket	1B6195	JA2	2	2						
3	Bolt—bracket to body (short)	HBZ0626	JA3	2	2						
4	Bolt—bracket to body (long)	HBZ0688	JA4	1	1						
5	Nut for bolt	FNZ106	JA5	8	8						
6	Washer for nut (spring)	LWZ306	JA6	8	8						
7	Clamp—half—steering column support	1B6199	JA7	2	2						
8	Piece—packing (rubber)	4B2502	JA8	1	1						
9	Bolt—short—for clamp half	52K1551	JA9	1	1						
10	Nut for bolt	FNZ104	JA10	1	1						
11	Washer for nut (spring)	LWZ304	JA11	1	1						
12	Bolt—long—for clamp half	HBZ0524	JA12	1	1						
13	Nut for bolt	FNZ105	JA13	1	1						
14	Washer for nut (spring)	LWZ305	JA14	1	1						
15	**Gear assembly—idler**	**1B6281**	**JA15**	1							
16	**Gear assembly—idler**	1B6286			1						
17	**Body—idler**	1B6282	JA16	2	2						
18	**Body—idler**	**1B6287**	**JA18**	1	1						
19	Bush	1B6257	JA19	1	1						
20	Seal—oil	1B6256	JA20	A/R	A/R	12					
21	**Shaft—idler**	**1B6258**	**JA21**	1	1						
22	Cover	1B6187	JA22	1	1						
23	Joint for cover	1B6188	JA23	1	1						
24	Screw for cover	HZS0506	JA24	8	8						
25	Washer for screw (spring)	LWZ305	JA25	8	8						
26	Plug—filler	2K8209	JA26	1	1						
27	Nut for idler shaft	51K870	JA27	1	1						
28	Washer for nut (plain)	PWZ112	JA28	1	1						
29	Screw—idler gear to body	HBZ0624	JA29	8	8						
30	Washer for screw (spring)	LWZ306		8	8						
31	Cover—dust—for oil seal (rubber)	1G6286		1	1						
32	**Lever—side- and cross-tube (idler gear)**	**1B6278**	**JA30**	1							
33	**Lever—side- and cross-tube (idler gear)**	1B6277	JA31		1						
34	**Rod—cross**	**1B6340**	JA32	1	1						
35	**End assembly—R.H.T.**	**1G6353**	**JA31**	1	1						
36	**End assembly—L.H.T.**	1G6354	JA32	1	1						
37	Nut (lock)—R.H.T.	51K820	JA33	1	1						
38	Nut (lock)—L.H.T.	51K365	JA34	1	1						
39	Nut for ball pin	FNZ307	JA35	2	2						
40	Lubricator	3H1709	JA36	2	2						
41	**Rod assembly—side**	**1B6292**	**JA37**	2	2						
42	Nut for ball pin	FNZ307	JA38	4	4						
43	Lubricator	3H1709	JA39	4	4						

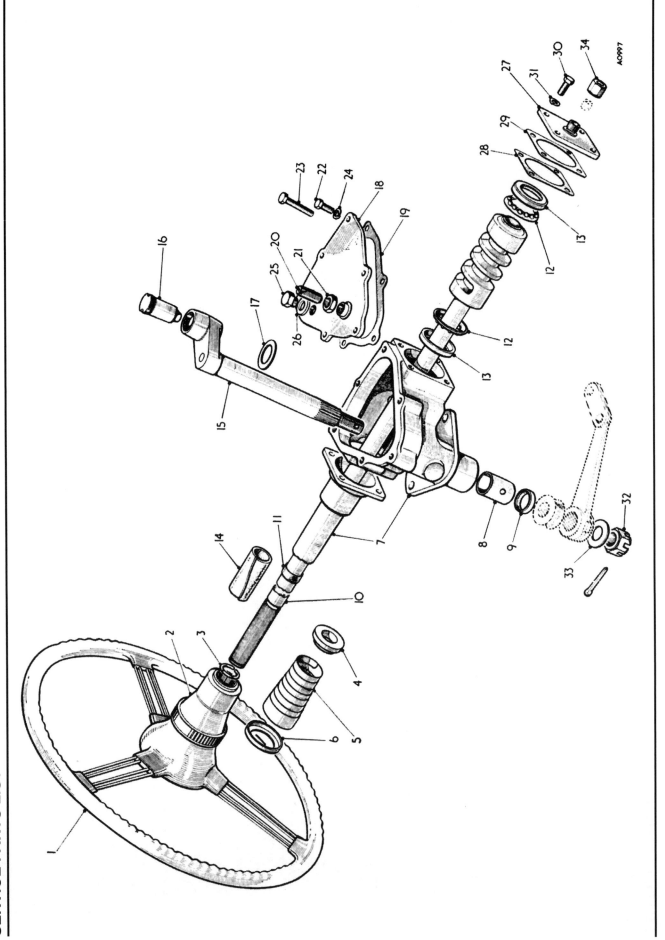

A0997

SERVICE PARTS LIST

Item No.	DESCRIPTION	Commencing (C) 501 Part Number	Illus. No.	Qty. per Vehicle RHD	Qty. per Vehicle LHD	Unit of Issue	Type of Vehicle	New Part Number	Change Point	Amdt. No.	REMARKS
	ADJUSTABLE STEERING (Optional Extra)										
1	**Wheel—steering**	**1B6299**	**JB1**	1	1						
2	Nut—clamping	1B6300	JB2	1	1						
3	Ring—spring	1F6153	JB3	1	1						
4	Support—telescopic spring dust cover	1B6214	JB4	1	1						
5	Cover—telescopic spring dust	1D6182	JB5	1	1						
6	Cup for dust cover	1B6301	JB6		1						
7	**Gear assembly—steering**	**AHB8314**			1						
8	**Gear assembly—steering**	**AHB8312**	**JB7**	1							
9	**Box and outer column**	17H6161			1						
10	**Box and outer column**	17H6163		1							
11	Bush	1B6257	JB8	1	1						
12	Seal—oil	7H6589	JB9	1	1						
13	**Column with cam**	17H6162	**JB10**		1						
14	**Column with cam**	17H6164		1							
15	Ring—(rubber)	7H6460	JB11	2	2						
16	Cage assembly—ball	7H6079	JB12	2	2						
17	Cup for ball cage	7H6116	JB13	2	2	6					
18	Bush—felt	ACA5297	JB14	1	1						
19	**Shaft—rocker**	**17H6106**	**JB15**	1	1						
20	Roller assembly—cam	7H6507	JB16	1	1						
21	Washer (Belleville)	7H6620	JB17	6	6						
22	**Cover—side**	**7H6599**	**JB18**	1	1						
23	**Cover—side**	7H6598		1	1						
24	Joint washer for side cover	17H6515	JB19	1	1	12					
25	Screw—thrust	17H6103	JB20	1	1						
26	Nut for screw (lock)	7H6155	JB21	1	1						
27	Bolt for side cover (¾″)	HNS0506	JB22	2	2						
28	Bolt for side cover (1¼″)	HBZ0512	JB23	2	2						
29	Washer for bolt (spring)	LWZ205	JB24	4	4	24					
30	Plug—oil	7H6391	JB25	1	1						
31	Washer for plug	7H6392	JB26	1	1						
32	**Cover—end**	**7H6267**	**JB27**	1	1						
33	Joint washer for end cover	7H6130	JB28	1	1						
34	Shim—.0024″ thick	7H6118	JB29	A/R	A/R						
35	Shim—.005″ thick	7H6128		A/R	A/R						
36	Shim—.010″ thick	7H6129		A/R	A/R						
37	Bolt for end cover	HNS0506	JB30	4	4						
38	Washer for bolt (spring)	LWZ205	JB31	4	4	24					
39	Nut—lever to gear	7H6436	JB32	1	1						
40	Washer for nut	7H6024	JB33	1	1						
41	Nut for stator tube	7H6167	JB34	1	1						

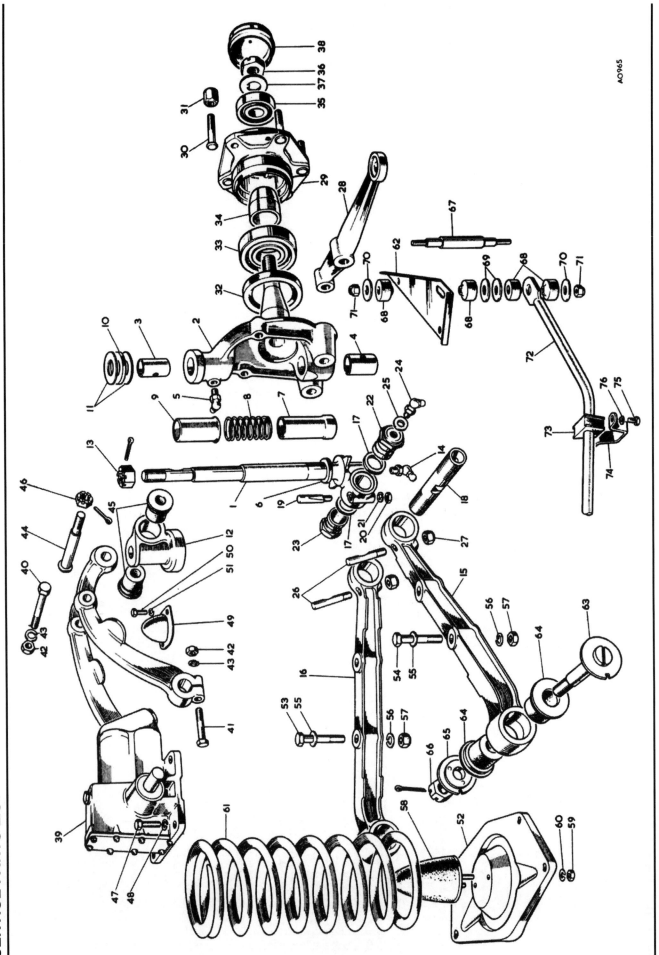

A0965

SERVICE PARTS LIST

AUSTIN-HEALEY 100 SIX (SERIES BN6)

FRONT AXLE AND SUSPENSION

Item No.	DESCRIPTION	Part Number (Commencing (C) 501)	Illus. No.	Qty RHD	Qty LHD	Unit of Issue	REMARKS
1	Front suspension assembly—R/H	N.S.P.		1	1		
2	Front suspension assembly—L/H	N.S.P.		1	1		
3	Pin—swivel	1G4345	K1	2	2		
4	Axle assembly—swivel	1B4517	K2	2	2		
5	Swivel bush (top)	1A4744	K3	2	2	12.	
6	Swivel bush (bottom)	1A4745	K4	2	2	12.	
7	Lubricator for swivel pin (top)	3H2192	K5	2	2		
8	Ring—cork—swivel axle pin	1A4746	K6	2	2	12.	
9	Tube—dust excluder (bottom)	1A4756	K7	2	2		
10	Spring for dust excluder	2K8951	K8	2	2		
11	Tube—dust excluder (top)	1G4271	K9	2	2		
12	Washer—thrust	1A4751	K10	2	2		
13	Washer—floating thrust—·052 to ·057"	1A4752	K11	A/R	A/R		
14	Washer—floating thrust—·058 to ·063"	1A4753		A/R	A/R		
15	Washer—floating thrust—·064 to ·069"	1A4754		A/R	A/R		
16	Trunnion—suspension link	1A4760	K12	2	2		
17	Nut—swivel axle pin	51K829	K13	2	2	36.	
18	Lubricator for swivel pin (lower)	8H8028	K14	2	2		
19	Link—lower—L/H front and R/H rear	1B4365	K15	2	2		
20	Link—lower—R/H front and L/H rear	1B4366	K16	2	2		
21	Ring for fulcrum pin—lower link	1G4505	K17	4	4	36.	
22	Pin—fulcrum—lower link	1A4788	K18	2	2	6.	
23	Pin—cotter—fulcrum pin to swivel pin	51K1764	K19	2	2		⎤ Alternatives
24	Pin—cotter—fulcrum pin to swivel pin	51K1770	K20	2	2		⎦
25	Nut for cotter	FNZ104	K21	2	2		
26	Washer for nut (spring)	LWZ204	K22	2	2	36.	
27	Bush—lower link front end	1G4346	K23	2	2	12.	
28	Bush—lower link rear end	1G4848	K24	2	2		
29	Lubricator for lower link front bush	8H8028	K25	2	2		
30	Washer for lubricator	2K4974	K26	4	4		
31	Pin—cotter—lower link to swivel pin fulcrum	1G4350	K27	4	4		
32	Nut for cotter	58K1662	K28	1	1		
33	Lever—steering—on swivel axle—R/H	1B4475	K29	1	1		
34	Lever—steering—on swivel axle—L/H	1B4476		1	1		
35	Hub assembly	1B4407	K30	10	10		
36	Stud—wheel	1G7435	K31	10	10	12.	
37	Nut for wheel stud	1G8075	K32	2	2	12.	
38	Seal—oil	8G554	K33	2	2		
39	Bearing for hub—inner	1G4400	K34	2	2		
40	Distance piece for bearing	1B4411		2	2		⎤ Alternatives
41	Distance piece for bearing	1B4552	K35	2	2		⎦ Disc wheels only
42	Bearing for hub—outer	1B4409	K36	2	2		
43	Nut for swivel axle	51K330	K37	2	2		
44	Washer for nut	1A4742	K38	2	2		
45	Cup—grease retainer	ATC4178		2	2		

(Modifications columns — Type of Vehicle, New Part Number, Change Point, Amdt. No. — all blank.)

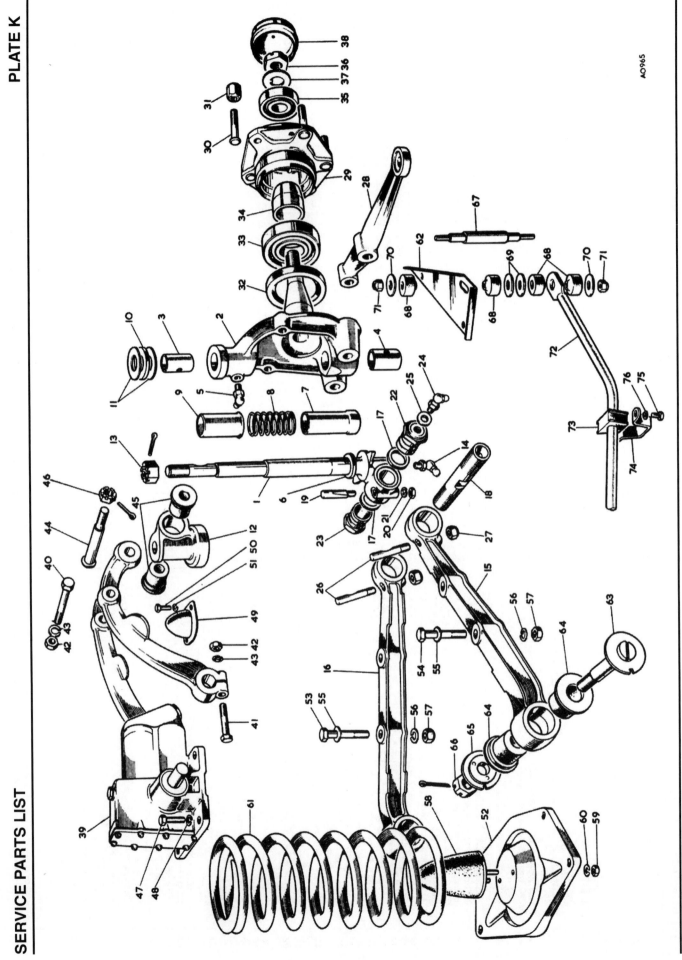

AO965

SERVICE PARTS LIST

AUSTIN-HEALEY 100 SIX (SERIES BN6)

Item No.	DESCRIPTION	Commencing (C) 501 Part Number	Illus. No.	Qty. per Vehicle RHD	LHD	Unit of Issue	Type of Vehicle	New Part Number	Change Point	Amdt. No.	REMARKS
	Front Axle and Suspension—*continued*										
1	**Hub assembly—R/H**	**1B4478**		1	1						
2	**Hub assembly—L/H**	**1B4481**		1	1						
3	Stud—wheel	1B4416		8	8						
4	Nut for wheel stud	FNZ507		8	8						
5	Washer for nut (spring)	LWZ307		8	8						
6	Seal—oil	8G554		2	2	12.					Wire wheels only
7	**Bearing for hub—inner**	**1B4399**		2	2						
8	Distance piece for bearing	1B4527		2	2						
9	Shim (·008")	1B4528		A/R	A/R						
10	Shim (·005")	1B4529		A/R	A/R						
11	Shim (·010")	1B4530		A/R	A/R						
12	**Bearing for hub—outer**	**1B4400**		2	2						
13	Nut to swivel axle	51K880		2	2						
14	Washer for nut	1B4892		2	2						
15	Cup—grease retainer	1B4816		2	2						
16	**Absorber—shock**	**1B4459**	**K39**	2	2						
17	Bolt for shock absorber arms	HBZ0620	K40	2	2						
18	Bolt—clamping—shock absorber arms to shaft.	HBZ0616	K41	2	2						
19	Nut for bolt	FNZ106	K42	4	4						
20	Washer for nut (spring)	LWZ306	K43	4	4						
21	Pin—fulcrum—trunnion	1G4349	K44	2	2						
22	Bearing—top link	8G621	K45	4	4	12.					
23	Nut for fulcrum pin	FNZ407	K46	2	2						

K.2

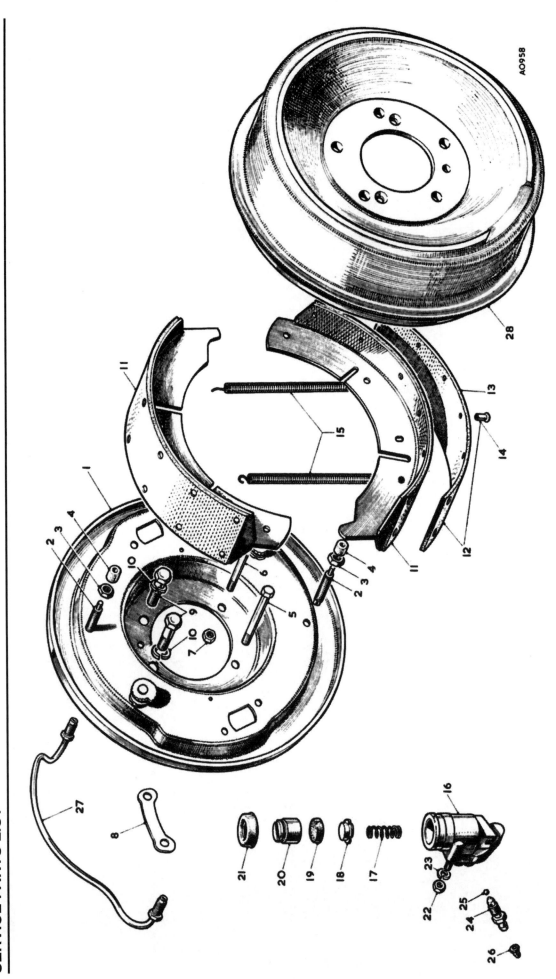

A0958

Item No.	Description	Part Number (Commencing (C) 501)	Illus. No.	RHD	LHD	Unit of Issue	Type of Vehicle	New Part Number	Change Point	Amdt. No.	REMARKS
	Front Axle and Suspension—*continued*										
1	**Plate—brake—R/H**	**1B4451**	**KA1**	1	1						Disc wheels only
2	**Plate—brake—L/H**	**1B4453**		1	1						Disc wheels only
3	**Plate—brake—R/H**	**1B4496**		1	1						Wire wheels only
4	**Plate—brake—L/H**	**1B4497**		1	1						Wire wheels only
5	Post—steady	7H4461	KA2	4	4						
6	Nut for steady post	FNZ205	KA3	4	4						
7	Bush for steady post (felt)	7H4429	KA4	4	4						
8	Bolt—brake plate and steering lever to axle (long)	HBZ0728	KA5	2	2						
9	Bolt—brake plate and steering lever to axle (short)	HBZ0726	KA6	2	2						
10	Nut for bolt	FNZ507	KA7	4	4						
11	Washer for bolt (lock)	1B4457	KA8	4	4						
12	Screw—brake plate to axle	1B4454	KA9	4	4						
13	Washer for screw (spring)	LWZ306	KA10	4	4						
14	**Shoe assembly—brake—R/H**	**8G8159**	**KA11**	1	1	set					
15	Shoe assembly—brake	N.S.P.		2	2						
16	**Shoe assembly—brake—L/H**	**8G8160**		1	1	set					
17	Shoe assembly—brake	N.S.P.		2	2						
18	**Liner with rivets**	**8G7069**	**KA12**	1	1	set					
19	Liner	N.S.P.	KA13	4	4						
20	Rivets	7H4989	KA14	48	48						
21	Spring—brake-shoe return	7H4259	KA15	4	4						
22	Spring—brake-shoe return	7H4581		4	4						
23	**Cylinder assembly—wheel—R/H**	**17H4003**		2	2						Disc wheels only
24	**Cylinder assembly—wheel—L/H**	**17H4004**		2	2						Wire wheels only
25	Body—R/H	N.S.P.	KA16	2	2						
26	Body—L/H	N.S.P.		2	2						Disc wheels only
27	Spring	7H4439	KA17	4	4						
28	Support—seal	17H4006	KA18	4	4						
29	Seal	7H4873	KA19	4	4						
30	Piston	17H4481	KA20	4	4						
31	Cover—dust—for piston	7H4745	KA21	4	4						
32	**Cylinder assembly—wheel—R/H**	**7H4584**		2	2						
33	**Cylinder assembly—wheel—L/H**	**7H4583**		2	2						
34	Body—R/H	N.S.P.		2	2						
35	Body—L/H	N.S.P.		2	2						
36	Spring	7H4406		4	4						Wire wheels only
37	Support—seal	17H4558		4	4						
38	Seal	7H4873		4	4						
39	Piston	7H4585		4	4						
40	Cover—dust—for piston	7H4600		4	4						
41	Nut—cylinder to brake plate	FNZ105	KA22	8	8						
42	Washer for nut (spring)	LWZ205	KA23	8	8						Disc wheels only
43	Nut—cylinder to brake plate	FNZI04		8	8	24					
44	Washer for nut (shakeproof)	17H4082		8	8						Wire wheels only

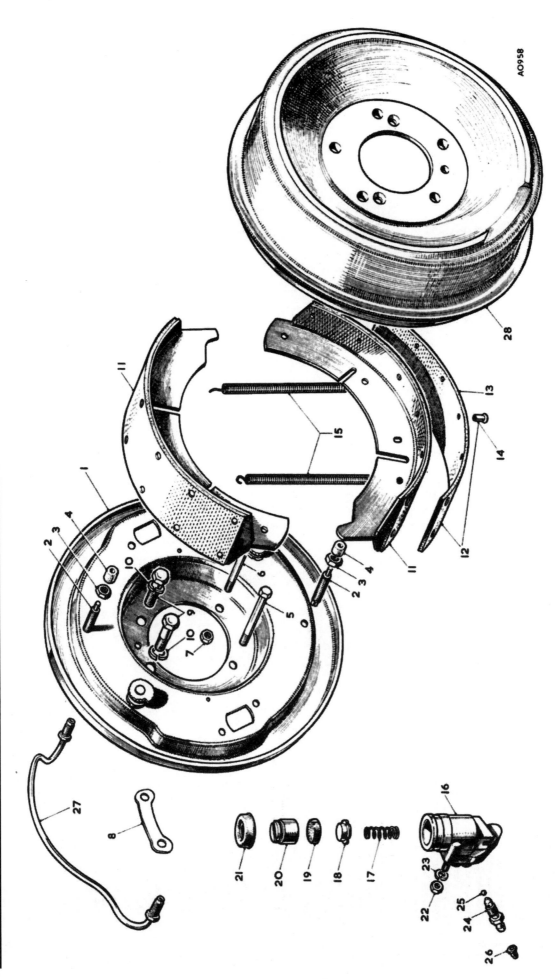

AO958

SERVICE PARTS LIST

AUSTIN-HEALEY 100 SIX (SERIES BN6)

Item No.	DESCRIPTION	Commencing (C) 501 Part Number	Illus. No.	Qty. per Vehicle RHD	Qty. per Vehicle LHD	Unit of Issue	Type of Vehicle	New Part Number	Change Point	Amdt. No.	REMARKS
	Front Axle and Suspension—continued										
1	Screw—bleeder	7H4973	KA24	2	2						Disc wheels only
2	Screw—bleeder	7H4868		2	2						Wire wheels only
3	Ball for bleed screw	7H4080	KA25	2	2						
4	Cover—dust—for bleed screw	7H4419	KA26	2	2						
5	**Pipe—brake—R/H**	1B4490	**KA27**	1	1						**Disc wheels only**
6	**Pipe—brake—L/H**	1B4490		1	1						**Disc wheels only**
7	**Pipe—brake—R/H**	1B8358		1	1						**Wire wheels only**
8	**Pipe—brake—L/H**	1B8358		1	1						**Wire wheels only**
9	**Drum—brake**	1B7422	**KA28**	2	2						**Disc wheels only**
10	Screw—drum to hub	CMZ0414		4	4						**Disc wheels only**
11	**Drum—brake**	1B4570		2	2						**Wire wheels only**
12	**Kit for wheel cylinder repair**	8G8201		1	1	set					Disc wheels only
13	Seal			4	4						Disc wheels only
14	Cover—dust—for piston			4	4						Disc wheels only
15	Ball for bleed screw			2	2						Disc wheels only
16	Cover—dust—for bleed screw			2	2						Disc wheels only
17	**Kit for wheel cylinder repair**	8G8145		1	1	set					Wire wheels only
18	Seal			4	4						Wire wheels only
19	Cover—dust—for piston			4	4						Wire wheels only
20	Ball for bleed screw			2	2						Wire wheels only
21	Cover—dust—for bleed screw			2	2						Wire wheels only

K.4

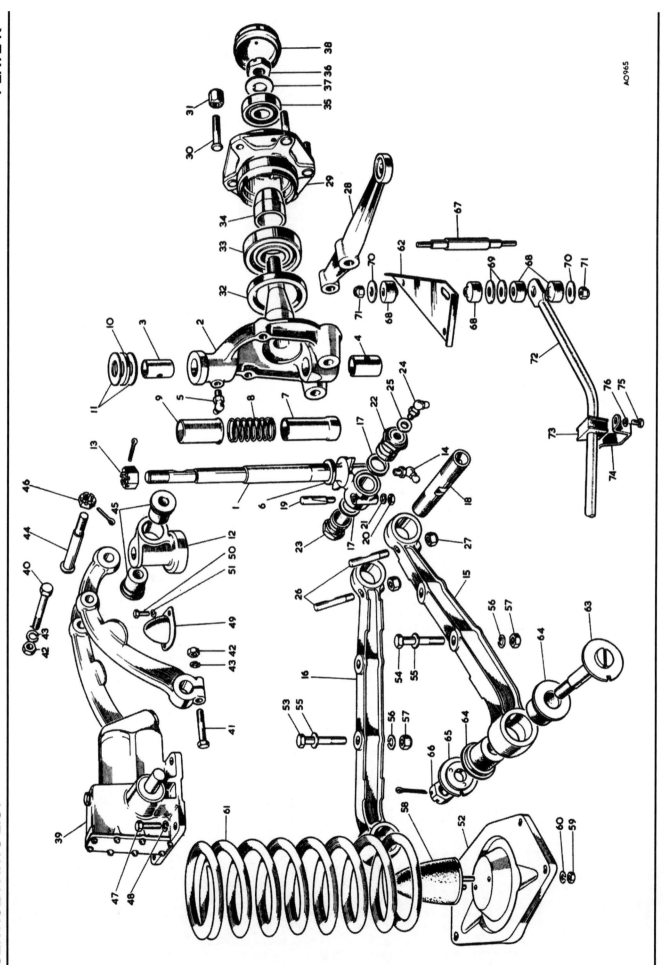

AO965

130

SERVICE PARTS LIST

AUSTIN-HEALEY 100 SIX (SERIES BN6)

Item No.	DESCRIPTION	Commencing (C) 501 Part Number	Illus. No.	Qty. per Vehicle RHD	LHD	Unit of Issue	Type of Vehicle	New Part Number	Change Point	Amdt. No.	REMARKS
	Front Axle and Suspension—*continued*										
1	Set screw—shock absorber to frame	HZS0608	K47	8	8						
2	Washer for screw (spring)	LWZ306	K48	8	8						
	Buffer—rebound										
3		1G4276	K49	2	2						
4	Screw—rebound buffer to frame	HZS0405	K50	4	4						
5	Washer for screw (spring)	LWZ304	K51	4	4						
6	Seat—spring	1G-4279	K52	2	2						
7	Bolt—spring seat to lower link	HBZ0618	K53	4	4						
8	Bolt—spring seat and anti-roll plate to lower link	HBZ0620	K54	4	4						
9	Washer for bolt	PWZ106	K55	8	8						
10	Washer for bolt (spring)	LWZ306	K56	8	8						
11	Nut for bolt	LNZ206	K57	8	8						
	Bumper—front suspension										
12		1B4501	K58	2	2						
13	Nut—suspension bumper to spring seat	FNZ105	K59	4	4						
14	Washer for nut (spring)	LWZ205	K60	4	4	24.					
	Spring—road (coil)										
15		1B4569	K61	2	2						
16	Plate—anti-roll bar—R/H	1B7354	K62	1	1						
17	Plate—anti-roll bar—L/H	1B7355	K62	1	1						
18	Pin—fulcrum—for lower links	1B4513	K63	4	4						
	Bearing for lower link										
19		8G622	K64	8	8	12.					
20	Washer for fulcrum pin	1A4785	K65	4	4						
21	Nut for fulcrum pin	FNZ408	K66	4	4						
22	Link—anti-roll bar	1B4486	K67	2	2						
23	Bush for link	3H8079	K68	8	8						
24	Washer—link bush (top)	2K6842	K69	4	4						
25	Washer—link bush (bottom)	6K9582	K70	4	4						
26	Nut for link (lock)	LNZ305	K71	4	4						
27	Bar—anti-roll	1B4525	K72	1	1						
28	Bearing for anti-roll bar (rubber)	1B4526	K73	2	2						
29	Strap—anti-roll bearing	1B7856	K74	2	2						
30	Set screw for bearing strap	HZS0506	K75	4	4						
31	Washer for screw (spring)	LWZ205	K76	4	4	24.					

PLATE L

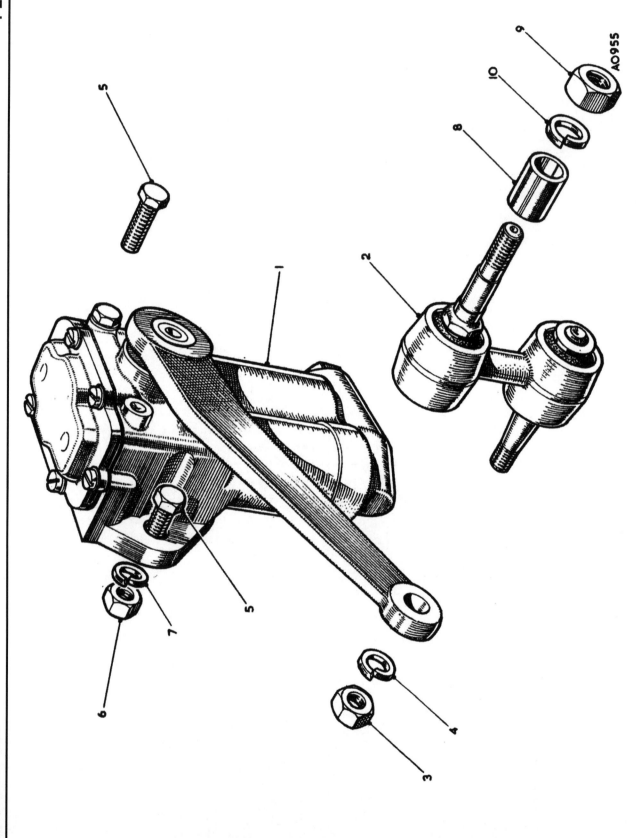

AO955

SERVICE PARTS LIST

AUSTIN-HEALEY 100 SIX (SERIES BN6)

REAR SHOCK ABSORBERS

Item No.	Description	Part Number (Commencing (C) 501)	Illus. No.	Qty. RHD	Qty. LHD
1	Shock absorber—rear R/H	1B7472	L1	1	1
2	Shock absorber—rear L/H	1B7473	L1	1	1
3	Link complete	1B7463	L2	2	2
4	Nut—link to arm	FNZ106	L3	2	2
5	Washer for nut (spring)	LWZ106	L4	4	4
6	Bolt—shock absorber to frame	53K1025	L5	4	4
7	Nut for bolt	FNZ506	L6	4	4
8	Washer for nut (spring)	LWZ106	L7	4	4
9	Distance tube—link to axle bracket	1B7464	L8	2	2
10	Nut for link pin	FNZ107	L9	2	2
11	Washer for nut (spring)	LWZ107	L10	2	2

133

L.1

A2407

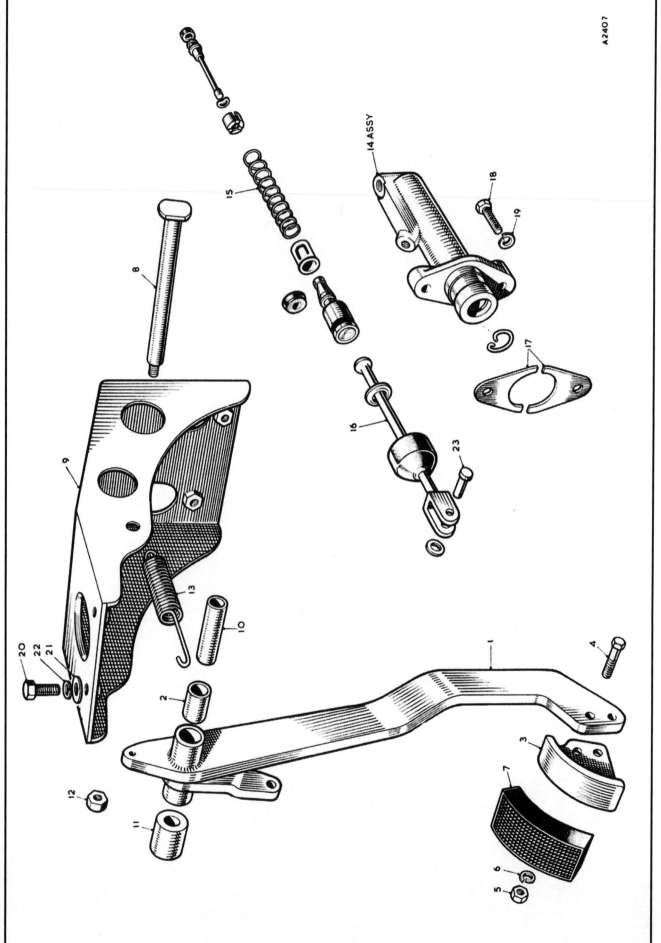

AUSTIN-HEALEY 100 SIX (SERIES BN6)

Item No.	DESCRIPTION	Commencing (C) 501 Part Number	Illus. No.	Qty. per Vehicle RHD	Qty. per Vehicle LHD	Unit of Issue	Type of Vehicle	New Part Number	Change Point	Amdt. No.	REMARKS
	BRAKE CONTROLS										
1	Pedal lever	11B5268	M1	1	1						
2	Bush	1G9810	M2	2	2						
3	Pad—pedal	1B8750	M3	1	1						
4	Bolt—pad to lever	LWZ304	M4	2	2						
5	Nut for bolt	FNZ104	M5	2	2						
6	Washer for nut (spring)	LWZ304	M6	2	2						
7	Rubber—brake pedal pad	1B8751	M7	1	1						
8	Shaft—brake and clutch pedal	11B5277	M8	1	1						
9	Bracket—brake and clutch pedal lever	11B5273	M9	1	1						
10	Sleeve for brake and clutch pedal shaft	1G9314	M10	2	2						
11	Distance piece	11B5279	M11	1	1						
12	Nut for shaft	LNZ205	M12	1	1						
13	Spring—brake and clutch pedal return	11B5283	M13	2	2						
14	**Master cylinder assembly**	11B5509	M14	1	1						
15	Spring	7H4944	M15	1	1						
16	Push-rod	17H4518	M16	1	1						
17	**Service kit for master cylinder**	17H4415	M17	1	1						
18	Packing piece—half—master cylinder	11B5188	M18	4	4						
19	Screw—master cylinder to pedal bracket	HZS0508	M19	4	4						
20	Washer for screw (spring)	LWZ205	M20	2	2	24.					
21	Screw—pedal bracket to pedal box	HZS0505	M21	2	2						
22	Washer for screw (plain)	PWZ205	M22	2	2						
23	Washer for screw (spring)	LWZ205	M23	2	2	24.					
24	Joint pin—pedal lever to master cylinder	CLZ0518	M24	1	1						

M.1

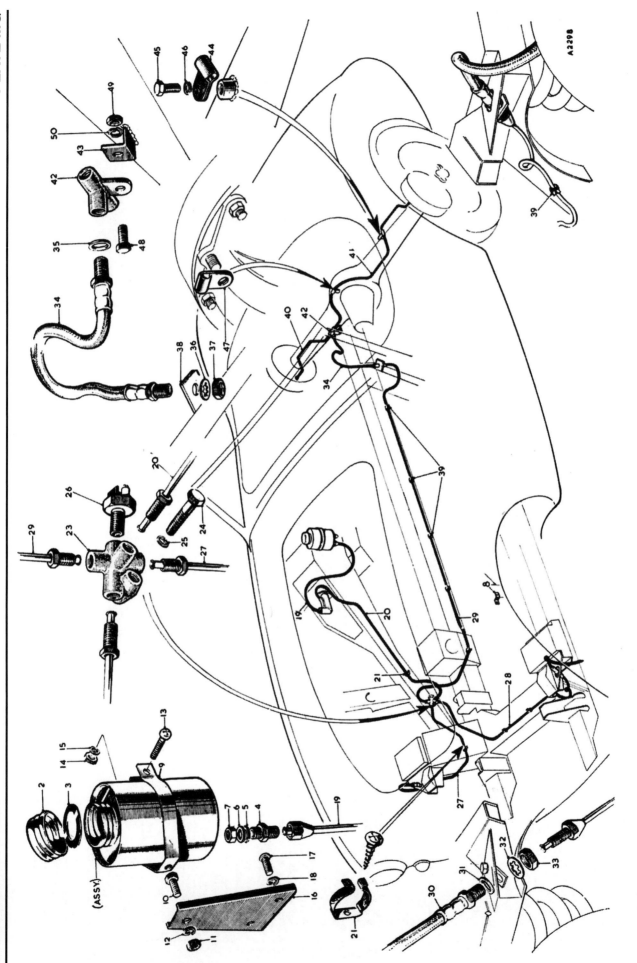

A2298

(ASSY.)

Item No.	DESCRIPTION	Commencing (C) 501 Part Number	Illus. No.	Qty. per Vehicle RHD	Qty. per Vehicle LHD	Unit of Issue	Type of Vehicle	New Part Number	Change Point	Amdt. No.	REMARKS
	SUPPLY TANK, PIPES, AND FITTINGS										
1	**Tank—dual supply**	**AGB5856**	**MA1**	1	1						
2	Cap—filler	7H4379	MA2	1	1						
3	Washer for filler cap	7H4726	MA3	1	1						
4	Adaptor	17H4238	MA4	2	2						
5	Gasket for adaptor	17H4180	MA5	2	2						
6	Washer for sealing inner body	17H4528	MA6	1	1						
7	Nut for adaptor	7H4867	MA7	2	2						
8	Bracket—tank to support channel	11B5521	MA8	1							
9	Clip—tank to bracket	8H599	MA9	1							
10	Bolt—clip to bracket	HZS0404	MA10	1	1						
11	Nut for bolt	FNZ104	MA11	1	1						
12	Washer for nut (spring)	LWZ204	MA12	1	1						
13	Screw—clip to supply tank	PMZ0814	MA13	1	1						
14	Nut for screw	FNZ108	MA14	1	1						
15	Washer for nut (spring)	LWZ208	MA15	1	1						
16	Bracket—tank to pedal box	11B5522	MA16	1							
17	Screw for bracket	HZS0403	MA17	2		36.					
18	Washer for screw (spring)	LWZ204	MA18	2							
19	**Pipe—supply tank to master cylinder**	**17H4519**	**MA19**	1							
20	**Pipe—supply tank to master cylinder**	**17H4515**			1						
21	Clip—pipe to front wheel arch panel	2H400		1							
22	Bolt for cup	PMZ0307		1							
23	Nut for bolt	FNZ103		1							
24	Washer for screw (spring)	LWZ203		1							
25	**Pipe—master cylinder to 5-way connection**	**17H4518**	**MA20**	1							
26	**Pipe—master cylinder to 5-way connection**	**17H4514**			1						
27	Clip—pipe to engine bearer strut	2H174	MA21	1							
28	Screw for clip	PTZ1004	MA22	1							
29	Connection—5-way	1B8026	MA23	1							
30	Screw—connection to boss	HBZ0410	MA24	1							
31	Washer for screw (spring)	LWZ304	MA25	1							
32	**Switch—stop light**	3H1894	**MA26**	1							
33	**Pipe—5-way connection to R/H front hose**	**17H4556**	**MA27**	1							
34	**Pipe—5-way connection to L/H front hose**	**17H4557**	**MA28**	1							
35	**Pipe—5-way connection to rear hose**	**17H4558**	**MA29**	1							
36	**Pipe—front flexible**	2A7227	MA30	2	2						
37	Gasket	8H2287	MA31	2	2						
38	Washer (shakeproof)	2K7131	MA32	2	2						
39	Nut	FNZ206	MA33	2	2						
40	**Pipe—rear flexible**	11B5543	MA34	1	1						
41	Gasket	8H2287	MA35	1	1						
42	Washer (shakeproof)	2K7131	MA36	1	1						
43	Nut	FNZ206	MA37	1	1						
44	Plate—locking	1B8965	MA38	1	1						
45	Clip for brake pipes	6K85	MA39	10	3						

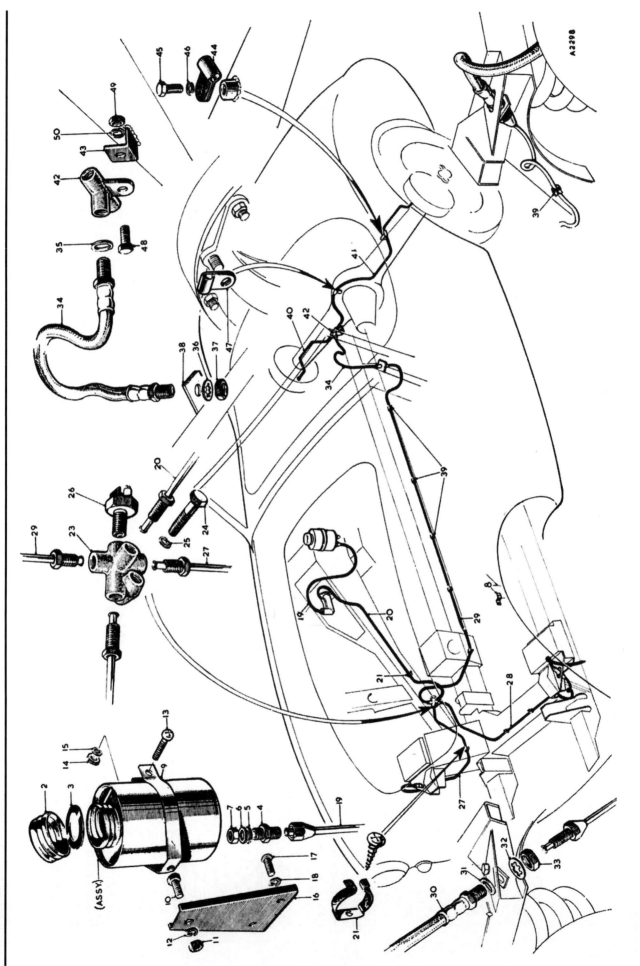

A2298

Item No.	DESCRIPTION	Part Number (Commencing (C) 501)	Illus. No.	Qty. per Vehicle RHD	Qty. per Vehicle LHD	Unit of Issue	Type of Vehicle	New Part Number	Change Point	Amdt. No.	REMARKS
	Supply Tank, Pipes, and Fittings—*continued*										
1	**Pipe—3-way junction rear to R/H brake**	17H4559	MA40	1	1						
2	**Pipe—3-way junction rear to L/H brake**	17H4560	MA41	1	1						
3	Connection—3-way	2A5846	MA42	1	1						
4	Bolt—8-way connection to axle case	HZS0506		1	1						
5	Washer for bolt (spring)	LWZ205		1	1	.24					
6	Nut for bolt	FNZ105		1	1						
7	Bracket extension	1B7527	MA43	1	1						
8	Clip—L/H rear brake pipe to boss on axle	2K5217	MA44	1	1						
9	Screw for clip	HZS0404	MA45	1	1						
10	Washer for screw (spring)	LWZ804	MA46	1	1						
11	Clip on gear carrier stud	2K5218	MA47	1	1						
12	Bolt—8-way piece to extension and bracket	HZS0506	MA48	2	2						
13	Nut for bolt	FNZ105	MA49	2	2						
14	Washer for nut (spring)	LWZ205	MA50	2	2	.24					

M.3

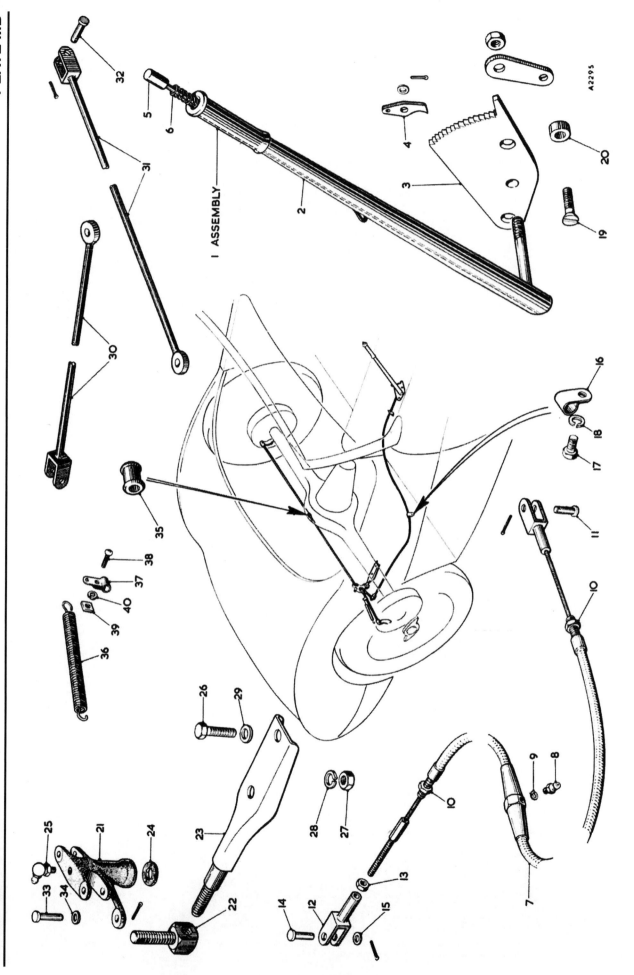

A2295

1 ASSEMBLY

SERVICE PARTS LIST

AUSTIN-HEALEY 100 SIX (SERIES BN6)

Item No.	DESCRIPTION	Commencing (C) 501 Part Number	Illus. No.	Qty. per Vehicle RHD	Qty. per Vehicle LHD	Unit of Issue	Type of Vehicle	New Part Number	Change Point	Amdt. No.	REMARKS
	HAND BRAKE MECHANISM										
1	**Assembly—hand brake**	**11B5282**	**MB1**	1	1						
2	Lever—hand brake	17H786	MB2	1	1						
3	Plate—ratchet	17H787	MB3	1	1						
4	Pawl for ratchet	17H788	MB4	1	1						
5	Button	17H789	MB5	1	1						
6	Spring	17H790	MB6	1	1						
7	**Cable—hand brake**	**11B5338**	**MB7**	1	1						
8	Nipple—grease	UHN305	MB8	1	1						
9	Washer for grease nipple (spring)	LWZ205	MB9	1	1						
10	Nut for cable	1B7864	MB10	2	2	24.					
11	Pin—joint—hand brake cable	2K5616	MB11	1	1						
12	End—fork	1B7362	MB12	1	1						
13	Locknut for fork end	FNZ204	MB13	1	1						
14	Pin—joint—balance lever	2K5221	MB14	1	1						
15	Washer for pin	PWZ105	MB15	1	1						
16	Clip—hand brake cable at heelboard	1B9074	MB16	1	1						⎱ Alternatives
17	Clip—hand brake cable at heelboard	PCR0609		1	1						⎰
18	Screw—clip to heelboard	HZS0403	MB17	1	1	86.					
19	Washer for screw (spring)	LWZ204	MB18	1	1						
20	Screw—hand brake to frame bracket	1B8895	MB19	2	2						
21	Piece—distance—hand brake to frame bracket	1B8896	MB20	2	2						
22	**Lever—balance**	**1G7485**	**MB21**	1	1						
23	Carrier—balance lever	1G7484	MB22	1	1						
24	Support with pin	1B7424	MB23	1	1						
25	Ring—felt	2K5213	MB24	1	1						
26	Nipple—grease	3H2192	MB25	1	1						
27	Bolt—support to bracket on axle	HZS0506	MB26	2	2						
28	Nut for bolt	FNZ105	MB27	2	2						
29	Washer for nut (spring)	LWZ305	MB28	2	2						
30	Washer for nut (plain)	PWZ105	MB29	2	2						
31	**Rod—short R/H cross**	**ATG7251**	**MB30**	1	1						
32	**Rod—long L/H cross**	**1G7549**	**MB31**	1	1						
33	Pin—joint—to backplate levers	2K6930	MB32	2	2						
34	Pin—joint—to balance lever	2K5248	MB33	2	2						
35	Ring for joint pins (felt)	2K5291	MB34	8	8	86.					
36	Ferrule for cross-rod steady (rubber)	1B5829	MB35	1	1						
37	Spring—pull-off	2H1641	MB36	2	2						
38	Clip for spring	1G7574	MB37	2	2						
39	Screw for clip	PMZ0806	MB38	2	2						
40	Nut for screw	NZS108	MB39	2	2						
41	Washer for nut (spring)	LWZ203	MB40	2	2						

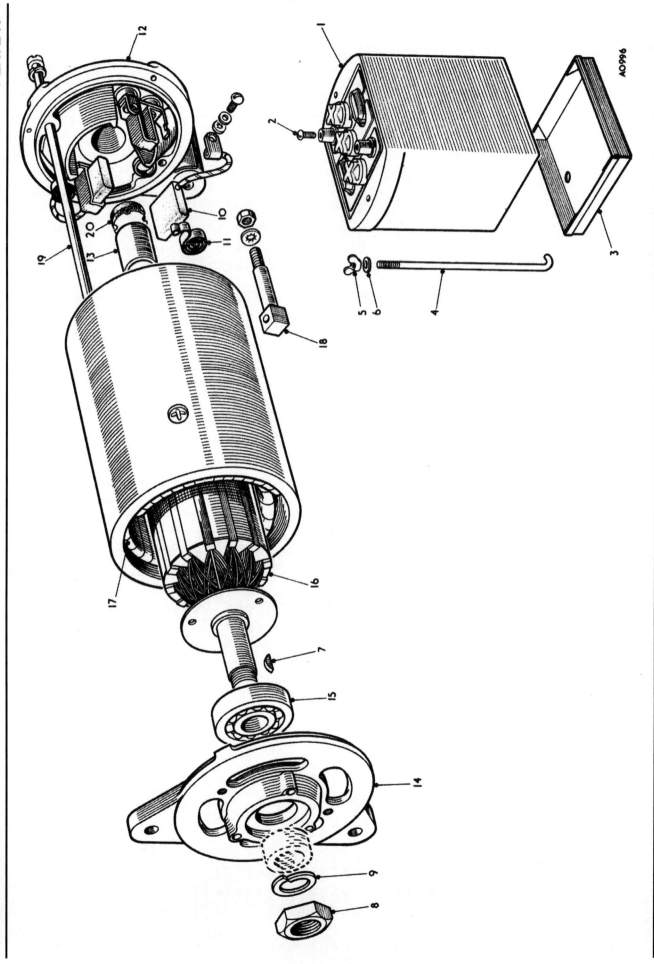

A0996

AUSTIN-HEALEY 100 SIX (SERIES BN6)

Item No.	DESCRIPTION	Part Number (Commencing (C) 501)	Illus. No.	Qty. per Vehicle RHD	Qty. per Vehicle LHD	Unit of Issue	Type of Vehicle	New Part Number	Change Point	Amdt. No.	REMARKS
	ELECTRICAL EQUIPMENT										
	BATTERY										
	Battery—6-volt	**N.S.P.**	**N1**	**2**	**2**						
1	Screw for battery lug	2K8645	N2	4	4						
2	Tray—battery	24B747	N3	2	2						
3	Rod—battery fixing	24B811	N4	4	4						
4	Nut for rod (wing)	WNZ104	N5	4	4						
5	Washer for nut (plain)	PWZ105	N6	4	4						
	DYNAMO										
	Dynamo	**11K100**	N7	1	1						
7	Key for pulley	WKN405	N8	1	1						
8	Nut for pulley	7H5023	N9	1	1						
9	Washer for nut (spring)	AJC5128	N10	1	1						
10	Brush	7H5016	N11	1	1	set					
11	Spring for brush	7H5020	N12	1	1	set					
12	Bracket—commutator end	17H5458	N13	1	1						
13	Bush—commutator end	17H5434	N14	1	1						
14	Bracket—drive end	7H5525	N15	1	1						
15	Bearing—drive end	7H5021	N16	1	1						
16	Armature	17H5238	N17	1	1	set					
17	Field coils	7H5025	N18	1	1						
18	Terminal	17H5438	N19	1	1						
19	Bolt for bracket	17H5180		2	2						
20	Sundry parts	7H5528	N20	1	1	set					
21	Oiler	87H5487		1	1						

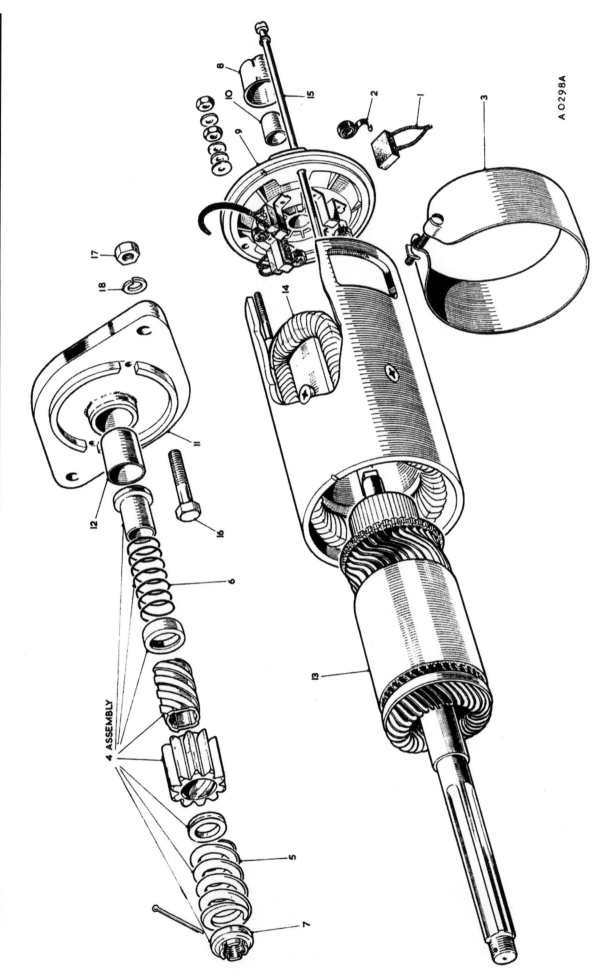

A 0298A

Item No.	DESCRIPTION	Commencing (C) 501 Part Number	Illus. No.	Qty. per Vehicle RHD	Qty. per Vehicle LHD	Unit of Issue	Type of Vehicle	New Part Number	Change Point	Amdt. No.	REMARKS
	Starter										
1	Starter	3H1281	NA1	1	1	set					
2	Brush	7H5002	NA3	2	2						
3	Band—cover	7H5000	NA4	1	1						
4	Pinion and barrel	7H5008	NA6	1	1						
5	Spring for pinion—return	7H5009	NA5	1	1						
6	Spring for pinion—main	7H5007	NA7	1	1						
7	Nut	7H5006	NA8	1	1						
8	Cap for shaft	7H5001	NA9	1	1						
9	Bracket—commutator end	7H5498	NA10	1	1						
10	Bush—commutator end	7H5004	NA2	1	1	set					
11	Spring—brush tension	7H5005	NA11	1	1						
12	Bracket—drive end	7H5010	NA12	1	1						
13	Bush—drive end	7H5011	NA13	1	1						
14	Armature	7H5012	NA14	1	1	set					
15	Coils—field	7H5018	NA15	1	1	set					
16	Bolt for bracket	7H5839		2	2						
17	Sundry parts	7H5156		1	1						
18	Bolt—starter to engine	HNS0615	NA16	2	2						
19	Nut for bolt	FNN106	NA17	2	2						
20	Washer for bolt (spring)	LWN206	NA18	2	2						

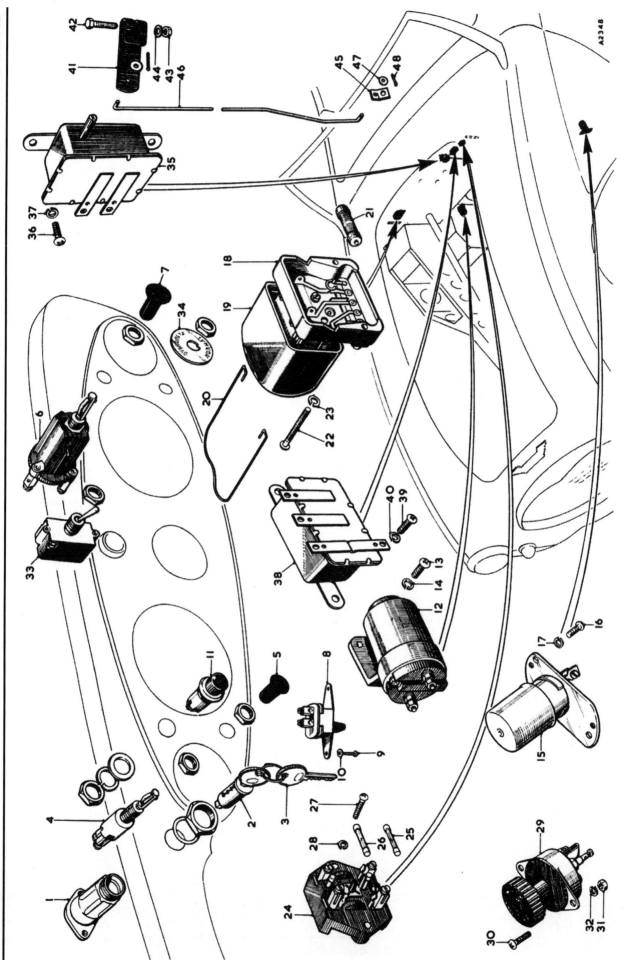

A2348

146

SERVICE PARTS LIST

AUSTIN-HEALEY 100 SIX (SERIES BN6)

Item No.	DESCRIPTION	Part Number	Illus. No.	RHD	LHD	Unit of Issue	Type of Vehicle	New Part Number	Change Point	Amdt. No.	REMARKS
	SWITCHES										
1	**Switch—ignition**	3H2824	NB1	1	1						
2	Lock and key	7H9830	NB2	1	1						
3	Key	ANK4646	NB3	1	1						
4	**Switch—windscreen wiper**	3H3095	NB4	1	1						
5	Knob	8H8096	NB5	1	1						
6	**Switch—head and sidelamp**	3H3098	NB6	1	1						
7	Knob	8H8099	NB7	1	1						
8	**Switch—panel light**	3H3100	NB8	1	1						
9	Screw—switch to fascia	6K9588	NB9	2	2						
10	Washer for screw (spring)	LWZ802	NB10	2	2						
11	**Switch—starter solenoid push**	3H3058	NB11	1	1						
12	**Switch—starter solenoid**	3H852	NB12	1	1						
13	Screw—switch to body	PMZ0306	NB13	2	2						
14	Washer for screw (spring)	LWZ203	NB14	2	2						
15	**Switch—dipper**	11G2007	NB15	1	1						
16	Screw—switch to dash	PMZ0306	NB16	2	2						
17	Washer for screw (spring)	LWZ203	NB17	2	2						
18	**Box—control**	3H1836	NB18	1	1						
19	Cover	7H5522	NB19	1	1						
20	Clip for cover	7H5128	NB20	1	1						
21	Resistance	7H5066	NB21	1	1						
22	Screw—control box to dash	PMZ0320	NB22	2	2						
23	Washer for screw (spring)	LWZ203	NB23	2	2						
24	**Box—fuse**	3H1910	NB24	1	1						
25	Fuse (35-amp.)	7H5067	NB25	2	2						
26	Fuse (50-amp.)	7H5540	NB26	2	2						
27	Screw—fusebox to dash	PMZ0207	NB27	2	2						
28	Washer for screw (spring)	LWZ203	NB28	2	2						
29	**Switch—battery master**	1B2804	NB29	1	1						
30	Screw—battery master switch to boot	PMZ0207	NB30	2	2						
31	Nut for screw	CNZ102	NB31	2	2						
32	Washer for nut (spring)	LWZ802	NB32	2	2						
33	**Switch—overdrive**	1B9030	NB33	1	1						
34	Escutcheon plate for overdrive switch	1B9081	NB84	1	1						
35	**Switch—throttle**	1B2837	NB35	1	1						
36	Screw—throttle switch to dash	PMZ0808	NB86	2	2						
37	Washer for screw (spring)	LWZ203	NB87	2	2		Overdrive				
38	**Relay for overdrive**	1B2836	NB38	1	1						
39	Screw—relay to dash	PMZ0808	NB39	2	2						
40	Washer for screw (spring)	LWZ203	NB40	2	2						
41	Lever—throttle switch (top)	11B2163	NB41	1	1						
42	Bolt—lever to throttle switch	53K129	NB42	1	1						
43	Nut for bolt	FNZ103	NB43	1	1						
44	Washer for nut (plain)	PWZ103	NB44	2	2						
45	Eye—throttle switch link	1B2721	NB45	1	1						
46	Link—throttle switch	11B2851	NB46	1	1						
47	Washer for link (plain)	PWZ102	NB47	2	2						
48	Split pin for link	2K1881	NB48	2	2						

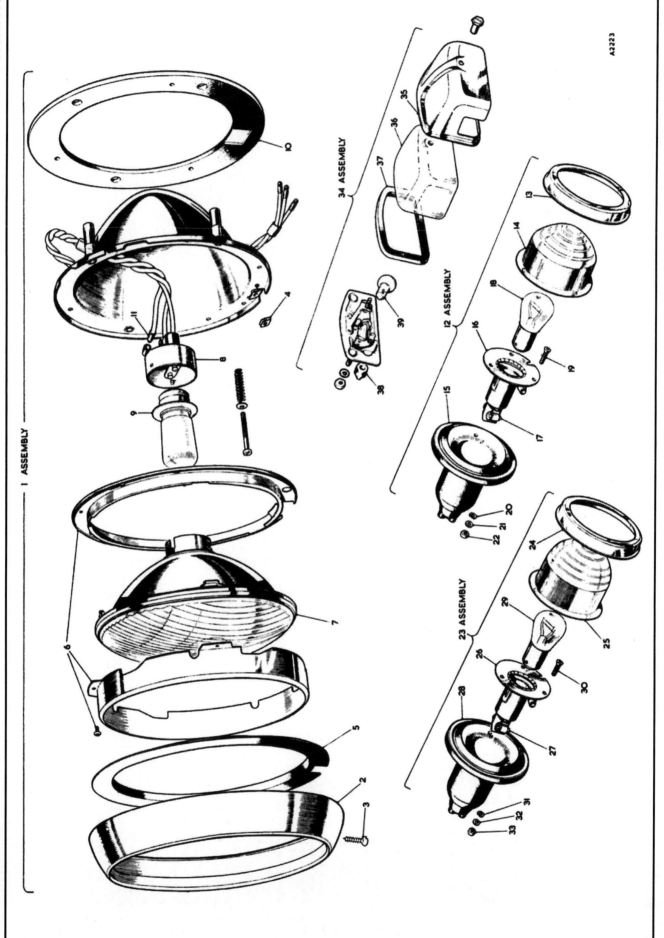

1 ASSEMBLY
12 ASSEMBLY
23 ASSEMBLY
34 ASSEMBLY

A2223

SERVICE PARTS LIST

AUSTIN-HEALEY 100 SIX (SERIES BN6)

Item No.	DESCRIPTION	Commencing (C) 501 Part Number	Illus. No.	Qty. per Vehicle RHD	Qty. per Vehicle LHD	Unit of Issue	Type of Vehicle	New Part Number	Change Point	Amdt. No.	REMARKS
	LAMPS (ROAD)										
1	Headlamp—left dip	1B9096	NC1	2							Except Europe
2	Headlamp—right dip ...(Not U.K.)	1B9095			2						Except Europe
3	Headlamp—vertical dip ...(Not U.K.)	1B9098			2						Except Europe and France
4	Headlamp (less bulb) ...(FRANCE)	1B9099			2						Europe except France
5	Rim assembly	37H5530	NC2	2	2						
6	Screw—rim fixing	AJA5081	NC3	2	2						
7	Nut for screw	AJA5083	NC4	2	2						
8	Excluder—dust	3H2962	NC5	2	2						
9	Rim and base assembly—inner	17H5205	NC6	2	2						
10	Light unit—left dip	17H5488	NC7	2							
11	Light unit—right dip	17H5375			2						
12	Light unit—vertical dip ...(FRANCE)	7H5485			2						
13	Light unit ...(FRANCE)	7H5486			2						
14	Back-shell assembly ...(FRANCE)	17H5146			2						
15	Bulb holder ...(FRANCE)	7H5062			2						
16	Sleeve—terminal ...(FRANCE)	7H5582			6						
17	Bulb holder	17H5306	NC8	2							
18	Sleeve—terminal	7H5582	NC11	2							
19	Adaptor (complete with cable) ...(N. AMERICA)	17H5244		2	2						
20	Gasket (rubber)	3H993	NC10	2	2						
21	Bulb—left dip	3H1892	NC9	2							
22	Bulb—right dip	3H1893			2						
23	Bulb—vertical dip	3H921			2						
24	Side and flasher lamp	1B9100	NC12	2	2						
25	Rim	7H5182	NC13	2	2						
26	Glass	87H5519	NC14	2	2						
27	Body (rubber)	87H5527	NC15	2	2						
28	Bulb holder and plate	27H5545	NC16	2	2						
29	Interior—bulb holder	17H5427	NC17	2	2						
30	Bulb	1F9026	NC18	2	2						
31	Screw fixing sidelamp	PMZ0207	NC19	6	6						
32	Washer for screw (spring)	LWZ802	NC20	6	6						
33	Washer for screw (plain)	PWZ102	NC21	6	6						
34	Nut for screw	CNZ102	NC22	6	6						

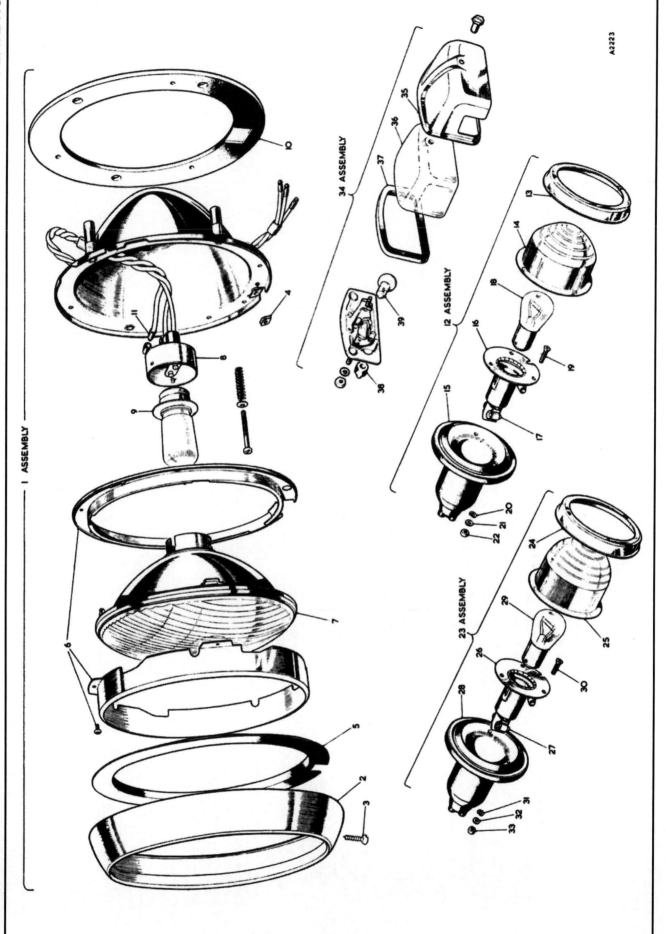

A2223

34 ASSEMBLY

1 ASSEMBLY

12 ASSEMBLY

23 ASSEMBLY

SERVICE PARTS LIST

Item No.	DESCRIPTION	Part Number (Commencing (C) 501)	Illus. No.	Qty. per Vehicle RHD	Qty. per Vehicle LHD	Unit of Issue	Type of Vehicle	New Part Number	Change Point	Amdt. No.	REMARKS
	Lamps (Road)—*continued*										
	Stop, tail, and flasher lamp complete	**1B9101**	**NC23**	**2**	**2**						
1	Rim	7H5182	NC24	2	2						
2	Glass	87H5581	NC25	2	2						
3	Bulb holder and plate	27H5545	NC26	2	2						
4	Interior—bulb holder	17H5427	NC27	2	2						
5	Body (rubber)	87H5527	NC28	2	2						
6	Bulb	1F9026	NC29	2	2						
7	Screw fixing lamp	PMZ0207	NC30	6	6						
8	Washer for screw (spring)	LWZ102	NC31	6	6						
9	Washer for screw (plain)	PWZ102	NC32	6	6						
10	Nut for screw	CNZ102	NC33	6	6						
11	**Number-plate lamp**	**3H1813**	**NC34**	**1**	**1**						
12	Cover	7H5185	NC35	1	1						
13	Glass	7H5121	NC36	1	1						
14	Gasket—glass seating	7H5122	NC37	1	1						
15	Grommet—cable	7H5164	NC38	1	1						
16	Sundry parts	7H5123		1	1	set					
17	Bulb	2H4817	NC39	1	1						
18	**Reflector—rear**	**1B9056**	**NC40**	**2**	**2**						
19	Rim	AJC5116	NC41	2	2						

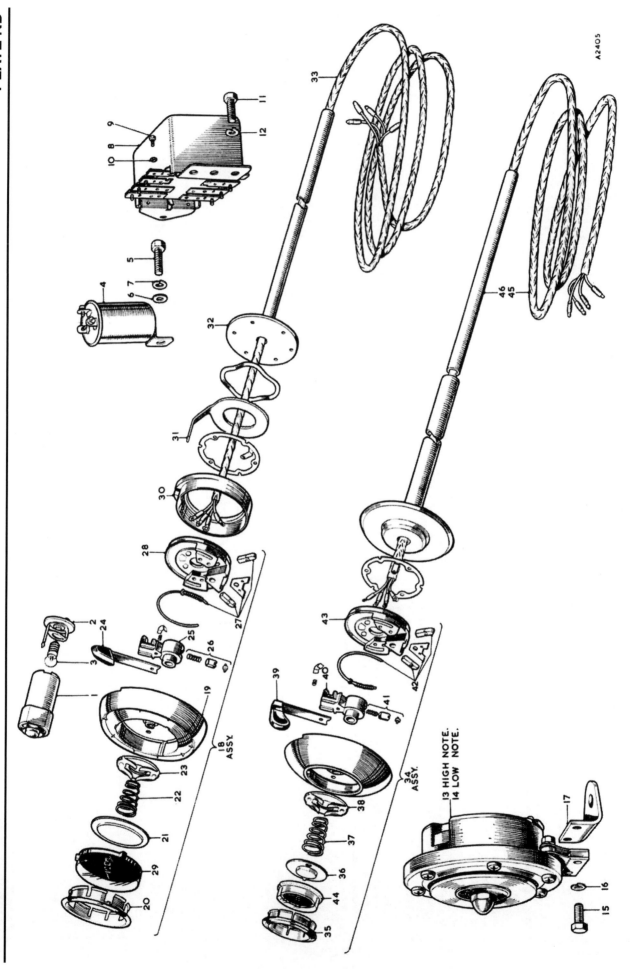

A24O5

13 HIGH NOTE.
14 LOW NOTE.

18 ASSY.

34 ASSY.

Item No.	DESCRIPTION	Commencing (C) 501 Part Number	Illus. No.	Qty. per Vehicle RHD	Qty. per Vehicle LHD	Unit of Issue	Remarks
	FLASHER, HORN, AND CONTROLS						
1	**Bezel and body—flasher indicator warning light**	**3H2765**	**ND1**	1	1		
2	Bulb holder	2H4978	ND2	1	1		
3	Bulb	2H4782	ND3	1	1		
4	**Flasher unit**	**11G9093**	**ND4**	1	1		
5	Screw—flasher unit to pedal box	PMZ0408	ND5	1	1		
6	Washer for screw (plain)	PWZ104	ND6	1	1		
7	Washer for screw (spring)	LWZ204	ND7	1	1		
8	**Relay—flasher**	**3H1454**	**ND8**	1	1		
9	Screw—terminal	17H5594	ND9	8	8		
10	Washer—terminal	27H5555	ND10	8	8		
11	Screw—relay to wheel arch	PMZ0308	ND11	3	3		
12	Washer for screw (spring)	LWZ208	ND12	3	3		
13	**Horn—high note**	**3H3059**	**ND13**	1	1		
14	**Horn—low note**	**3H3060**	**ND14**	1	1		
15	Bolt—horn to front cross-member	HZS0405	ND15	4	4		
16	Washer for bolt (spring)	LWZ304	ND16	4	4		
17	Plate—tapped	AHB8290	ND17	2	2		
18	**Horn and direction indicator control**	**1B6346**		1	1		
19	Top cover assembly	47H5244	ND28	1	1		
20	Moulding—top cover	47H5240	ND18	1	1		
21	Ring—horn-push retaining	47H5241	ND19	1	1		
22	Plate—horn-push contact	47H5242	ND20	1	1		
23	Spring—horn-push	7H5189	ND21	1	1		
24	Contact assembly—horn-push	7H5188	ND22	1	1		
25	Lever—trafficator	47H5243	ND23	1	1		
26	Rotor and plunger—switch	7H5469	ND24	1	1		
27	Plunger assembly—rotor	7H5142	ND25	1	1		
28	Pawls and springs	7H5143	ND26	1	1	set	
29	Base assembly—switch	7H5140	ND27	1	1		
30	Horn-push	47H5245	ND29	1	1		
31	Sundry parts	7H5512	ND30	1	1	set	
32	Ring—striker	7H5471	ND31	1	1		
33	Bracket—striker ring location	7H5472	ND32	1	1		
34	Stator tube and plate assembly	47H5246	ND33	1	1		
35	Cable	47H5247		1	1		
36	**Horn and direction indicator control**	**1B6303**	ND43	1	1		
37	Top cover assembly	47H5010	ND34	1	1		
38	Ring—horn-push retaining	7H5468	ND35	1	1		
39	Plate—horn-push contact	AJA5006	ND36	1	1		
40	Spring—horn-push	7H5189	ND37	1	1		
41	Contact assembly—horn-push	7H5188	ND38	1	1		
42	Lever—trafficator	27H5556	ND39	1	1		
43	Rotor and plunger-switch	7H5469	ND40	1	1		
44	Plunger assembly—rotor	7H5142	ND41	1	1		
45	Pawls and springs	7H5143	ND42	1	1	set	
46	Base assembly—switch	27H5557	ND44	1	1		
47	Horn-push	47H5011		1	1		
48	Sundry parts	7H5512	ND45	1	1	set	
49	Cable	17H5259	ND46	1	1		
50	Stator tube	1B6226		1	1		

Note: The REMARKS column contains a bracketed annotation "Adjustable steering" spanning the second "Horn and direction indicator control" group (items 37–49). The MODIFICATIONS columns (New Part Number, Change Point, Amdt. No.) and the Type of Vehicle column are blank for all rows.

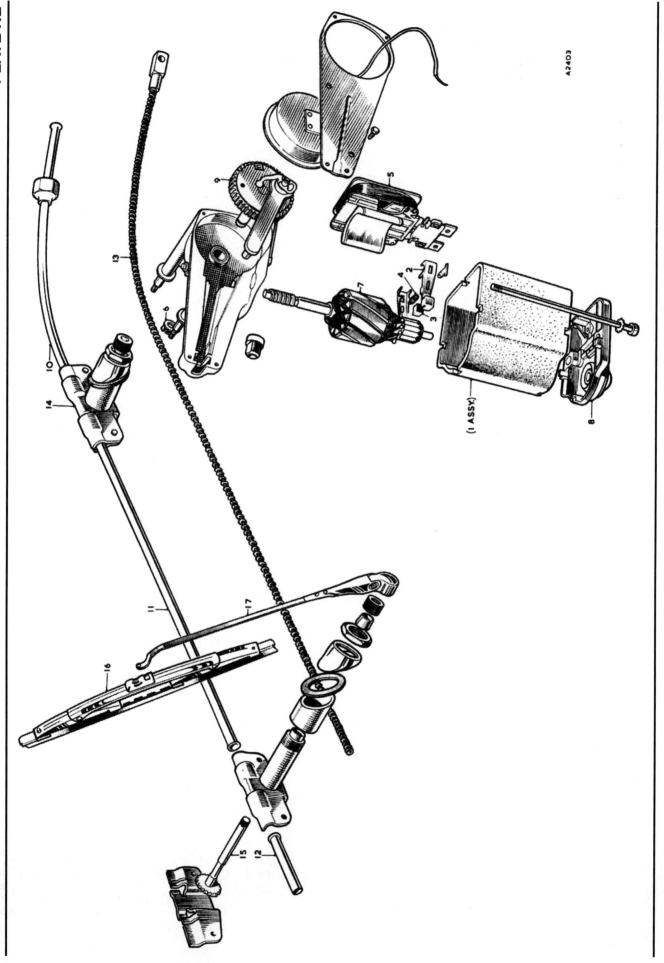

A2403

(1 ASSY.)

154

Item No.	DESCRIPTION	Commencing (C) 501		Qty. per Vehicle		Unit of Issue	Type of Vehicle	MODIFICATIONS			REMARKS
		Part Number	Illus. No.	RHD	LHD			New Part Number	Change Point	Amdt. No.	
	WINDSCREEN WIPER										
1	**Motor—windscreen wiper**	**37H5308**	**NE1**	1	1						
2	Brush gear	17H5896	NE2	1	1						
3	Brush	7H5180	NE3	1	1	set					
4	Spring—brush	27H5309	NE4	1	1	set					
5	Coil assembly	37H5288	NE5	1	1						
6	Washer—bolt fixing	7H5568	NE6	2	2						
7	Armature	17H5255	NE7	1	1						
8	Switch—adjusting	17H5442	NE8	1	1						
9	Shaft and gear	37H5487	NE9	1	1						
10	Fixing parts	17H5481		1	1	set					
11	Sundry parts	17H5441		1	1	set					
12	**Casing—outer—motor to wheelbox**	**14B5589**	**NE10**	1	1						
13	Casing—outer—wheelbox to wheelbox	14B5508	NE11	1	1						
14	Casing—outer—wheelbox extension	14G3722	NE12	1	1						
15	**Cross-head and rack assembly**	**37H5169**	**NE13**	1	1						
16	**Wheelbox**	**14B5568**	**NE14**	2	2						
17	Spindle and gear	AJH5079	NE15	2	2						
18	**Blade—wiper**	**AHH5417**	**NE16**	2	2						
19	**Arm—wiper**	**14B5596**	**NE17**	2							
20	**Arm—wiper**	**14B5597**			2						

SERVICE PARTS LIST

AUSTIN-HEALEY 100 SIX (SERIES BN6)

Item No.	DESCRIPTION	Commencing (C) 501 Part Number	Illus. No.	Qty. per Vehicle RHD	Qty. per Vehicle LHD	Unit of Issue	Type of Vehicle	New Part Number	Change Point	Amdt. No.	REMARKS
	CABLES AND CONNECTIONS										
1	**Cable—main harness**	**1B9102**		1	1			**AHB8286**	**Com. (C) 3460**		
2	Clip—main harness to filler piece	PCR0807		1	1						
3	Clip—main harness to dash	PCR1007		1	1						
4	Screw for clip	PMZ0808		1	1						
5	Washer for screw (spring)	LWZ203		1	1						
6	Clip—main harness to reinforcement panel	PCR0707		1	1						
7	Clip—main harness to L/H inner wheel arch	PCR0707		1	1						
8	Clip—main harness to R/H reinforcement	PCR0707		3	3						
9	Clip—main harness stop light switch	PCR0507		1	1						
10	Clip—main harness to L/H side of cross-brace	PCR1007		1	1						
11	Screw for clip	PMZ0808		1	1						
12	Nut for screw	FNZ103		1	1						
13	Washer for nut (spring)	LWZ203		1	1						
14	Clip—main harness to R/H side of cross-brace	PCR0707		1	1						
15	Screw for clip	PMZ0808		1	1						
16	Nut for screw	FNZ103		1	1						
17	Washer for nut (spring)	LWZ203		1	1						
18	Clip—main harness to relay on flitch fixings	PCR1007		1	1						
19	Clip—main harness solenoid switch	PCR0407		1	1						
20	**Cable—dipper switch harness**	**1B2847**		1	1						
21	Grommet for dipper switch harness	RFN303		2	2						
22	Clip—main and dipper switch harness to dash	11K9095		1	1						
23	Screw for clip	PMZ0808		1	1						
24	Washer for screw (spring)	LWZ203		1	1						
25	**Cable—chassis harness**	**1B9179**		1	1			**AHB8287**	**Com. (O) 3460** / Fin. (C) 3459		
26	Clip—chassis harness to L/H side-member	PCR0407		3	3				Fin. (C) 3459		
27	Clip—chassis harness to L/H side-member	PCR0607		3/5	3/5						Quantity increased at (C) 3460
28	Clip—chassis harness to L/H side-member	PCR0707		3	3						
29	Clip—chassis harness to L/H inner front wheel arch panel	PCR0407		1	1						
30	Clip—chassis harness to boot floor	PCR0407		1	1						
31	Clip—chassis harness to under side of boot floor	PCR0407		2	2						
32	Clip—chassis harness to engine cover	PCR0507		2	2						
33	Screw for clip	PMZ0808		2	2						
34	Nut for screw	FNZ108		2	2						
35	Washer for nut (spring)	LWZ203		2	2						
36	Clip—chassis harness to L/H reinforcement piece	PCR0407		1	1						
37	Clip—chassis harness to boot vertical panel	PCR0407		1	1						
38	Screw for clip	PMZ0804		1	1						
39	Washer for screw (spring)	LWZ203		1	1						
40	Clip—chassis harness to bump rubber box	PCR0507		2	2						
41	Grommet for chassis harness	RFN405		2	2						
42	Ring for sidelamp cables (rubber)	1G2673		2	2						
43	Clip—edge—headlamp cable to cross-brace	11K9181		2	2						
44	Clip—stator tube cable to cross-brace	PCR0407		1	1						

N.8

SERVICE PARTS LIST

AUSTIN-HEALEY 100 SIX (SERIES BN6)

Item No.	DESCRIPTION	Part Number (Commencing (C) 501)	Illus. No.	RHD	LHD	Unit of Issue	Type of Vehicle	New Part Number	Change Point	Amdt. No.	REMARKS
	Cables and Connections—*continued*										
1	**Cable—boot harness**	**1B2796**		1	1						
2	Clip—boot harness to rear of boot	PCR0507		4	4						
3	**Cable—battery negative to starter solenoid switch**	**1B2800**		1	1						
4	Clip—battery negative cable to R/H side-member	PCR0707		6	6						
5	Clip—battery negative cable to R/H side-member	PCR0713		1	1						
6	Clip—battery negative cable to heelboard panel	PCR0609		1	1						
7	Screw for clip	HZS0403		1	1	36.					
8	Nut for screw	FNZ104		1	1						
9	Washer for nut (spring)	LWZ204		1	1						
10	Clip—battery negative cable to engine side cover	PCR0707		1	1						
11	Screw for clip	PMZ0308		1	1						
12	Nut for screw	FNZ103		1	1						
13	Washer for nut	LWZ203		1	1						
14	**Cable—starter solenoid switch to starter**	**1B2801**		1	1						
15	Cap—starter solenoid switch terminal insulating	8G548		2	2						
16	**Cable—battery positive to master switch**	**1B9180**		1	1			AHB8288	] Com. (C) **3460**		
17	**Cable—battery link**	**1B2810**		1	1			AHB8289	]		
18	Clip—battery link cable to body	PCR0807		1	1						
19	Screw for clip	PMZ0808		1	1						
20	Nut for screw	FNZ103		1	1						
21	Washer for nut (spring)	LWZ203		1	1						
22	**Cable—battery master switch to earth**	**1B9078**		1	1						
23	Screw—cable to frame	HZS0604		1	1						
24	Washer for screw (spring)	LWZ206		1	1						
25	**Cable—engine earth**	**2K6167**		1	1						
26	Screw—cable to frame	HZS0604		1	1						
27	Washer for screw (spring)	LWZ206		1	1						
28	Clip—tank unit cable to boot vertical panel	PCR0407		1	1						
29	Grommet—tank unit cable through boot vertical panel	3F90		1	1						
30	Grommet—number-plate lamp cable through rear panel	3H2144		1	1						
31	Drive screw for cable clip	PTZ1004		34/28	34/28						Quantity increased at (C) 3460
32	Cable—overdrive harness	1B9104		1	1		Overdrive				
33	Clip—overdrive harness to dash	PCR0407		1	1						
34	Screw for clip	PMZ0808		1	1						
35	Washer for screw (spring)	LWZ208		1	1						
36	Clip—overdrive harness to gearbox side cover	PCR0811		1	1						
37	Clip—chassis and overdrive harness to engine side cover—top	PCR0607		1	1						
38	Screw for clip	PMZ0308		1	1						
39	Nut for screw	FNZ103		1	1						
40	Washer for nut (spring)	LWZ208		1	1						

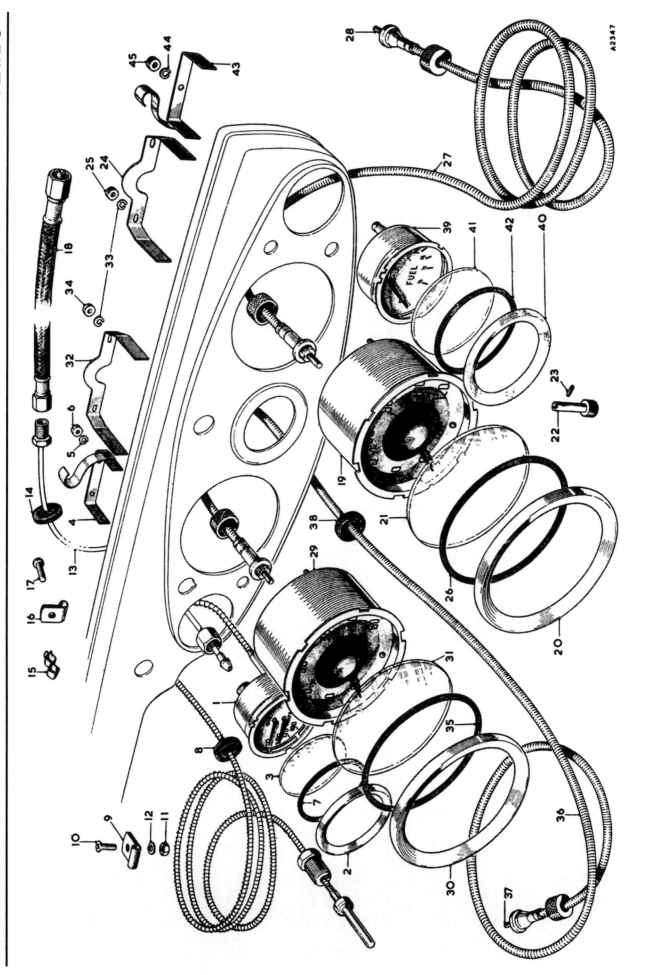

A2347

INSTRUMENTS

Item No.	DESCRIPTION	Commencing (C) 501 Part Number	Illus. No.	Qty. RHD	Qty. LHD	Unit of Issue	Type of Vehicle	New Part Number	Change Point	Amdt. No.	REMARKS
1	**Gauge—oil pressure and radiator thermometer**	**1B9064**	**01**	1	1			**AMB5758**	**Com. (C) 2030**		
2	Bezel	AJH5182	O2	1	1						
3	Glass	17H1068	O3	1	1						
4	Strap—fixing	27H992	O4	1	1						
5	Washer (spring)	27H387	O5	2	2						
6	Nut (thumb)	17H982	O6	2	2						
7	Ring (rubber)	17H1642	O7	1	1						
8	Grommet—tube through dash	3H2615	O8	1	1						
9	Clip—thermo capillary tube to bonnet surround	PCR0307	O9	4	4						
10	Screw fixing clip	CMZ0307	O10	4	4						
11	Nut for screw	FNZ108	O11	4	4						⎰ Fin. (C) 2029
12	Washer for nut (spring)	LWZ203	O12	2	2						
13	Clip—thermo capillary tube			1	1			BHA4081	Com. (C) 2080		
14	**Pipe—oil gauge**	**11B2188**	**013**	1	—						
15	**Pipe—oil gauge**	**11B2186**		—	1						
16	Grommet—pipe through dash	RFN403	O14	1	1						
17	Clip for pipe	6K85	O15	2	2						
18	Clip for pipe	2K5215	O16	1	1						
19	Screw for clip	PMZ0807	O17	2	2						
20	**Hose—flexible**	**8G637**	**018**	1	1						
21	**Speedometer (miles)**	**1B9059**	**019**	1	1						
22	**Speedometer (kilometres)**	**1B9060**			1						
23	Speedometer (miles)	1B9057		1	1		Overdrive				
24	Speedometer (kilometres)	1B9058			1		Overdrive				
25	Bezel	27H397	O20	1	1						
26	Glass	AJH5177	O21	1	1						
27	Trip stem assembly	17H1684	O22	1	1						
28	Screw for trip stem	17H1658	O23	1	1						
29	Strap—fixing	27H429	O24	1	1						
30	Nut—thumb	17H1304	O25	2	2						
31	Ring (rubber)	AJH5178	O26	1	1						
32	**Cable—speedometer**	**2A9039**	O27	1	1						
33	Cable—outer	17H690	O28	1	1						
34	Cable—inner	17H689		1	1						
35	Cable—speedometer	1H9049		1	1		Overdrive				
36	Cable—outer	17H1496		1	1		Overdrive				
37	Cable—inner	17H844		1	1		Overdrive				
38	**Tachometer**	**1B9188**	**029**	1	1						
39	Bezel	27H397	O80	1	1						
40	Glass	AJH5177	O81	1	1						
41	Strap—fixing	27H429	O82	1	1						
42	Washer (spring)	17H1341	O83	2	2						
43	Nut (thumb)	17H1804	O84	2	2						
44	Ring (rubber)	AJH5178	O85	1	1						

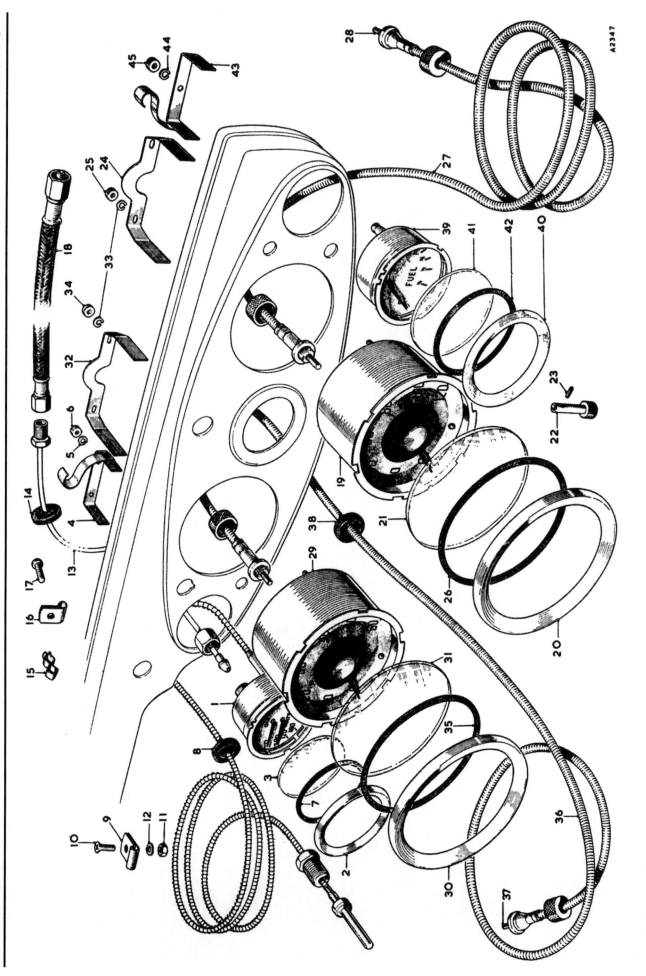

A2347

Item No.	DESCRIPTION	Commencing (C) 501		Qty. per Vehicle		Unit of Issue	Type of Vehicle	MODIFICATIONS			REMARKS
		Part Number	Illus. No.	RHD	LHD			New Part Number	Change Point	Amdt. No.	
	Instruments—*continued*										
	Cable—tachometer	**1B9140**		1							
1	Cable—outer	27H984	O86	1							
2	Cable—inner	27H985	O87	1							
3	**Cable—tachometer**	**1B9141**			1						
4	Cable—outer	17H1343			1						
5	Cable—inner	17H630			1						
6	Grommet—cable through dash	RFN403	O38	1	1						
7	**Gauge—fuel**	**1B9061**	**O39**	1	1						
8	Bezel	AJH5182	O40	1	1						
9	Glass	17H1068	O41	1	1						
10	Ring (rubber)	17H1642	O42	1	1						
11	Strap—fixing—and lamp holder complete	17H1822	O43	1	1						
12	Washer (spring)	27H887	O44	1	1						
13	Nut (thumb)	17H982	O45	1	1						

O.2

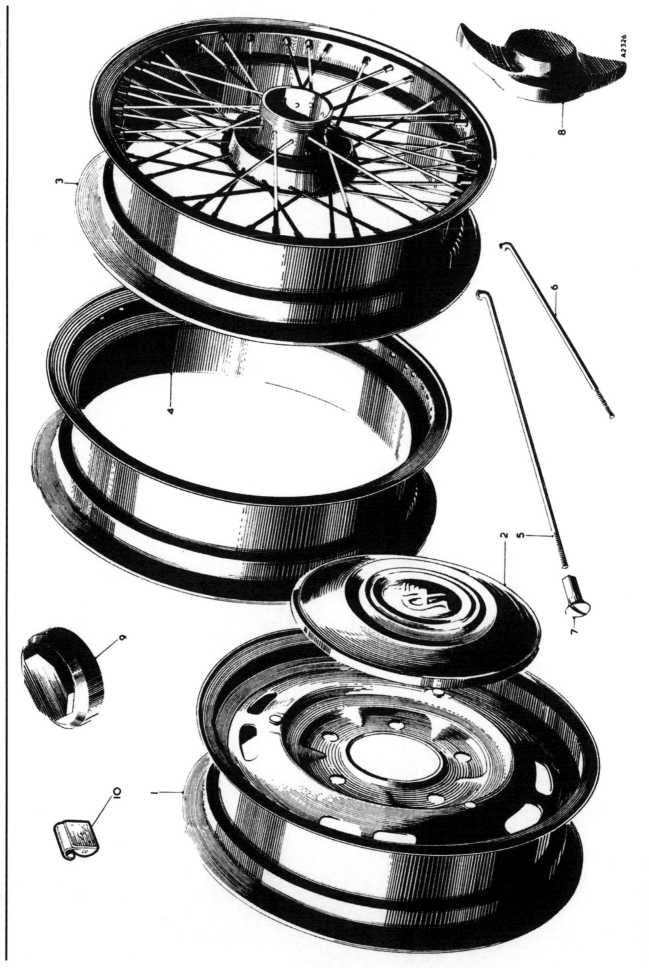

A2326

WHEELS

Item No.	DESCRIPTION	Commencing (C) 501 Part Number	Illus. No.	Qty. per Vehicle RHD	Qty. per Vehicle LHD	Unit of Issue	Type of Vehicle	New Part Number	Change Point	Amdt. No.	REMARKS
1	Wheel—disc	1B8057	P1	5	5						
2	Cap for disc wheel	1G8084	P2	4	4						
3	Wheel—wire	1B8048	P3	5	5						
4	Rim—wire wheel	7H1804	P4	5	5	6					
5	Spoke—long	7H1805	P5	80	80						
6	Spoke—short	7H1806	P6	160	160						
7	Nipple for spoke	7H1709	P7	240	240						
8	Cap for wire wheel—R/H side (L.H.T.)	1B8077	P8	2	2						
9	Cap for wire wheel—L/H side (R.H.T.)	1B8078		2	2						
10	Cap for wire wheel—R/H side	AHH8008	P9	2	2						Germany only
11	Cap for wire wheel—L/H side	AHH8009		2	2						
12	Weight—wheel balance—½ oz.	1B8036	P10	A/R	A/R						
13	Weight—wheel balance—1 oz.	1B8037		A/R	A/R						
14	Weight—wheel balance—1½ oz.	1B8038		A/R	A/R						
15	Weight—wheel balance—2 oz.	1B8039		A/R	A/R						
16	Weight—wheel balance—2½ oz.	1B8040		A/R	A/R						
17	Weight—wheel balance—3 oz.	1B8041		A/R	A/R						

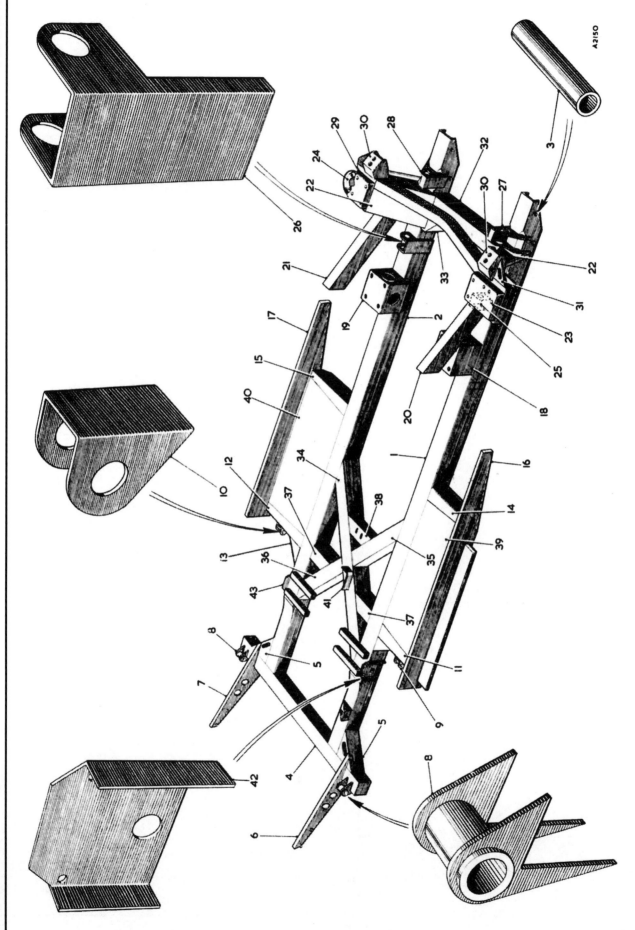

A2150

SERVICE PARTS LIST

AUSTIN-HEALEY 100 SIX (SERIES BN6)

BODY SHELL

Item No.	DESCRIPTION	Commencing (C) 501 Part Number	Illus. No.	Qty. per Vehicle RHD	Qty. per Vehicle LHD	Unit of Issue	Type of Vehicle	New Part Number	Change Point	Amdt. No.	REMARKS
1	Shell—body	4B4922A									
2	Frame assembly—chassis with front end assembly and rear end assembly	AHB5605		1	1						
	Frame—chassis	11B5529		1	1						
3	Side-member—R/H	11B5202	R1	1	1						
4	Side-member—L/H	11B5205	R2	1	1						
5	Tube—front bumper mounting	11B5212	R3	4	4						
6	Cross-member—rear	1B8641	R4	1	1						
7	Gusset—rear cross-member	1B8658	R5	2	2						
8	Bracket—rear bumper—R/H	11B5252	R6	1	1						
9	Bracket—rear bumper—L/H	11B5254	R7	1	1						
10	Bracket—rear spring rear	1B8648	R8	2	2						
11	Bracket—rear spring front R/H	1B8688	R9	1	1						
12	Bracket—rear spring front L/H	1B8689	R10	1	1						
13	Bracket—body mounting rear R/H	11B5225	R11	1	1						
14	Bracket—body mounting rear L/H	11B5228	R12	1	1						
15	Gusset—body bracket	1B8693	R13	2	2						
16	Bracket—body mounting front R/H	1B8698	R14	1	1						
17	Bracket—body mounting front L/H	1B8699	R15	1	1						
18	Sill—body—R/H	11B5264	R16	1	1						
19	Sill—body—L/H	11B5265	R17	1	1						
20	Platform—engine front mounting—R/H	11B5214	R18	1	1						
21	Platform—engine front mounting—L/H	11B5217	R19	1	1						
22	Strut—engine bearer—R/H	1B8670	R20	1	1						
23	Strut—engine bearer—L/H	1B8672	R21	1	1						
24	Housing—front suspension	1B8766	R22	2	2						
25	Adaptor—suspension housing—R/H	1B8839	R23	1	1						
26	Adaptor—suspension housing—L/H	1B8840	R24	1	1						
27	Bracket—lower link rear R/H	11B5251	R25	1	1						
28	Bracket—lower link rear L/H	1B8685	R26	1	1						
29	Bracket—lower link front R/H	11B5218	R27	1	1						
30	Bracket—lower link front L/H	11B5220	R28	1	1						
31	Cup for bumper	1A9203	R29	2	2						
32	Bracket—steering	1B8731	R30	2	2						
33	Gusset—steering bracket	11B5148	R31	2	2						
34	Member complete—cross-brace	11B5119		1	1						
35	Member—front	1B8703	R32	1	1						
36	Gusset—front cross-member	1B8777	R33	2	2						
37	Cross-brace—main beam	11B5120	R34	1	1						
38	Cross-brace—half beam front	11B5123	R35	1	1						
39	Cross-brace—half beam rear	11B5126	R36	1	1						
40	Stiffener—cross-brace	11B5128	R37	2	2						
41	Member—engine rear mounting support	11B5119	R38	1	1						
42	Panel—side floor—R/H	11B5228	R39	1	1						
43	Panel—side floor—L/H	11B5224	R40	1	1						
44	Bracket—hand brake	11B5236	R41	1	1						
45	Bracket—rear shock absorber mounting—R/H	11B5580	R42	1	1						
46	Bracket—rear shock absorber mounting—L/H	11B5534	R43	1	1						

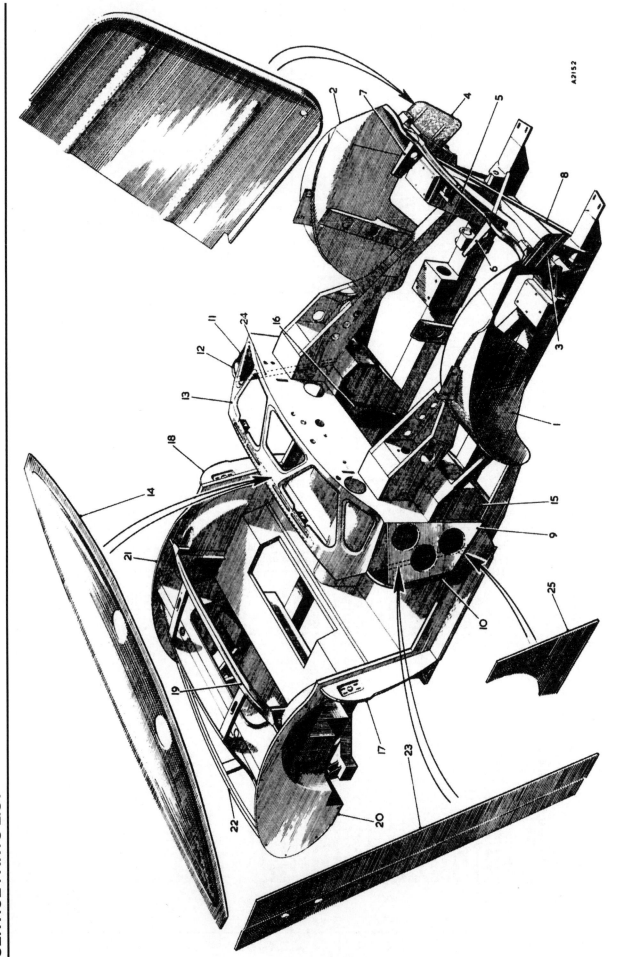

A2152

AUSTIN-HEALEY 100 SIX (SERIES BN6)

Item No.	DESCRIPTION	Part Number Commencing (C) 501	Illus. No.	Qty. per Vehicle RHD	Qty. per Vehicle LHD	Unit of Issue	Type of Vehicle	MODIFICATIONS New Part Number	MODIFICATIONS Change Point	MODIFICATIONS Amdt. No.	REMARKS
	Body Shell—*continued*										
	Front end assembly	**AHB5391**									
1	Wheel arch assembly—R/H	4B7427	RA1	1	1						
2	Wheel arch assembly—L/H	4B7428	RA2	1	1						
3	Wheel arch splash panel—R/H	14B6461	RA3	1	1						
4	Wheel arch splash panel—L/H	14B6462	RA4	1	1						
5	Cowl and cross-brace assembly	4B9853	RA5	1	1						
6	Bracket—radiator steady R/H	14B5811	RA6	1	1						
7	Bracket—radiator steady L/H	14B5812	RA7	1	1						
8	Cross-brace assembly—centre	4B9866	RA8	1	1						
9	Scuttle side panel assembly—R/H	4B9856	RA9	1	1						
10	Hinge pillar assembly—R/H	4B9854	RA10	1	1						
11	Scuttle side panel assembly—L/H	4B9857	RA11	1	1						
12	Hinge pillar assembly—L/H	4B9855	RA12	1	1						
13	Scuttle top inner panel	4B9858	RA13	1	1						
14	Demister channel assembly	4B9865	RA14	1	1						
15	Dash and pedal box assembly	4B9859	RA15	1	1						
16	Panel—reinforcement—gearbox cover extension assembly	AHB8285	RA16	1	1						
	Rear end assembly	**4B2050**									
17	Shut pillar assembly—R/H	AHB5892	RA17	1	1						
18	Shut pillar assembly—L/H	AHB5893	RA18	1	1						
19	Rail reinforcement assembly	AHB5894	RA19	1	1						
20	Rear quarter panel inner assembly—R/H	AHB5895	RA20	1	1						
21	Rear quarter panel inner assembly—L/H	AHB5896	RA21	1	1						
22	Rear skirt rail assembly	4B9864	RA22	1	1						
23	Extension plate—scuttle side panel—R/H	24B1682	RA23	1	1						
24	Extension plate—scuttle side panel—L/H	24B1683	RA24	1	1						
25	Gusset plate—scuttle side to sill	24B1684	RA25	2	2						

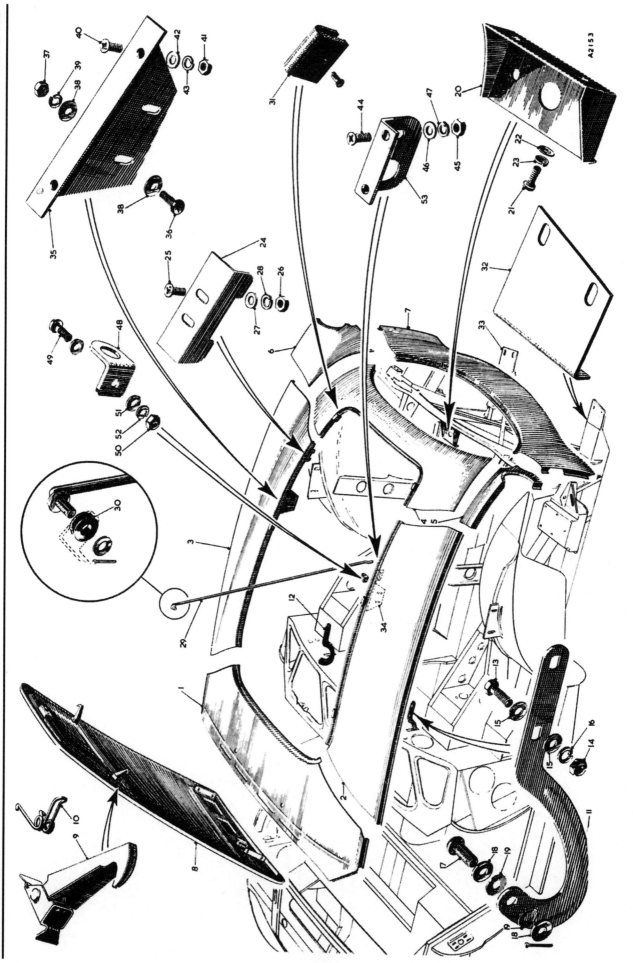

A2153

Item No.	DESCRIPTION	Commencing (C) 501 Part Number	Illus. No.	Qty. per Vehicle RHD	Qty. per Vehicle LHD	Unit of Issue	Type of Vehicle	New Part Number	Change Point	Amdt. No.	REMARKS
	Body Shell—*continued*										
	Bonnet surround assembly	**4B1085**		**1**	**1**						
1	Scuttle top panel outer	14B5722	RB1	1	1						
2	Front wing inner panel—R/H	14B5723	RB2	1	1						
3	Front wing inner panel—L/H	14B5724	RB3	1	1						
4	Cowl front top panel	14B5725	RB4	1	1						
5	Cowl side panel—R/H	14B5726	RB5	1	1						
6	Cowl side panel—L/H	14B5727	RB6	1	1						
7	Cowl front bottom panel	14B5728	RB7	1	1						
8	**Bonnet top assembly**	**4B1089**	RB8	1	1						
9	Hook assembly—bonnet	14A366	RB9	2	2						
10	Spring	4B8646	RB10	2	2						
11	**Hinge—bonnet—R/H**	**14G3692**	RB11	1	1						
12	**Hinge—bonnet—L/H**	**14G3693**	RB12	1	1						
13	Screw fixing hinge	HZS0406	RB13	4	4						
14	Nut for screw	FNZ104	RB14	8	8	12.					
15	Washer for nut (plain)	PWZ104	RB15	8	8						
16	Washer for nut (spring)	LWZ204	RB16	4	4						
17	Pin—clevis	CLZ0511	RB17	2	2						
18	Washer for pin (plain)	PWZ105	RB18	4	4						
19	Washer (anti-rattle)	AWZ105	RB19	4	4						
20	Bracket—bonnet lock support	14B5861	RB20	1	1						
21	Screw fixing bracket	PMZ0810	RB21	2	2						
22	Washer for screw (plain)	PWZ103	RB22	2	2						
23	Washer for screw (spring)	LWZ203	RB23	2	2						
24	Striker—bonnet hook safety catch	14B8812	RB24	2	2						
25	Screw fixing striker	CMZ0808	RB25	4	4						
26	Nut for screw	FNZ103	RB26	4	4						
27	Washer for nut (plain)	PWZ103	RB27	4	4						
28	Washer for nut (spring)	LWZ203	RB28	4	4						
29	Prop rod	AHB5748	RB29	1	1						
30	Ferrule (rubber)	2H1046	RB30	1	1						
31	Buffer (rubber)—bonnet surround	14B766	RB31	5	5						
32	Bracket—bonnet surround to chassis—R/H	14B7661	RB32	1	1						
33	Bracket—bonnet surround to chassis—L/H	14B7662	RB33	1	1						
34	Plate—bonnet opening support—R/H	14B2005	RB34	1	1						
35	Plate—bonnet opening support—L/H	14B2006	RB35	1	1						
36	Screws fixing plates	PMZ0808	RB36	4	4						
37	Nut for screw	FNZ103	RB37	4	4						
38	Washer for nut (plain)—large	PWZ203	RB38	8	8						
39	Washer for nut (spring)	LWZ203	RB39	4	4						

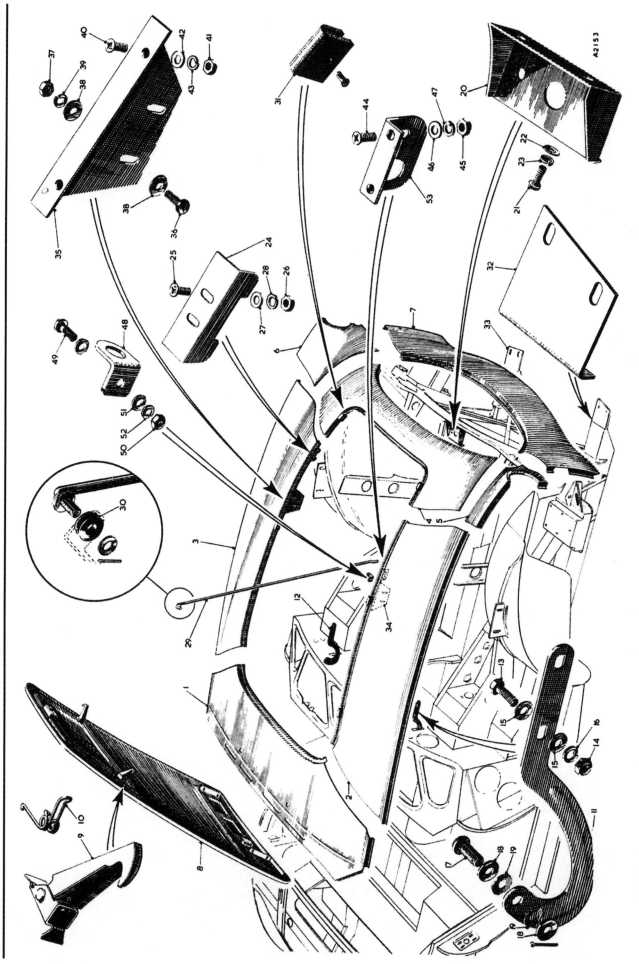

A2153

SERVICE PARTS LIST

AUSTIN-HEALEY 100 SIX (SERIES BN6)

Item No.	DESCRIPTION	Commencing (C) 501 Part Number	Illus. No.	Qty. per Vehicle RHD	LHD	Unit of Issue	Type of Vehicle	New Part Number	Change Point	Amdt. No.	REMARKS
	Body Shell—*continued*										
1	Screw fixing plate	CMN0808	RB40	4	4						
2	Nut for screw	FNZ108	RB41	4	4						
3	Washer for nut (plain)	PWZ103	RB42	4	4						
4	Washer for nut (spring)	LWZ203	RB43	4	4						
5	Screw fixing bracket	CMN0810	RB44	2	2						
6	Nut for screw	FNN103	RB45	2	2						
7	Washer for nut (plain)	PWN103	RB46	2	2						
8	Washer for nut (spring)	LWN208	RB47	2	2	24.					
9	Bracket—remote control rod support	14B6806	RB48	1	1						
10	Screw fixing bracket	PMZ0308	RB49	1	1						
11	Nut for screw	FNZ108	RB50	1	1						
12	Washer for nut (plain)	PWZ103	RB51	2	2						
13	Washer for nut (spring)	LWZ208	RB52	1	1						
14	Bracket—prop rod support	24B778	RB53	1	1						

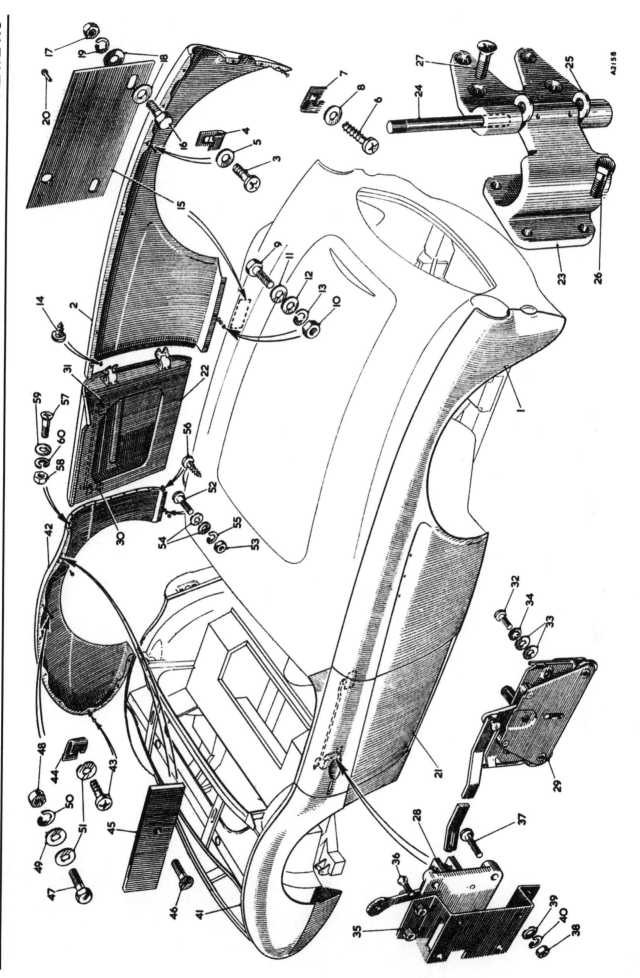

A2158

AUSTIN-HEALEY 100 SIX (SERIES BN6)

Item No.	DESCRIPTION	Part Number (Commencing (C) 501)	Illus. No.	Qty. per Vehicle RHD	Qty. per Vehicle LHD	Unit of Issue	Type of Vehicle	New Part Number	Change Point	Amdt. No.	REMARKS
	Body Shell—*continued*										
1	**Wing assembly—R/H**	4B1087	RC1	1	1						
2	**Wing assembly—L/H**	4B1088	RC2	1	1						
3	Bolt fixing wing (⅜″ × ¼″)	ABZ0407	RC3	12	12						
4	Nut for bolt (Spire)	6K9817	RC4	12	12						
5	Washer for nut (plain 'D')	2K9993	RC5	12	12						
6	Bolt (⅜″ × ¼″)	6K9818	RC6	6	6						
7	Nut for bolt (Spire)	PFS514	RC7	6	6						
8	Washer for nut (plain 'D')	2K9993	RC8	6	6						
9	Screw (¾″ × ¼″)	HZS0406	RC9	6	6						
10	Nut for screw	FNZ104	RC10	6	6						
11	Washer for nut (plain 'D')	2K9993	RC11	6	6						
12	Washer for nut (plain)	PWZ104	RC12	6	6	12					
13	Washer for nut (spring)	LWZ204	RC13	6	6						
14	Screw (No. 6 × ⅜″)	PTZ603	RC14	14	14						
15	Bracket—front wing support	14B6453	RC15	2	2						
16	Screw fixing bracket	HZS0406	RC16	4	4						
17	Nut for screw	FNZ104	RC17	4	4						
18	Washer (special)	2K9051	RC18	8	8						
19	Washer for nut (spring)	LWZ204	RC19	4	4						
20	Rivet	6K9717	RC20	6	6						
21	**Door shell assembly—R/H**	4B1083	RC21	1	1						
22	**Door shell assembly—L/H**	4B2053	RC22	1	1						
23	**Hinge—door**	14B5896	RC23	4	4						
24	Pin—hinge	14B3732	RC24	4	4						
25	Washer for hinge pin	2K9005	RC25	8	8						
26	Screw—hinge to door	HZS0508	RC26	16	16						
27	Screw—hinge to body	CMZ0516	RC27	16	16						
28	**Lock unit—R/H**	14B7481	RC28	1	1						
29	Remote control unit—R/H	14B6822	RC29	1	1						
30	**Lock unit—L/H**	14B7482	RC30	1	1						
31	Remote control unit—L/H	14B6823	RC31	1	1						
32	Screw fixing lock and remote control	PPZ0306	RC32	6	6						
33	Washer for screw (plain)	PWZ103	RC33	12	12						
34	Washer for screw (shakeproof)	2K8232	RC34	6	6						
35	Bracket—door lock fixing R/H	14B7483	RC35	1	1						
36	Bracket—door lock fixing—L/H	14B7484		1	1						
37	Screw fixing bracket	CMZ0308	RC36	4	4						
38	Screw fixing lock and remote control	RMZ0310	RC37	8	8						
39	Nut for screw	FNZ103	RC38	8	8						
40	Washer for nut (plain)	PWZ103	RC39	8	8						
41	Washer for nut (spring)	LWZ203	RC40	8	8						

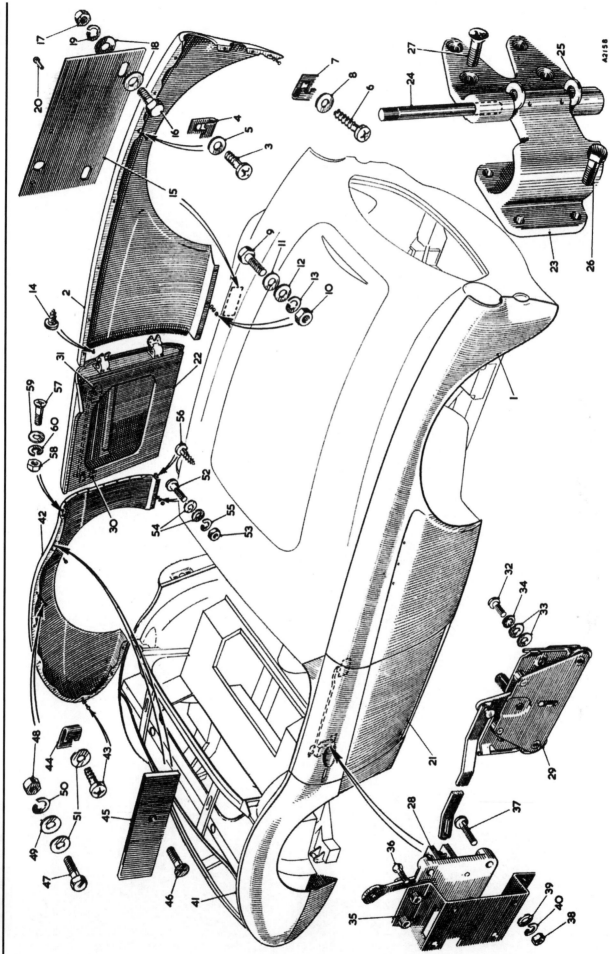

A2158

Item No.	DESCRIPTION	Commencing (C) 501		Qty. per Vehicle		Unit of Issue	Type of Vehicle	MODIFICATIONS			REMARKS
		Part Number	Illus. No.	RHD	LHD			New Part Number	Change Point	Amdt. No.	
	Body Shell—*continued*										
1	Rear quarter panel assembly—R/H	4B1091	RC41	1	1						
2	Rear quarter panel assembly—L/H	4B1092	RC42	1	1						
3	Bolt fixing quarter panel	ABZ0407	RC43	18	18						
4	Spire nut	6K9817	RC44	13	13						
5	Tapped plate	14B2546	RC45	2	2						
6	Screw ($\frac{1}{4}'' \times \frac{5}{8}''$)	CMN0410	RC46	2	2						
7	Screw ($\frac{1}{4}'' \times \frac{3}{4}''$)	HNS0406	RC47	1	1						
8	Nut for screw	FNN104	RC48	1	1						
9	Washer for nut (plain)	PWN104	RC49	1	1						
10	Washer for nut (spring)	LWN204	RC50	1	1						
11	Washer (plain 'D')	2K9993	RC51	14	14						
12	Screw (No. 10 UNF × $\frac{5}{8}''$)	PMN0810	RC52	4	4						
13	Nut for screw	FNN103	RC53	4	4						
14	Washer for nut (plain)	PWN108	RC54	8	8	24					
15	Washer for nut (spring)	LWN203	RC55	4	4						
16	Screw (No. 8 × $\frac{5}{8}''$)	PTN805	RC56	2	2						
17	Screw (No. 10 × $\frac{1}{2}''$)	CMN0308	RC57	16	16						
18	Nut for screw	FNN103	RC58	16	16						
19	Washer for nut (plain)	PWN203	RC59	16	16						
20	Washer for nut (spring)	LWN203	RC60	16	16	24					

R.6

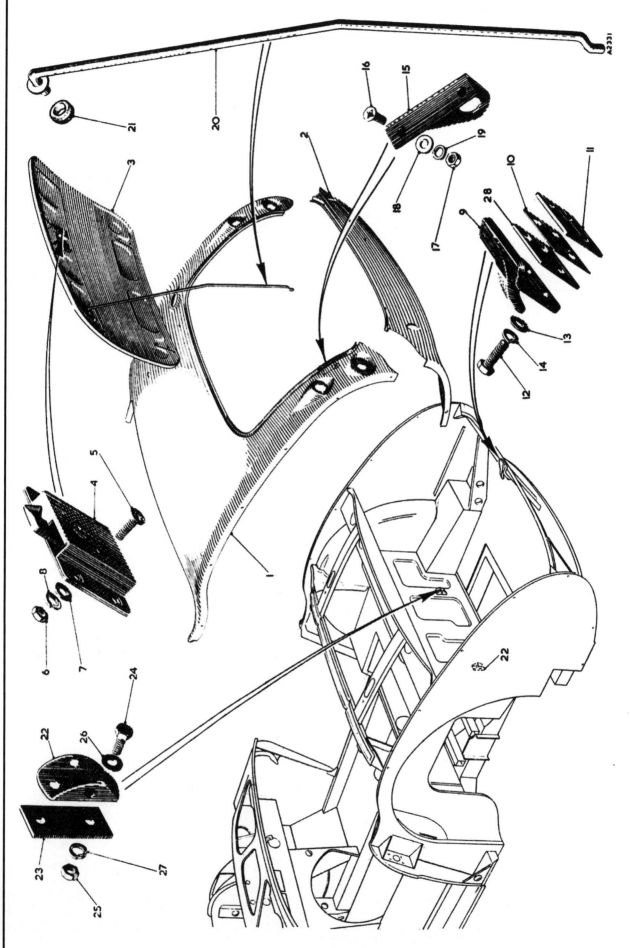

A2331

SERVICE PARTS LIST

AUSTIN-HEALEY 100 SIX (SERIES BN6)

Item No.	DESCRIPTION	Part Number Commencing (C) 501	Illus. No.	Qty. per Vehicle RHD	Qty. per Vehicle LHD	Unit of Issue	Type of Vehicle	New Part Number	Change Point	Amdt. No.	REMARKS
	Body Shell—*continued*										
	Tonneau assembly	**4B2048**	**RD1**	1	1						
1	Panel—rear skirt	14B5739	RD2	1	1						
2	**Lid—boot**	**4B1090**	**RD3**	1	1						
3	**Lock**	**14B1718**	**RD4**	1	1						
4	Screw fixing lock	CMZ0412	RD5	4	4						
5	Nut for screw	FNZ104	RD6	4	4	12					
6	Washer for nut (plain)	PWZ104	RD7	4	4						
7	Washer for nut (spring)	LWZ204	RD8	4	4						
8	Striker—boot lid	14B1719	RD9	1	1						
9	Plate—packing	14B2809	RD28	A/R	A/R						
10	Packing piece	14B6817	RD10	1	1						
11	Plate—tapped	14B2038	RD11	1	1						
12	Screw fixing striker	HZS0407	RD12	3	3						
13	Washer for screw (plain)	PWZ104	RD13	3	3	12					
14	Washer for screw (spring)	LWZ204	RD14	3	3						
15	Bracket—prop rod support	14B6407	RD15	1	1						
16	Screw fixing bracket	CMN0308	RD16	2	2						
17	Nut for screw	FNN103	RD17	2	2						
18	Washer for nut (plain)	PWN103	RD18	2	2						
19	Washer for nut (spring)	LWN203	RD19	2	2	24					
20	Rod—boot lid prop	14B6597	RD20	1	1						
21	Ferrule for rod (rubber)	2H1046	RD21	1	1						
22	Bracket—fuel tank strap fixing	14B1884	RD22	2	2						
23	Plate—stiffening	14B2531	RD23	2	2						
24	Screw fixing bracket and plate	HNS0405	RD24	4	4						
25	Nut for screw	FNN104	RD25	4	4						
26	Washer for nut (plain)	PWN104	RD26	4	4						
27	Washer for nut (spring)	LWN204	RD27	4	4						

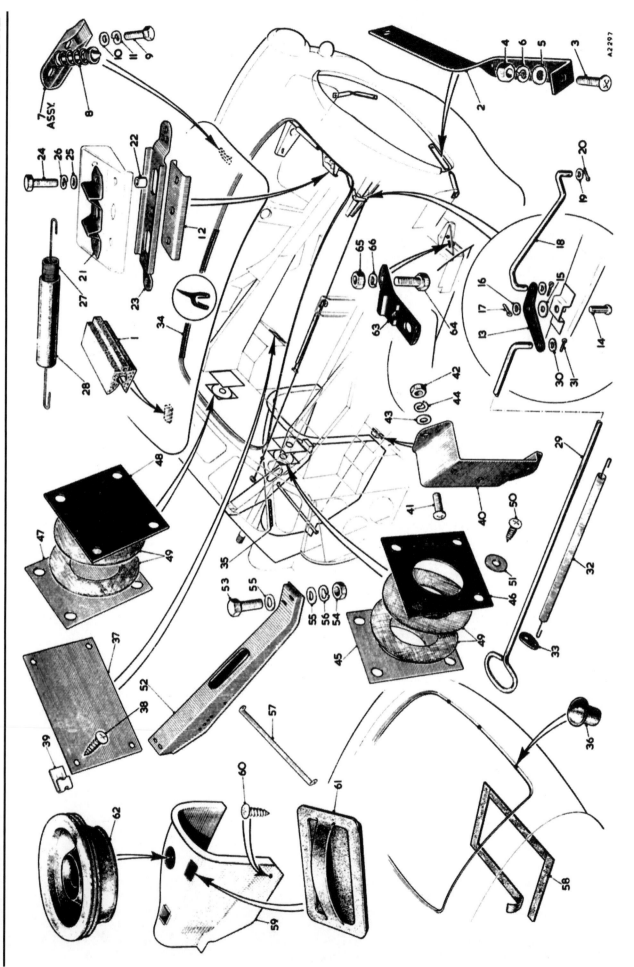

A2297

178

Item No.	DESCRIPTION	Part Number Commencing (C) 501	Illus. No.	Qty. per Vehicle RHD	LHD	Unit of Issue	Type of Vehicle	New Part Number	Change Point	Amdt. No.	REMARKS
	Body Shell—*continued*										
1	Stop—bonnet prop rod (rubber)	2H9215	RE1	1	1						
2	Bracket—steady—front wheel arch splash panel	14B8818	RE2	2	2						
3	Screw fixing bracket	PMZ0306	RE3	2	2						
4	Nut for screw	FNZ103	RE4	2	2						
5	Washer for nut (plain)	PWZ103	RE5	2	2						
6	Washer for nut (spring)	LWZ203	RE6	2	2						
7	**Striker pin assembly—bonnet catch**	**14B2845**	**RE7**	1	1						
8	Spring—striker pin	14B2846	RE8	1	1						
9	Screw—fixing pin assembly	HZS0405	RE9	2	2						
10	Washer for screw (plain)	PWZ104	RE10	2	2	12.					
11	Washer for screw (spring)	LWZ204	RE11	2	2						
12	Slider support assembly	ADH456	RE12	1	1						
13	Lever	ADA457	RE18	1	1						
14	Clevis pin fixing lever	CLZ0313	RE14	1	1						
15	Washer for pin—large (plain)	PWZ203	RE15	1	1						
16	Washer for pin (plain)	PWZ103	RE16	1	1						
17	Cotter pin	ZPS0204	RE17	1	1						
18	Connecting rod—lever to bonnet catch slider	14B6754	RE18	1	1						
19	Washer for rod (plain)	PWZ103	RE19	2	2						
20	Cotter pin	ZPS0204	RE20	1	1						
21	Plate—guide	ADA463	RE21	1	1						
22	Distance tube	ADA464	RE22	2	2						
23	Slider—bonnet catch	ADA461	RE23	1	1						
24	Screw fixing plate, tube, and slider	HZS0407	RE24	2	2	12.					
25	Washer for screw (plain)	PWZ104	RE25	2	2						
26	Washer for screw (spring)	LWZ204	RE26	2	2						
27	Spring—tension—bonnet catch	ADA466	RE27	1	1						
28	Sleeve for spring (rubber)	ADA467	RE28	1	1						
29	Rod—bonnet lock remote control	14B6805	RE29	1	1						
30	Washer for rod (plain)	PWZ103	RE80	1	1						
31	Cotter pin	ZPS0204	RE81	1	1						
32	Spring—anti-rattle	ADA2450	RE82	1	1						
33	Bracket—anchor	ACA5814	RE83	1	1						
34	Strip—bonnet surround sealing—L/H	24B758	RE34	1	1						
35	Strip—scuttle—top panel sealing	14B2871	RE85	2	2				Fin. (C) **4800**		
36	Buffer in rear skirt panel (rubber)	4G8595	RE36	3	3						
37	Plate—blanking—pedal accommodation box assembly	4B3223	RE87	1	1						
38	Screw fixing plate	PTZ803	RE38	4	4						
39	Nut for screw—spring ('J' type)	PFS5528	RE89	4	4						
40	Bracket—dipper switch	1A1880	RE40	1	1						
41	Screw fixing bracket	PMZ0410	RE41	2	2						
42	Nut for screw	FNZ104	RE42	2	2						
43	Washer for nut (plain)	PWZ104	RE43	2	2	12.					
44	Washer for nut (spring)	LWZ204	RE44	2	2						

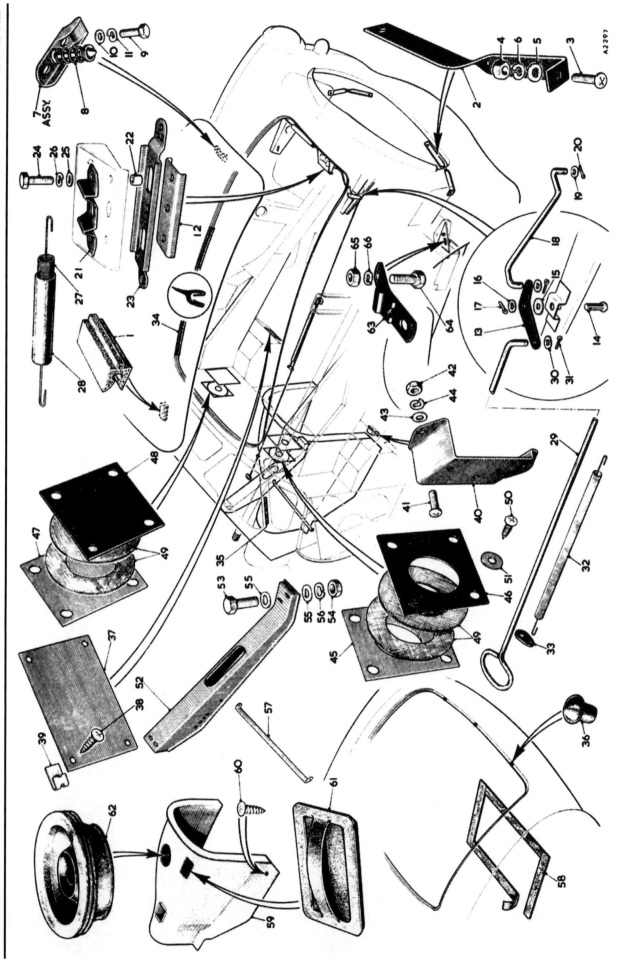

AUSTIN-HEALEY 100 SIX (SERIES BN6)

Item No.	DESCRIPTION	Commencing (C) 501 Part Number	Illus. No.	Qty. per Vehicle RHD	Qty. per Vehicle LHD	Unit of Issue	Type of Vehicle	New Part Number	Change Point	Amdt. No.	REMARKS
	Body Shell—*continued*										
1	Plate—sealing—steering column (inner)	14B1815	RE45	1	1						
2	Plate—sealing—steering column (outer)	14B7544	RE46	1	1						
3	Plate—blanking—steering column (inner)	14B2512	RE47	1	1						
4	Plate—blanking—steering column (outer)	14B7545	RE48	1	1						
5	Felt for sealing and blanking plates	14B2513	RE49	4	4						
6	Screw fixing plates	PTZ603	RE50	16	16						
7	Washer for screw (special)	53K3157	RE51	16	16						
8	Bracket fixing steering column	14B2547	RE52	1	1						
9	Screw fixing bracket	HNS0505	RE53	4	4						
10	Nut for screw	FNN105	RE54	4	4						
11	Washer for nut (plain)	PWN105	RE55	8	8	12.					
12	Washer for nut (spring)	LWN205	RE56	4	4						
13	Bracket—steering column steady	14B7458	RE57	1	1						
14	Rubber—sealing—fuel tank mounting	14B6632	RE58	1	1						
15	**Cover assembly—gearbox**	4B3178	RE59	1	1						
16	Screw fixing cover	PTZ806	RE60	4	4						
17	Plug—gearbox cover (rubber)	4G4920	RE61	1	1						
18	Grommet—gear lever	14B8877	RE62	1	1						
19	Bracket—front brake hose	11B5149	RE63	2	2						
20	Bolt for bracket	HZS0406	RE64	2	2						
21	Nut for bolt	FNZ104	RE65	2	2						
22	Washer for nut (spring)	LWZ204	RE66	2	2						
23	Panel—front apron			1	1			14B5785	Com. (C) 4022		

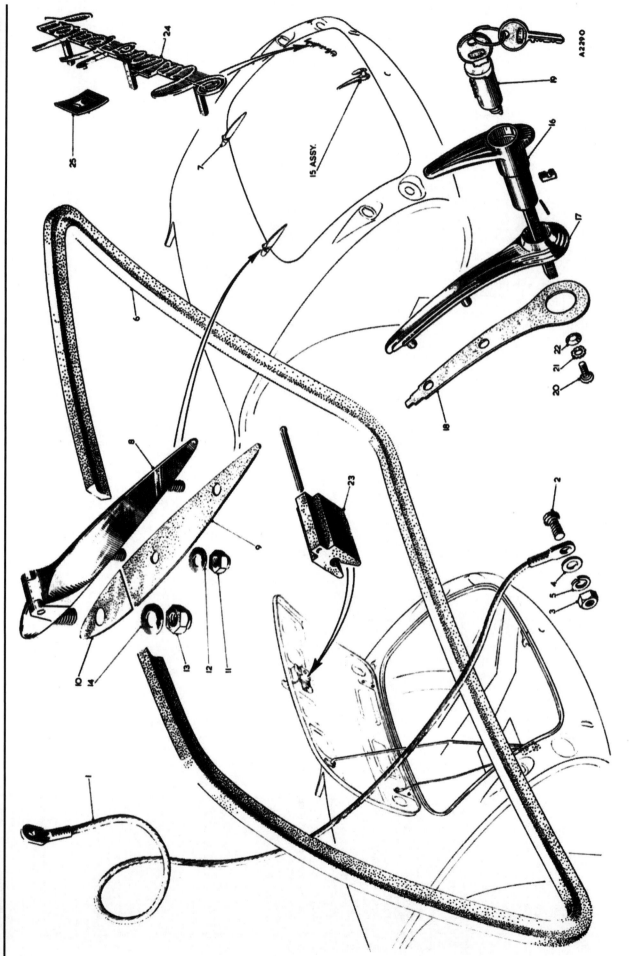

A2290

SERVICE PARTS LIST

AUSTIN-HEALEY 100 SIX (SERIES BN6)

Item No.	DESCRIPTION	Commencing (C) 501 Part Number	Illus. No.	Qty. per Vehicle RHD	Qty. per Vehicle LHD	Unit of Issue	Type of Vehicle	New Part Number	Change Point	Amdt. No.	REMARKS
	BOOT LID FITTINGS										
1	**Cable—boot lid control**	**14B8692**	**RF1**	1	1						
2	Screw fixing cable	RMZ0410	RF2	1	1						
3	Nut for screw	FNZ104	RF3	1	1						
4	Washer for nut (plain)	PWZ104	RF4	1	1	12					
5	Washer for nut (spring)	LWZ204	RF5	1	1						
6	Rubber—sealing	14B7466	RF6	1	1						
7	**Hinge—boot lid—R/H**	**14B1725**	**RF7**	1	1						
8	**Hinge—boot lid—L/H**	**14B1726**	**RF8**	1	1						
9	Washer—seating (male)	14B3462	RF9	2	2						
10	Washer—seating (female)	14B3463	RF10	2	2						
11	Nut fixing hinge to outer panel	58K1661	RF11	4	4						
12	Washer for nut (plain)	PWZ104	RF12	4	4	12					
13	Nut fixing hinge to top panel	58K1662	RF13	2	2						
14	Washer for nut (plain)	PWZ105	RF14	2	2						
15	**Handle assembly—locking**	**14B1963**	**RF15**	1	1						
16	Handle	14B1721	RF16	1	1						
17	Escutcheon	14B1722	RF17	1	1						
18	Washer for escutcheon	14B1964	RF18	1	1						
19	Barrel for lock	7H9830	RF19	1	1						
20	Key	ANK4646	RF20	2	2						
21	Screw fixing handle	PMZ0806	RF21	2	2						
22	Washer for screw (shakeproof)	2K8609	RF22	2	2						
23	Washer (cup)	6K9426	RF28	2	2						
24	Stop for prop rod (rubber)	2H9215	RF24	1	1						
25	Nameplate	14B3823	RF25	1	1						
26	Push-on fix	PFS106		8	8	12					

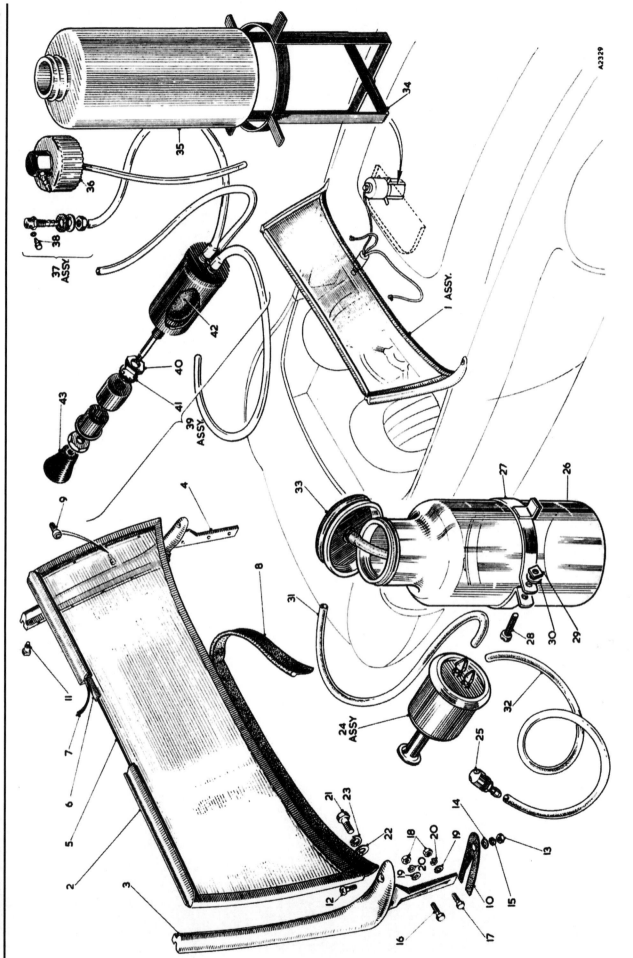

A2329

SERVICE PARTS LIST

Item No.	Description	Part Number (Commencing (C) 501)	Illus. No.	Qty. RHD	Qty. LHD	Unit of Issue	New Part Number	Change Point
	WINDSCREEN							
1	**Windscreen assembly**	**24B624**	**RG1**	1	1			
2	Frame—windscreen	24B625	RG2	1	1			
3	Pillar—R/H	14B5889	RG3	1	1			
4	Pillar—L/H	14B5890	RG4	1	1			
5	Glass	14B5891	RG5	1	1			
6	Rubber—glazing	AHB5833	RG6	1	1			
7	Rubber—glazing—top rail	AHB8382	RG7	1	1			
8	Strip—rubber	24B503	RG8	1	1			
9	Seal—bottom weather	14B5892	RG9	8	8			
10	Screw—frame to pillar	54K195	RG10	2	2			
11	Pad—pillar foot (rubber)	14B6743	RG11	2	2			
12	Stud—retaining toggle clamp	14B7660	RG12	2	2			
13	Screw—pillar to scuttle top panel	RMP0416	RG13	2	2			
14	Nut for screw	FNZ104	RG14	2	2			
15	Washer for nut (plain)	PWZ204	RG15	2	2			
16	Washer for nut (spring)	LWZ204	RG16	2	2			
17	Screw—windscreen to scuttle side panel	HZS0408	RG17	3	3			
18	Screw—windscreen to scuttle side panel	HZS0410	RG18	1	1			
19	Nut for screw	FNZ104	RG19	4	4	12		
20	Washer for nut (plain)	PWZ104	RG20	4	4			
21	Washer for nut (spring)	LWZ204	RG21	4	4			
22	Screw—1¼" × ⅝"	HZS0510	RG22	2	2			
23	Washer for screw (plain)	PWZ106	RG23	2	2			
24	Washer for screw (spring)	LWZ205		2	2	24		
	WINDSCREEN WASHER							
25	**Washer—windscreen**	**14B7784**	RG24	1	1			
26	Pump assembly	17H577	RG25	1	1			
27	Jet—delivery	17H578	RG26	1	1			
28	Reservoir	17H579	RG27	1	1			
29	Bracket—reservoir	17H581	RG28	1	1			
30	Screw—bracket to reservoir	PMZ0316	RG29	1	1			
31	Nut for screw	FNZ103	RG30	2	2			
32	Washer for nut (plain)	PWZ103	RG31	1	1			
33	Tube—suction (rubber)	14B8634	RG32	1	1			
34	Tube—delivery (rubber)	14B8635	RG33	1	1			
35	Container cap and tube assembly	27H9662	RG34	1	1			
36	**Washer—windscreen**			1	1		**AHB5945**	
37	Bracket		RG35	1	1		27H9671	
38	Container		RG36	1	1		7H9779	
39	Cap assembly—container		RG37	1	1		7H9785	
40	Jet mounting assembly		RG38	2	2		27H9622	Fin. (C) 1182
41	Jet		RG39	2	2		27H9623	Com. (C) 1188
42	Control assembly		RG40	1	1		27H9654	
43	Nut—back		RG41	1	1		27H9655	
44	Washer—shakeproof		RG42	1	1		7H9782	
45	Bulb—rubber		RG43	1	1		27H9626	
46	Knob			1	1		27H9625	

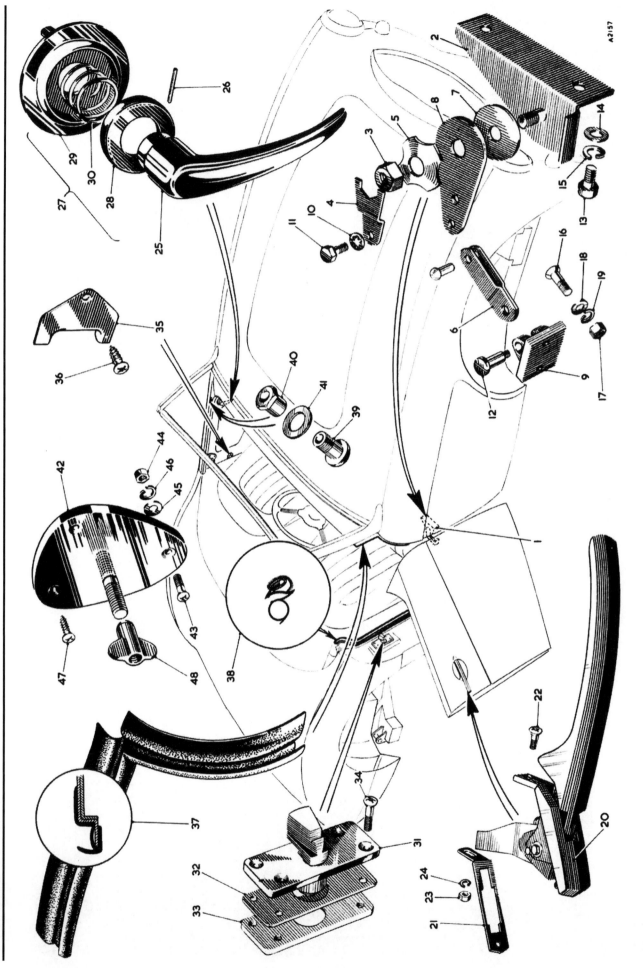

A2157

SERVICE PARTS LIST

AUSTIN-HEALEY 100 SIX (SERIES BN6)

Item No.	DESCRIPTION	Commencing (C) 501 Part Number	Illus. No.	Qty. per Vehicle RHD	Qty. per Vehicle LHD	Unit of Issue	Type of Vehicle	New Part Number	Change Point	Amdt. No.	REMARKS
	DOOR FITTINGS										
1	**Check assembly—R/H**	**14B7554**	**RH1**	1	1						
2	**Check assembly—L/H**	**14B7555**		1	1						
3	Bracket and stud assembly—R/H	14B7556	RH2	1	1						
4	Nut for stud (L.H.T.)	58K1191	RH3	1	1						
5	Bracket and stud assembly—L/H	14B7557		1	1						
6	Nut for stud (R.H.T.)	58K1712		1	1						
7	Spanner—friction	14B7562	RH4	2	2						
8	Washer (spring)	14B7563	RH5	2	2						
9	Link—connection	14B7564	RH6	2	2						
10	Disc—friction	14B7565	RH7	2	2						
11	Arm	14B7566	RH8	2	2						
12	Bracket—check strap	14B4466	RH9	2	2						
13	Washer—internal (shakeproof)	2K8609	RH10	2	2						
14	Screw	58K122	RH11	2	2						
15	Shouldered screw	54K3495	RH12	2	2						
16	Screw—check assembly to hinge pillar	HZS0406	RH18	4	4	12					
17	Washer for screw (plain)	PWZ104	RH14	4	4						
18	Washer for screw (spring)	LWZ304	RH15	4	4						
19	Screw—check assembly to door	RMP0810	RH16	4	4						
20	Nut for screw	FNZ103	RH17	4	4						
21	Washer for screw (plain)	PWZ103	RH18	4	4						
22	Washer for screw (spring)	LWZ203	RH19	4	4						
23	**Handle—door—plain—R/H**	**24B612**	**RH20**	1	1						
24	**Handle—door—plain—L/H**	**24B613**		1	1						
25	Washer—seating	14B9476	RH21	2	2						
26	Screw—fixing door handle to door panel	RMP0808	RH22	2	2						
27	Nut for screw	FNZ108	RH23	2	2						
28	Washer for nut (spring)	LWZ208	RH24	2	2						
29	**Handle—remote control**	**ADG1673**	**RH25**	2	2						
30	Pin—securing handle	ADG1811	RH26	2	2						
31	Escutcheon assembly	ADG709	RH27	2	2						
32	Shell—front	ADB8657	RH28	2	2						
33	Shell—back	ADB554	RH29	2	2						
34	Spring	ADB557	RH30	2	2						
35	Striker—door lock	14B2841	RH31	2	2						
36	Plate—packing	14B2842	RH82	2	2						
37	Plate—tapped	14B2848	RH83	2	2						
38	Screw fixing striker	RMP0812	RH84	8	8						

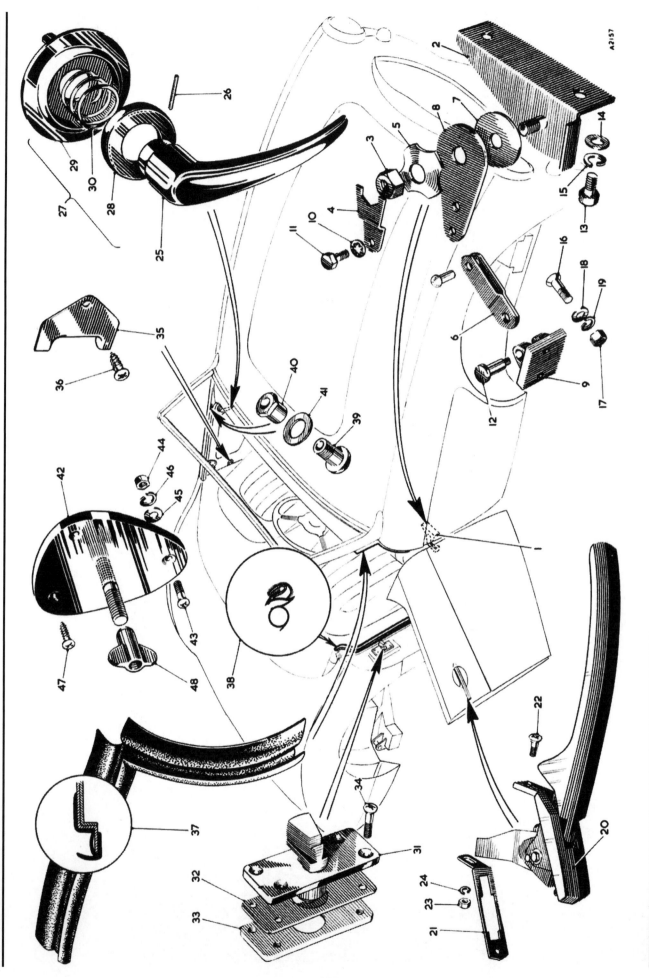

A2157

SERVICE PARTS LIST

AUSTIN-HEALEY 100 SIX (SERIES BN6)

Item No.	DESCRIPTION	Commencing (C) 501 Part Number	Illus. No.	Qty. per Vehicle RHD	Qty. per Vehicle LHD	Unit of Issue	Type of Vehicle	New Part Number	Change Point	Amdt. No.	REMARKS
	Door Fittings—*continued*										
1	Plate—lock catch	14B2544	RH35	2	2						
2	Screw fixing plate	54K3014	RH36	2	2						
3	Sealing rubber—door to scuttle—R/H	24B690	RH37	1	1						
4	Sealing rubber—door to scuttle—L/H	24B691	RH37	1	1						
5	**Sealing rubber—door aperture surround (Red)**	**AHB5398**	**RH38**	**2**	**2**						
6	Sealing rubber—door aperture surround (Blue)	AHB8307		2	2						
7	Sealing rubber—door aperture surround (Black)	AHB8308		2	2						
8	Sealing rubber—door aperture surround (Grey)	AHB8309		2	2						
9	**Socket body for side window**	**14B7648**	**RH39**	**2**	**2**						
10	Spacing nut fixing socket	14B7649	RH40	2	2						
11	Washer for nut	14B7651	RH41	2	2						
12	**Plate assembly for side window—securing**	**24B1656**	**RH42**	**2**	**2**						
13	Screw fixing plate	RPP0810	RH43	4	4						
14	Nut for screw	FNZ103	RH44	4	4						
15	Washer for nut (plain)	PWZ103	RH45	4	4						
16	Washer for nut (spring)	LWZ203	RH46	4	4						
17	Screw fixing plate	54K3413	RH47	2	2						
18	Nut fixing window (wing)	24B540	RH48	4	4						

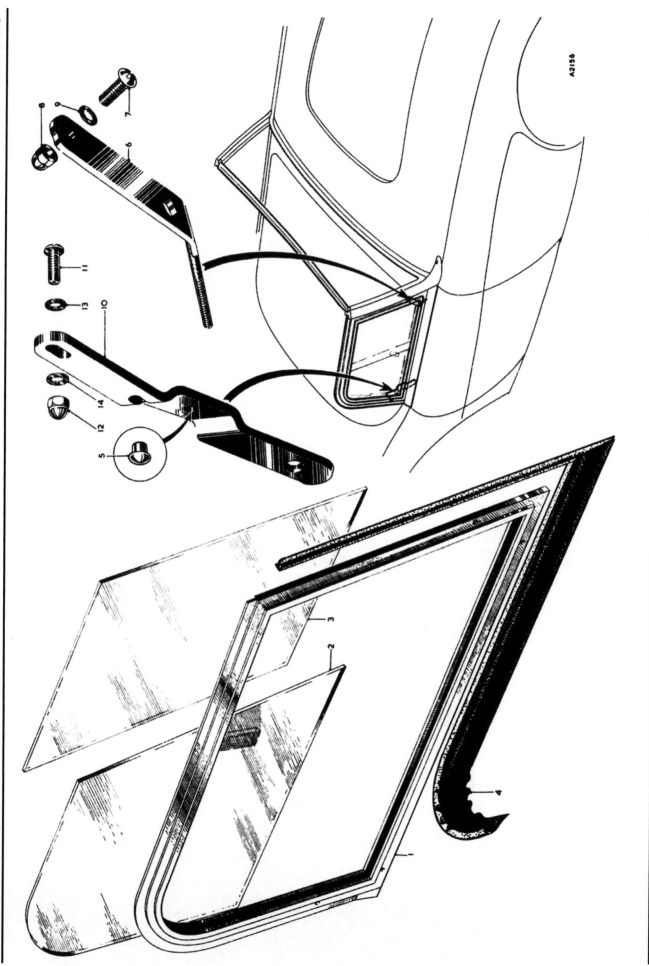

A2156

190

SERVICE PARTS LIST

AUSTIN-HEALEY 100 SIX (SERIES BN6)

Item No.	DESCRIPTION	Commencing (C) 501 Part Number	Illus. No.	Qty. per Vehicle RHD	Qty. per Vehicle LHD	Unit of Issue	Type of Vehicle	New Part Number	Change Point	Amdt. No.	REMARKS
	WINDOWS										
1	**Window—side—R/H**	**24B635**		1	1						
2	Frame—R/H	24B637	RJ1	1	1						
3	Window—sliding—R/H	14B8712	RJ2	1	1						
4	Window—fixed—R/H	14B7744	RJ3	1	1						
5	Weatherstrip—R/H	14B7755	RJ4	1	1						
6	Buffer—rubber	4G8595	RJ5	1	1						
7	Bracket—securing (front)—R/H	24B558	RJ6	1	1						
8	Screw—fixing bracket to frame	14B7764	RJ7	2	2						
9	Nut for screw (dome)	14B7762	RJ8	2	2						
10	Washer for nut (shakeproof)	2K8609	RJ9	2	2						
11	Bracket—securing (rear)—R/H	24B617	RJ10	1	1						
12	Screw—fixing bracket to frame	14B7764	RJ11	2	2						
13	Nut for screw (plain)	14B7762	RJ12	2	2						
14	Washer for nut (plain)	PWZ103	RJ13	2	2						
15	Washer for nut (shakeproof)	2K8609	RJ14	2	2						
16	**Window—side—L/H**	**24B636**		1	1						
17	Frame—L/H	24B638		1	1						
18	Window—sliding—L/H	14B8718		1	1						
19	Window—fixed—L/H	14B7744		1	1						
20	Weatherstrip—L/H	14B7756		1	1						
21	Buffer (rubber)	4G8595		1	1						
22	Bracket—securing (front)—L/H	24B554		1	1						
23	Screw—fixing bracket to frame	14B7764		2	2						
24	Nut for screw (dome)	14B7762		2	2						
25	Washer for nut (shakeproof)	2K8609		1	1						
26	Bracket—securing (rear)—L/H	24B618		1	1						
27	Screw—fixing bracket to frame	14B7764		2	2						
28	Nut for screw (dome)	14B7762		2	2						
29	Washer for nut (plain)	PWZ103		2	2						
30	Washer for nut (shakeproof)	2K8609		2	2						

R.14

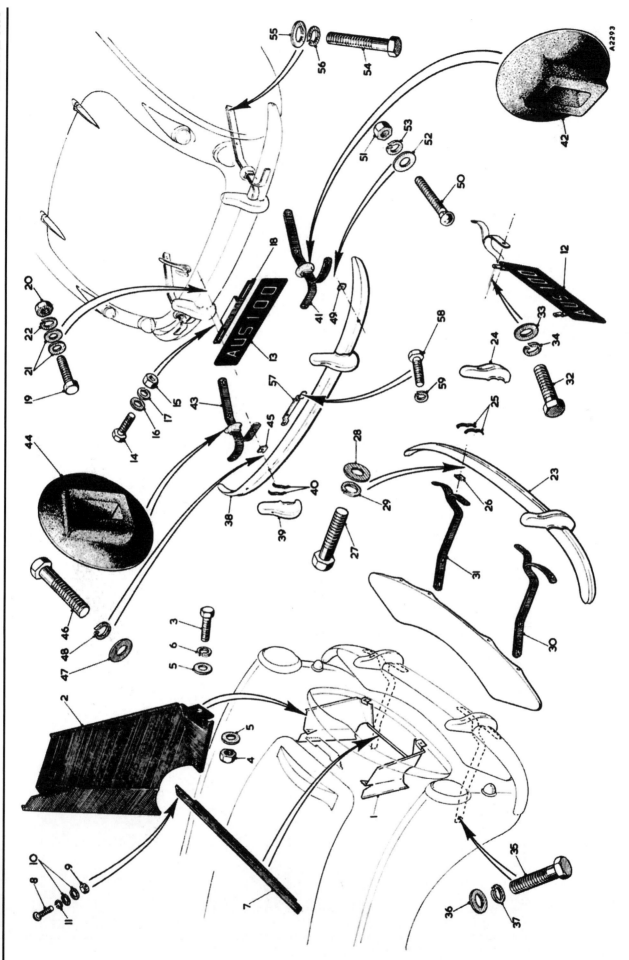

A2293

AUSTIN-HEALEY 100 SIX (SERIES BN6)

Item No.	DESCRIPTION	Commencing (C) 501		Qty. per Vehicle		Unit of Issue	Type of Vehicle	MODIFICATIONS			REMARKS
		Part Number	Illus. No.	RHD	LHD			New Part Number	Change Point	Amdt. No.	
	BONNET FITTINGS										
1	**Deflector assembly—air intake—R/H**	**4B4204**	**RK1**	1	1						
2	**Deflector assembly—air intake—L/H**	**4B4205**	**RK2**	1	1						
3	Screw fixing deflector assembly	HZS0406	RK3	2	2						
4	Nut for screw	FNZ104	RK4	4	4						
5	Washer for nut (plain)	6K9823	RK5	2	2						
6	Washer for nut (spring)	LWZ204	RK6	2	2						
7	Tie-bar—deflector	24B601	RK7	1	1						
8	Screw fixing tie-bar	PMZ0808	RK8	2	2						
9	Nut for screw	FNZ103	RK9	2	2						
10	Washer for nut (plain)	PWZ103	RK10	4	4						
11	Washer for nut (spring)	LWZ208	RK11	2	2						

R.15

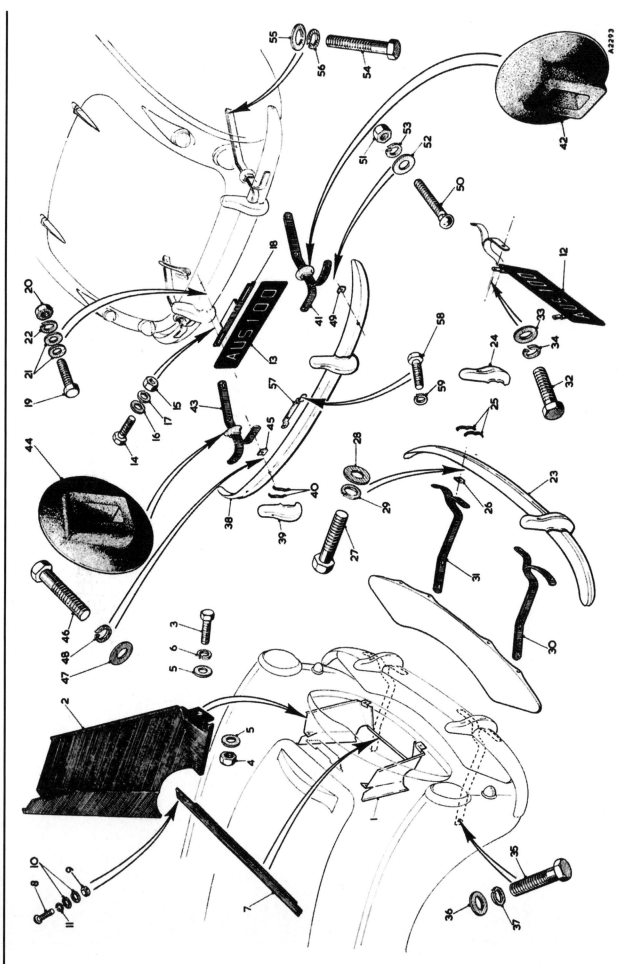

A2293

SERVICE PARTS LIST

AUSTIN-HEALEY 100 SIX (SERIES BN6)

Item No.	DESCRIPTION	Part Number	Illus. No.	RHD	LHD	Unit of Issue	Type of Vehicle	New Part Number	Change Point	Amdt. No.	REMARKS
	NUMBER-PLATES AND FITTINGS										
1	**Plate—front number**	**1B8937**	**RK12**	1							
2	**Plate—rear number**	**1B8940**	**RK13**	1							
3	Bolt—rear number-plate to bracket	HZS0404	RK14	2							
4	Nut for bolt	FNZ104	RK15	2							
5	Washer for bolt (plain)	PWZ204	RK16	2							
6	Washer for bolt (spring)	LWZ204	RK17	2							
7	Bracket—rear number-plate	14B2742	RK18	1	1						
8	Screw fixing bracket	HZS0405	RK19	2	2						
9	Nut for screw	FNZ104	RK20	2	2						
10	Washer for screw (plain)	PWZ104	RK21	4	4	12					
11	Washer for screw (spring)	LWZ204	RK22	2	2						

195   R.16

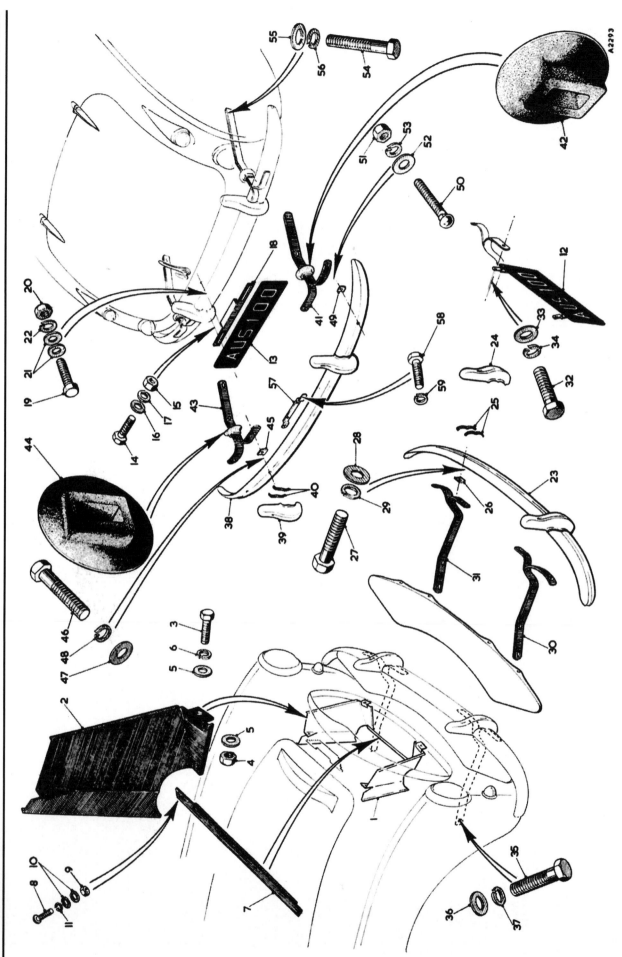

A2293

Item No.	DESCRIPTION	Commencing (C) 501		Qty. per Vehicle		Unit of Issue	Type of Vehicle	MODIFICATIONS			REMARKS
		Part Number	Illus. No.	RHD	LHD			New Part Number	Change Point	Amdt. No.	
	BUMPERS AND FITTINGS										
1	**Bar—front bumper**	**11B5303**	**RK23**	1	1						
2	**Over-rider assembly**	**11B5308**	**RK24**	2	2						
3	Seating for over-rider	11B5809	RK25	4	4						
4	Packing piece—over-rider to bumper bar	1G9799	RK26	2	2						
5	Screw—over-rider to bumper bar	HZS0610	RK27	2	2						
6	Washer for screw (plain)	PWZ106	RK28	2	2						
7	Washer for screw (spring)	LWZ206	RK29	2	2						
8	Spring bar assembly—front R/H	17H9701	RK30	1	1						
9	Spring bar assembly—front L/H	17H9702	RK81	1	1						
10	Screw—spring bar and number-plate bracket to bumper bar	HZS0608	RK82	4	4						
11	Washer for screw (plain)	PWZ106	RK88	4	4						
12	Washer for screw (spring)	LWZ206	RK84	4	4						
13	Set screw—front bumper to frame	HBZ0611	RK85	4	4						
14	Washer for screw (plain)	PWZ106	RK36	4	4						
15	Washer for screw (spring)	LWZ206	RK87	4	4						
16	**Bar—rear bumper**	**11B5312**	**RK38**	1	1						
17	**Over-rider assembly**	**11B5308**	**RK39**	2	2						
18	Seating for over-rider	11B5809	RK40	4	4						
19	Spring bar assembly—rear R/H	17H9099	RK41	1	1						
20	Grommet—spring bar—R/H	1A9307	RK42	1	1						
21	Spring bar assembly—rear L/H	17H9700	RK48	1	1						
22	Grommet—spring bar—L/H	1A9308	RK44	1	1						
23	Packing piece—inner spring bar to bumper bar	1G9799	RK45	2	2						
24	Bolt—inner spring bar to bumper bar and over-rider	HBZ0612	RK46	2	2						
25	Washer for bolt (plain)	PWZ106	RK47	2	2						
26	Washer for bolt (spring)	LWZ206	RK48	2	2						
27	Packing piece—outer spring bar to bumper bar	1G9799	RK49	2	2						
28	Beetle bolt—outer spring bar to bumper bar	1G9707	RK50	2	2						
29	Nut for bolt	FNZ106	RK51	2	2						
30	Washer for nut (plain)	PWZ106	RK52	2	2						
31	Washer for nut (spring)	LWZ206	RK53	2	2						
32	Set screw—rear bumper to frame	HBZ0611	RK54	4	4						
33	Washer for screw (plain)	PWZ106	RK55	4	4						
34	Washer for screw (spring)	LWZ206	RK56	4	4						
35	Bracket—rear number-plate illumination lamp	14B1941	RK57	1	1						
36	Set screw—bracket to bumper bar	HZS0405	RK58	2	2						
37	Washer for screw (spring)	LWZ204	RK59	2	2						

A232 7

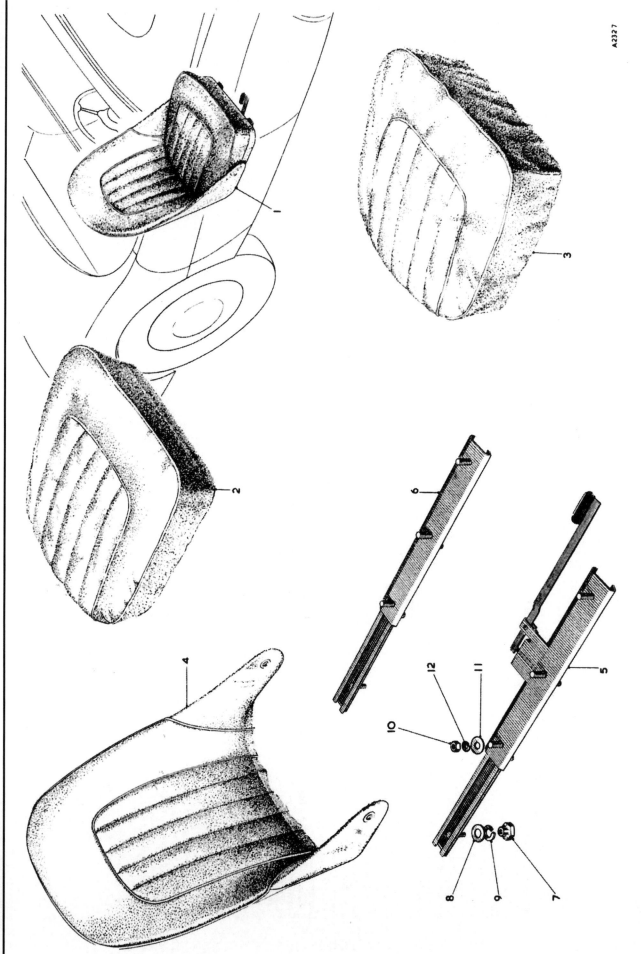

198

SEAT AND SEAT FITTINGS

Item No.	DESCRIPTION	Commencing (C) 501 Part Number	Illus. No.	Qty. per Vehicle RHD	Qty. per Vehicle LHD	Unit of Issue	Type of Vehicle	New Part Number	Change Point	Amdt. No.	REMARKS
1	Seat assembly—bucket—R/H—Red with Ivory White piping	4B4206	RM1	1	1						
2	Seat assembly—bucket—R/H—Red with Black piping	AHB5538		1	1						
3	Seat assembly—bucket—R/H—Blue with Ivory White piping	AHB5539		1	1						
4	Seat assembly—bucket—R/H—Black with Ivory White piping	AHB5540		1	1						
5	Seat assembly—bucket—R/H—Black with Yellow piping	AHB5541		1	1						
6	Seat assembly—bucket—R/H—Grey with Green piping	AHB5542		1	1						
7	Seat assembly—bucket—R/H—Grey with Red piping	AHB5543		1	1						
8	Seat assembly—bucket—R/H—Yellow with Black piping	AHB5544		1	1						
9	Cushion assembly—bucket seat—R/H—Red with Ivory White piping	14B1382	RM2	1	1						
10	Cushion assembly—bucket seat—R/H—Red with Black piping	AHB5545		1	1						
11	Cushion assembly—bucket seat—R/H—Blue with Ivory White piping	AHB5546		1	1						
12	Cushion assembly—bucket seat—R/H—Black with Ivory White piping	AHB5547		1	1						
13	Cushion assembly—bucket seat—R/H—Black with Yellow piping	AHB5548		1	1						
14	Cushion assembly—bucket seat—R/H—Grey with Green piping	AHB5549		1	1						
15	Cushion assembly—bucket seat—R/H—Grey with Red piping	AHB5550		1	1						
16	Cushion assembly—bucket seat—R/H—Yellow with Black piping	AHB5551		1	1						
17	Cover assembly—cushion—R/H—Red with Ivory White piping	14B1387	RM3	1	1						
18	Cover assembly—cushion—R/H—Red with Black piping	AHB5552		1	1						
19	Cover assembly—cushion—R/H—Blue with Ivory White piping	AHB5553		1	1						
20	Cover assembly—cushion—R/H—Black with Ivory White piping	AHB5554		1	1						
21	Cover assembly—cushion—R/H—Black with Yellow piping	AHB5555		1	1						
22	Cover assembly—cushion—R/H—Grey with Green piping	AHB5556		1	1						
23	Cover assembly—cushion—R/H—Grey with Red piping	AHB5557		1	1						
24	Cover assembly—cushion—R/H—Yellow with Black piping	AHB5558		1	1						

A232 7

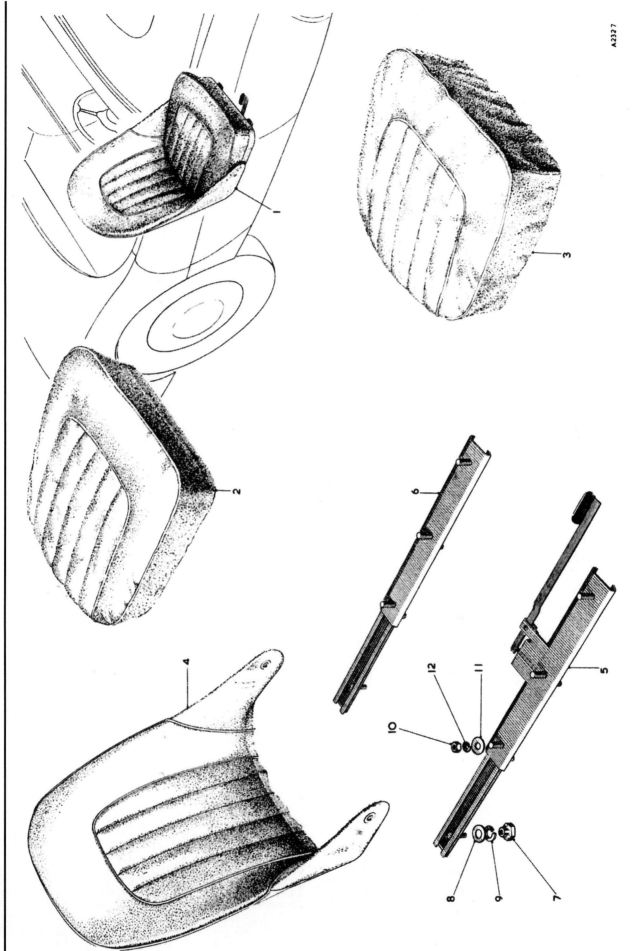

Item No.	DESCRIPTION	Commencing (C) 501 Part Number	Illus. No.	Qty. per Vehicle RHD	Qty. per Vehicle LHD	Unit of Issue	Type of Vehicle	New Part Number	Change Point	Amdt. No.	REMARKS
	Seat and Seat Fittings—*continued*										
1	**Seat assembly—bucket—L/H—Red with Ivory White piping**	**4B4207**		1	1						
2	Seat assembly—bucket—L/H—Red with Black piping	AHB5559		1	1						
3	Seat assembly—bucket—L/H—Blue with Ivory White piping	AHB5560		1	1						
4	Seat assembly—bucket—L/H—Black with Ivory White piping	AHB5561		1	1						
5	Seat assembly—bucket—L/H—Black with Yellow piping	AHB5562		1	1						
6	Seat assembly—bucket—L/H—Grey with Green piping	AHB5563		1	1						
7	Seat assembly—bucket—L/H—Grey with Red piping	AHB5564		1	1						
8	Seat assembly—bucket—L/H—Yellow with Black piping	AHB5565		1	1						
9	**Cushion assembly—bucket seat—L/H—Red with Ivory White piping**	**14B1383**		1	1						
10	Cushion assembly—bucket seat—L/H—Red with Black piping	AHB5566		1	1						
11	Cushion assembly—bucket seat—L/H—Blue with Ivory White piping	AHB5567		1	1						
12	Cushion assembly—bucket seat—L/H—Black with Ivory White piping	AHB5568		1	1						
13	Cushion assembly—bucket seat—L/H—Black with Yellow piping	AHB5569		1	1						
14	Cushion assembly—bucket seat—L/H—Grey with Green piping	AHB5570		1	1						
15	Cushion assembly—bucket seat—L/H—Grey with Red piping	AHB5571		1	1						
16	Cushion assembly—bucket seat—L/H—Yellow with Black piping	AHB5572		1	1						

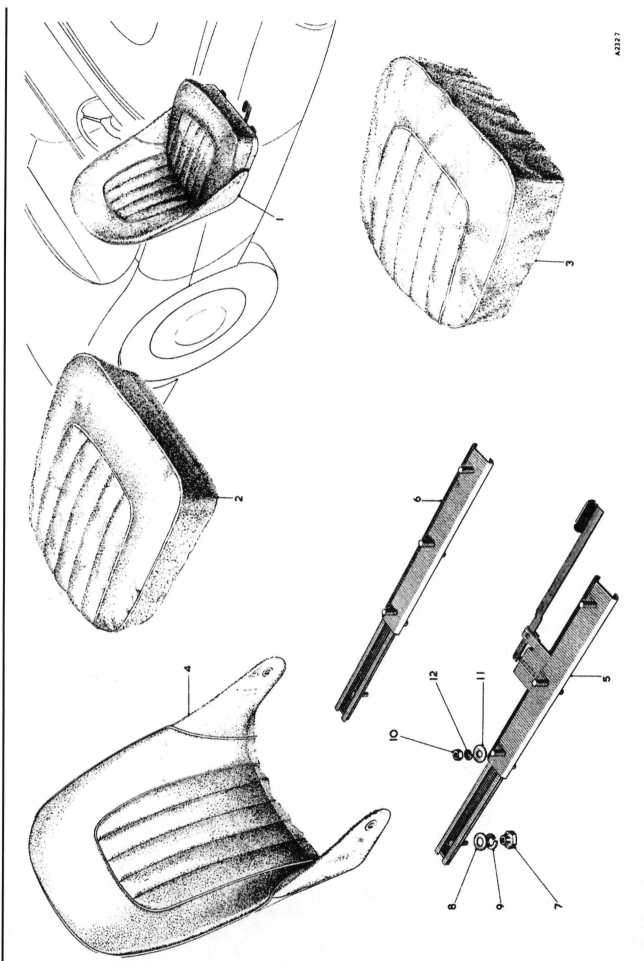

A232 7

SERVICE PARTS LIST

AUSTIN-HEALEY 100 SIX (SERIES BN6)

Item No.	DESCRIPTION	Commencing (C) 501 Part Number	Illus. No.	Qty. per Vehicle RHD	Qty. per Vehicle LHD	Unit of Issue	Type of Vehicle	New Part Number	Change Point	Amdt. No.	REMARKS
	Seat and Seat Fittings—*continued*										
1	**Cover assembly—cushion—L/H—Red with Ivory White piping**	**14B1388**		1	1						
2	Cover assembly—cushion—L/H—Red with Black piping	AHB5573		1	1						
3	Cover assembly—cushion—L/H—Blue with Ivory White piping	AHB5574		1	1						
4	Cover assembly—cushion—L/H—Black with Ivory White piping	AHB5575		1	1						
5	Cover assembly—cushion—L/H—Black with Yellow piping	AHB5576		1	1						
6	Cover assembly—cushion—L/H—Grey with Green piping	AHB5577		1	1						
7	Cover assembly—cushion—L/H—Grey with Red piping	AHB5578		1	1						
8	Cover assembly—cushion—L/H—Yellow with Black piping	AHB5579		1	1						
9	**Cover assembly—squab—Red with Ivory White piping**	**14B1386**	**RM4**	2	2						
10	Cover assembly—squab—Red with Black piping	AHB5580		2	2						
11	Cover assembly—squab—Blue with Ivory White piping	AHB5581		2	2						
12	Cover assembly—squab—Black with Ivory White piping	AHB5582		2	2						
13	Cover assembly—squab—Black with Yellow piping	AHB5583		2	2						
14	Cover assembly—squab—Grey with Green piping	AHB5584		2	2						
15	Cover assembly—squab—Grey with Red piping	AHB5585		2	2						
16	Cover assembly—squab—Yellow with Black piping	AHB5586		2	2						
17	**Slide assembly with lever—R/H**	**14B2774**	**RM5**	1	1						
18	**Slide assembly with lever—L/H**	**14B2767**		1	1						
19	Slide assembly—plain	14B2768	RM6	2	2						
20	'T' nut—slide to floor	14B2877	RM7	12	12						
21	Washer for nut (plain)	PWZ106	RM8	12	12						
22	Washer for nut (spring)	LWZ206	RM9	12	12						
23	Nut—slide to seat	FNZ104	RM10	12	12						
24	Washer for nut—large (plain)	PWZ204	RM11	12	12						
25	Washer for nut (spring)	LWZ204	RM12	12	12						

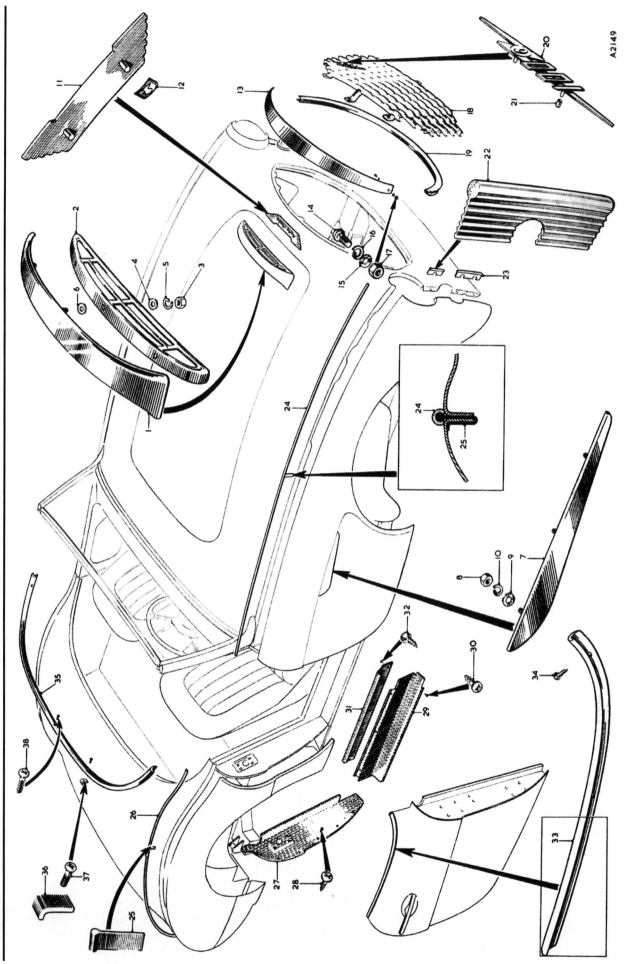

A2149

SERVICE PARTS LIST

AUSTIN-HEALEY 100 SIX (SERIES BN6)

Item No.	DESCRIPTION	Part Number (Commencing (C) 501)	Illus. No.	Qty. per Vehicle RHD	Qty. per Vehicle LHD	Unit of Issue	Type of Vehicle	New Part Number	Change Point	Amdt. No.	REMARKS
	BODY MOULDINGS										
1	**Surround air intake assembly**	**14B5777**	**RN1**	1	1						
2	**Grille air intake**	**14B5779**	**RN2**	1	1						
3	Nut fixing surround and grille	FNZ103	RN3	3	3						
4	Washer for nut (plain)	PWZ103	RN4	3	3						
5	Washer for nut (spring)	LWZ203	RN5	3	3						
6	Packing washer	14B9484	RN6	3	3						
7	Flash—body side—R/H	14B1727	RN7	1	1						
8	Flash—body side—L/H	14B1728		1	1						
9	Nut fixing flash	FNZ103	RN8	6	6						
10	Washer for nut (plain)	PWZ103	RN9	6	6						
11	Washer for nut (spring)	LWZ203	RN10	6	6						
12	Austin-Healey badge	14B1728	RN11	1	1						
13	Push-on fix for badge	14B1998	RN12	2	2						
14	Hood—radiator grille	14B5773	RN13	1	1						
15	Screw fixing hood	PMP0308	RN14	2	2						
16	Washer for screw (plain)	PWZ103	RN15	2	2						
17	Washer for screw (spring)	LWZ203	RN16	2	2						
18	Nut for screw	FNZ104	RN17	2	2						
19	**Grille assembly—radiator**	**14B5759**	**RN18**	1	1						
20	**Moulding—radiator grille**	**14B5796**	**RN19**	1	1						
21	100 Six flash	14B5772	RN20	1	1						
22	Clip—locking—fixing flash (tubular)	97H510	RN21	2	2						
23	Piping—front wing upper (plastic)	14B6824	RN22	2	2						
24	Piping—front wing lower (plastic)	14B6825	RN23	2	2						
25	Piping—front wing	14B6729	RN24	2	2						
26	Tab fixing piping to front wing	4G7614	RN25	24	24						
27	Piping—rear quarter	14B1708	RN26	2	2						
28	Tab fixing piping	4G7614	RN27	16	16						
29	Cover-plate—shut pillar panel—R/H	24B876		1	1						
30	Cover-plate—shut pillar panel—L/H	24B877		1	1						
31	Screw fixing cover-plate	54K3024	RN28	12	12						
32	Screw fixing cover-plate	AHB8384		2	2						
33	Cover-plate—sill panel—outer R/H	24B878	RN29	1	1						
34	Cover-plate—sill panel—outer L/H	24B879		1	1						
35	Screw fixing cover-plate	54K3024	RN30	16	16						
36	Cover-plate—sill panel—inner R/H	24B880	RN31	1	1						
37	Cover-plate—sill panel—inner L/H	24B881		1	1						
38	Screw fixing tread plate	54K3024	RN32	8	8						
39	**Moulding—door cockpit—R/H**	**14B5876**	**RN33**	1	1						
40	**Moulding—door cockpit—L/H**	**14B5877**		1	1						
41	Screw fixing moulding	RTP806	RN34	6	6						
42	**Moulding—cockpit—rear**	**24B774**	**RN35**	1	1						
43	Plate—tapped (cockpit rear moulding)	14B7785	RN36	5	5						
44	Screw fixing moulding (¾")	RPP0312	RN37	4	4						
45	Screw fixing moulding (⅜")	RJP1005	RN38	3	3						
46	Plate—hard top surround finisher—R/H	24B1677		1	1						
47	Plate—hard top surround finisher—L/H	24B1678		1	1						
48	Plate—hood surround socket finisher	24B1679		2	2						

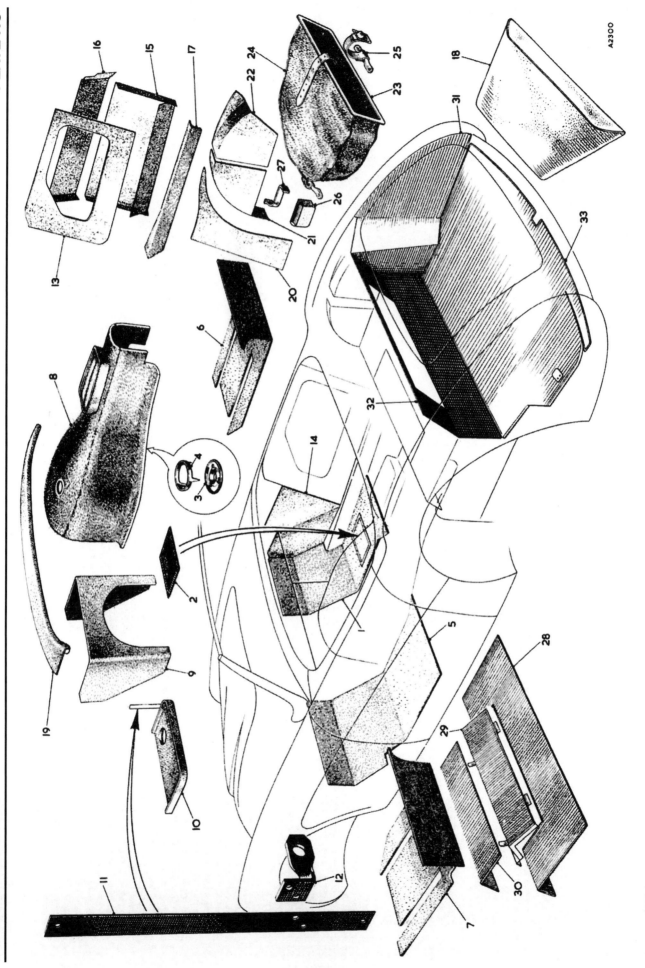

A2300

SERVICE PARTS LIST

AUSTIN-HEALEY 100 SIX (SERIES BN6)

Item No.	DESCRIPTION	Commencing (C) 501 Part Number	Illus. No.	Qty. per Vehicle RHD	Qty. per Vehicle LHD	Unit of Issue	Type of Vehicle	New Part Number	Change Point	Amdt. No.	REMARKS
	TRIMMING										
1	**Carpet—front floor—R/H—Red**	**4B3180**	**RO1**	1							
2	Carpet—front floor—R/H—Blue	AHB5410		1							
3	Carpet—front floor—R/H—Black	AHB5411		1							
4	Carpet—front floor—R/H—Green	AHB5412		1							
5	Pad—heel (rubber)	2H6961	RO2	1							
6	Fastener	2H8445	RO3	4							
7	Ring—spiked	2H6136	RO4	4							
8	**Carpet—front floor—L/H—Red**	**4B3181**	**RO5**	1							
9	Carpet—front floor—L/H—Blue	AHB5413		1							
10	Carpet—front floor—L/H—Black	AHB5414		1							
11	Carpet—front floor—L/H—Green	AHB5415		1							
12	Fastener	2H8445		4							
13	Ring—spiked	2H6136		4							
14	**Carpet—front floor—R/H—Red**	**4B3182**			1						
15	Carpet—front floor—R/H—Blue	AHB5416			1						
16	Carpet—front floor—R/H—Black	AHB5417			1						
17	Carpet—front floor—R/H—Green	AHB5418			1						
18	Fastener	2H8445			4						
19	Ring—spiked	2H6136			4						
20	**Carpet—front floor—L/H—Red**	**4B3183**			1						
21	Carpet—front floor—L/H—Blue	AHB5419			1						
22	Carpet—front floor—L/H—Black	AHB5420			1						
23	Carpet—front floor—L/H—Green	AHB5421			1						
24	Pad—heel (rubber)	2H6961			4						
25	Fastener	2H8445			4						
26	Ring—spiked	2H6136			4						
27	**Carpet—rear floor—R/H—Red**	**24B1795**	**RO6**	1	1						
28	Carpet—rear floor—R/H—Blue	AHB5895		1	1						
29	Carpet—rear floor—R/H—Black	AHB5896		1	1						
30	Carpet—rear floor—R/H—Green	AHB5897		1	1						
31	**Carpet—rear floor—L/H—Red**	**24B1796**	**RO7**	1	1						
32	Carpet—rear floor—L/H—Blue	AHB5898		1	1						
33	Carpet—rear floor—L/H—Black	AHB5899		1	1						
34	Carpet—rear floor—L/H—Green	AHB5900		1	1						
35	**Carpet—gearbox—Red and arm-rest pad assembly— Red with Black piping**	**AHB5947**	**RO8**	1	1						
36	Carpet—gearbox—Red and arm-rest pad assembly— Grey with Red piping	AHB8293		1	1						
37	Carpet—gearbox—Red and arm-rest pad assembly— Red with White piping	AHB8294		1	1						
38	Carpet—gearbox—Blue and arm-rest pad assembly— Blue with White piping	AHB5948		1	1						
39	Carpet—gearbox—Black and arm-rest pad assembly —Red with Black piping	AHB5949		1	1						
40	Carpet—gearbox—Black and arm-rest pad assembly —Black with White piping	AHB8295		1	1						

R.22

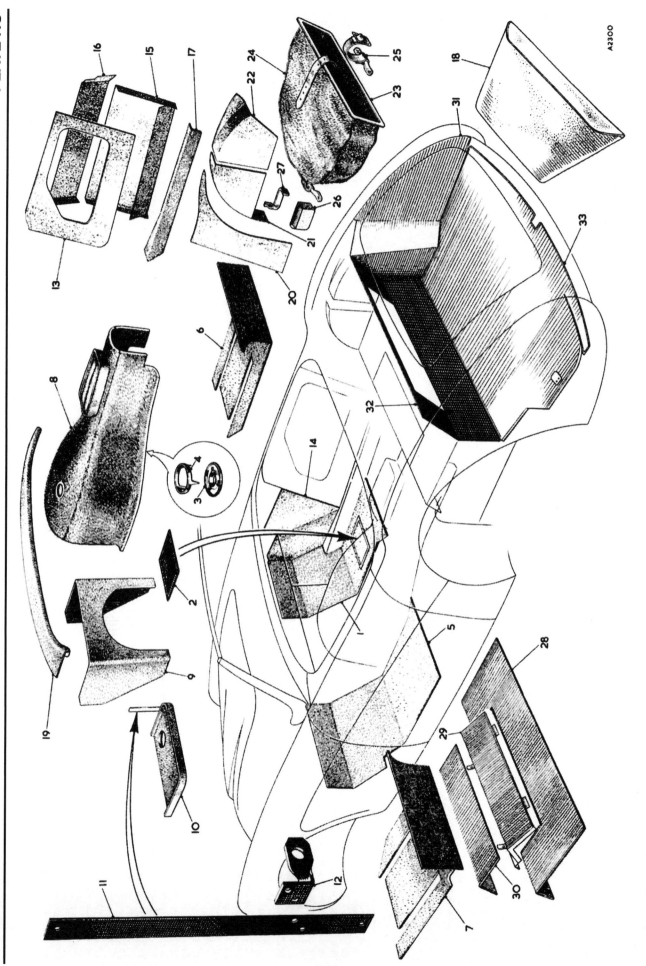

A2300

SERVICE PARTS LIST

AUSTIN-HEALEY 100 SIX (SERIES BN6)

Item No.	DESCRIPTION	Commencing (C) 501 Part Number	Illus. No.	Qty. per Vehicle RHD	Qty. per Vehicle LHD	Unit of Issue	Type of Vehicle	New Part Number	Change Point	Amdt. No.	REMARKS
	Trimming—*continued*										
1	Carpet—gearbox—Black and arm-rest pad assembly	AHB8296									
	—Black with Yellow piping			1	1						
2	Carpet—gearbox—Black and arm-rest pad assembly	AHB8297									
	—Yellow with Black piping			1	1						
3	Carpet—gearbox—Green and arm-rest pad assembly										
	—Grey with Green piping	AHB5950		1	1						
4	Fastener	2H8445		7	7						
5	Ring—spiked	2H6186		7	7						
6	**Extension assembly—gearbox cover—Red**	4B3179	RO9	1	1						
7	Extension assembly—gearbox cover—Blue	AHB8298		1	1						
8	Extension assembly—gearbox cover—Black	AHB8299		1	1						
9	Extension assembly—gearbox cover—Green	AHB8301		1	1						
10	Screw fixing cover (1")	PTZ808		9	9						
11	Screw fixing cover (¾")	PTZ806		4	4						
12	Rubber—gearbox cover sealing	14B5628		1	1						
13	**Tray assembly—parcel—Red with Red carpet**	4B3172	RO010	1							
14	Tray assembly—parcel—Red with Black carpet	AHB8860		1							
15	Tray assembly—parcel—Blue with Blue carpet	AHB5434		1							
16	Tray assembly—parcel—Black with Black carpet	AHB5435		1							
17	Tray assembly—parcel—Grey with Green carpet	AHB5436		1							
18	Tray assembly—parcel—Grey with Red carpet	AHB8859		1							
19	Tray assembly—parcel—Yellow with Black carpet	AHB5437		1							
20	**Tray assembly—parcel—Red with Red carpet**	4B4124			1						
21	Tray assembly—parcel—Red with Black carpet	AHB8871			1						
22	Tray assembly—parcel—Blue with Blue carpet	AHB5438			1						
23	Tray assembly—parcel—Black with Black carpet	AHB5439			1						
24	Tray assembly—parcel—Grey with Green carpet	AHB5440			1						
25	Tray assembly—parcel—Grey with Red carpet	AHB8872			1						
26	Tray assembly—parcel—Yellow with Black carpet	AHB5441			1						
27	Screw fixing tray	PMP0308		1	1						
28	Nut for screw	FNZ103		1	1						
29	Washer for nut (plain)	PWZ103		1	1						
30	Washer for nut (spring)	LWZ203		1	1						
31	Screw fixing tray (⅜")	PTZ803		4	4						
32	Screw fixing tray (½")	PTZ804		8	8						
33	Bracket—parcel tray support	14B6816	RO11	1	1						
34	Screw fixing bracket	PMZ0807		1	1						
35	Nut for screw	FNZ103		1	1						
36	Washer for nut (plain)	PWZ103		1	1						
37	Washer for nut (spring)	LWZ203		1	1						
38	Bracket—choke control	14B7581	RO12	1	1						
39	Screw—choke control bracket to parcel tray support bracket	PMZ0808		2	2						
40	Nut for screw	FNZ103		2	2						
41	Washer for nut (plain)	PWZ103		4	4						
42	Washer for nut (spring)	LWZ203		2	2						
43	**Liner assembly—door—R/H—Red**	4B3207	RO13	1	1						
44	Liner assembly—door—R/H—Blue	AHB5442		1	1						
45	Liner assembly—door—R/H—Black	AHB5443		1	1						
46	Liner assembly—door—R/H—Grey	AHB5444		1	1						

R.23

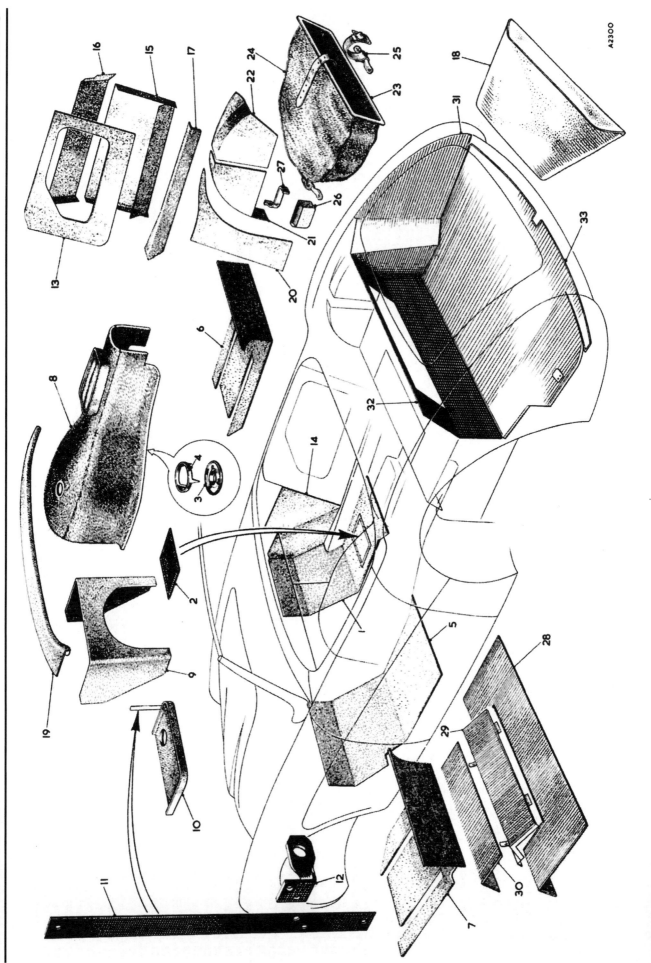

A2300

SERVICE PARTS LIST

Item No.	DESCRIPTION	Commencing (C) 501 Part Number	Illus. No.	Qty. per Vehicle RHD	Qty. per Vehicle LHD	Unit of Issue	Type of Vehicle	New Part Number	Change Point	Amdt. No.	REMARKS
	Trimming—*continued*										
1	Liner assembly—door—R/H—Yellow	AHB5445		1	1						
2	**Liner assembly—door—L/H—Red**	**4B3208**		1	1						
3	Liner assembly—door—L/H—Blue	AHB5446		1	1						
4	Liner assembly—door—L/H—Black	AHB5447		1	1						
5	Liner assembly—door—L/H—Grey	AHB5448		1	1						
6	Liner assembly—door—L/H—Yellow	AHB5449		1	1						
7	Screw fixing liner	54K3014		24	24						
8	Washer for screw	6K9062		24	24						
9	**Liner assembly—scuttle—R/H—Red**	**4B3215**	RO14	1	1						
10	Liner assembly—scuttle—R/H—Blue	AHB5450		1	1						
11	Liner assembly—scuttle—R/H—Black	AHB5451		1	1						
12	Liner assembly—scuttle—R/H—Grey	AHB5452		1	1						
13	Liner assembly—scuttle—R/H—Yellow	AHB5453		1	1						
14	**Liner assembly—scuttle—L/H—Red**	**4B3247**		1	1						
15	Liner assembly—scuttle—L/H—Blue	AHB5454		1	1						
16	Liner assembly—scuttle—L/H—Black	AHB5455		1	1						
17	Liner assembly—scuttle—L/H—Grey	AHB5456		1	1						
18	Liner assembly—scuttle—L/H—Yellow	AHB5457		1	1						
19	Screw fixing liner (½″)	54K3014		7	7						
20	Screw fixing liner (¾″)	54K3016		3	3						
21	Washer for screw	6K9062		10	10						
22	**Liner assembly—door inner lower—R/H—Red**	**4B3217**	RO15	1	1						
23	Liner assembly—door inner lower—R/H—Blue	AHB5458		1	1						
24	Liner assembly—door inner lower—R/H—Black	AHB5459		1	1						
25	Liner assembly—door inner lower—R/H—Grey	AHB5460		1	1						
26	Liner assembly—door inner lower—R/H—Yellow	AHB5461		1	1						
27	**Liner assembly—door inner lower—L/H—Red**	**4B3218**		1	1						
28	Liner assembly—door inner lower—L/H—Blue	AHB5462		1	1						
29	Liner assembly—door inner lower—L/H—Black	AHB5463		1	1						
30	Liner assembly—door inner lower—L/H—Grey	AHB5464		1	1						
31	Liner assembly—door inner lower—L/H—Yellow	AHB5465		1	1						
32	**Liner assembly—door inner upper—R/H—Red**	**4B3219**	RO16	1	1						
33	Liner assembly—door inner upper—R/H—Blue	AHB5466		1	1						
34	Liner assembly—door inner upper—R/H—Black	AHB5467		1	1						
35	Liner assembly—door inner upper—R/H—Grey	AHB5468		1	1						
36	Liner assembly—door inner upper—R/H—Yellow	AHB5469		1	1						
37	**Liner assembly—door inner upper—L/H—Red**	**4B3220**		1	1						
38	Liner assembly—door inner upper—L/H—Blue	AHB5470		1	1						
39	Liner assembly—door inner upper—L/H—Black	AHB5471		1	1						
40	Liner assembly—door inner upper—L/H—Grey	AHB5472		1	1						
41	Liner assembly—door inner upper—L/H—Yellow	AHB5473		1	1						
42	Screw fixing liner	RWP605		6	6						
43	Washer for screw	6K9062		6	6						
44	**Fillet assembly—door inner lower—R/H—Red**	**4B3221**	RO17	1	1						
45	Fillet assembly—door inner lower—R/H—Blue	AHB5474		1	1						
46	Fillet assembly—door inner lower—R/H—Black	AHB5475		1	1						
47	Fillet assembly—door inner lower—R/H—Grey	AHB5476		1	1						
48	Fillet assembly—door inner lower—R/H—Yellow	AHB5477		1	1						

MODIFICATIONS

R.24

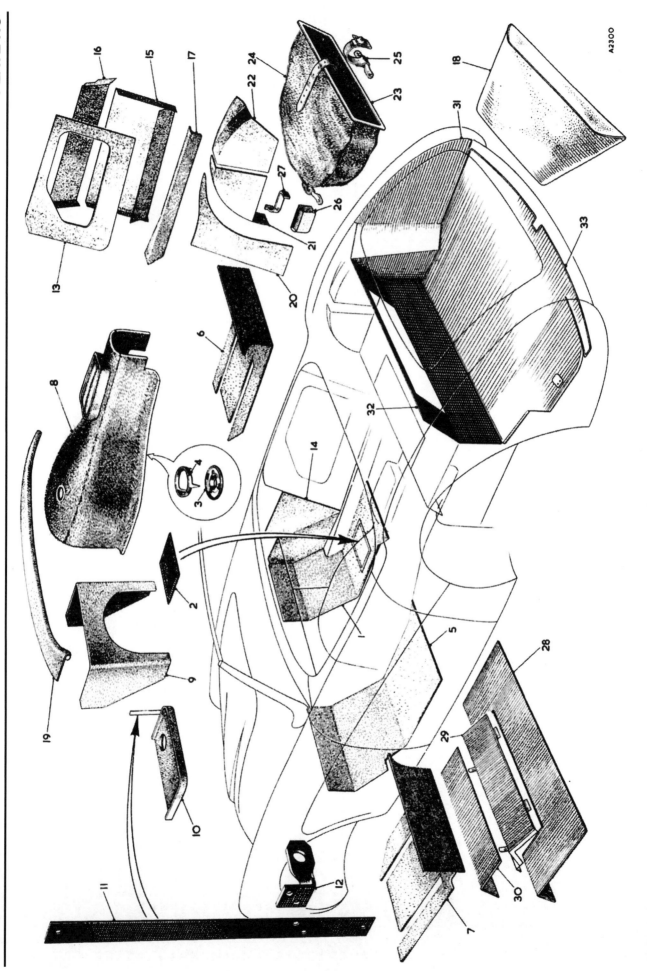

A2300

Item No.	DESCRIPTION	Part Number Commencing (C) 501	Illus. No.	Qty. per Vehicle RHD	Qty. per Vehicle LHD	Unit of Issue	Type of Vehicle	New Part Number	Change Point	Amdt. No.	REMARKS
	Trimming—*continued*										
1	**Fillet assembly—door inner lower—L/H—Red**	**4B3222**		1	1						
2	Fillet assembly—door inner lower—L/H—Blue	AHB5478		1	1						
3	Fillet assembly—door inner lower—L/H—Black	AHB5479		1	1						
4	Fillet assembly—door inner lower—L/H—Grey	AHB5480		1	1						
5	Fillet assembly—door inner lower—L/H—Yellow	AHB5481		1	1						
6	**Case assembly—side window—Red**	**4B4119**	R018	1	1						
7	Case assembly—side window—Blue	AHB5482		1	1						
8	Case assembly—side window—Black	AHB5483		1	1						
9	Case assembly—side window—Grey	AHB5484		1	1						
10	Case assembly—side window—Yellow	AHB5485		1	1						
11	**Liner assembly—scuttle top—Red with White piping**	**4B4211**	R019	1	1						
12	Liner assembly—scuttle top—Red with Black piping	AHB8886		1	1						
13	Liner assembly—scuttle top—Blue with White piping	AHB5486		1	1						
14	Liner assembly—scuttle top—Black with White piping	AHB5487		1							
15	Liner assembly—scuttle top—Black with Yellow piping	AHB8887		1							
16	Liner assembly—scuttle top—Grey with Green piping	AHB5488		1	1						
17	Liner assembly—scuttle top—Grey with Red piping	AHB8888		1	1						
18	Liner assembly—scuttle top—Yellow with Black piping	AHB5489		1							
19	Screw fixing liner (⅜")	CTP605		2	2						
20	Washer for screw	6K9062		2	2						
21	Turn-button (single)	8F2480		2	2						
22	Screw fixing turn-button (¾")	RTP606		4	4						
23	Fastener—bottom portion	14B2878		1	1						
24	**Liner assembly—rear quarter cockpit—R/H—Red**	**4B5123**	R020	1	1						
25	Liner assembly—rear quarter cockpit—R/H—Blue	AHB5490		1	1						
26	Liner assembly—rear quarter cockpit—R/H—Black	AHB5491		1	1						
27	Liner assembly—rear quarter cockpit—R/H—Grey	AHB5492		1	1						
28	Liner assembly—rear quarter cockpit—R/H—Yellow	AHB5493		1	1						
29	**Liner assembly—rear quarter cockpit—L/H—Red**	**4B5124**		1	1						
30	Liner assembly—rear quarter cockpit—L/H—Blue	AHB5494		1	1						
31	Liner assembly—rear quarter cockpit—L/H—Black	AHB5495		1	1						
32	Liner assembly—rear quarter cockpit—L/H—Grey	AHB5496		1	1						
33	Liner assembly—rear quarter cockpit—L/H—Yellow	AHB5497		1	1						
34	Screw fixing liner (⅜")	CWZ806		10	10						
35	Screw fixing liner (½")	RJP605		6	6						
36	Screw fixing liner (⅜")	RJP604		4	4						
37	Washer for screw (countersunk)	6K9062		10	10						
38	Screw fixing liner (1¼")	CTZ610		4	4						

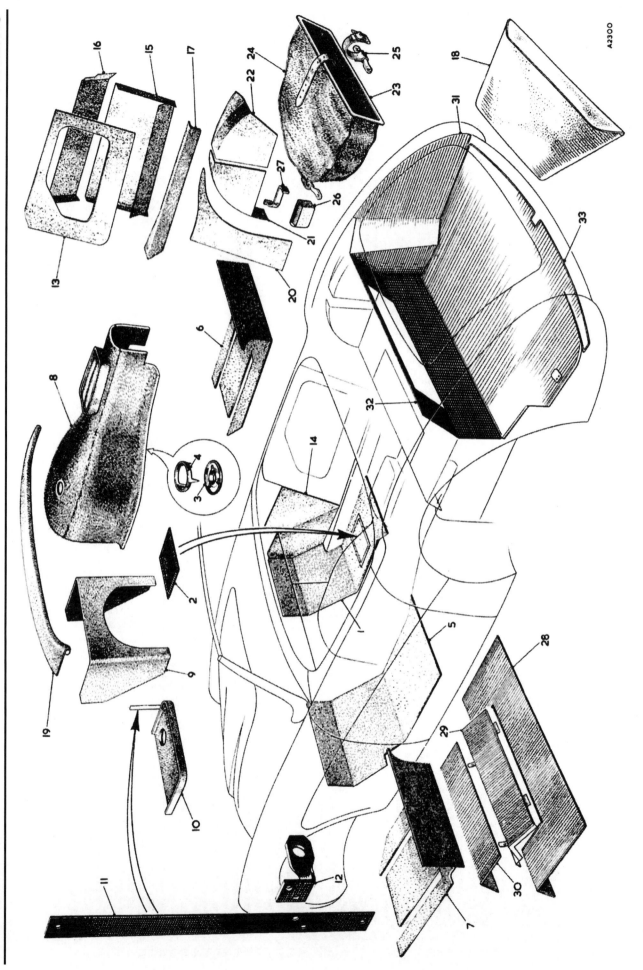

A2300

SERVICE PARTS LIST

AUSTIN-HEALEY 100 SIX (SERIES BN6)

Item No.	DESCRIPTION	Part Number Commencing (C) 501	Illus. No.	Qty. per Vehicle RHD	Qty. per Vehicle LHD	Unit of Issue	Type of Vehicle	MODIFICATIONS New Part Number	MODIFICATIONS Change Point	MODIFICATIONS Amdt. No.	REMARKS
	Trimming—*continued*										
1	**Liner assembly—rear wheel arch cockpit—R/H—Red**	4B5125	R021	1	1						
2	Liner assembly—rear wheel arch cockpit—R/H—Blue	AHB5498		1	1						
3	Liner assembly—rear wheel arch cockpit—R/H—Black	AHB5499		1	1						
4	Liner assembly—rear wheel arch cockpit—R/H—Grey	AHB5500		1	1						
5	Liner assembly—rear wheel arch cockpit—R/H—Yellow	AHB5501		1	1						
6	**Liner assembly—rear wheel arch cockpit—L/H—Red**	4B5126		1	1						
7	Liner assembly—rear wheel arch cockpit—L/H—Blue	AHB5502		1	1						
8	Liner assembly—rear wheel arch cockpit—L/H—Black	AHB5503		1	1						
9	Liner assembly—rear wheel arch cockpit—L/H—Grey	AHB5504		1	1						
10	Liner assembly—rear wheel arch cockpit—L/H—Yellow	AHB5505		1	1						
11	Screw fixing liner (¾")	RJP604		2	2						
12	Washer for screw	6K9062		2	2						
13	**Liner assembly—rear wheel arch—R/H—Red**	4B5127	R022	1	1						
14	Liner assembly—rear wheel arch—R/H—Blue	AHB5506		1	1						
15	Liner assembly—rear wheel arch—R/H—Black	AHB5507		1	1						
16	Liner assembly—rear wheel arch—R/H—Grey	AHB5508		1	1						
17	Liner assembly—rear wheel arch—R/H—Yellow	AHB5509		1	1						
18	**Liner assembly—rear wheel arch—L/H—Red**	4B5128		1	1						
19	Liner assembly—rear wheel arch—L/H—Blue	AHB5510		1	1						
20	Liner assembly—rear wheel arch—L/H—Black	AHB5511		1	1						
21	Liner assembly—rear wheel arch—L/H—Grey	AHB5512		1	1						
22	Liner assembly—rear wheel arch—L/H—Yellow	AHB5513		1	1						
23	**Cover assembly—spare wheel—Red**	4B5122	R023	1	1						
24	Cover assembly—spare wheel—Blue	AHB5514		1	1						
25	Cover assembly—spare wheel—Black	AHB5515		1	1						
26	Cover assembly—spare wheel—Grey	AHB5516		1	1						
27	Cover assembly—spare wheel—Yellow	AHB5517		1	1						
28	**Strap assembly—spare wheel securing—long**	24B785	R024	1	1						
29	Screw fixing strap	RMP0308		2	2						
30	Nut for screw	FNZ103		2	2						
31	Washer for nut (plain)	PWZ103		2	2						
32	**Strap assembly—spare wheel securing—short**	24B787	R025	1	1						
33	Screw fixing strap	RMP0310		2	2						
34	Washer for screw (plain)	PWZ103		2	2						
35	Washer for screw (spring)	LWZ203		2	2						

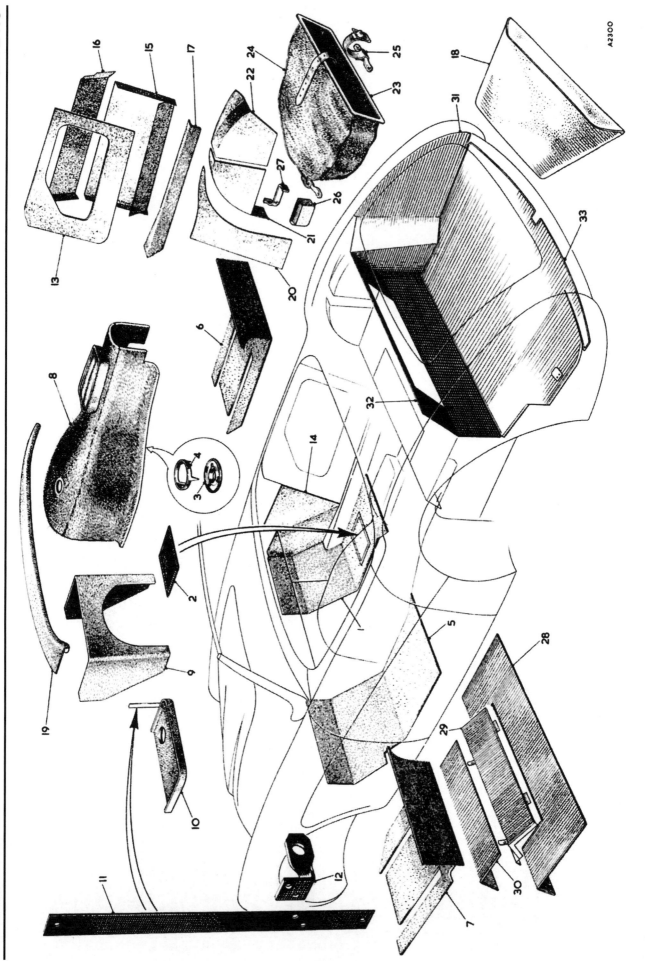

A2300

SERVICE PARTS LIST

Item No.	DESCRIPTION	Part Number Commencing (C) 501	Illus. No.	Qty. per Vehicle RHD	Qty. per Vehicle LHD	Unit of Issue	Type of Vehicle	New Part Number	Change Point	Amdt. No.	REMARKS
	Trimming—continued										
1	**Box assembly—hood stowage R/H—Red**	**4B5139**	**RO26**	1	1						
2	Box assembly—hood stowage—R/H—Blue	AHB5518		1	1						
3	Box assembly—hood stowage—R/H—Black	AHB5519		1	1						
4	Box assembly—hood stowage—R/H—Grey	AHB5520		1	1						
5	Box assembly—hood stowage—R/H—Yellow	AHB55521		1	1						
6	**Box assembly—hood stowage—L/H—Red**	**4B5140**		1	1						
7	Box assembly—hood stowage—L/H—Blue	AHB55522		1	1						
8	Box assembly—hood stowage—L/H—Black	AHB55523		1	1						
9	Box assembly—hood stowage—L/H—Grey	AHB55524		1	1						
10	Box assembly—hood stowage—L/H—Yellow	AHB55525		1	1						
11	Screw fixing box	54K3215		6	6						
12	**Strap—hood stowage retaining—Red**	**4B5143**	**RO27**	2	2						
13	Strap—hood stowage retaining—Blue	AHB55526		2	2						
14	Strap—hood stowage retaining—Black	AHB55527		2	2						
15	Strap—hood stowage retaining—Grey	AHB55528		2	2						
16	Strap—hood stowage retaining—Yellow	AHB55529		2	2						
17	Screw fixing strap (‡)	54K2995		4	4						
18	Screw fixing strap (‡)	RPW606		2	2						
19	**Covering assembly—rear bulkhead—Red**	**4B5142**	**RO28**	1	1						
20	Covering assembly—rear bulkhead—Blue	AHB5580		1	1						
21	Covering assembly—rear bulkhead—Black	AHB5581		1	1						
22	Covering assembly—rear bulkhead—Grey	AHB55582		1	1						
23	**Panel assembly—battery access—Red**	**4B4210**	**RO29**	1	1						
24	Panel assembly—battery access—Blue	AHB55584		1	1						
25	Panel assembly—battery access—Black	AHB55585		1	1						
26	Panel assembly—battery access—Grey	AHB55586		1	1						
27	**Covering assembly—battery access panel—Red**	**AHB8302**	**RO30**	1	1						
28	Covering assembly—battery access panel—Blue	AHB8803		1	1						
29	Covering assembly—battery access panel—Black	AHB88804		1	1						
30	Covering assembly—battery access panel—Grey	AHB88805		1	1						
31	Screw fixing panel	PMZ0306		4	4						
32	Nut for screw	FNZ103		4	4						
33	Washer for nut (plain)	PWZ103		4	4						
34	Washer for nut (spring)	LWZ208		4	4						
35	**Liner assembly—boot rear quarter—R/H—Black**	**4B5119**	**RO31**	1	1						
36	**Liner assembly—boot rear quarter—L/H—Black**	**4B5120**	**RO32**	1	1						
37	**Liner assembly—boot axle cover panel—Black**	**4B5121**		1	1						
38	**Liner assembly—boot floor and tool compartment— Black**	**4B5118**	**RO33**	1	1						
39	Screw fixing boot floor liner	RTP604		9	9						
40	Washer for screw	6K9062		9	9						

217

R.27

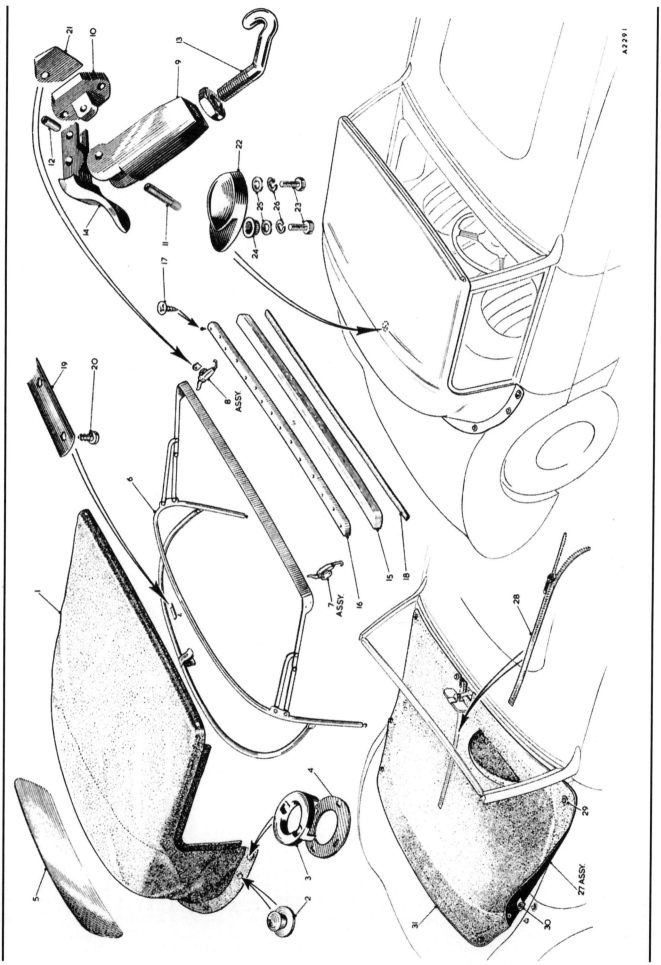

A 2 2 9 I

Item No.	DESCRIPTION	Part Number Commencing (C) 501	Illus. No.	Qty. per Vehicle RHD	Qty. per Vehicle LHD	Unit of Issue	Type of Vehicle	New Part Number	Change Point	Amdt. No.	REMARKS
	HOOD AND TONNEAU COVER										
1	**Hood assembly—Blue**	**4B4216**		1	1						
2	Hood assembly—Black	AHB5598		1	1						
3	Hood assembly—Grey	AHB5599		1	1						
4	**Hood cover assembly—Blue**	**14B1385**	**RP1**	1	1						
5	Hood cover assembly—Black	AHB5600		1	1						
6	Hood cover assembly—Grey	AHB5601		1	1						
7	Fastener—top portion	14B2465	RP2	4	4						
8	Eyelet	8F2408	RP3	2	2						
9	Washer—eyelet	8F2409	RP4	2	2						
10	Back-light	24B1777	RP5	1	1						
11	Frame assembly	24B1588	RP6	1	1						
12	Clamp assembly—toggle—R/H	24B1709	RP7	1	1						
13	Clamp assembly—toggle—L/H	24B1710	RP8	1	1						
14	Body	24B1712	RP9	2	2						
15	Fixing base	24B1713	RP10	2	2						
16	Pin—large	24B1714	RP11	2	2						
17	Pin—small	24B1715	RP12	2	2						
18	Hook—R/H	24B1716	RP13	1	1						
19	Hook—L/H	24B1717	RP14	1	1						
20	Handle—toggle clamp	24B1711	RP15	2	2						
21	Hood stick and finisher assembly—Black	AHB5799		1	1						
22	Hood stick and finisher assembly—Grey	AHB5800		1	1						
23	Hood stick and finisher assembly—Blue	AHB5944		1	1						
24	Retaining rail—hood stick	24B789	RP16	1	1						
25	Screw fixing rail	CWN804	RP17	15	15						
26	Sealing rubber—hood stick	14B8472	RP18	1	1						
27	Clip fixing hood cover to frame	AHB5407	RP19	2	2						
28	Screw fixing clip	PTZ603	RP20	4	4						
29	Packer—toggle clamp assembly	AHB5943	RP21	2	2						
30	Retainer—hood cover	14B1780	RP22	2	2						
31	Screw fixing retainer	58K124	RP23	4	4						
32	Washer for screw (cap)	2K9798	RP24	2	2						
33	Washer for screw (plain)	PWZ103	RP25	4	4						
34	Washer for screw (spring)	LWZ203	RP26	4	4						
35	**Tonneau cover assembly—Blue**	**4B5133**	**RP27**	1							
36	Tonneau cover assembly—Black	AHB5594		1							
37	Tonneau cover assembly—Grey	AHB5595		1							
38	**Tonneau cover assembly—Blue**	**4B5134**			1						
39	Tonneau cover assembly—Black	AHB5596			1						
40	Tonneau cover assembly—Grey	AHB5597			1						
41	Fastener—zip	14B8699	RP28	1	1						
42	Eyelet	8F2408	RP29	4	4						
43	Washer for eyelet	2F2409	RP30	4	4						
44	Fastener—top portion	14B2465	RP31	5	5						

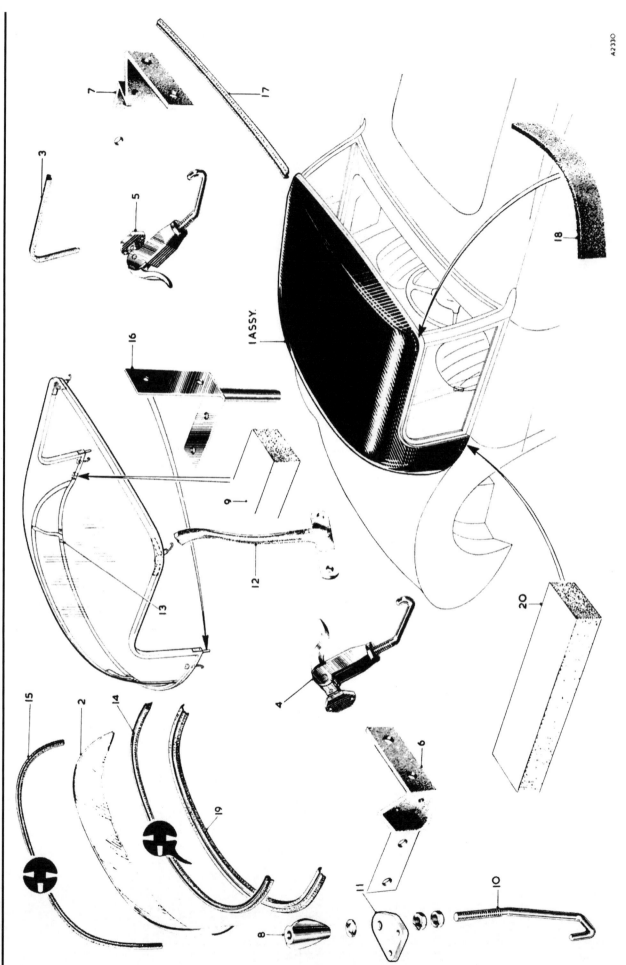

A2330

I ASSY.

SERVICE PARTS LIST

AUSTIN-HEALEY 100 SIX (SERIES BN6)

Item No.	DESCRIPTION	Commencing (C) 501 Part Number	Illus. No.	Qty. per Vehicle RHD	Qty. per Vehicle LHD	Unit of Issue	Type of Vehicle	New Part Number	Change Point	Amdt. No.	REMARKS
	HARD TOP (Optional Extra)										
1	Hard top—Black	AHB5606	RQ1	1	1						
2	Hard top—Ivory White	AHB5602		1	1						
3	Hard top—Colorado Red	AHB5603		1	1						
4	Hard top—Florida Green	AHB5604		1	1						
5	Hard top—Blue	AHB8749		1	1						
6	Hard top—Primed	27H9893		1	1						
7	Back-light	27H9772	RQ2	1	1						
8	Rubber—cant rail sealing	27H9598	RQ3	2	2						
9	Catch—toggle—R/H	24B1709	RQ4	1	1						
10	Catch—toggle—L/H	24B1710	RQ5	1	1						
11	Bracket—corner—R/H	27H9673	RQ6	1	1						
12	Bracket—corner—L/H	27H9674	RQ7	1	1						
13	Wing nut	27H9591	RQ8	2	2						
14	Pad—quarter casing to hard top (rubber)	27H9592	RQ9	4	4						
15	Hook—securing	27H9773	RQ10	2	2						
16	Plate—securing	27H9774	RQ11	2	2						
17	Pillar support—R/H	27H9587	RQ12	1	1						
18	Pillar support—L/H	27H9588	RQ13	1	1						
19	Rubber—back-light glazing (bottom)	27H9595	RQ14	1	1						
20	Rubber—back-light glazing (top)	27H9594	RQ15	1	1						
21	Spigot—locating—R/H	27H9894	RQ16	1	1						
22	Spigot—locating—L/H	27H9895		1	1						
23	Rubber—header rail sealing	27H9597	RQ17	1	1						
24	Buffer (rubber)	27H9601	RQ18	2	2						
25	Rubber—hard top to body sealing	27H9776	RQ19	1	1						
26	Pad—cockpit rail sealing	27H9777	RQ20	2	2						

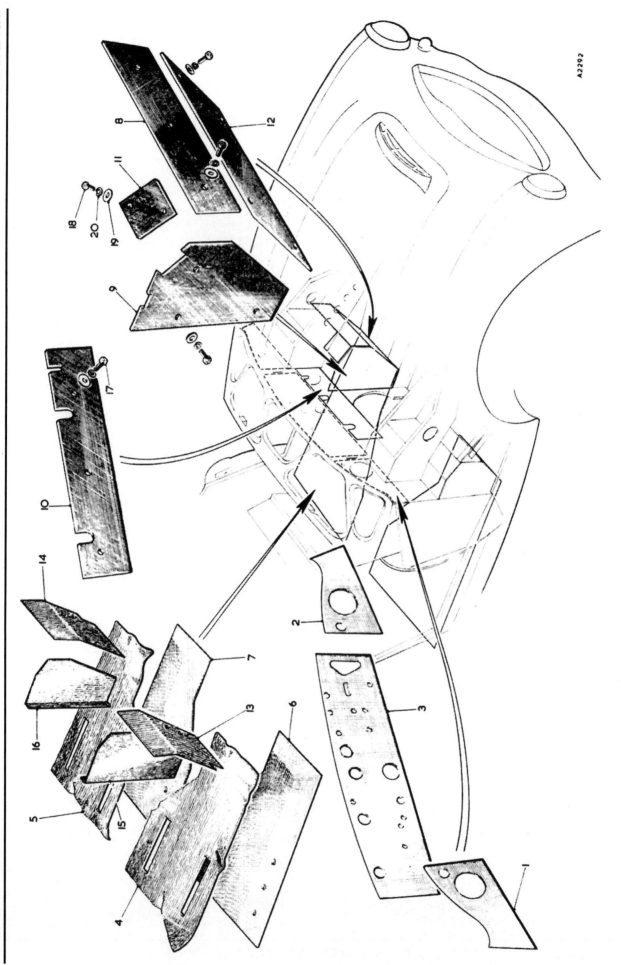

A2292

SERVICE PARTS LIST

AUSTIN-HEALEY 100 SIX (SERIES BN6)

Item No.	DESCRIPTION	Part Number Commencing (C) 501	Illus. No.	Qty. per Vehicle RHD	Qty. per Vehicle LHD	Unit of Issue	Type of Vehicle	New Part Number	Change Point	Amdt. No.	REMARKS
	FELTS AND INSULATIONS										
1	Insulation for dash front—R/H	14B7474	RR1	1	1						
2	Insulation for dash front—L/H	14B7475	RR2	1	1						
3	Insulation for dash front—centre	14B7476	RR3	1	1						
4	Covering for floor—R/H (felt)	24B1793	RR4	1	1						
5	Covering for floor—L/H (felt)	24B1794	RR5	1	1						
6	Insulation for floor—R/H	24B1791	RR6	1	1						
7	Insulation for floor—L/H	24B1792	RR7	1	1						
8	Covering for pedal box—front—L/H (asbestos)	14B6760	RR8	1	1						
9	Covering for pedal box—side—L/H (asbestos)	14B6761	RR9	1	1						
10	Covering for dash front panel (asbestos)	14B7804	RR10	1	1						
11	Covering for pedal box—front—R/H (asbestos)	14B6759	RR11	1	1						
12	Covering for pedal box—front—L/H lower (asbestos)	14B6828	RR12	1	1						
13	Covering for pedal box front panel—R/H (felt)	14B7584	RR13	1	1						
14	Covering for pedal box front panel—L/H (felt)	14B7585	RR14	1	1						
15	Covering for pedal box inner panel—R/H (felt)	14B7586	RR15	1	1						
16	Covering for pedal box inner panel—L/H (felt)	14B7587	RR16	1	1						
17	Screw for fixing coverings (¼")	PMZ0308	RR17	2	2						
18	Screw for fixing coverings (⅜")	PMZ0310	RR18	13	13						
19	Washer for screw (special)	53K3151	RR19	15	15						
20	Washer for screw (spring)	LWZ203	RR20	15	15						
	BULK MATERIAL—TRIM										
21	Carpet—Black	ADE589		A/R	A/R						
22	Carpet—Red	ADE565		A/R	A/R						
23	Carpet—Blue	AHB8782		A/R	A/R						
24	Carpet—Green	AHB8783		A/R	A/R						
25	Leathercloth—Red	5D8827		A/R	A/R						
26	Leathercloth—Blue	5D8828		A/R	A/R						
27	Leathercloth—Black	5D8826		A/R	A/R						
28	Leathercloth—Grey	5D8513		A/R	A/R						
29	Leathercloth—Yellow	5D8627		A/R	A/R						

R.30

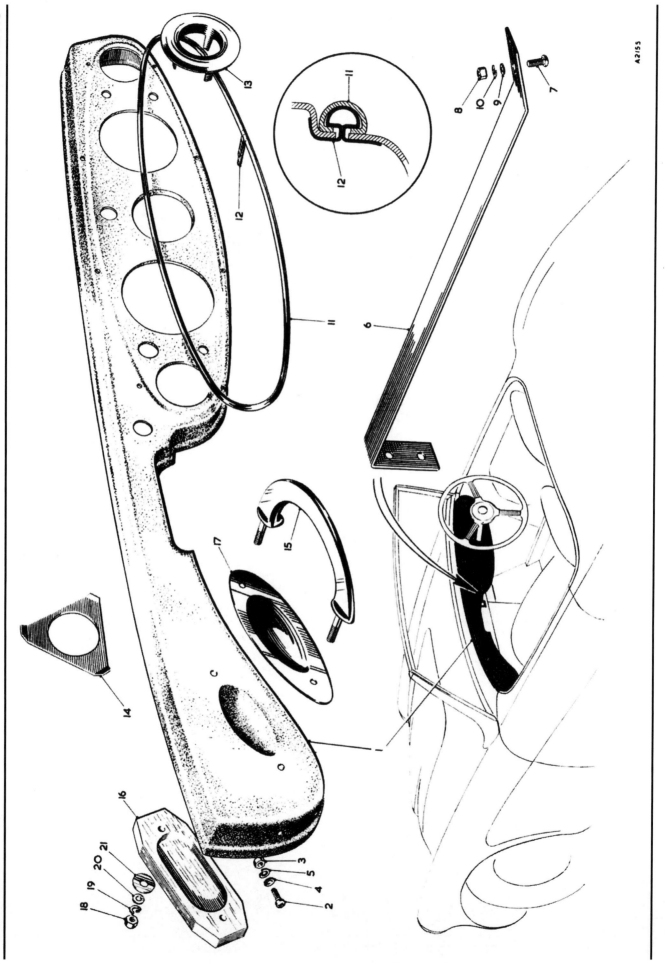

A2155

SERVICE PARTS LIST

Item No.	DESCRIPTION	Commencing (C) 501 Part Number	Illus. No.	Qty. per Vehicle RHD	LHD	Unit of Issue	Type of Vehicle	New Part Number	Change Point	Amdt. No.	REMARKS
	FASCIA DETAILS										
1	**Panel—fascia**	**24B697**	**RS1**	1							
2	**Panel—fascia**	24B726	RS1		1						
3	Screw fixing panel	PMP0812	RS2	4	4						
4	Nut for screw	FNZ103	RS3	4	4						
5	Washer for nut (plain)	PWZ103	RS4	4	4						
6	Washer for nut (spring)	LWZ203	RS5	4	4						
7	Bracket—fascia support	14B7579	RS6	1	1						
8	Screw fixing bracket	PMP0308	RS7	1	1						
9	Nut for screw	FNZ103	RS8	1	1						
10	Washer for nut (plain)	PWZ103	RS9	1	1						
11	Washer for nut (spring)	LWZ203	RS10	1	1						
12	**Moulding—instrument panel**	**14B6740**	**RS11**	1	1						
13	Clip fixing moulding	14G5854	RS12	8	8						
14	Escutcheon—steering column aperture	24B725	RS13	1	1						
15	Plate—escutcheon retaining	AHB5406	RS14	1	1						
16	Handle—grab	14B1729	RS15	1	1						
17	Strip—packing	14B5776	RS16	1	1						
18	Escutcheon for handle	14B5775	RS17	1	1						
19	Nut fixing handle, strip, and escutcheon	FNZ104	RS18	2	2						
20	Washer for nut (spring)	LWZ204	RS19	2	2						
21	Washer for nut—small (plain)	PWZ104	RS20	2	2	12					
22	Washer for nut—large (plain)	PWZ204	RS21	2	2						

R.31

A2299

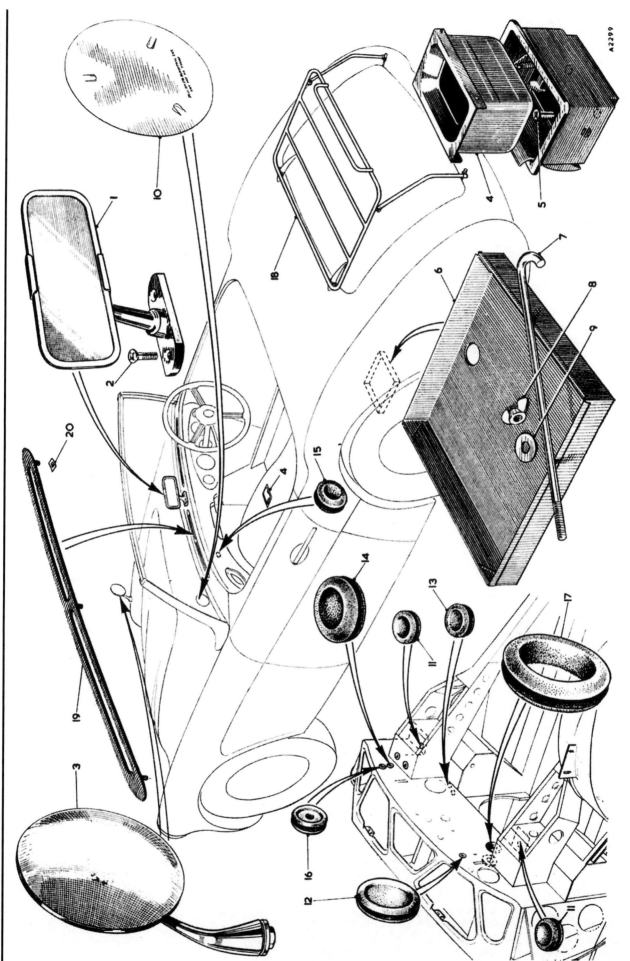

226

SERVICE PARTS LIST

SUNDRIES

Item No.	Description	Commencing (C) 501 Part Number	Illus. No.	Qty. per Vehicle RHD	Qty. per Vehicle LHD	Unit of Issue	Type of Vehicle	New Part Number	Change Point	Amdt. No.	REMARKS
1	Mirror—driving	14B1867	RT1	1	1						
2	Screw fixing mirror	RPP0812	RT2	2	2						
3	Mirror—wing	BHA4066	RT3	2	2						Optional extra
4	Ashtray	14B2016	RT4	1	2						
5	Screw fixing ashtray	CMZ0208	RT5	2	2						
6	Tray—battery	24B747	RT6	2	2						
7	Rod—battery fixing	24B811	RT7	4	4						
8	Nut for rod (wing)	WNZ104	RT8	4	4						
9	Washer for nut (plain)	PWZ105	RT9	4	4						
10	Holder—licence	14A3823	RT10	1	1						
11	Grommet for blanking dipper switch harness holes (rubber)	4G2541	RT11	2	2						
12	Grommet in dash front panel (rubber)	4G3575	RT12	1	1						
13	Grommet for blanking steering column bracket holes (rubber)	4G6492	RT13	2	2						
14	Grommet for blanking pendent pedal bracket holes (rubber)	4G6492	RT13	2	2						
15	Grommet for blanking oil gauge pipe hole (rubber)	4G2541	RT14	1	1						
16	Grommet for blanking hole in cold air duct panel (rubber)	4G6492	RT15	1	1						
17	Grommet fitted in dash for air control cable (rubber)	RFN303	RT16	1	1						
18	Ferrule fitted in dash panel for steering column (rubber)	3H2506	RT17	2	2						
19	Carrier—luggage	17H9932	RT18	1	1						⎤ Optional extra
20	Lighter—cigar	AHH5759		1	1						⎦
21	Mask assembly—demister	4B8521	RT19	2	2						
22	Push-on fix	PFS106	RT20	6	6						

R.32

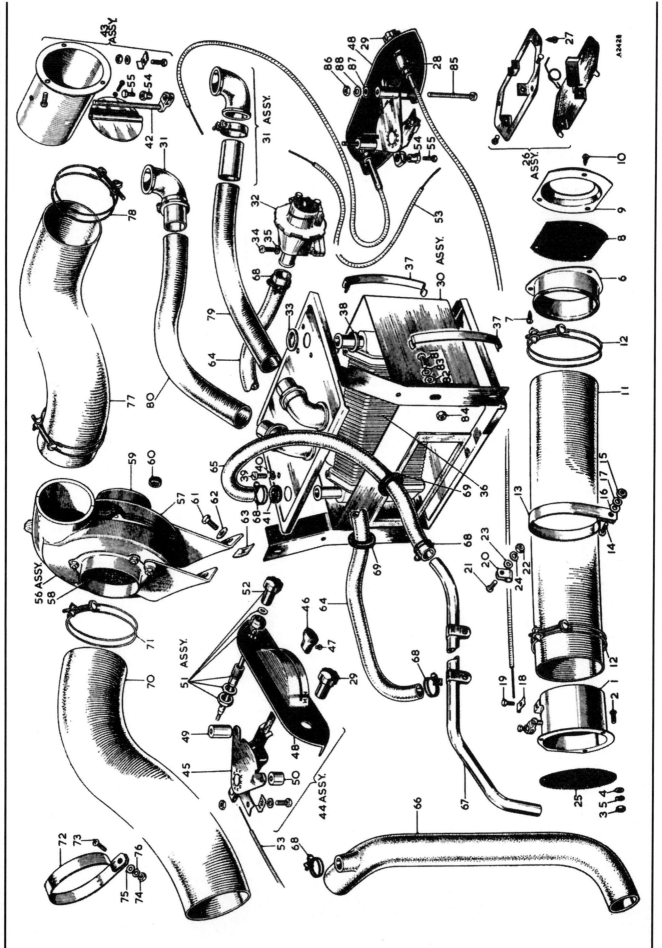

A2424

SERVICE PARTS LIST

Item No.	DESCRIPTION	Part Number (Commencing (C) 501)	Illus. No.	Qty. per Vehicle RHD	Qty. per Vehicle LHD	Unit of Issue	Type of Vehicle	New Part Number	Change Point	Amdt. No.	REMARKS
	HEATING AND VENTILATING EQUIPMENT										
	Air intake assembly										
1	**Air intake assembly**	**14B7711**	**RU1**	1	1						
2	Screw fixing air intake assembly	PMZ0308	RU2	3	3						
3	Nut for screw	FNZ103	RU3	3	3						
4	Washer for nut (plain)	PWZ103	RU4	3	3						
5	Washer for nut (spring)	LWZ208	RU5	3	3						
6	Flange—air intake	14B7712	RU6	1	1						
7	Screw fixing flange	PTZ1003	RU7	3	3						
8	Gauze—cold air duct panel	14B8780	RU8	1	1						
9	Bezel—cold air duct panel	14B8781	RU9	1	1						
10	Screw fixing gauze and bezel	PTZ603	RU10	3	3						
11	**Hose—air**	**14B2749**	**RU11**	1	1						
12	Clip for hose	14G800	RU12	2	2						
13	Clip fixing air hose to front wheel arch	14B1917	RU13	1	1						
14	Screw fixing clip	PMZ0810	RU14	1	1						
15	Nut for screw	FNZ103	RU15	1	1						
16	Washer for nut (plain)	PWZ103	RU16	1	1						
17	Washer for nut (spring)	LWZ208	RU17	1	1						
18	Clamp—cable	14G6451	RU18	2	2						
19	Screw fixing clamp	53K155	RU19	4	4						
20	Clip	PCR0807	RU20	1	1						
21	Screw fixing clip	CMZ0308	RU21	1	1						
22	Nut for screw	FNZ103	RU22	1	1						
23	Washer for nut (plain)	PWZ103	RU28	1	1						
24	Washer for nut (spring)	LWZ208	RU24	1	1						
25	Gauze—air valve	4G6575	RU25	1	1						
26	**Door assembly—outlet**	**13H59**	**RU26**	2	2						
27	Screw fixing door	PTZ603	RU27	8	8						
28	**Push-pull control—air intake**	**14B7782**	**RU28**	1	1						
29	Knob	17H1493	RU29	1							
30	**Push-pull control—air intake**	**14B7779**			1						
31	Knob	17H1493			1						

R.33

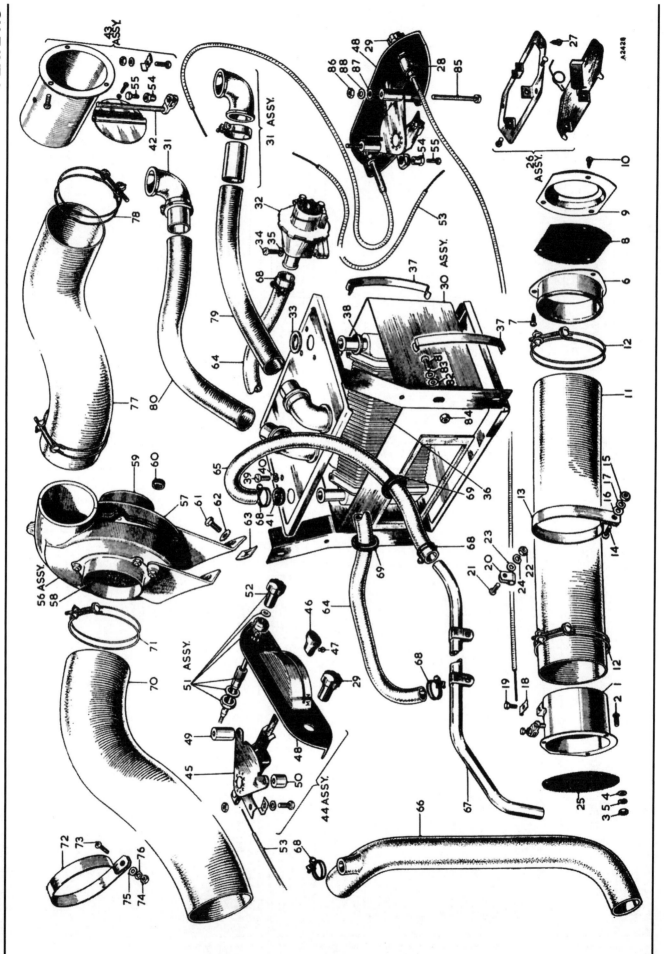

A.2428

Heating and Ventilating Equipment—*continued*

HEATER (Optional Extra)

Item No.	DESCRIPTION	Commencing (C) 501 Part Number	Illus. No.	Qty. per Vehicle RHD	Qty. per Vehicle LHD	Unit of Issue	Type of Vehicle	New Part Number	Change Point	Amdt. No.	REMARKS
1	**Heater kit set**	**8G9048**	**RU30**								
2	**Heater unit assembly**	**14B6599**	**RU30**	1	1						
3	Elbow assembly	14G8499	RU31	2	2						
4	Valve—water	27H1171	RU32	1	1						
5	Ring—valve seal	27H614	RU33	1	1						
6	Screw fixing valve	27H1172	RU34	2	2						
7	Washer for screw (spring)	27H611	RU35	4	4						
8	Radiator and seals	27H1173	RU36	1	1						
9	Clip—spring	27H1174	RU37	8	8						
10	Ring—radiator seal	27H614	RU38	1	1						
11	Screw fixing radiator	27H1242	RU39	2	2						
12	Washer for screw (spring)	27H611	RU40	2	2						
13	Grommet	17H1591	RU41	1	1						
14	Arm and spindle	27H1176	RU42	1	1						
15	Valve assembly—air inlet	27H1177	RU43	1	1						
16	**Control assembly—lever**	**14B6600**	**RU44**	1	1						
17	Lever—control	18H78	RU45	1	1						
18	Knob—control lever	18H76	RU46	1	1						
19	Screw for knob	53K1802	RU47	1	1						
20	Panel—control lever	18H77	RU48	1	1						
21	Spacer (long)	24B632	RU49	2	2						
22	Spacer (short)	24B688	RU50	2	2						
23	Push-pull assembly	14B7780	RU51	1	1						
24	Knob	17H1494	RU52	1	1						
25	Cable—heater control	14B7776	RU53		1						
26	Push-pull assembly	14B7781		1							
27	Knob	17H1494		1							
28	Cable—heater control	14B7777	RU54		1						
29	Trunnion for cable	14B7810	RU55	8	8						
30	Screw for trunnion	53K155	RU56	8	8						
31	**Blower assembly**	**14B6598**	**RU57**	1	1						
32	Casing	17H819	RU58	1	1						
33	Mesh intake	17H1597	RU59	1	1						
34	Motor	27H1178	RU60	1	1						
35	Grommet	27H1179	RU61	4	4						
36	Bolt fixing blower assembly	ABZ0407	RU62	4	4						
37	Washer for bolt (special)	6K9488	RU63	4	4						
38	Nut (Spire speed)	6K9817		4	4						
39	Hose—heater box to engine (feed)	1D1780	RU64	1	1						
40	Hose—heater box to engine (return)	14B7550	RU65	1	1						

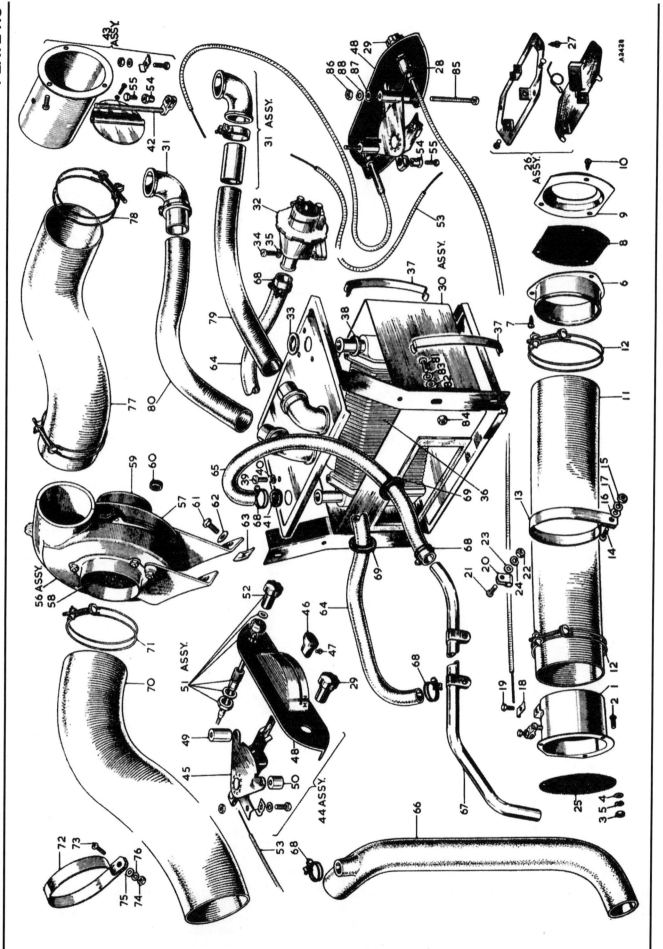

A2428

SERVICE PARTS LIST

Item No.	DESCRIPTION	Commencing (C) 501		Qty. per Vehicle		Unit of Issue	Type of Vehicle	MODIFICATIONS			REMARKS
		Part Number	Illus. No.	RHD	LHD			New Part Number	Change Point	Amdt. No.	
	Heater—*continued*										
1	Connection—water—radiator to water pump	11B2117	RU66	1	1						
2	Pipe—water—heater to water connection	11B624	RU67	1	1						
3	Clip for hose	8G531	RU68	5	5						
4	Grommet—hose through dash	14B9820	RU69	2	2						
5	Hose—cold air	14B9821	RU70	1	1						
6	Clip for hose	14G800	RU71	1	1						
7	Clip—air hose to front wheel arch	AHH5714	RU72	1	1						
8	Screw fixing clip	PMZ0810	RU73	1	1						
9	Nut for screw	FNZ103	RU74	1	1						
10	Washer for nut (plain)	PWZ103	RU75	1	1						
11	Washer for nut (spring)	LWZ203	RU76	1	1						
12	Hose—heater (30"×3¼")	14B6601	RU77	1	1						
13	Clip for hose	14G5630	RU78	2	2						
14	Hose—heater to demister (11¼"×1¼")	14B6602	RU79	1	1						
15	Hose—heater to demister (18¼"×1¼")	14B6603	RU80	1	1						
16	Screw—heater to cold air duct panel	PMZ0808	RU81	6	6						
17	Washer for screw (plain)	PWZ103	RU82	6	6						
18	Washer for screw (spring)	LWZ203	RU83	6	6						
19	Nut	FNZ103	RU84	2	2						
20	Screw—control assembly to fascia panel	PMZ0828	RU85	2	2						
21	Nut for screw	FNZ103	RU86	2	2						
22	Washer for nut (plain)	PWZ103	RU87	2	2						
23	Washer for nut (spring)	LWZ203	RU88	2	2						

R.35

SERVICE PARTS LIST

Item No.	DESCRIPTION	Commencing (C) 501 Part Number	Illus. No.	Qty. per Vehicle RHD	Qty. per Vehicle LHD	Unit of Issue	Type of Vehicle	New Part Number	Change Point	Amdt. No.	REMARKS
	TOOL KIT										
1	Toolbag	2A5412		1	1						
2	Screwdriver	2H4614		1	1						
3	Tyre valve tool	2H1083		1	1						
4	Ignition gauge and screwdriver	3H2648		1	1						
5	Spanner—sparking plug (box)	1B8995		1	1						
6	Gauge—sparking plug and tappet clearance	2A5419		1	1						
7	Brace—wheel	1B8907		1	1						
8	Gun—grease	13H50		1	1						
9	Jack—lifting	2H2099		1	1						
10	Shaft and handle	11B5196		1	1						
11	Spanner for hub cap	AHH5839		1	1						Germany only
12	Extractor—front hub cap	1B4889		1	1						Wire wheels
13	Hammer—copper	11B5166		1	1						

S.1

234

SERVICE PARTS LIST

AUSTIN-HEALEY 100 SIX (SERIES BN6)

Item No.	DESCRIPTION	Commencing (C) 501 Part Number	Illus. No.	Qty. per Vehicle RHD	Qty. per Vehicle LHD	Unit of Issue	Type of Vehicle	New Part Number	Change Point	Amdt. No.	REMARKS
	SERVICE TOOLS										
	ENGINE AND CLUTCH										
1	Remover—crankshaft gear, pulley, and propeller shaft flange	18G2		1	1						
2	Legs—gear remover (replacements for 18G2)	18G2A		1	1						
3	Bush—engine front cover locating	18G3		1	1						
4	Replacer—crankshaft gear and pulley	18G16		1	1						
5	Remover and replacer—valve rocker bush	18G21		1	1						
6	Handle—valve seat cutter and pilot	18G27		1	1						
7	Grinding-in tool—valve	18G29		1	1						
8	Pad—suction—valve grinding-in tool	18G29A		1	1						
9	Remover—main bearing cap (basic tool)	18G42A		1	1						
10	Adaptor—main bearing cap remover	18G42B		1	1						
11	Compressor—piston ring	18G55A		1	1						
12	Remover and replacer—water pump bearing	18G61		1	1						
13	Grinding-in tool—oil pump release valve	18G69		1	1						
14	Centralizer—clutch	18G79		1	1						
15	Gauging fixture—clutch assembly	18G99A		1	1						
16	Compressor—valve spring	18G106		1	1						
17	Reamer—camshaft liner (basic tool)	18G123A		1	1						
18	Cutter—camshaft liner reamer	18G123C		1	1						
19	Cutter—camshaft liner reamer	18G123D		1	1						
20	Cutter—camshaft liner reamer	18G123E		1	1						
21	Cutter—camshaft liner reamer	18G123F		1	1						
22	Pilot—camshaft liner reamer	18G123L		1	1						
23	Pilot—camshaft liner reamer	18G123R		1	1						
24	Pilot—camshaft liner reamer	18G123T		1	1						
25	Pilot—camshaft liner reamer	18G123AA		1	1						
26	Pilot—camshaft liner reamer	18G123AB		1	1						
27	Box for camshaft reamers (fibre)	18G123AL		1	1						
28	Remover and replacer—camshaft liner	18G124A		1	1						
29	Adaptor—camshaft liner remover	18G124C		1	1						
30	Adaptor—camshaft liner remover	18G124D		1	1						
31	Adaptor—camshaft liner remover	18G124E		1	1						
32	Adaptor—camshaft liner remover	18G124F		1	1						
33	Adaptor—camshaft liner remover	18G124H		1	1						
34	Adaptor—camshaft liner remover	18G124L		1	1						
35	Pilot—valve seat cutter	18G174D		1	1						
36	Adaptor—radiator reverse-flush	18G187		1	1						
	GEARBOX										
37	Synchromesh assembly ring	18G262		1	1						
38	Synchromesh assembly ring	18G263		1	1						
39	Remover—gearbox rear oil seal (basic tool)	18G389		1	1						
40	Adaptor—gearbox rear oil seal remover	18G389D		1	1						

SERVICE PARTS LIST

Item No.	DESCRIPTION	Commencing (C) 501 Part Number	Illus. No.	Qty. per Vehicle RHD	Qty. per Vehicle LHD	Unit of Issue	Type of Vehicle	New Part Number	Change Point	Amdt. No.	REMARKS
	Service Tools—continued										
	OVERDRIVE—LAYCOCK										
1	Replacer—oil seal	18G177		1	1						
2	Roller clutch assembly ring	18G178		1	1						
3	Compressor—accumulator housing piston ring	18G179		1	1						
4	Compressor—operating piston ring	18G180		1	1						
5	Guide—accumulator housing ring	18G181		1	1						
6	Remover—accumulator housing	18G182		1	1						
7	Remover—oil pump body	18G183		1	1						
8	Replacer—oil pump body	18G184		1	1						
9	Dummy—mainshaft	18G185		1	1						
10	Replacer—main bearing	18G186		1	1						
11	Gauge complete—hydraulic pressure	18G251		1	1						
12	Gauge only—hydraulic pressure	18G251A		1	1						
13	Pipe—hydraulic pressure gauge	18G251B		1	1						
14	Union—hydraulic pressure gauge pipe	18G251C		1	1						
	FRONT SUSPENSION										
15	Remover—hub assembly	18G8		1	1						
16	Adaptor—front hub remover—L/H	18G8H		1	1						
17	Extension—front hub remover centre screw	18G8J		1	1						
18	Adaptor—front hub remover—R/H	18G8K		1	1						
19	Adaptor—front hub bearing inner race remover	18G8L		1	1						
20	Compressor—front suspension spring	18G37		1	1						
21	Plate—front suspension checking	18G56		1	1						
22	Reamer—swivel axle bush—top	18G64		1	1						
23	Reamer—swivel axle bush—bottom	18G65		1	1						
24	Wrench—swivel axle bush reamer	18G68		1	1						
25	Remover—steering-arm	18G75A		1	1						
26	Remover and replacer—swivel axle bush	18G85		1	1						
27	Fixture—front suspension assembly	18G89		1	1						
	STEERING										
28	Separator—steering ball joint	18G125		1	1						
29	Spanner—steering-wheel nut	18G512		1	1						

S.3

SERVICE PARTS LIST

Item No.	DESCRIPTION	Commencing (C) 501 Part Number	Illus. No.	Qty. per Vehicle RHD	LHD	Unit of Issue	Type of Vehicle	New Part Number	Change Point	Amdt. No.	REMARKS
	Service Tools—*continued*										
	REAR AXLE AND REAR SUSPENSION										
1	Wrench—bevel pinion flange	18G34A		1							
2	Remover—differential bearing (basic tool)	18G47C		1	1						
3	Adaptor—differential bearing remover	18G47R		1	1						
4	Replacer—bearing and oil seal (basic tool)	18G184		1	1						
5	Adaptor—rear hub oil seal replacer	18G184AQ		1	1						
6	Adaptor—rear hub bearing remover	18G184K		1	1						
7	Gauge—bevel pinion setting	18G191		1	1						
8	Gauge—differential bearing	18G191A		1	1						
9	Gauge—bevel pinion bearing preload	18G207		1	1						
10	Remover—front and rear hub (basic tool)	18G220		1	1						
11	Adaptor—hub remover	18G220A		1	1						
12	Adaptor ring—hub remover	18G220D		1	1						
13	Pad—hub remover thrust	18G220E		1	1						
14	Spanner—rear hub nut	18G258		1	1						
15	Remover—bevel pinion bearing outer race (basic tool)	18G264		1	1						
16	Adaptor—bevel pinion bearing outer race remover	18G264D		1	1						
17	Adaptor—bevel pinion bearing outer race remover	18G264H		1	1						
18	Box—partitioned (fibre)	18G264K		1	1						
	MISCELLANEOUS										
19	Wrench—torque—30 to 140 lb. ft.	18G872		1	1						
20	Wrench—torque—2 to 8 lb. ft.	18G586		1	1						
21	Wrench—torque—5 to 30 lb. ft.	18G587		1	1						
	LITERATURE										
	Schedule of Repair Times	AKD967		1	1						
	Schedule of Repair Charges	AKD969		1	1						
	Maintenance Service Voucher Book	AKD970		1	1						
	Driver's Handbook	AKD947		1	1						
	Service Parts List	AKD855		1	1						
	Workshop Manual	97H1489		1	1						
	B.M.C. Master Price List	AKD698		1	1						
	Service Tool Catalogue	AKD659		1	1						
	Service Literature Catalogue	AKD858B		1	1						

Distributed by Brooklands Books Ltd., PO Box 146, Cobham,
Surrey KT11 1LG, England Phone: 01932 865051
E-mail: sales@brooklands-books.com www.brooklandsbooks.com

Part No. AKD 855

S.U. CARBURETTER
SERVICE PARTS LIST

	Model Application	Specification No.	Type	Section
AUSTIN-HEALEY	100/6 (Series BN6)	AUC 866	HD6	SF

CARBURETTER THROTTLE SIZES

Type	Throttle Diameter
HD6	$1\frac{3}{4}''$ (4·44 cm)

CARBURETTER PISTON SPRING IDENTIFICATION

Paint Colour on End Coil	Load at Length		Part No.
Blue	$2\frac{1}{2}$ oz (70·9 gm)	$2\frac{5}{8}''$ (6·67 cm)	AUC 4587
Red	$4\frac{1}{2}$ oz (127·6 gm)	$2\frac{5}{8}''$ (6·67 cm)	AUC 4387
Yellow	8 oz (226·8 gm)	$2\frac{3}{4}''$ (6·98 cm)	AUC 1167
Green	12 oz (340·2 gm)	$3''$ (7·62 cm)	AUC 1170
Red and Green	$11\frac{1}{4}$ oz (318·9 gm)	$3\frac{7}{8}''$ (9·84 cm)	AUC 4826
Red and Light Blue	18 oz (510·3 gm)	$3\frac{7}{8}''$ (9·84 cm)	AUC 4818

CARBURETTER JET NEEDLES

On most carburetter specifications that appear in this Service Parts List the rich, standard, and weak jet needles have been listed. In some cases only the rich or weak needles have been listed together with the standard jet needle.   The standard jet needle is fitted to all new S.U. carburetter assemblies and installations.

When ordering it is essential to quote the needle code letters and/or numbers together with the appropriate part number.

Example :   **Needle—jet**
        Rich (RH)..AUD 1291
        Standard (OA6) ....AUD 1276
        Weak (OA7) ....AUD 1277

Extract from Part No. AKD 5036

B.M.C. SERVICE LIMITED
COWLEY · OXFORD · ENGLAND

Telephone	–	–	–	–	–	–	Oxford 77777
Telex	–	–	–	BMC Serv Oxford 83145 and 83146			
Telegrams	–	–	–	BMC Serv Telex, Oxford			
Cables	–	–	–	BMC Serv Telex Oxford, England			
Codes	–	–	Bentley's, Bentley's Second Phrase, A.B.C.				

(5th and 6th Editions), Western Union and Private

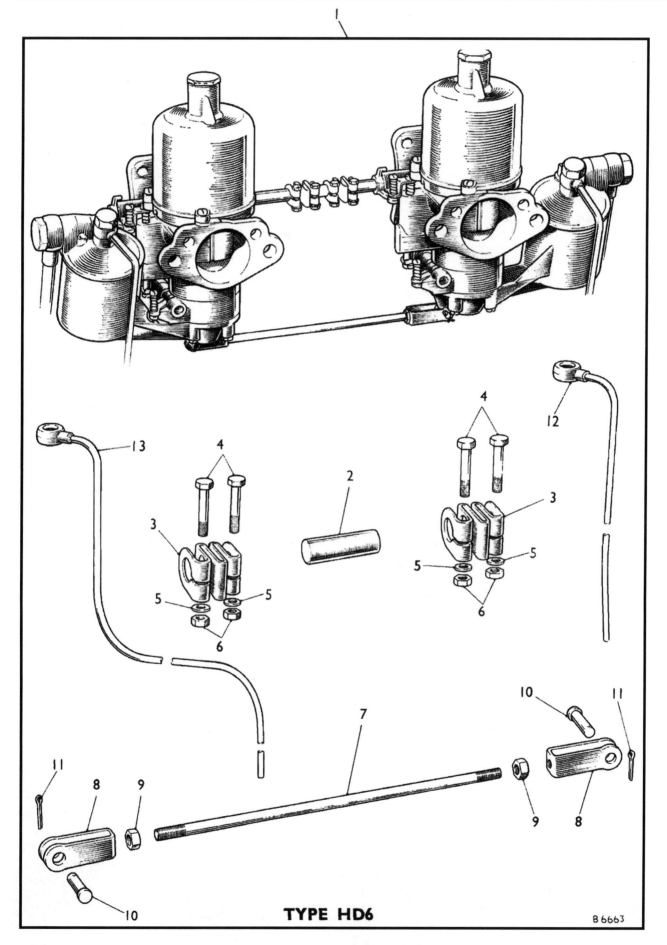

TYPE HD6

B 6663

	DESCRIPTION	Part No.	Illus. No.	Quantity	Stock recoms. DIST. Exp.	UK	D	Change Point	REMARKS

CARBURETTERS—TYPE HD6

			Page	*Plate*
TWIN INSTALLATION				
AUC 866			SF 7–SF 11	F 4–F 6

Type HD6
Twin Installation

Description	Part No.	Illus. No.	Quantity	Dist. Exp/UK	Remarks
Carburetter installation	AUC 866	1	1 pr	★ ★	
Rod—throttle spindle connecting	AUC 2419	2	1		
Coupling—rod	AUC 4384	3	2		
Bolt—coupling	AUC 2672	4	4		
Washer—plain	AUC 4612	5	4		
Nut—bolt	AJD 8014 Z	6	4		Part No. change; was AUC 2673
Rod—jet lever connecting	AUC 2867	7	1		
Fork—rod to jet lever	AUC 2256	8	2		
Nut—rod	AJD 8012 Z	9	2		Part No. change; was AUC 2156
Pin—fork to jet lever	AUC 2108	10	2		
Pin—split	CPS 0204	11	2		Part No. change; was AUC 2109
Pipe—air vent and overflow—front	AUC 8366	12	1		
Pipe—air vent and overflow—rear	AUC 8367	13	1		

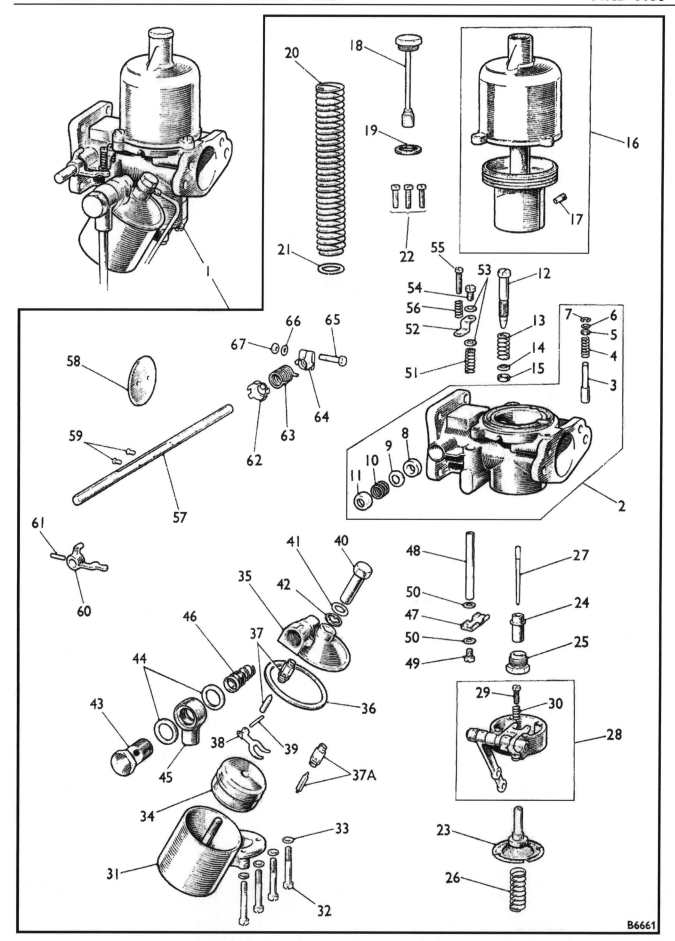

B6661

	DESCRIPTION	Part No.	Illus. No.	Quantity	Stock recoms. DIST. Exp.	UK	D	Change Point	REMARKS
	Type HD6—*continued*								
	Twin Installation—*continued*								
	Carburetter assembly—front	AUC 9040	1	1					
	Body assembly	AUC 8243	2	1					
	Pin—piston lifting	AUC 2065	3	1	★	★			
	Spring—pin	AUC 2066	4	1	★	★			
	Washer (neoprene)	AUC 4943	5	1					
	Washer (brass)	AUC 4944	6	1					
	Circlip—pin	AUC 1250	7	1					
	Gland (cork)	AUC 2098	8	2					
	Washer—dished	AUC 2096	9	2					
	Spring	AUC 2097	10	2					
	Retainer—spring	AUC 2010	11	2					
	Valve—slow running	AUC 2028	12	1					
	Spring—valve	AUC 2027	13	1					
	Washer—dished (brass)	AUC 2030	14	1					
	Washer—gland (neoprene)	AUC 2029	15	1					
	Chamber and piston assembly	AUC 8075	16	1					⎤ Alternatives
	Chamber and piston assembly	AUD 9189	16	1					⎦
	Screw—needle locking	AUC 2057	17	1					
	Cap and damper	AUC 8102	18	1	★	★			
	Washer (fibre)	AUC 4900	19	1	★	★			
	Spring—piston—Yellow	AUC 1167	20	1	★	★			
	Washer—thrust—spring	AUC 3071	21	1					
	Screw—chamber to body	AUC 2175	22	3					
	Jet	AUC 8155	23	1	★	★			
	Bearing—jet	AUC 2001	24	1	★	★			
	Screw—jet locking	AUC 2002	25	1					
	Spring—jet return	AUC 2006	26	1					
	Needle—jet								
	Rich (RD)	AUD 1288	27	1	★	★			
	Standard (CV)	AUD 1112	27	1	★	★			
	Weak (SQ)	AUD 1332	27	1	★	★			
	Housing assembly—jet	AUC 8149	28	1					
	Screw—stop	AUC 2521	29	1					
	Spring—screw	AUC 2451	30	1					
	Chamber—float	AUC 4067	31	1					
	Bolt—chamber to body	AUC 2110	32	4					
	Washer—shakeproof	LWN 403	33	4					Part No. change; was AUA 4643
	Float	AUC 1123	34	1	★	★			
	Lid—float chamber	AUC 4260	35	1					
	Washer—lid	AUC 1147	36	1	★	★			
	Needle and seat	AUC 8170	37	1					Not available; use AUD 9096
	Needle and seat	AUD 9096	37A	1	★	★			
	Lever—hinged	AUC 1980	38	1					
	Pin—hinged lever	AUC 1152	39	1					
	Nut—cap—lid	AUC 1867	40	1					
	Washer (aluminium)	AUC 1557	41	1					
	Washer (fibre)	AUC 1928	42	1	★	★			
	Bolt—banjo	AUC 2698	43	1					
	Washer (fibre)	AUC 2141	44	2	★	★			

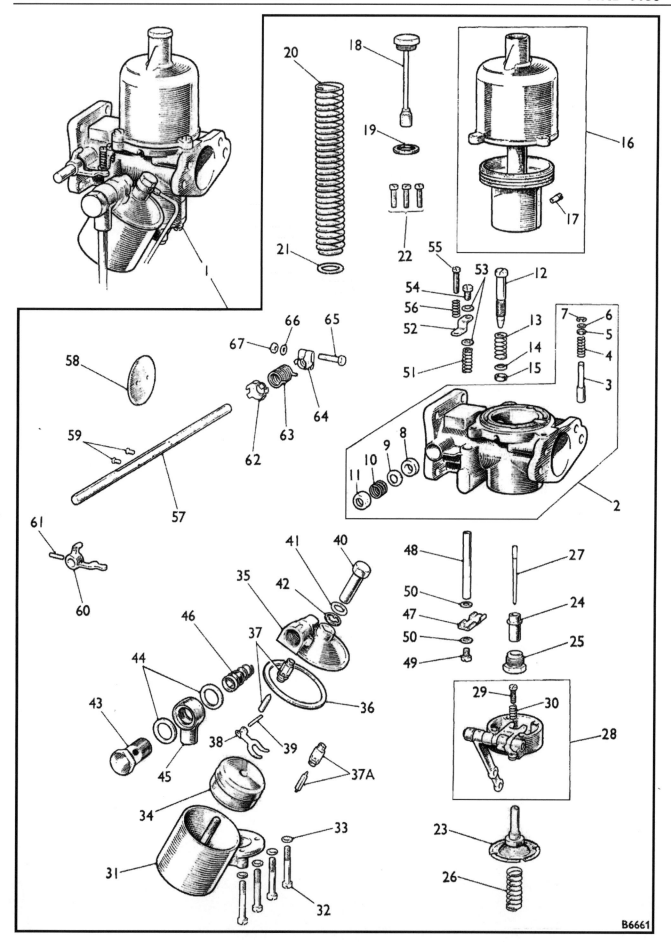

B6661

		DESCRIPTION	Part No.	Illus. No.	Quantity	Stock recoms. DIST. Exp.	UK	D	Change Point	REMARKS

Type HD6—*continued*
Twin Installation—*continued*

DESCRIPTION	Part No.	Illus. No.	Quantity	REMARKS
Union—banjo	AUC 1866	45	1	
Filter	AUC 2139	46	1	
Shoe—cam	AUC 2031	47	1	
Rod—shoe	AUC 2018	48	1	
Screw—rod to shoe	AUC 4790	49	1	
Washer—shakeproof	LWN 403	50	2	Part No. change; was AUA 4648
Spring—rod	AUC 2020	51	1	
Plate—top	AUC 2019	52	1	
Washer—shakeproof	LWN 403	53	2	Part No. change; was AUA 4643
Screw—plate retaining	AUC 4790	54	1	
Screw—stop adjusting	AUC 3464	55	1	
Spring—screw	AUC 2451	56	1	
Spindle—throttle	AUC 4859	57	1	
Disc—throttle	AUC 3280	58	1	
Screw—disc	AUC 1358	59	2	
Lever—throttle stop	AUC 2023	60	1	
Pin—taper—lever	AUC 2106	61	1	
Plate—return spring anchor	AUC 1087	62	1	
Spring—spindle return	AUC 4781	63	1	
Clip—end	AUC 4771	64	1	
Bolt—clip	AUC 2672	65	1	
Washer—plain	AUC 4612	66	1	
Nut—bolt	AJD 8014 Z	67	1	Part No. change; was AUC 2673

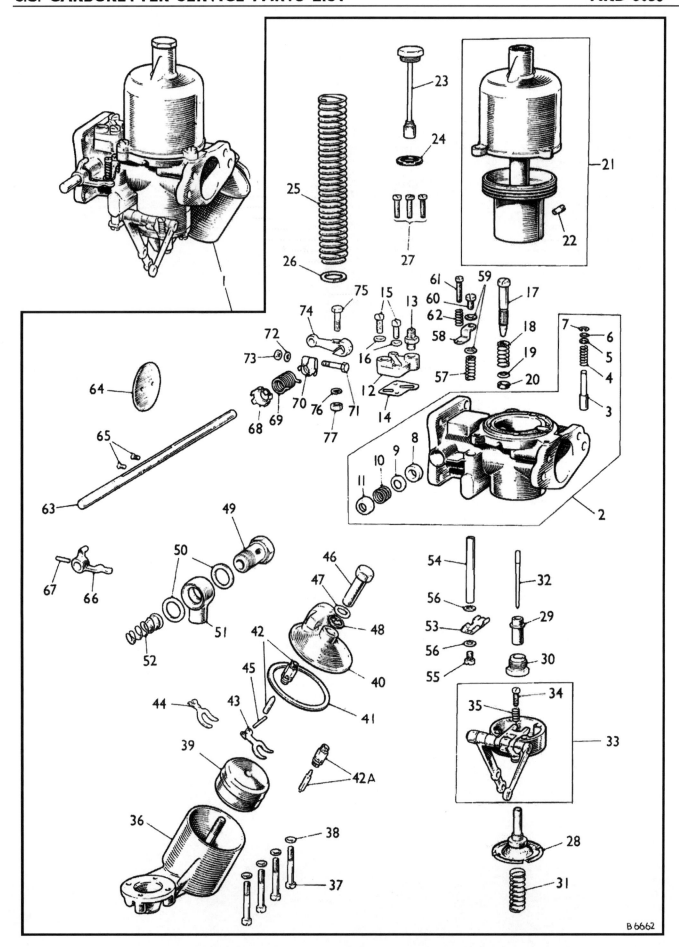

DESCRIPTION	Part No.	Illus. No.	Quantity	Exp.	UK	D	Change Point	REMARKS
Type HD6—*continued*								
Twin Installation—*continued*								
Carburetter assembly—rear	AUC 9041	1	1					
Body assembly	AUC 8242	2	1					
Pin—piston lifting	AUC 2065	3	1	★	★			
Spring—pin	AUC 2066	4	1	★	★			
Washer (neoprene)	AUC 4943	5	1					
Washer (brass)	AUC 4944	6	1					
Circlip—pin	AUC 1250	7	1					
Gland (cork)	AUC 2098	8	2					
Washer—dished	AUC 2096	9	2					
Spring	AUC 2097	10	2					
Retainer—spring	AUC 2010	11	2					
Adaptor—auto ignition	AUC 2044	12	1					
Union—auto ignition	AUC 4490	13	1					
Gasket—adaptor	AUC 2014	14	1	★	★			
Screw—adaptor	AUC 2175	15	2					
Washer—shakeproof	LWN 403	16	2					Part No. change; was AUA 4643
Valve—slow running	AUC 2028	17	1					
Spring—valve	AUC 2027	18	1					
Washer—dished (brass)	AUC 2030	19	1					
Washer—gland (neoprene)	AUC 2029	20	1					
Chamber and piston assembly	AUC 8075	21	1					⎤ Alternatives
Chamber and piston assembly	AUD 9189	21	1					⎦
Screw—needle locking	AUC 2057	22	1					
Cap and damper	AUC 8102	23	1	★	★			
Washer (fibre)	AUC 4900	24	1	★	★			
Spring—piston—Yellow	AUC 1167	25	1	★	★			
Washer—thrust—spring	AUC 3071	26	1					
Screw—chamber to body	AUC 2175	27	3					
Jet	AUC 8155	28	1	★	★			
Bearing—jet	AUC 2001	29	1	★	★			
Screw—jet locking	AUC 2002	30	1					
Spring—jet return	AUC 2006	31	1					
Needle—jet								
Rich (RD)	AUD 1288	32	1	★	★			
Standard (CV)	AUD 1112	32	1	★	★			
Weak (SQ)	AUD 1332	32	1	★	★			
Housing assembly—jet	AUC 8206	33	1					
Screw—stop	AUC 2521	34	1					
Spring—screw	AUC 2451	35	1					
Chamber—float	AUC 4067	36	1					
Bolt—chamber to body	AUC 2110	37	4					
Washer—shakeproof	LWN 403	38	4					Part No. change; was AUA 4643
Float	AUC 1123	39	1	★	★			
Lid—float chamber	AUC 4261	40	1					Not available; use AUD 2284 with 1 off hinged lever AUD 2285
Lid—float chamber	AUD 2284	40	1					
Washer—lid	AUC 1147	41	1	★	★			
Needle and seat	AUC 8170	42	1					Not available; use AUD 9096
Needle and seat	AUD 9096	42A	1	★	★			
Lever—hinged	AUC 1980	43	1					
Lever—hinged	AUD 2285	44	1					For use with AUD 2284
Pin—hinged lever	AUC 1152	45	1					
Nut—cap—lid	AUC 1867	46	1					
Washer (aluminium)	AUC 1557	47	1					
Washer (fibre)	AUC 1928	48	1	★	★			
Bolt—banjo	AUC 2698	49	1					
Washer (fibre)	AUC 2141	50	2	★	★			

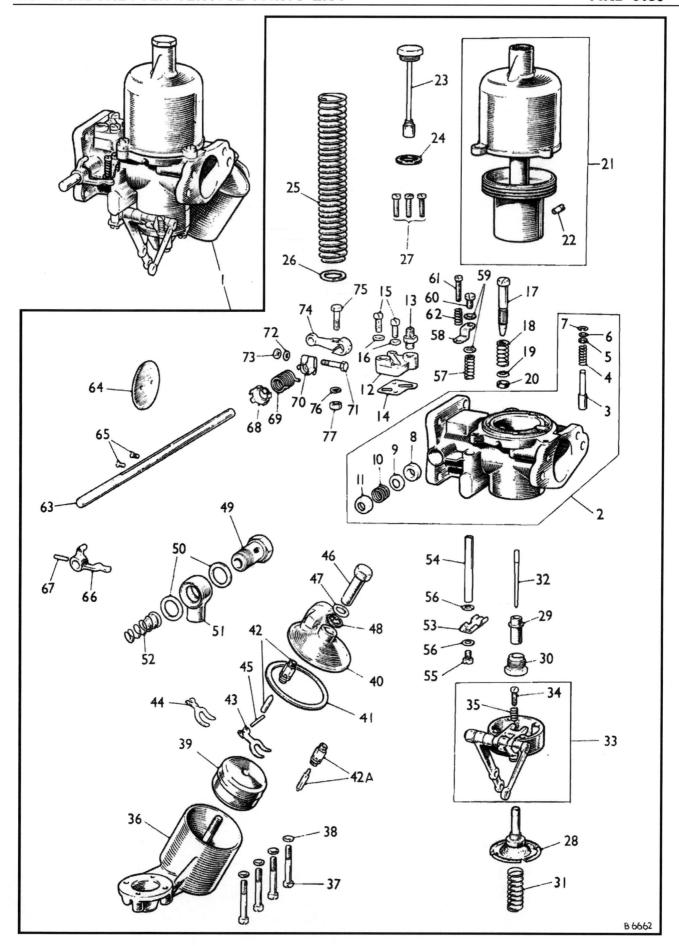

B 6662

				DESCRIPTION	Part No.	Illus. No.	Quantity	Stock recoms. DIST. Exp.	UK	D	Change Point	REMARKS

Type HD6—*continued*
Twin Installation—*continued*

DESCRIPTION	Part No.	Illus. No.	Quantity	REMARKS
Union—banjo	AUC 1866	51	1	
Filter	AUC 2139	52	1	
Shoe—cam	AUC 2031	53	1	
Rod—shoe	AUC 2018	54	1	
Screw—rod to shoe	AUC 4790	55	1	
Washer—shakeproof	LWN 403	56	2	Part No. change; was AUA 4643
Spring—rod	AUC 2020	57	1	
Plate—top	AUC 2019	58	1	
Washer—shakeproof	LWN 403	59	2	Part No. change; was AUA 4643
Screw—plate retaining	AUC 4790	60	1	
Screw—stop adjusting	AUC 3464	61	1	
Spring—screw	AUC 2451	62	1	
Spindle—throttle	AUC 4839	63	1	
Disc—throttle	AUC 3280	64	1	
Screw—disc	AUC 1358	65	2	
Lever—throttle stop	AUC 2023	66	1	
Pin—taper—lever	AUC 2106	67	1	
Plate—return spring anchor	AUC 1037	68	1	
Spring—spindle return	AUC 4781	69	1	
Clip—end	AUC 4771	70	1	
Bolt—clip	AUC 2672	71	1	
Washer—plain	AUC 4612	72	1	
Nut—bolt	AJD 8014 Z	73	1	Part No. change; was AUC 2673
Lever—throttle	AUC 1196	74	1	
Bolt—lever	AJD 1042	75	1	Part No. change; was AUC 2694
Washer—spring	LWZ 303	76		Part No. change; was AUC 2246
Nut—bolt	AJD 8012 Z	77	1	Part No. change; was AUC 2156

Brooklands Books Ltd., PO Box 904,
Amersham, Bucks, HP6 9JA, UK
www.brooklandsbooks.com

Extract from Part No. AKD 5036

Brooklands Books Ltd., PO Box 904,
Amersham, Bucks, HP6 9JA, UK
www.brooklandsbooks.com

Part No. AKD 855 and Extract from Part No. AKD 5036

ISBN: 9781783180486   AH66PC   4W4/4T15

OFFICIAL TECHNICAL BOOKS

Brooklands Technical Books has been formed to supply owners, restorers and professional repairers with official factory literature.

Model	Original Part No.	ISBN
Workshop Manuals		
Austin-Healey 100 BN1 & BN2	97H997D	9780907073925
Austin-Healey 100/6 & 3000	AKD1179	9780948207471
(100/6 - BN4, BN6, 3000 MK. 1, 2, 3 - BN7, BT7, BJ7 & BJ8)		
Austin-Healey Sprite Mk. 1 Frogeye	AKD4884	9781855201262
Austin-Healey Sprite Mk. 2, Mk. 3 & Mk. 4 and	AKD4021	9781855201255
MG Midget Mk. 1, Mk. 2 & Mk. 3		
Parts Catalogues / Service Parts Lists		
Austin-Healey 100 BN1 & BN2	1050 Edition 3	9781783180363
Austin-Healey 100/6 BN4	AKD1423	9781783180493
Austin-Healey 100/6 BN6	AKD855 Ed.2	9781783180486
Austin-Healey 3000 Mk. 1 and Mk. 2 (BN7 & BT7)	AKD1151 Ed.5	9781783180370
Mk. 1 BN7 & BT7 Car no. 101 to 13750,		
Mk. 2 BN7 Car no. 13751 to 18888,		
Mk. 2 BT7 Car no. 13751 to 19853		
Austin-Healey 3000 Mk. 2 and Mk. 3 (BJ7 & BJ8)	AKD 3523 & AKD 3524	9781783180387
BJ7 Mk. 2 Car no. 17551 to 25314 and		
BJ8 Mk. 3 Car no. 25315 to 43026		
Austin-Healey Sprite Mk. 1 & Mk. 2 and	AKD 3566 & AKD 3567	9781783180509
MG Midget Mk. 1		
Austin-Healey Sprite Mk. 3 & Mk. 4 and	AKD 3513 & AKD 3514	9781783180554
MG Midget Mk. 2 & Mk. 3 (Mechanical & Body Edition 1969)		
Austin-Healey Sprite Mk. 3 & Mk. 4 and	AKM 0036	9780948207419
MG Midget Mk. 2 & Mk. 3 (Feb 1977 Edition)		
Handbooks		
Austin-Healey 100	97H996E	9781869826352
Austin-Healey 100/6	97H996H	9781870642903
Austin-Healey 3000 Mk 1 & 2	AKD3915A	9781869826369
Austin-Healey 3000 Mk 3	AKD4094B	9781869826376
Austin-Healey Sprite Mk 1 'Frogeye'	97H1583A	9780948207945

Also Available

Austin-Healey 100/6 & 3000 Mk. 1, 2 & 3 Owners Workshop Manual	9781783180455
Austin-Healey Sprite Mk. 1, 2, 3 & 4	9781855201255
MG Midget 1, 2, 3 & 1500 1958-1980 Owners Workshop Manual Glovebox Edition	
Austin-Healey Sprite Mk. 1, 2, 3 & 4	9781783180332
MG Midget 1, 2, 3 & 1500 1958-1980 Owners Workshop Manual	

Carburetters

SU Carburetters Tuning Tips & Techniques	9781855202559

Restoration Guide

Restoring Sprite & Midgets	9781855205987

Road Test Series

Austin-Healey 100 & 100/6 Gold Portfolio 1952-1959	9781855200487
Austin-Healey 3000 Road Test Portfolio	9791783180394
Austin-Healey Frogeye Sprite Road Test Portfolio 1958-1961	9781783180530
Austin-Healey Sprite Gold Portfolio 1958-1971	9781855203716

From Austin-Healey specialists, Amazon and all good motoring bookshops.

www.brooklandsbooks.com